the
Mainstream

the
Mainstream

A Critique of Ideology in American Politics and Everyday Life

Edited by Herbert G. Reid
The University of Kentucky

David McKay Company, Inc. • New York

Up the Mainstream:
A Critique of Ideology in American Politics and Everyday Life

INTERNATIONAL STANDARD BOOK NUMBER: 0-679-30229-8

LIBRARY OF CONGRESS CATALOG CARD NUMBER: 72-90988

MANUFACTURED IN THE UNITED STATES OF AMERICA

DESIGNED BY ANGELA FOOTE

FOR AMY AND TRENT

Preface

This book has been designed especially for supplementary use in courses in American political thought and contemporary ideologies and issues. It should also prove valuable in courses in American government and political culture, American civilization, political sociology and political behavior, and twentieth-century American history.

Several recent textbooks for the study of American politics have begun with variations on the theme "The times are out of joint." The American political system is undergoing a crisis of legitimacy that makes one wonder why it was not anticipated more often in social science works of, say, twenty years ago. One reason may be that a critical concept of ideology was so seldom applied in the study of our political life. Today, political phenomena are, in some ways, less effectively integrated by institutional forms—a situation in which two tendencies of political development are dialectically interrelated. There is a dangerous tendency of one major trend of public policy to make "official" a version of the American ideology which a few years ago was so much taken for granted that it was often deemed the nonideological firmament of pragmatic genius. There is also a hopeful tendency, evident especially among the young, an impulse to comprehend the society as a whole that would expand the public sense of political possibility.

However, the campus form of this impulse generally has short-circuited as the cry for "relevance" has opened up the curriculum to miscellaneous "problem courses" and to a spate of texts and readers stressing ecological destruction, racism, Vietnam, etc. *Up the Mainstream* is designed to redeem recent student concern with "relevance" to daily life by uncovering and probing the *deep roots* of such problems. The student has a right to expect and demand *general and critical* interpretations that confront the yawning gap between theory and practice and that aid in organizing and penetrating the political events that go on around him or her and in taking action with respect to them. Youthful criticism of everyday life, to be politically significant, must be informed by a critical concept of ideology. This book provides some materials essential to an "ideology critique" of past American politics and of emerging trends of our advanced industrial society.

Many collections of readings on American politics and society bombard the student with surface-level "facts" that put into glaring contrast civics-book ideals and the real world beyond the campus. Such books tend both to reflect and reinforce the familiar American political tension between the cults of technology and moralism. By design or not, as such anthologies reflect a technologistic preoccupation with certain kinds of facts, they encourage a moralistic approach to political activity. If subjective activism is a problem of some politically concerned students, it may actually be related to the "objectivism" of much academic research and teaching.

This book goes beyond the primitive political reflection involved in divulging facts (especially cold, lifeless statistics) in a thin framework of contrast to related ethical and political ideals. Its chief purpose is to take seriously the assumptions, norms, and ideas on which "mainstream" politics depends, as its flow contributes to the maintenance of a politico-economic system that often pollutes the social possibilities and historical consciousness of the citizenry and its public landscape. *Up the Mainstream* suggests fundamental materials and directions for replenishing an underground stream of political thought that attempts to alter fundamentally the direction of mainstream ideology and the social order defined by it. It provides several illustrations of the necessary concepts, values, and perspectives for a new democratic theory in the formative stages. It emphasizes the strongest currents of the mainstream ideology which, operating as a cultural hegemony, tend persistently to submerge these prefigurations of a new culture and society. The Editor would not deny the possibility of the forceful current or osmotic power of the political and economic mainstream turning these efforts into a stagnant eddy of populistic frustration or a whirlpool of mindless activism. *Up the Mainstream* is a way of "keeping the faith" that this need not necessarily or inevitably be the fate of a new democratic thought and movement.

I wish to express my thanks and appreciation to the following friends and students, all colleagues, for their encouraging comments and helpful suggestions at various stages in the preparation of the manuscript: Richard Couto, Erling Eng, Fred Fleron, Jerry Gaines, Randal Ihara, John Nelson, David Patten, David Walls, Margaret Wendelsdorf, Kenneth Winter, and Ernest Yanarella. I am especially indebted to Lou Jean Fleron for her thoughtful review of the introductory essays and discriminating suggestions for their final preparation. For critical commentaries on this book in an early stage of its development, I am grateful to Alan Wolfe and Michael Weinstein. I am sure it would be a more challenging book if I had had time to take into better account some suggestions by Norman Birnbaum, Erling Eng, and Denis Goulet. I would like to thank Trent Schroyer for making available to me the manuscript of *The Critique of Domination: The Origins and Development of Critical Theory* (to be published by George Braziller, Inc.) which facilitated my study of the Frankfurt School's theory of "ideology critique" and has hopefully borne some fruit in the present work. Finally, I must acknowledge the diligent editorial assistance of Mr. Edward Artinian at David McKay Company.

HERBERT G. REID
Lexington, Kentucky

Contents

Part Three

The American Dream and the Democratic Mirage: The Facts of Anti-Development   154

Part Four

The Rhetoric of Equality in the Mobilization of Political Bias and Official Violence   227

Part Five

The Emergence of Technocratic Ideology in the Super-industrial Society   286

the Mainstream

Part One Mainstream Ideology as a System of Cultural Hegemony: Political Domination in Everyday Life

The subject of this book is the American ideology that forms a cultural background for mainstream politics. After the 1972 presidential election some prominent political analysts claimed that Senator George Mc-Govern lost essentially because he was viewed by many voters as outside the mainstream of American political thought. This voter image of Senator McGovern was consciously used, if not created, by the successful effort to reelect Richard Nixon. The dominant ideology prevented many voters from accurately perceiving Senator McGovern as a mainstream liberal who sup-ported existing institutional arrangements and procedures. Reform liberals must devote considerable campaign time to demonstrating their basic commitment to the American ideology; they must persuade the people that they do support the structures which allegedly embody the "American way," protect our "high standard of living," provide for our "national security," and so on. The goal of this book is to describe the American ideology and to show how it dominates thought about politics in everyday life, closing off alternative possibilities.

Not only do many Americans have an aversion to any view that might be "socialist," "radical," or "extremist," they are also at times uncomfortable about describing themselves as "conservative" or "liberal." The dominant ideological tradition has fostered a widespread notion of American politics as uniquely nonideological and pragmatic. This notion that our politics are characterized by a pragmatic "genius," which eliminates any need for ideology, has been encouraged by some social scientists. Yet the claim that American politics are nonideological is itself ideological, because it contains an antiintellectual bias and plays down basic conflicts of principle. Vague no-tions of "democracy" and "capitalism" as fundamentally American have served as substitutes for serious political thought. From Tocqueville to Marcuse, critics of American society have observed that it is not easy for most Americans to affirm political beliefs ranging beyond limited practical con-

2

cerns. This is evident in the ways we conceive of the world as well as in our more immediate feelings and attitudes. (Tocqueville, writing about 1830, commented on both the general lack of interest in theoretical science and the distaste for poetry in America.) A common distrust of "theory" may conceal a determination to get along in politics with a particular, traditional theory unrecognized as such. However, in recent years it has become difficult not to see that the pragmatic veneer of mainstream politics conceals a volcano of fundamental social and cultural conflict rather than an iceberg of institutionalized political wisdom.

But those conflicts have remained largely unarticulated. As Louis Hartz has shown, prerevolutionary America, unlike Europe, lacked a feudal aristocratic class and the historical struggles against it and so there was little social soil for the cultivation and growth either of radical socialism or of traditional conservatism. America has seemed to be a timeless Utopia. In fact, the typical American political mind has tended to be frozen from the historical moment of its conception. Liberalism (the historical ideology epitomized in the thought of John Locke) has not been a stage of our history but the whole of it. Social change has proceeded but the general public has had little benefit of a hard conflict of major political ideas and principles. The growth of concentrated economic power in industrializing America brought an increase of social tensions and barriers. But the plight of exploited groups was hardly improved, because such betterment could only come through actions based on a coherent and critical ideology outside of the dominant liberal-capitalist framework.

An amorphous middle class has been a major historical agent of the dominant ideology. This ideology, discussed in the selection by C. Wright Mills, was comprised of beliefs in individualism, private property, natural rights, legalism, a market-oriented doctrine of equality of opportunity, and a general privatistic orientation toward social life. The middle classes have continued to express their abstract devotion to these ideological principles even as the American dream loses its basis in reality. The "silent majority" may be "silent" for good reason. Its members have nothing approaching a viable theory of their increasingly technological and organizational society. Instead of the securely successful, self-reliant sovereign citizen of liberal individualism, the technocorporate society reveals (or hides?) a semisovereign, frustrated, and confused citizen confronting bureaucratic power and consumer culture. Many people accept governmental programs they cannot justify in terms of their individualistic political beliefs. They know they cannot afford to dispense with the operational programs of the welfare state (for example, social security and medicare) which have been developed to alleviate the contradictions between the technocorporate society of everyday life and the good society idealized in the old liberal code of American belief. But this code or credo endures as the skeleton of their political identity and continues to dominate political rhetoric. It was this skeleton that was rattled by Senator McGovern and by the elite coalition opposing him in the recent election. Senator McGovern's liberalism was seen by many voters not as giving new flesh to old bones but as creating instead a "socialist" or "radical" political monster. In Louis Hartz's terms, President Nixon invoked the liberal enchantment of the American dream of individual success and prosperity through hard work and business enterprise. (See the selection by Johnson in part 3 of this volume.) Senator McGovern, with a great deal of "help" from his opponents, tended to evoke for many middle-class voters the liberal terror of "subversive socialism." He was perceived by many to be clearly outside the mainstream of American political thought. At the same time, for many of McGovern's supporters he represented the best in the liberal tradition and perhaps for some its last hope.

In recent years, journalists have reported a mass of evidence of discontent, disorientation, and uncertainty about the system. A Louis Harris poll in the summer of 1972 showed the level of public alienation to be 47 percent higher than anytime since Harris began probing it in 1966. A new generation of scholars has given increasing attention to what seems to be a mounting crisis of public authority. The literature discussing the so-called generation gap and the conflict between new and old cultures is even better known to the reading public. Nevertheless, as the 1972 election makes quite clear, the cultural hegemony (dominance) of mainstream ideology persists.

The persisting notions of individualism, success, and equality that make up the mainstream ideology have tended to eradicate concepts that might help develop a more realistic American self-image and that could challenge and reformulate the legitimacy of the dominant technocorporate order. The growing *rage* that some people apparently feel toward the system may be blunted by acceptance of the mainstream *model* of politics which obscures its source. The elites of the technocorporate state make this model appear as the objective, eternal form of politics. But violence looms as an inevitable alternative for a people whose political thinking has rotted or frozen.

A persistent belief of our political culture is that the voice of rational political order speaks the language of narrowly defined and short-range "interest." Extreme caution is urged whenever any other language (apart from the rhetoric of patriotism) is articulated. Political thought and political action that are not linked to limited economic goals have been suspected of subverting political order itself. A meaningful politics emerging from hard conflict of ideas and from actions based on *real* (basic and long-range) interests has not been a significant reality in our political history; for many it has been an object of suspicion or fear. This allegedly practical approach to political life is related to the individualist faith prominent in America's social history, in which economic self-interest has been seen as the chief motive in human affairs. This faith is also connected historically to a doctrine of fixed, unchanging human nature epitomized in the thought of Calvin and Hobbes and given impetus by the conditions of an emergent market (capitalist) society. The first selection in this volume, by Norman Birnbaum, points up the importance of early bourgeois notions of politics and society and the historical omnipresence of the market in the everyday culture of American life. Selections by Mills, Veblen, Bottomore, and Johnson elaborate on this theme.

Political conflict has thus involved a narrow range of issues for the public majority. The educational system and the mass media are generally devoid of serious criticism of the political system. Publications with limited circulation, such as the *New York Review of Books* and the *Nation,* sometimes offer fundamental criticisms, but the big newspapers and mass magazines restrict themselves to limited fault-finding on specific policies. The general environment of popular culture encourages a commitment to the *status quo,* and most people remain immersed in an established political system, fundamentally unaware of radical alternatives. The omnipresent immediacy of interest-group bargaining and business as usual has been so great that any wider and richer vision of human development has been hard to sustain. The business orientation of American politics has tended to push ideological bias below the surface level of general political controversy and popular political opinion. It has not been easy to detect the relationship of our pragmatic mainstream politics to these ideological principles operating unconsciously within the conformist culture discussed by observers from Tocqueville to Hartz and Marcuse.

The first three selections in part 1 examine the question of how and why liberal ideals have become irrelevant to a viable theory of modern society. The selections by C. Wright Mills and Murray Edelman indicate how American liberalism has become a set of trite phrases—an "official language for all public statement" used by organized elites to paper over conflicts and to reassure the mass public. The final selection in part 1 by the Radical Action Cooperative assesses the consequences of mainstream ideology in daily life. Mainstream ideology has tended to become a system of "cultural hegemony"—a body of thought that controls tastes and judgments in every institution of society and closes off alternative possibilities.[1]

Those who wish to avoid being limited by the mainstream ideology must search for ways to criticize this ideology and its consequences in the politics of everyday life. Criticism of ideology involves the attempt to understand how human beings are dominated in everyday life and how this domination is concealed by rhetoric. A starting point is the recognition that the cultural tradition, symbolic heritage, and everyday vocabulary of a political

---

1. Gwyn A. Williams, "The Concept of 'Egemonia' in the Thought of Antonio Gramsci: Some Notes on Interpretation," *Journal of the History of Ideas* 21 (1960): 587.

system are not unbiased, neutral, or objective instruments for the participation and action of citizens. (Consider the Dahrendorf, Edelman, and Mills selections in this regard.) American capitalist-liberal mainstream ideology has
provided so-called common-sense assumptions essential to the maintenance
of established hierarchical institutions. The leaders of our technocorporate institutions and their spokesmen have enforced their values and interests
through a persuasive and coercive mechanism in which mainstream ideology
is an important element. Elite manipulation and coercion aimed at imposing
capitalist order in times of social unrest have supplemented an astonishing
ideological incorporation of nonelites into the social system throughout
American history. The selections by Bruce Johnson and John William Ward
analyze how the mobilization of cultural bias through appeals to mainstream
myths has been an important dimension of the use of official violence by
dominant elites. This mobilization mechanism is also a basic ideological
process in other institutions of twentieth-century industrial society.

   Murray Edelman's selection attempts to show that secrecy or simple
lack of public awareness cannot fully explain the apathy of the general public
toward policies clearly disadvantageous to it. In fact, defining the problem as
invisibility (for example, inadequate information) leads to proposing remedies
that reveal a *myth* that all social groups have equal access to neutral
education and cultural means of political sophistication. The formula of "get
the facts" and "go vote" only increases the problems of political awareness
and action. Elections tend to become one more device for the legitimation of a
system in which effective action is increasingly taken by experts, many of
whom belong to the higher circles of power and privilege. Many students are
rightly suspicious of a get-the-facts-and-vote approach in political education.

   In the new technocorporate state culture has become increasingly tied
to the interests and values of ruling elites. Not only does mainstream ideology
function to justify the political goals of these elites, but it also permeates
education, the family, the mass media, religious organizations, and other institutions that have traditionally been thought of as independent from politics.
Theodor Adorno notes that ideology today gives us "advertisements for the
world" as it is, while Jacques Ellul observes that sociological propaganda
which influences the very way in which human beings relate to one another in
ordinary life has become more important than traditional political propaganda
which justifies the legitimacy of rulers.[2] Jules Henry holds that advertising in
the United States is a philosophical system which teaches that personal salvation can be attained through purchasing more and more consumer goods
manufactured by the huge business corporations. Advertising, then, is a form
of sociological propaganda that programs the individual to pursue private and

---

   2. The Adorno quote is from *Prisms*, trans. Samuel and Sherry Weber (London: Neville
Spearman, 1967), pp. 31–34. The reference to Jacques Ellul is in regard to his study *Propaganda*
(New York: Alfred A. Knopf, 1965).

selfish ends that can never be satisfied—there are always more products to buy. Along with the *status quo* bias of mainstream ideology goes the growing importance of technocracy—the idea that social problems can be solved best by scientific managers representing established organizations. Under this view, basic policy choices should not be debated by wide publics. Instead, policy decisions should be sold to the masses by professional symbol manipulators. In the field of political science this tendency toward one-dimensional social engineering has taken the form of a call to reconcile democratic theory with reality, rather than to bring reality closer to democratic ideals.

This volume is designed not to apologize for mainstream ideology but to encourage critical explanation and analysis. Economic, political, and social analyses of mainstream thought provide a basis for the development of what European social theorist Jurgen Habermas calls the "ideology critique" of daily life. Members of the now-defunct Radical Action Cooperative (see selection 5) speak for a growing number of students when they state:

> Not to criticize daily life is only to prolong its impoverishment. This mistake is made not only by status-quo oriented social scientists but also by potential revolutionaries. They downgrade the significance of daily life just because it is so impoverished and underdeveloped. Criticism is thwarted, moreover, by both the mystification of daily life and the restrictions imposed on behavior by "law and order."

If by 1976 (or 2076 for that matter) there is anything approaching a new revolutionary spirit in American politics, it will have been infused by those who have overcome our aversion to critical political theory. Philosophical renewal in our political culture, of course, will not suffice; it must be connected to the struggle against a well-established cultural hegemony and the simultaneous reordering of public priorities. What this involves in connection with some of our domestic problems is illuminated by Ralph Ellison:

> Perhaps more than any other people, Americans have been locked in a deadly struggle with time, with history. We've fled the past and trained ourselves to suppress, if not forget, troublesome details of the national memory, and a great part of our optimism, like our progress, has been bought at the cost of ignoring the processes through which we've arrived at any given moment in our national existence.[3]

In her study of revolution, Hannah Arendt holds that a "failure of remembrance" is mainly responsible for the great fear of revolution that has characterized postwar American foreign policy. She refers to the "desperate attempts at stabilization of the status quo" and the resulting misuse of American power and prestige to support "obsolete and corrupt political regimes that long since had become objects of hatred and contempt among their own citizens."[4] In an alternative interpretation, Gabriel Kolko pursues the

3. Ralph Ellison, *Shadow and Act* (New York: Signet, 1966), p. 243.

roots of American foreign policy in the "unique economic interests and aspirations of the United States in the world, and the degree to which it benefits
or loses within the existing distribution and structure of power and the world
economy."[5] Kolko's perspective reminds us that the "failure to remember"
does not take place in some privileged cultural realm outside the reach of
power relations. However, neither is the "failure to remember" merely an
ideological reflex of certain historically specific interests. Memory of the
collective past requires a social framework, including shared meanings which
function in the context of stratified social and political organizations.

A critical historical explanation of the failure of social memory is not
an easy task, although its significance in recent social ills has become hard to
ignore. What various black, Indian, women's liberation, and other leaders have
been trying to show, sometimes first of all to themselves, is that historical
events and present social, political and economic inequalities are closely inter-
twined. Images of history are biased in favor of the values of elites. Witness
the treatment of minority groups in the mass media and the stereotypes of
popular culture. However, the liberation movements face serious obstacles in
their attempts to oppose a viable and critical alternative to the mainstream
ideology. The historical background of continuous exploitation is frequently
obscured by romantic and superficial idealizations of the past which play upon
widespread fears and anxieties. The tendency for the subjects of the
technocorporate state to accept counterfeit and comforting images of the
past is illustrated by the current nostalgia craze (e.g., the "old-time" Coca-
Cola glasses). Appeals to nostalgia and sentimentality about the mythical
"good old days" block awareness of a history of human suffering and conflict.
These appeals also serve as tools for merchandising goods and as justifications for triviality and wastefulness.

American political thought has been remarkably deficient in
generating concepts and norms that go beyond the immediate experience of a
society given over to the quest for efficiency in the name of profit. The
"missing traits" of the American self-image discussed in the selection by Ralf
Dahrendorf indicate our lack of the political and historical awareness essential
for a genuinely democratic critique of the technocorporate state. A critical
theory of mainstream ideology must examine how power relations and
system norms and processes tend to obscure the concepts that might illuminate unnecessarily deterministic and elitist structures, both symbolic and
organizational, on which the legitimacy and stability of the technocorporate
state hinge. A critical theory of mainstream ideology "renders possible the development of concepts which de-stabilize and transcend the closed universe
by comprehending it as historical universe."[6] That most of us, as C. Wright

4. Hannah Arendt, *On Revloution* (New York: Viking 1965) p. 291.
5. Gabriel Kolko, *The Roots of American Foreign Policy* (Boston: Beacon Press, 1969), p.
49. See also pp. 8–11.
6. Herbert Marcuse, *One-Dimensional Man* (Boston: Beacon, 1964), p. 99.

Mills says, "now live as spectators in a world without political interlude" *may* imply the existence of new bases for communal types of political solidarity, identity, and action that have been heretofore frail and transient. However, in light of some of the things learned on this trip "up the mainstream," it will come as no surprise that various efforts to give concrete expression to new forms of social life often meet with coercion and closed-mindedness. For the time being, then, it may be important to stress that mere awareness of the dominance of mainstream ideology is a first step toward liberating oneself from blind conformity to elite dictates. The primary purpose of this book is to facilitate the development of a critical theory of ideology which encompasses but goes beyond the good common sense of American pragmatic politics in the movement toward a truly democratic society.

NORMAN BIRNBAUM
Problems of Social Consciousness in America

If there is one basic American disorder, it certainly entails our inadequate and distorted social consciousness. The sources of defect and distortion are many. Perhaps these go back to the very roots of our culture. It is historically false to argue that the Puritans in New England were without a social ethic: the Mayflower Compact was an exercise in social theology. However, the importation to this country of early bourgeois notions of community and polity combined with the development of a market unrestrained by pre-capitalist institutions and traditions. It eventually resulted in the society's continuing inability to find a social ethic adapted to its real situation. Our social ethic has always evinced a serious lag with respect to the social contradictions it has had to master. It is quite true that no one any longer will promulgate imbecilities like the assertion that the family farm is the backbone of America; the struggle in 1970 over welfare-state institutions which hardly represent an advance

Source: Excerpt from Norman Birnbaum, "Late Capitalism in the United States," in George Fischer, ed., *The Revival of American Socialism* (New York: Oxford University Press, 1971), pp. 133–53. Copyright © by Norman Birnbaum. Reprinted by permission.

over Bismark's nineteenth-century social policies does suggest that there are still serious historical discrepancies in our public vision.

The first source of these defects must be found in the strange fate of high culture in America. By high culture I mean that tradition of systematic reflection on man, society, and nature developed in the medieval church and the medieval universities and continued at times within and at times without the universities by those intellectuals who assumed the responsibility for the custody of tradition. America has had groups which have manifested a high culture but rarely like the European elite with its community of discourse with their society's intellectual and cultural elite. (Marx's own cultural attitudes would no doubt horrify many dues-paying members of our own New University Conference.) The history of immigration to the United States has been the history of a constant infusion of groups cut off from European high culture. This has been particularly, although not exclusively, true of much of the American working class. The market, therefore, and life goals and life styles derived from the working of market forces, have imposed themselves on most of the American population as an institutional context which could not be imagined away. Critical notions based on other perspectives for human life, as developed by intellectuals who were instinctually anticapitalist, have met incomprehension, hostility, and even murderous hatred. The secularization of American Protestantism (and of the other American religions) has been so profound that not alone a flattening but a virtual eradication of the metaphysical horizon has reduced most of the American population to the point at which it cannot imagine a concrete transcendence of its conditions of existence. Revising Marx, we may say that precisely the absence of religion has contributed to a state of political quietism in America.

The social classes in America have generally lacked the cultural resources to develop self-conscious and articulated images of their own interests. The southern slaveholders and the New England merchants did for a period develop coherent ideologies. These were not generalized, indeed they could not be generalized, to cover any substantial section of an expanding society—even if they were consonant with the culture, life style, and interests of the groups at issue. It is significant that American liberalism has been a curious fusion of entrepreneurial materialism on the one hand and vulgar egoism on the other—whatever its ideal or more civilizing elements. These last have frequently remained in the realm of moral pronouncement and moral criticism, a realm to which the intellectuals were confined until the emergence, at the beginning of this century, of a true technical intelligentsia. Briefly put, the fragmentation of class struggle in America, the ethnic diversity of the population, have contributed to the prevention of a true cultural homogenization of the population. The homogenization which has now taken place is rather an imposed one and not necessarily an entirely profound one.

Another way of looking at this is to assert that America has developed no political conception of a general will, no genuine notion of a polity and political life. Mills in *White Collar* called our attention to Aristotle's definition of an "idiot" as a private man with no communal or general interests. The reduction of a considerable section of the American population to this sort of idiocy can be seen as due to the interaction of two factors: long-term cultural values (or their absence) and the heavy pressure of a manufactured mass culture. In the circumstances, the wonder is not that America has never had a full-scale or enduring movement of social criticism expressed in political terms, but that so much social criticism and so much radical politics have emerged in our history.

American society, then, lacks the ideological resources to make a correct estimate of its historical situation. Popular notions of social causality remain relatively primitive, however much suspicions and intimations of exploitation move large groups. The targets of popular hostility are frequently displaced. The intellectuals do speak to a larger group—but a good deal of the intellectuals' public is so bound to white-collar or technocratic occupational routine that its perceptions of social contradiction remain, for the moment at least, without serious political consequences. In the circumstances, attacking policemen with lead pipes does not seem to be an entirely appropriate response to the problems of mass political education.

RALF DAHRENDORF

The American Self-Image: Missing Traits and Their Prospects

There can be no doubt that the reception of European sociology in the United States was selective, nor can there be any doubt that the sample selected was not representative. American sociology displays what L. and H. Rosenmayr call "blackout phenomena,"[1] and it shares these blank spots with the self-image of American society. Characteristically,

Source: Excerpt from Ralf Dahrendorf, "European Sociology and the American Self-Image," *European Journal of Sociology* 2 (1961): 324–66. Reprinted by permission.

those traits which are prominent in European sociology but have nevertheless played but a minor part in American thought, must be expressed
not in terms of ideas (such as "democracy" or "individualism"), but as
concepts—although the use of each of these concepts invokes a host of
connotations and attitudes to society. Six such concepts, and their problematic role in American thought, will be discussed in this section: *class,
violence, elite, revolution, history,* and *intellectuals.* These concepts,
all of which have at best an ambiguous place in American thought, might
be associated with the names of European sociologists, too: among
others, with those of Marx, Pareto, Mosca, Sorel, Landauer, Benda,
Mannheim, Alfred Weber. But the attempt to associate any one of
these names specifically with but one of the six concepts would be even
more arbitrary than the association of names and ideas above.

In terms of the self-image of a society, what are "missing traits"
from the point of view of the "official," the dominant ethos, are usually
the values of minorities. In fact, the following discussion is a discussion
of the ethos of the radical minority in American social thought and
politics. Thus, the "missing traits" not only constitute a background
that gives contours to the actual values of American society and their
origin, but they also describe the contradictions inherent in American—
as in any other—society. Those who employed the concepts discussed in
this section, and adhered to the ideas with which they are associated,
were deviants in their own society; but as deviants they may have contributed more to its development than the uncritical conformists.

(a) Class.

If Edward Shils were to rewrite his account of *The Present State of
American Sociology* after thirteen years, one of the statements he would
have to qualify would be that about class: "Neither class relations in the
power sphere nor inter-class ascent and descent have been systematically
studied by American sociologists."[2] Perhaps, in a subtle sense, this
statement is still correct. But ostensibly a great deal of research has been
devoted, in the last decade, to the subjects of class, status, and power,
including social mobility between classes. There is the *Yankee City
Series*, and several monographs by its main author, W. Lloyd Warner,
including one on *Social Class in America;* there is R. Centers' study of
The Psychology of Social Classes; there are numerous lesser studies of
specific aspects of class and mobility; and there are two great summaries in the form of a Reader on *Class, Status and Power,* and a monograph on *Social Mobility in Industrial Society,* both by R. Bendix and
S. M. Lipset.

However, the first thing that strikes the European student of Amer-

ican research in the field of class, is that it is lacking in the sense of urgency which is so evident in its European counterpart. In the United
States, class is no more than one among other criteria of self-interpretation (and as such, it is clearly less important than, say, color). This detached attitude is in part due to the fact that in America the concept of
class underwent a radical change in meaning. Whereas in Europe, the
notions of class, economic position, and class struggle are quite inseparable, it does not sound at all peculiar to American ears to hear that "social class in America is not the same as economic class"[3] or to discuss
Sumner's question of *What Social Classes Owe to Each Other.*[4] There
are, to be sure, influential American critics of this neglect of the economic aspects of class and the problem of class conflict. Several years
ago, S. M. Lipset and R. Bendix published a profound critique of American studies of class and their underlying ideological bias (of conservatism)[5]; C. Wright Mills never tires to remind his countrymen of the significance of class in the European sense for American society; earlier
Robert Lynd presented both empirical data and analysis to underline the
reality of class conflicts in America.[6] But these men represent the very
minority with which we are concerned in this section. So far, they have
stood for what the American self-image is not; for the ordinary American, class is not a prime category of self-interpretation.

The place of class in American society and social analysis is of
course part of the more general problem of the impact of Marxism on
American thought. This is a problem that defies simple generalizations,
even if they are as cautious as that of L. and H. Rosenmayr: "There is
nothing in the USA that could correspond to the flood of political, historical and sociological discussion of Marxism in Europe between
1860 and 1930."[7] What about the discussion of the role of the state or of
early American socialism? Even the early meetings of the American
Sociological Society were dominated by discussions of acute "social
problems" and of solutions offered for them.[8] All that can confidently
be said is that the influence of Marx was inferior to that of many other
European social scientists, including Tocqueville and Spencer, Simmel
and Weber. In so far as there was any influence at all, it usually consisted
in more or less violent reactions against Marx. "The study of social
classes," state S. M. Lipset and R. Bendix, "has suffered in the past from
the proclivity of social scientists to react against the influence of
Marx."[9] This may be true for the United States, but it is utterly incor-
rect for Europe. In Europe, social science and, one suspects, the self-
image of many societies, have been influenced by Marx more than by
any other single social scientist. In the United States Marx seemed, for a
long time, simply not applicable; and when people tried to apply his
thought to American problems more recently, they violated a taboo of
American values.

Perhaps the question of why all this is so is the same as Sombart's famous question: *Why Is There No Socialism in the United States?* In a letter to Weydemeyer in 1852, Marx acknowledged that "in the United States, bourgeois society has not yet matured," and that the class struggle is therefore not yet apparent.[10] But of course, Marx thought that this was merely a matter of time. Half a century later, Sombart argued along much the same lines. He saw four reasons for the absence of socialism in the United States: the standard of living of the workers, the "democratic" character of American society, the unauthoritarian character of employer-worker relations, and the significance of geographical and social mobility for working-class life.[11] However, Sombart concluded his analysis with the prediction "that all the factors which have held up the development of socialism in the United States to the present day are in the process of disappearing or being reversed, so that in all probability socialism will grow to full bloom in the Union during the next generation."[12] It would take a lot of sophistry to prove that Sombart's prediction has come true. Fifty years later, it would in fact still seem valid that "although social classes are rank orders placing people and their families in higher and lower orders, they do not permanently fix the status of either the individual or his family in America."[13] At the same time, the very fact that Sombart's prediction once appeared reasonably plausible points to the existence of a strand in American history which, although neglected by sociology and public consciousness, has left its imprint on contemporary American society.

(b) Violence.

One of the reasons why the "undeveloped areas" (to quote Shils[14]) of American sociology as well as the American self-image can be described more accurately in terms of concepts than of ideas is that they refer to factual conditions of American society rather than to its ideology. It is no secret (at least to a "European sociologist") that social values do not always reflect the factual substratum of the society in which they are held; they may also conceal it by presenting an image of order and beauty where there is in fact disorganization and ugliness. Nowhere is this more true than with respect to the role of violence in American society. One of the first impressions that strike the foreign visitor to the United States even today is the amount of violence characteristic of American life. Crime statistics (even if they are occasionally inflated by police chiefs who want to increase their budgets), the incidence of fighting in public places, the atmosphere of political struggles as well as of competition in business and between individuals are curiously in accord with the prevailing emphasis on "action" in television plays and films. As Laski said more than a decade ago: "The American tradition is one in which veneration for law is at least equalled by the widespread habit of a violence which disregards the habits of law."[15] Laski tried to explain this too: "Partly, that violence is the inevitable accompaniment of a frontier civilisation [...] Partly also, the violence derives from the mixture of races and philosophies out of which, at so swift a pace, America has emerged. It is connected very directly with the fact that it was so easy, if the law was put aside, to make one's way to wealth on so immense a scale [....]"[16] But looking at American sociology, or at the American self-image, one would not think that violence really plays so large a part in American life—unless the very absence of any recognition of violence testifies by the laws of psychoanalysis, to its significance. That Americans have been hesitant to interpret their own society in Marx's terms of class and class struggle, we have seen. Few American authors refer to Sorel's *Reflections on Violence* (and when I recommended the book to some American graduates in sociology, I found them deeply shocked after reading it). Simmel has played a considerable role for many of the early American sociologists, but the chapter of his *Sociology* concerned with conflict was translated only a few years ago;[17] and one not untypical author adds to his reference to Coser's discussion of Simmel's theory of conflict the apology that he "should have been, but was not familiar" with this theory.[18] Coser himself has some interesting comments to offer on the neglect of conflict in American sociology.[19] In its formative years, he claims, conflict was in fact recognized as a source of progress. But since the 1920s, the study of conflict was increasingly neglected. This was due, Coser believes, to changes in the position and self-image of American sociologists, and especially to their increasing association with public bureaucracies, as well as to "the fear of social conflict and the call to unity which seems to pervade much of the current intellectual trends."[20]

Conflict is of course not necessarily violent. It is possible to approve of conflict and to disapprove of violence. In the United States, however, there seems to be so much disapproval of both, and so much insistence on "love of peace," that doubts must be raised about the "rationality" and the viability of the American self-image at this point. Where democracy is understood to mean representative government, it is invariably also understood to mean conflict. Wherever, on the other hand, consensus, stability, and unity are over-emphasized, a society becomes very vulnerable to the really disruptive effects of internal strife. If it were not for that thin but important stratum of American intellectuals who, throughout the last decades, have kept the Hobbesian solution of the Hobbesian problem of order alive, American society would be even harder pushed today in its efforts to cope with what potential and actual violence there is in its structure.

(c) Elite.

The student of American sociology cannot but realize that a number of names of outstanding European sociologists—including those of Sorel, Pareto, Mosca, Michels—are, if not exactly taboo, yet mentioned comparatively rarely and often apologetically. Where they are referred to, it is frequently secondary and minor aspects of their works which are quoted, although all four have by now been translated, and there are excellent monographs by American authors on at least two of them.[21] One of the reasons for this comparative reticence is understandable: all these authors were, or were said to be, associated with Italian fascism. It seems to me, though, that there is another reason, and one that is not only less justifiable, but also left implicit. Sorel, Pareto, Mosca, Michels were all concerned with the phenomenon of elites, of ruling classes, their emergence, circulation, and impact on society. As with class in general, however, so it appears to be with ruling classes in particular. It is, as Meisel expresses it, "the American majority opinion: ruling classes may exist in Europe, or in Asia, but it cannot happen here."[22] This is an old American belief which Laski traces back to "the victory of Jefferson in the great election of 1800" which "meant that the idea of an America would triumph in which the notion of an *élite* to whom government was confided would have no place."[23] Obviously, elites are incompatible with the American idea of democracy: where all are equal, the chosen few have no place. Yet the silence about the concept of elites in American thought is suspicious.[24]

The belief that one is ruled by a small group of men who monopolize the reins of power is an element of the self-image of many, if not most European societies. In European sociology, however, this image occurs in the main with authors who have to be described as conservative in their political orientation: from Vilfredo Pareto to Raymond Aron. It is characteristic of radical social and political theory in Europe to insist on the role of the many (discarded as passive "masses" by Mosca and Pareto) in the shaping of history. Not even Marx was an elite theorist in any meaningful sense. These positions are curiously reversed in the United States. Here, it is the radicals who are preoccupied with the notion of elites, and assert the existence of a "leisure class" or a "power elite," for by these assertions they contradict every valid value of their environment.[25] If C. Wright Mills is right—many an American seems to tell himself—then everything one has thought about one's country must be wrong; therefore, Mills cannot be right. And yet, a lingering suspicion remains that he may be right after all—and it is difficult to cope with this fear if one has avoided looking at society in terms of ruling elites at all.

Between Mills' "elite to end all elites," as Meisel nicely puts it,[26] and the watered-down concept of elite employed in, say, the Hoover Elite Studies (which are in any case not concerned with the United States but with the rest of the world),[27] there is a notion of governing elites which is indispensable at least to the sociologist's, if not to every citizen's understanding of society. The belief in the common man becomes Utopian, if it is not associated with recognition of the realities of power under whatever social and political conditions.[28] Whether C. Wright Mills is right or not in his assertion of a homogeneous power elite removed not only from the public eye but also from a parliamentary control in the United States, he has, I think, done his countrymen a great service by reminding them of an aspect of European sociology which has so far found dangerously little resonance in American self-interpretation.

(d) Revolution.

In a sense, the three lacunae of American values discussed so far in this section converge in the concept of revolution. In any case, European analysts and theorists of revolution were always concerned with elites, classes, and violence. Once again, however, American scholars have managed to give a phenomenon, which is ostensibly the same as that studied by their European colleagues, a strikingly different interpretation. For a long time, Americans thought of revolution—i.e., the American revolution—as an event involving no more violence than the Boston Tea Party, carried on by the active masses of the population, and leading to the establishment of a classless democracy. Only recently has this idyllic notion of revolution been put to the test, and found somewhat lacking. The Russian Revolution and its numerous successors in our own century have caused many Americans to revise their own happy view of this phenomenon. And while American society was, in the nineteenth century, rather well disposed to the idea of revolution, American reactions to present-day Cuba suggest that in this respect too, the last decades have been decades of change. Thus the role of the notion of revolution for the American self-image is above all an illustration of the decline of the American Creed of the nineteenth century.

Raymond Bruckberger, a French traveller to the United States, markedly less perceptive and equally markedly more romantic than his great predecessor a century ago, has recently restated the old American view of revolution in all naïveté. In his book (which is characteristically entitled *La République américaine* in the original, *Images of America* in the English and *Amerika—Die Revolution des Jahrhunderts* in the German version) he claims: "More than of the political sovereignty of a people, the most perfect expression of which is a revolution, one can say of every genuine revolution that it originated from God, but comes to light in the people and can only be fulfilled by the people."[29] The American revolution, of course, was a "genuine revolution" (as was, no doubt, the French), and one that is outstanding because "it happened in the sphere of social principles, of the mutual rights and obligations of men and nations."[30] It is the little attribute "genuine" that distinguishes Bruckberger from most Americans of the last century: nowadays, one has to reckon with events called revolutions but characterized by force and unfreedom, rather than "social principles." Perhaps no other study signifies the turning point of American thinking about revolution as well as Brinton's *Anatomy of Revolution.* Ostensibly Brinton is trying to formulate a theory of revolution that applies to the English as well as the French, the American as well as the Russian case. In fact, however, he finds himself arguing at great length that whereas the English, French and Russian revolutions may have involved a Reign of Terror and a post-Thermidorean dictatorship, the "American revolution" was spared this terrible fate.[31] Thus it would seem that there are "good" and "bad" revolutions, and that the "American revolution" is one (the only?) example of a "good revolution." Might it not have been rather more in keeping with Brinton's theoretical intent to abandon the popular interpretation of the attainment of independence by the Thirteen States as a revolution and call it by its proper name, a war of independence? But perhaps Brinton did not want to go quite so far in destroying the traditional self-image. Since his book was first published in 1938, the theme of revolution has played a decreasing role in American social science. Even in 1948, Shils could point to "the study of revolutions" as one of the "undeveloped areas" in American sociology;[32] today, it is hardly ever mentioned at all.

Of course, the role of revolutions in national self-images is always ambivalent. When L. and H. Rosenmayr refer to the American tradition as one of "revolution incarnated in law,"[33] they describe what is in fact by necessity characteristic of all societies deriving their values from a revolution. It is inevitable that a process of what Max Weber called *Veralltäglichung,* of reducing the exceptional to everyday dimensions and thereby destroying its dynamics, sets in with respect to the memory of revolutions. From this point of view, the fate of the concept of revolution in American thought is perhaps not altogether surprising. On the other hand, the abandonment of the sweet American notion of revolution in face of the harsher reality of comparable events in the contemporary world, and the corresponding neglect of those European sociologists who had placed great emphasis on the study of violent and radical social and political change, accord well with the growing prevalence of a somewhat anxious conservatism. For the dynamic conservative of the nineteenth century it was possible to combine the ideas of the revolutionary origin of American society and of its organic stability in one system of values; for the worried conservative of our own times, the idea of revolution involves so many frighteningly explosive connotations that he prefers to interpret his own society entirely in terms of integration, community, and stability.

(e) History.

"An awareness of history is always a part of any culturally alert national life; but I believe that what underlies this overpowering nostalgia of the last fifteen years is a keen feeling of insecurity," wrote Hofstadter in 1948.[34] Many modern observers are agreed that Americans are as conscious of their political tradition as any other people. But it must remain doubtful whether this concern with the American past involves any deeper understanding of the historicity of all human societies including that of America. To refer to "history" as one of the blank spots in American national consciousness, cannot mean that Americans show no interest in their own history; the contrary is true. It can and does mean, however, that interest in the past does not lead, in America, to an appreciation of the changeability of all things human. America is perhaps the only country in the world in which there are many who believe that Utopia can come true. This is understandable, since so many Utopias so nearly came true in the United States. At the same time, it is a very unhistorical way of looking at reality.

The absence of historical consciousness in American sociology is a frequent complaint of its critics. Thus C. Wright Mills devotes a whole chapter to the "uses of history" in his *Sociological Imagination* in which he charges American sociologists with producing too many "a-historical" studies.[35] More than a decade earlier, E. A. Shils had regretfully stated that "American sociologists are notoriously deficient" with respect to historical knowledge.[36] More recently, and more specifically, M. Stein concluded that "American sociology, unlike its European counterpart, has always displayed impatience with the ineradicable historicity of much sociological data."[37] The relations between sociology and history are complicated even when they are good, and there is no use denying that similar objections are quite familiar to European sociologists too. Nor is it easy to tell what historically conscious sociological research would actually look like—for what is meant by this demand must obviously be more than that the history of every phenomenon under investigation is taken into account in the analysis of its present condition. Perhaps, the point of the criticism of a-historical sociology as well as of the thesis that history is a blank spot in the American self-image is really not a matter of merely recognizing change, but of recognizing it for what it is—a force uncertain in direction which may turn good to bad and bad to good, which is somewhere beyond the possibilities of human control, and which has to be reckoned with wherever we deal with social data. In this sense, I would say that many Americans, sociologists and otherwise, have failed to come to terms with history.

(f) Intellectuals.

No subject has been debated more passionately by American intellectuals in the last decades, than that of American intellectuals. The persistence of this debate is all the more remarkable since there is really very little disagreement among its participants. Everybody—that is, of course, every intellectual—seems to agree that intellectuals in the United States are hard done by, suffer from low social and economic status, exert no influence whatever on American politics, and are generally ignored by society, if not attacked by the prevailing values of "anti-intellectualism." Agreement on these points is so general, and is so much a role expectation of the American intellectual, that S. M. Lipset's essay on "American intellectuals, their politics and status" came as a real shock to many and broke a sacred rule.[38] Lipset claims that, first, the status of American intellectuals is by no means as low as most of them like to believe, that, secondly, they exert considerable influence on their society, and that, thirdly, in pretending to be undervalued by their society they betray a sneaking sympathy for the very aristocracy of rank which they fight in their explicit political convictions. But shocking as it may have been to many of those concerned, to the (more or less) impartial outside observer Lipset's essay has done much to clear the somewhat misty air over the problem of American intellectuals.

It seems clear now (as indeed one would have expected to find), that the position of intellectuals in American society was different at different times. At the height of the rugged individualism of capitalist expansion, there was no place for intellectuals in American society. Unlike the situations in those countries which have belatedly started to develop an industrial economy, an autonomous bourgeoisie dominated the American scene, and its values explicitly denied the luxury of useless activities such as thinking, writing, painting, and the like. N. Birnbaum thinks that he can trace this period in American politics too: none of the presidents between Jackson and Th. Roosevelt "was an intellectual, not even Lincoln; in the staff of none of the presidents, including that of

Lincoln, was the number of intellectuals of importance; none of them was influenced or indeed unsettled by general ideas."[39] More recently, there arose a new vogue of anti-intellectualism, culminating in the McCarthy persecutions, the object of which was (and still is, to some extent) the alleged "leftism" of intellectual politics. At the same time, intellectuals have taken an active part in American politics under at least three presidents—Wilson, F. D. Roosevelt, and now Kennedy—and they have never lost their importance since the First World War. Thus, Lionel Trilling's general statement that in "American culture"—the self-image of the country—"there exists an opposition between reality and mind and [. . .] one must enlist oneself in the party of reality,"[40] is at best partly correct, for especially in the last decades there have been many who enlisted in the party of mind and have not done badly in the process.

Not only are there important differences in the position of American intellectuals over time, but at any one time this group is also by no means as homogeneous as its members would have the outside world believe. Throughout his article, Lipset takes the fact to be conclusively proven that American intellectuals have been consistently "leftist" in their political orientation; but toward the end he suddenly suggests that very recently, in the last few years or so, there has been a vogue of conservatism among intellectuals everywhere, including the United States. In this, he is by no means alone; N. Birnbaum, for example, but also E. Shils and R. Hofstadter and many others share this view. The trouble is, however, that half a century ago more radical social scientists—say, Lester Ward or Thorstein Veblen—felt much the same about their contemporaries, and that probably radicals everywhere find the present unbearably slow-moving and conservative. Very likely, the truth of the matter is that at any one time there are conservative and radical intellectuals. Their distribution may change, but as a social group or stratum the intelligentsia is probably less uniform than any other group, if only because so many of its members are "free-floating" in the sense of having broken with their ascriptive and primary ties. Thus the analysis of the position of intellectuals has to go beyond all too simple generalizations.

Social scientists are no exception to this pattern. But—and this is why I have included in the present analysis the subject of intellectuals —as we survey the history of American social science, and especially of American sociology, a remarkable fact emerges. Throughout the history of American sociology there were those who felt committed to a better future and those who were by and large satisfied with the present. There were—to use Merton's unfortunate, but symptomatic terms—the "rebels" and "retreatists" who wanted to change the basic values of their society as well as the accepted means for their realization, and the "innovators" who were content with minor adjustments of reality to the undisputed values of their society.[41] In America, however, unlike other countries, the latter constituted, from the beginnings of Sumner and Small and Giddings and others, the overwhelming majority of the sociological profession.[42] Lipset rightly quotes Geiger's statement which applies to all European countries:

> Of all groups in the intelligentsia, the social scientists are most sensitive to the power dimension in society, and also the most exposed to the attacks on intellectual freedom by those in power [. . .] Therefore, we can expect that [. . .] a significant number of social scientists [. . .] would be attracted to the left in one or another of its forms.[43]

By this standard, only a few American social scientists could be called social scientists; or, more precisely, many American social scientists are not really intellectuals at all. American sociology began with the concern with "social problems," and with devising ways and means to solve these problems. Explicit or implicit "social engineering" is a persistent feature of American sociology. The continental European division of "sociology" and "social policy" as university disciplines has never been introduced in the United States. As a result, American sociologists have tended to orient themselves to policies of improvement: improvement of enterprises and prisons, cities and schools, hospitals and slums, etc. etc. By this very orientation, they have come to be "innovators," agents of the adaptation of social reality to the values from which it has deviated, "dynamic conservatives." It is clear that in this context the tradition that leads from Ward and Veblen to Lynd and Mills is a marginal tradition, and that the profession does (and did) all it can to dissociate itself from the imaginative few who can think of other values than those embodied in the status quo.

We are here concerned with European sociology and the American self-image; in this context, we do not have to decide whether American intellectuals in general have tended to be conservative or progressive. However, American sociologists have a special relevance for our problem. In so far as European sociology has been at all influential in the United States, American sociology has been an important intermediary. I have tried to show that in this traffic a number of concepts and ideas have been more or less systematically neglected, although they played and continue to play a prominent role in the thinking of European sociologists; the concepts of class, violence, and elite, the ideas of revolution, of history, and of the intellectual as "rebel." If our analysis of American sociology is at all plausible, it provides an explanation for this consequential neglect. American sociologists have, apart from a small "intellectual" minority marginal to the group, failed to absorb those ideas of European sociologists which threatened their undisputed acceptance of the values of their society. They have thereby rendered their society the dubious service of apparently protecting it from some of the more unsettling ideas of modern times.

NOTES

1. Leopold and Hilde Rosenmayr, *Introduction* to Roscoe and Gisela Hinkle, *Die Entwicklung der Amerikanischen Soziologie* (Munich: Oldenbourg, 1960), p. 15ff.

2. Edward Shils, *The Present State of American Sociology* (Glencoe, Ill.: Free Press, 1948), p. 21.

3. W. Lloyd Warner, *American Life—Dream and Reality* (Chicago: University of Chicago Press, 1953), p. 53.

4. Title of one of Sumner's books, a "social Darwinian classic." Richard Hofstadter, *Social Darwinism in American Thought* (Boston: Beacon Press, 1959), p. 8.

5. Seymour Martin Lipset and Reinhard Bendix, "Social Status and Social Structure," *British Journal of Sociology* 2 (1951).

6. Cf. C. Wright Mills, *White Collar: The American Middle Class* (New York: Oxford University Press, 1951), and *The Power Elite* (New York: Oxford University Press, 1956); Robert and Helen Lynd, *Middletown* (New York: Harcourt Brace, 1929) and, above all, *Middletown in Transition* (New York: Harcourt Brace, 1937).

7. L. and H. Rosenmayr, *Introduction*, p. 16.

8. Cf., e.g., L. Coser, *The Functions of Social Conflict* (London: Routledge & Kegan Paul, 1956), p. 15ff.

9. Lipset and Bendix, "Social Status and Social Structure," p. 151.

10. Letter by Karl Marx to Josef Weydemeyer of March 5, 1852.

11. This is the briefest summary of Sombart's brilliant analysis, *Warum gibt es in den Vereinigten Staaten keinen Sozialismus?* (Tübingen, 1906), especially pp. 124–42.

12. Ibid., p. 141ff.

13. Warner, *American Life*, p. 54.

14. Cf. Shils, *Present State of American Sociology*, p. 52ff.

15. Harold Laski, *The American Democracy* (London: Allen & Unwin, 1949), p. 31.

16. Ibid., p. 31ff.

17. Georg Simmel, *Conflict and Web of Group Affiliations*, trans. K. H. Wolff (Glencoe, Ill.: Free Press, 1955).

18. Thus James H. Meisel, *The Myth of the Ruling Class* (Ann Arbor: University of Michigan Press, 1958), p. 424, n. 64.

19. Coser, *Functions of Social Conflict*, chap. 1.

20. Ibid., p. 28.

21. Lawrence J. Henderson, *Pareto's General Sociology* (Cambridge, Mass.: Harvard University Press, 1935), and Meisel, *Myth of the Ruling Class,* with the subtitle "Gaetano Mosca and the Elite."

22. Meisel, *Myth of the Ruling Class,* p. 360.

23. Laski, *American Democracy,* p. 9.

24. There is an apparent contradiction between my thesis that the concept of elite has been neglected in American sociology and A. Brodersen's statement ("Strukturprobleme der heutigen amerikanischen Gessellschaft," *Hamburger Jahrbuch für Wirtschafts und Gesellschaftspolitik* 4 (1959): 40): "Concepts like "ruling class" were so far [. . .] usually avoided in American sociology. Instead another concept was adopted much more eagerly and used almost indiscriminately for almost every kind of of structural analysis. I am thinking of the concept of elite." Brodersen's first statement shows that we are agreed in principle; as to the latter, Brodersen fails to present enough evidence to substantiate it, although he has a point insofar as there are a few authors who try to do to the concept of elite what American sociology did to the concept of class: reduce it to a neutral, and rather sterile meaning.

25. For a discussion of elite theories and theorists in America see Meisel, "Conclusions," *Myth of the Ruling Class.*

26. Ibid., p. 360.

27. The "elite studies" of the Hoover Institute at Stanford University provide excellent data on German, Soviet and other political leaders; but the concept of elite employed by them is devoid of any meaning.

28. It is unfortunate from this point of view, that C. J. Friedrich, the author of *The New Image of the Common Man* (Boston: Beacon Press, 1950), should be "fairly representative of the American majority opinion." (Meisel, *Myth of the Ruling Class,* p. 360.)

29. Quoted from the German version of R. L. Bruckberger, *Amerika— Die Revolution des Jahrhunderts* (Frankfurt: S. Fischer, 1960), p. 101.

30. Ibid., p. 60.

31. Brinton puts his case rather cleverly in the following way: having discussed the rise to power of "Cromwell, Bonaparte, Stalin," he adds the— clearly rhetorical—statement: "Indeed, in the Federalist period in the United States, there were Jeffersonians ungrateful enough to suggest that Washington was a perfectly good example of the tyrant born of revolution" (*The Anatomy of Revolution,* rev. ed. [New York: Vintage Books, 1957], p. 218). In fairness it must be added that Brinton has asked himself whether the American revolution is really a case in point, and although he has decided that it is, he has not done so without reservation.

32. Shils, *American Sociology,* p. 53.

33. L. and H. Rosenmayr, *Introduction,* p. 13.

34. Richard Hofstadter, *The American Political Tradition* (New York: Alfred A. Knopf, 1948), p. v.

35. C. Wright Mills, *The Sociological Imagination* (New York: Oxford University Press, 1959), chap. 8.

36. Shils, *American Sociology,* p. 53.

37. M. Stein, *The Eclipse of Community* (Princeton: Princeton University Press, 1960), p. 95.

38. Seymour Martin Lipset, "American Intellectuals, Their Politics and Status," *Political Man* (Garden City, N.Y.: Doubleday, 1960).

39. Norman Birnbaum, "Die Intellektuellen in der gegenwärtigen Politik der Vereinigten Staaten," *Zeitschrift fur Politik,* 1957, p. 126.

40. Lionel Trilling, "Reality in America," *The Liberal Imagination* (Garden City, N.Y.: Doubleday, 1957), p. 8.

41. Cf. Robert King Merton, "Social Structure and Anomie," *Social Theory and Social Structure* (Glencoe, Ill.: Free Press, 1958).

42. This is why not only the relation between Sumner and Spencer, but also that between Small and Schmoller is so significant: in Germany, Schmoller was a representative not of "sociology," but of "social policy" (*Sozialpolitik*) which was the theory of Bismarck's dynamic conservatism. German sociology developed in active opposition to this school of thought.

43. Th. Geiger, *Aufgabe und Stellung der Intelligenz in der Gesellschaft* (Stuttgart: F. Ekke, 1949), p. 124.

C. WRIGHT MILLS

Liberal Values in the Modern World

Most of us now live as spectators in a world without political interlude: fear of total permanent war stops our kind of morally oriented politics. Our spectatorship means that personal, active experience often seems politically useless and even unreal. This is a time when frustration seems to be in direct ratio to understanding, a time of cultural mediocrity when the levels of public sensibility have sunk below sight. It is a time of irresponsibility, organized and unorganized; when common sense, anchored in fast-outmoded experience, has become myopic and irrelevant. Nobody feels secure in a simple place; nobody feels secure and there is no simple place.

It is a time when no terms of acceptance are available, but also no terms of rejection: those on top seem stunned, distracted, and bewildered, and don't know what to do. But what is much more damaging to us: those on the bottom are also without leaders, without counter-ideas, don't know what to do, do not have real demands to make of those in key positions of power.

Source: From *Power, Politics and People: The Collected Essays of C. Wright Mills,* edited by Irving Louis Horowitz. Copyright © 1963 by the Estate of C. Wright Mills. Reprinted by permission of Oxford University Press, Inc.

Whatever the political promises of labor and leftward forces 15 years ago, they have not been fulfilled; whatever leadership they have developed has hidden itself for illusory safety, or been buried by events it neither understands nor wishes to control. Organized labor in the forties and early fifties has been mainly another adaptive and adapting element. What goes on domestically may briefly be described in terms of the main drift toward a permanent war economy in a garrison state.

Internationally, of course, the world of nations has been polarized into two dead-locked powers, with no prospects of a structured peace, with a penumbra of variously graded and variously dependent satellites, puppets, and vacuums. For the first time in its easy history, the United States finds itself a nation in a military neighborhood, having common frontiers with a big rival. The United States is a sea and air power from an external position; wherever it turns, it faces a vast land-power with an internal position. In the meantime, Europe has become a virtual colony, held by military force and economic dependence, And neither in the West nor in the East do U.S. spokesmen seem to have ideas and policies that have genuine appeal to the people residing there.

Internationally and domestically, the death of political ideas in the United States coincides with the general intellectual vacuum to underpin our malaise. Insofar as ideas are involved in our political impasse, these ideas center in the nature and present day situation of liberalism. For liberalism is at once the main line of our intellectual heritage and our official political philosophy. I shall not here attempt a full analysis of liberalism's connection with the modern malaise. I only want to lay out some key themes, which I believe must be taken into account in any examination of liberalism today.

I

Like any social philosophy, liberalism can conveniently be understood and discussed: (1) as an articulation of *ideals* which, no matter what its level of generality, operates as a sort of moral optic and set of guidelines for judgments of men, movements and events; (2) as a *theory*, explicit or implied, of how a society works, of its important elements and how they are related, of its key conflicts and how they are resolved; (3) as a social phenomenon, that is, as an *ideology* or political rhetoric— justifying certain institutions and practices, demanding and expecting others. In these terms, what is the situation of liberalism today?

As a set of articulated *ideals*, liberalism has been and is a major part of "the secular tradition of the west." As a political *rhetoric*, liberalism has been the ideology of the rising middle class. As a *theory* of society, liberalism is confined in relevance to the heroic epoch of the middle class. These points are connected, for as a carrier of ideals, liberalism has been detached from any tenable theory of modern society, and however engaging in its received condition, it is no longer a useful guide-line to the future. For the eighteenth and part of the nineteenth centuries, liberal theory did clarify and offer insight; for the twentieth century, it just as often confuses.

II

Liberalism, as a set of ideals, is still viable, and even compelling to Western men. That is one reason why it has become a common denominator of American political rhetoric; but there is another reason. The ideals of liberalism have been divorced from any realities of modern social structure that might serve as the means of their realization. Everybody can easily agree on general ends; it is more difficult to agree on means and the relevance of various means to the ends articulated. The detachment of liberalism from the facts of a going society make it an excellent mask for those who do not, cannot, or will not do what would have to be done to realize its ideals.

As a kind of political rhetoric, liberalism has been banalized: now it is commonly used by everyone who talks in public for every divergent and contradictory purpose. Today we hear liberals say that one liberal can be "for," and another liberal "against," a vast range of contradictory political propositions. What this means is that liberalism as a common denominator of American political rhetoric, is without coherent content; that, in the process of its banalization, its goals have been so formalized as to provide no clear moral optic. The crisis of liberalism (and of American political reflection) is due to liberalism's success in becoming the official language for all public statement. To this fact was added its use in the New Deal Era when, in close contact with power, liberalism became administrative. Its crisis in lack of clarity is underpinned by its use by all interests, classes, and parties.

It is in this situation that professional liberals sometimes make a fetish of indecision, which they would call open-mindedness, as against inflexibility; of the absence of criteria, which they would call tolerance, as against dogmatism; of the formality and hence political irrelevance of criteria, which they would call "speaking broadly," as against "details."

We may not, of course, dismiss liberalism merely because it is a common denominator of political rhetoric. Its wide use as justification limits the choices and, to some extent, guides the decisions of those in authority. For if it is the common denominator, all powerful decisions made in the open must be justified in its terms, and this may restrain the deciders even if they do not "believe in it." For men are influenced in their use of authority by the rhetoric they feel they must employ. The leaders as well as the led, and even the mythmakers, are influenced by prevailing rhetorics of justification.

Liberals have repeatedly articulated a secular humanism, stressing the priceless value of the individual personality, and the right of each individual to be dealt with in accordance with rational and understandable laws, to which all power is also subject. They have been humanist in the sense that they see man as the measure of all things: policies and events are good or bad in terms of their effect on men; institutions and societies are to be judged in terms of what they mean to and for the individual human being. Liberals have assumed that men should control their own life-fates. It is in terms of this value that the entire concern with consent to authority and the opposition to violence should be understood. All loyalties to specific movements and organizations tend, for the liberal, to be conditional upon his own principles, rather than blindly to an organization. Liberals have assumed that there are rational ways to acquire knowledge, and that substantive reason, anchored in the individual, provides the way out.

As a set of such ideals, liberalism has very heavily contributed to the big tradition of the West, but it is not the sole carrier of this tradition; it is not to be identified with it. And it is a real question whether today it is the most whole-hearted carrier of it, for it is to be greatly doubted that, as a theory of society, liberalism is in a position to lead or help men carry these ideals into realization.

So, if as ideal, liberalism is the secular tradition of the West, as a theory of society, which enables these ideals, it is the ideology of one class inside one epoch. If the moral force of liberalism is still stimulating, its sociological content is weak; it has no theory of society adequate to its moral aims.

III

The assumptions of liberal theories about society, have to do with how liberal values could be anchored, with how they could operate as guide to policy. The liberal ideals of the eighteenth and nineteenth centuries were anchored in several basic assumptions about the condition of modern society that are no longer simple or clear:

(i) Liberalism has assumed that both freedom and security, its key values, flourish in a world of small entrepreneurs. But it is quite clear that one of the most decisive changes over the last hundred years is the enormous increase in the scale of property units. This has meant that the ideals of liberty and of security have changed: absolute liberty to control property has become tyranny. The meaning of freedom, positively put, has to be restated now, not as independence, but as control over that upon which the individual is dependent. Security, once resting on the small holding, has become, in the world of large property, anxiety—anxiety produced by the concentration of process and by the manner of living without expectation of owning. Positively, security must be group-guaranteed; individual men can no longer provide for their own futures.

If a particular ideal of freedom assumes for its realization the dominance of a scatter of small property, then, the social meaning of this ideal is quite different from a statement of freedom that assumes a situation of concentrated property. It is in its theory of society, tacit or explicit, that we find the political content of a social philosophy. If men assume the dominance of huge-scale property, and yet state eighteenth-century ideals, they are off base. In the kindergarten of political philosophy one learns that the idea of freedom *in general* is more serviceable as politically irrelevant rhetoric than ideal. Twentieth-century problems cannot be solved by eighteenth-century phrases. Liberty is not an a-priori individual fact, and it has been a social achievement only when liberal ideals have fortunately coincided with social realities.

Order can be reconciled with liberty by an underlying common sentiment, or by a balance of harmoniously competing groups. Common sentiment can grow from slow-paced tradition or be imposed from a powerful center. Competitive balance can be maintained only if each faction remains small enough and equal enough to compete freely. But now there is no common sentiment, and there is no balance, but a lop-sided competition between and among dominant factions and midget interests.

Liberalism, in the nineteenth-century epoch of its triumph, never really took into account the changing economic foundations of the political ideals and forms it espoused. That simple fact goes far to explain the decline of liberalism in authoritative cogency. This is the fact upon which Marxism has been correctly focused and upon which it has capitalized.

(ii) Many classic liberals, perhaps especially of the Rousseauian and Jeffersonian persuasion, have assumed the predominance of rural or "small city states," in brief, of a small-scale community. Liberal discussion of the general will, and liberal notions of "public opinion" usually rest on such assumptions. We no longer live in this sort of small-scale world.

(iii) A third assumption about society, characteristic of classic liberalism, has been the stress upon the autonomy of different institutional orders. In the beginning, as with Locke, it would split off religious institutions from the political, so that the political justifications, whatever they may be, had to be secular. Later on, the economic order was split from the political order, in the classic case of laissez-faire, perhaps coming to a head in the early philosophical radicals in England. But that was not the end of making different institutional orders autonomous. The kinship order was also to be split from the other orders so that there was a free marriage market, just as there was a free commodity market.

Moreover, in each of these orders a similar principle was upheld: that of individual freedom of choice—as an economic agent; as a presumptuous political man, who had to be shown before he would obey; as a man on the marriage market making a free contract with his partner; and so on.

But what has happened is the fusion of several institutional orders; the co-ordination of the major orders has become the contemporary reality. We see in the United States today an increased coincidence and fusion of the economic, political, and military orders.

(iv) A fourth underlying sociological assumption, probably the most subtle and far-reaching, certainly the most philosophically relevant, is that the individual is the seat of rationality. When liberals speak of rationality and "the increase of enlightenment," they have assumed that the individual will be increased in stature and dignity because *his* power to reason and *his* knowledge will be increased. But the decisive fact here, as signified quite well by such writers as Max Weber and Karl Mannheim, is that the seat of rationality has shifted from the individual and is now in the big institution. The increase of enlightenment does not necessarily wise up the individual. This has to do with the distinction of substantive from formal rationality, in short, the growth of a bureaucratic organization of knowledge. The prevailing character as well as the distribution of rationality now leads to a whole set of questions to which we have no contemporary liberal answers. This modern weakness and irrationality of the individual, and especially his political apathy, is crucial for liberalism; for liberalism has classically relied on the reasoning individual as its lever for progressive change.

(v) Tied in with the belief in the growth of the individual's substantive rationality is the belief in the explicitness of authority. Men, as individuals or as groups of individuals, could learn to know who exercised power and so could debate it or obey. But today, one of the crucial political problems "for experts," as for laymen, is to locate exactly who has the power.

It is fashionable now, especially among those who have left what radical circles remain, to suppose that "there is no ruling class," just as it was fashionable in the thirties to suppose a set of class villains to be the source of all social injustice and public malaise. I should be as far from supposing that some enemy could be firmly located, that some one or two set of men were responsible, as I should be from supposing that it is all merely impersonal, tragic drift. The view that all is blind drift is largely a fatalist projection of one's own feeling of impotence and perhaps a salve of guilt about it. The view that all is due to the conspiracy of an easily locatable enemy is also a hurried projection from the difficult effort to understand how structural shifts open opportunities to various elites and how various elites take advantage or fail to take advantage of them. To accept either view is to relax the effort rationally to understand in detail how it is.

There are obviously gradations of power and opportunities among modern populations, which is not to say that all ruling powers are united, or that they fully know what they do, or that they are consciously joined in conspiracy. One can, however, be more concerned with their structural position and the consequences of their decisive actions than with the extent of their awareness or the impurity of their motives. But such analysis has not been part of the liberal tradition, nor does this tradition provide decisive help in undertaking it.

IV

The root problem of any "democratic" or "liberal"—or even humanist—ideals is that they are in fact statements of hope or demands or preferences of an intellectual elite psychologically capable of individually fulfilling them, but they are projected for a population which in the twentieth century is not at present capable of fulfilling them.

What is inferred from this depends, in part, upon what is seen to be the causes of this mass incapability, and, in part, simply upon the degree of sanguinity. In nineteenth-century liberalism, the causes were seen largely as ignorance; so the answer was education. This was true of classic liberalism and, in part, of classic socialism, although the meaning and the further reasons for ignorance were more sophisticatedly worked out by socialist than by liberal writers. In the twentieth century, serious thinkers have further developed this socialist view, whether or not they know it as socialist, and have come to see that the whole structure of modern society, in particular its bureaucratic and communication systems virtually expropriate from all but a small intellectual elite the capacity for individual freedom in any adequate psychological meaning of the term.

The intellectual question for liberals, then, rests on the confrontation of the old individual ideals with new social and psychological facts. The old social anchors of individual freedom and individual security of small scattered properties and small-scale communities are gone; the roots of these values in autonomously operating institutions are dried up; the seat of rationality is no longer unambiguously the individual; the centers of power are as often hidden as explicit. And so the question becomes whether the ideals themselves must be given up or drastically revised, or whether there are ways of re-articulating them that retain their old moral force in a world that moral liberals never made.

MURRAY EDELMAN

Symbols and Political Quiescence

Few forms of explanation of political phenomena are more common than the assertion that the success of some group was facilitated by the "apathy" of other groups with opposing interests. If apathy is not an observable phenomenon in a political context because it connotes an individual's mental state, quiescence is observable. It is the purpose of this essay to specify some conditions associated with political quiescence in the formation of business regulation policies. Although the same general conditions are apparently applicable to the formation of public policies in any area, the argument and the examples used here focus upon the field of government regulation of business in order to make the subject manageable and to permit more intensive treatment.

Political quiescence toward a policy area can be assumed to be a function either of lack of interest—whether it is simple indifference or stems rather from a sense of futility about the practical prospects of securing obviously desirable changes—or of the satisfaction of whatever interest the quiescent group may have in the policy in question. Our concern here is with the forms of satisfaction. In analyzing the various means by which it can come to pass, the following discussion distinguishes between interests in resources (whether goods or freedoms to act) and interests in symbols connoting the suppression of threats to the group in question. Few political scientists would doubt, on the basis of common sense evidence, that public policies have value to interested groups both as symbols and as instruments for the allocation of more

Source: American Political Science Review 54 (September 1960): 695–704. Reprinted by permission of the publisher and the author.

tangible values. The political process has been much less thoroughly studied as a purveyor of symbols, however; and there is a good deal of evidence, to be presented below, that symbols are a more central component of the process than is commonly recognized in political scientists' explicit or implicit models.[1]

Three related hypotheses will be considered:

(1) The interests of organized groups in tangible resources or in substantive power are less easily satiable than are interests in symbolic reassurance.

(2) Necessary conditions associated with the occurrance of the latter type of interest are:

(a) the existence of economic conditions in some measure threatening the security of a large group;

(b) the absence of organization for the purpose of furthering the common interest of that group;

(c) widespread political responses suggesting the prevalence of inaccurate, oversimplified, and distorted perceptions of the issue.

(3) The pattern of political activity represented by lack of organization, distorted perception, interests in symbolic reassurance, and quiescence is a key element in the ability of organized groups to use political agencies in order to make good their claims on tangible resources and power, thus continuing the threat to the unorganized.

Available evidence bearing on these hypotheses will be marshalled as follows. First, some widely accepted propositions regarding group claims, quiescence, and techniques for satisfying group interests in governmental regulation of business will be summarized. Next, some pertinent experimental and empirical findings of other disciplines will be considered. Finally we will explore the possibility of integrating the various findings and applying them to the propositions listed above.

I

If the regulatory process is examined in terms of a divergence between political and legal promises on the one hand and resource allocations and group reactions on the other hand, the largely symbolic character of the entire process becomes apparent. What do the studies of government regulation of business tell us of the role and functions of that amorphous group who have an interest in these policies in the sense that they are affected by them, but who are not rationally organized to pursue their interest? The following generalizations would probably be accepted by most students, perhaps with occasional changes of emphasis:

(1) Tangible resources and benefits are frequently not distributed to unorganized political group interests as promised in regulatory statutes and the propaganda attending their enactment.

This is not true of legal fictions, but rather of the values held out to (or demanded by) groups which regard themselves as disadvantaged and which presumably anticipate benefits from a regulatory policy. There is virtually unanimous agreement among students of the anti-trust laws, the Clayton and Federal Trade Commission acts, the Interstate Commerce acts, the public utility statutes and the right-to-work laws, for example, that through much of the history of their administration these statutes have been ineffective in the sense that many of the values they promised have not in fact been realized. The story has not been uniform, of course; but the general point hardly needs detailed documentation at this late date. Herring, Leiserson, Truman, and Bernstein[2] all conclude that few regulatory policies have been pursued unless they proved acceptable to the regulated groups or served the interests of these groups. Within the past decade Redford, Bernstein[3] and others have offered a "life cycle" theory of regulatory history, showing a more or less regular pattern of loss of vigor by regulatory agencies. For purposes of the present argument it need not be assumed that this always happens but only that it frequently happens in important cases.[4]

(2) When it does happen, the deprived groups often display little tendency to protest or to assert their awareness of the deprivation.

The fervent display of public wrath, or enthusiasm, in the course of the initial legislative attack on forces seen as threatening "the little man" is a common American spectacle. It is about as predictable as the subsequent lapse of the same fervor. Again, it does not always occur, but it happens often enough to call for thorough explanation. The leading students of regulatory processes have all remarked upon it; but most of these scholars, who ordinarily display a close regard for rigor and full exploration, dismiss this highly significant political behavior rather casually. Thus, Redford declares that, "In the course of time the administrator finds that the initial public drive and congressional sentiment behind his directive has wilted and that political support for change from the existing pattern is lacking."[5]

Although the presumed beneficiaries of regulatory legislation often show little or no concern with its failure to protect them, they are nevertheless assumed to constitute a potential base of political support for the retention of these statutes in the law books. The professional politician is probably quite correct when he acts on the assumption that his advocacy of this regulatory legislation, in principle, is a widely popular move, even though actual resource allocations inconsistent with the promise of the statutes are met with quiescence. These responses (support of the statute; apathy toward failure to allocate resources as the statute promises) define the meanings of the law so far as the presumed beneficiaries are concerned.[6] It is the frequent inconsistency between the two types of response that is puzzling.

(3) The most intensive dissemination of symbols commonly attends the enactment of legislation which is most meaningless in its effects upon resource allocation. In the legislative history of particular regulatory statutes the provisions least significant for resource allocation are most widely publicized and the most significant provisions are least widely publicized.

The statutes listed under Proposition 1 as having promised something substantially different from what was delivered are also the ones which have been most intensively publicized as symbolizing protection of widely shared interests. Trust-busting, "Labor's Magna Carta" (the Clayton Act), protection against price discrimination and deceptive trade practices, protection against excessive public utility charges, tight control of union bureaucracies (or, by other groups, the "slave labor law"), federal income taxation according to "ability to pay," are the terms and symbols widely disseminated to the public as descriptive of much of the leading federal and state regulation of the last seven decades; and they are precisely the descriptions shown by careful students to be most misleading. Nor is it any less misleading if one quotes the exact language of the most widely publicized specific provisions of these laws: Section 1 of the Sherman Act, Sections 6 and 20 of the Clayton Act, or the closed shop, secondary boycott, or emergency strike provisions of Taft-Hartley, for example. In none of these instances would a reading of either the text of the statutory provision or the attendant claims and publicity enable an observer to predict even the direction of future regulatory policy, let alone its precise objectives.

Other features of these statutes also stand as the symbols of threats stalemated, if not checkmated, by the forces of right and justice. Typically, a preamble (which does not pretend to be more than symbolic, even in legal theory) includes strong assurances that the public or the public interest will be protected. And the most widely publicized regulatory provisions always include other nonoperational standards connoting fairness, balance, or equity.

If one asks, on the other hand, for examples of changes in resource allocations that have been influenced substantially and directly by public policy, it quickly appears that the outstanding examples have been publicized relatively little. One thinks of such legislation as the silver purchase provisions; the court definitions of the word "lawful" in the Clayton Act's labor sections; the procedural provisions of Taft-Hartley and the Railway Labor Act; the severe postwar cuts in Grazing Service appropriations; and changes in the parity formula requiring that such items as interest, taxes, freight rates and wages be included as components of the index of prices paid by farmers.

Illuminating descriptions of the operational meaning of statutory mandates are found in Truman's study and in Earl Latham's *The Group Basis of Politics*.[7] Both emphasize the importance of contending groups and organizations in day-to-day decision-making as the dynamic element in policy formation; and both distinguish this element from statutory language as such.[8]

We are only beginning to get some serious studies of the familiarity of voters with current public issues and of the intensity of their feelings about issues; but successful political professionals have evidently long acted on the assumption that there is in fact relatively little familiarity, that expressions of deep concern are rare, that quiescence is common, and that, in general, the congressman can count upon stereotyped reactions rather than persistent, organized pursuit of material interests on the part of most constituents.[9]

(4) Policies severely denying resources to large numbers of people can be pursued indefinitely without serious controversy.

The silver purchase policy, the farm policy, and a great many other subsidies are obvious examples. The anti-trust laws, utility regulations, and other statutes ostensibly intended to protect the small operator or the consumer are less obvious examples; though there is ample evidence, some of it cited below, that these usually support the proposition as well.

The federal income tax law offers a rather neat example of the divergence between a widely publicized symbol and actual resource allocation patterns. The historic constitutional struggle leading up to the Sixteenth Amendment, the warm defenses of the principle of ability to pay, and the frequent attacks upon the principle through such widely discussed proposals as that for a 25 percent limit on rates have made the federal tax law a major symbol of justice. While the fervent rhetoric from both sides turns upon the symbol of a progressive tax and bolsters the assumption that the system is highly progressive, the bite of the law into people's resources depends upon quite other provisions and activities that are little publicized and that often seriously qualify its progressive character. Special tax treatments arise from such devices as family partnerships, gifts *inter vivos*, income-splitting, multiple trusts, percentage depletion, and deferred compensation.

Tax evasion alone goes far toward making the symbol of "ability to pay" hollow semantically though potent symbolically. While 95 percent of income from wages and salaries is taxed as provided by law, taxes are actually collected on only 67 percent of taxable income from interest, dividends, and fiduciary investments and on only about 36 percent of taxable farm income.[10] By and large, the recipients of larger incomes can most easily benefit from exemptions, avoidances and evasions. This may be desirable public policy, but it certainly marks a disparity between symbol and effect upon resources.

II

These phenomena are significant for the study of the political process for two reasons. First, there is a substantial degree of consistency in the group interest patterns associated with policies on highly diverse subject matters. Second, they suggest that nonrational reaction to symbols among people sharing a common governmental interest is a key element in the process. The disciplines of sociology, social psychology, and semantics have produced some pertinent data on the second point; and to some of this material we turn next.

Harold Lasswell wrote three decades ago that "[P]olitics is the process by which the irrational bases of society are brought out into the open." He marshalled some support in case studies for several propositions that have since been confirmed with richer and more direct experimental evidence. "The rational and dialectical phases of politics," he said, "are subsidiary to the process of redefining an emotional consensus." He argued that "widespread and disturbing changes in the life-situation of many members of society" produce adjustment problems which are resolved largely through symbolization; and he suggested that "[P]olitical demands probably bear but a limited relevance to social needs."[11]

The frame of reference suggested by these statements is sometimes accepted by political scientists today when they study voting behavior and when they analyze the legislative process. Its bearing on policy formation in the administrative process is not so widely recognized. It is true that cognition and rationality are central to administrative procedures to a degree not true of legislation or voting. But this is not at all the same thing as saying that administrative policies or administrative politics are necessarily insulated from the "process of redefining an emotional consensus."

Let us consider now some experimental findings and conclusions specifying conditions under which groups or personality types are prone to respond strongly to symbolic appeals and to distort or ignore reality in a fashion that can be politically significant.

(1) People read their own meanings into situations that are unclear or provocative of emotion. As phrased by Fensterheim, "The less well defined the stimulus situation, or the more emotionally laden, the greater will be the contribution of the perceiver."[12] This proposition is no

longer doubted by psychologists. It is the justification for so-called projective techniques and is supported by a great deal of experimental evidence.

Now it is precisely in emotionally laden and poorly defined situations that the most widely and loudly publicized public regulatory policies are launched and administered. If, as we have every reason to suppose, there is little cognitive familiarity with issues, the "interest" of most of the public is likely to be a function of other socio-psychological factors. What these other factors are is suggested by certain additional findings.

(2) It is characteristic of large numbers of people in our society that they see and think in terms of stereotypes, personalization, and oversimplifications; that they cannot recognize or tolerate ambiguous and complex situations; and that they accordingly respond chiefly to symbols that over-simplify and distort. This form of behavior (together with other characteristics less relevant to the political process) is especially likely to occur where there is insecurity occasioned by failure to adjust to real or perceived problems.[13] Frenkel-Brunswik has noted that "such objective factors as economic conditions" may contribute to the appearance of the syndrome, and hence to its importance as a widespread group phenomenon attending the formulation of public policy.[14] Such behavior is sufficiently persistent and widespread to be politically significant only when there is social reinforcement of faith in the symbol. When insecurity is individual, without communication and reinforcement from others, there is little correlation with ethnocentricity or its characteristics.[15]

A different kind of study suggests the extent to which reality can become irrelevant for persons very strongly committed to an emotion-satisfying symbol. Festinger and his associates, as participant-observers, studied a group of fifteen persons who were persuaded that the world would come to an end on a particular day in 1956 and that they as believers would be carried away in a flying saucer. With few exceptions the participants refused to give up their belief even after the appointed day had passed. The Festinger study concludes that commitment to a belief is likely to be strengthened and reaffirmed in the face of clear disproof of its validity where there is a strong prior commitment (many of the individuals involved had actually given away their worldly goods) and where there is continuing social support of the commitment by others (two members who lost faith lived in environments in which they had no further contact with fellow-members of the group; those who retained their faith had continued to see each other). What we know of previous messianic movements of this sort supports this hypothesis.[16]

(3) Emotional commitment to a symbol is associated with content-

ment and quiescence regarding problems that would otherwise arouse concern.

It is a striking fact that this effect has been noticed and stressed by careful observers in a number of disparate fields, using quite different data and methods. Adorno reports it as an important finding of the *Authoritarian Personality* study:

Since political and economic events make themselves felt apparently down to the most private and intimate realms of the individual, there is reliance upon stereotype and similar avoidances of reality to alleviate psychologically the feeling of anxiety and uncertainty and provide the individual with the illusion of some kind of intellectual security.[17]

In addition to the support it gets from psychological experiment, the phenomenon has been remarked by scholars in the fields of semantics, organizational theory, and political science. Albert Salomon points out that "Manipulation of social images makes it possible for members of society to believe that they live not in a jungle, but in a well organized and good society."[18] Harold Lasswell put it as follows:

It should not be hastily assumed that because a particular set of controversies passes out of the public mind that the implied problems were solved in any fundamental sense. Quite often a solution is a magical solution which changes nothing in the conditions affecting the tension level of the community, and which merely permits the community to distract its attention to another set of equally irrelevant symbols. The number of statutes which pass the legislature or the number of decrees which are handed down by the executive, but which change nothing in the permanent practices of society, is a rough index of the role of magic in politics. . . .Political symboliation has its catharsis function. . . .[19]

Chester Barnard, an uncommonly astute analyst of his own long experience as an executive, concluded that:

Neither authority nor cooperative disposition . . . will stand much overt division on formal issues in the present stage of human development. Most laws, executive orders, decisions, etc., are in effect formal notice that all is well— there is agreement, authority is not questioned.[20]

Charles Morris, a leading logician and student of semantics, has analyzed the role of language in shaping social behavior and inculcating satisfaction with existing power relationships. He points to the possibility that exploited groups will "actively resist changes in the very sign structure by which they are exploited." Defining such behavior as "socially pathic," he makes the following comment:

The signs in question may relieve certain anxieties in the members of society with respect to the social behavior in which they are engaged, and so be cherished for this satisfaction even though the signs hinder or even make impossible the actual realization of the goals of such social behavior itself.[21]

Kenneth Burke makes much the same point. Designating political rhetoric as "secular prayer," he declares that its function is "to sharpen up the pointless and blunt the too sharply pointed."[22] Elsewhere, he points out that laws themselves serve this function, alleging that positive law is *itself* "the test of a judgment's judiciousness."[23]

(4) An active demand for increased economic resources or fewer political restrictions on action is not always operative. It is, rather, a function of comparison and contrast with reference groups, usually those not far removed in socioeconomic status.

This is, of course, one of the most firmly established propositions about social dynamics; one that has been supported by macro-sociological analysis,[24] by psychological experiment,[25] and by observation of the political process, particularly through contrast between politically quiescent and protest or revolutionary activity.[26]

The proposition helps explain failure to demand additional resources where such behavior is socially sanctioned and supported. It also helps explain the insatiability of the demand by some organized groups for additional resources (i.e., the absence of quiescence) where there is competition for such resources among rival organizations and where it is acquisitiveness that is socially supported.

(5) The phenomena discussed above (the supplying of meaning in vague situations, stereotypes, oversimplification, political quiescence) are in large measure associated with social, economic, or cultural factors affecting large segments of the population. They acquire political meaning as group phenomena.

Even among the psychologists, some of whom have at times been notably insensitive to socialization and environment as explanations and phases of the individual "traits" they claim to "identify" or "isolate," there are impressive experimental findings to support the proposition. In analyzing the interview material of his *Authoritarian Personality* study, Adorno concluded that "our general cultural climate" is basic in political ideology and in stereotyped political thinking; and he catalogued some standardizing aspects of that climate.[27] His finding, quoted above, regarding the relation of symbols to quiescence is also phrased to emphasize its social character. Lindesmith and Strauss make a similar point, emphasizing the association between symbols and the reference groups to which people adhere.[28]

Another type of research has demonstrated that because interests are typically bound up with people's social situation, attitudes are not typically changed by ex parte appeals. The function of propaganda is rather to activate socially rooted interests. One empirical study which arrives at this conclusion sums up the thesis as follows:

Political writers have the task of providing "rational" men with good and acceptable reasons to dress up the choice which is more effectively determined by underlying social affiliations.[29]

George Herbert Mead makes the fundamental point that symbolization itself has no meaning apart from social activity: "Symbolization constitutes objects . . . which would not exist except for the context of social relationships wherein symbolization occurs."[30]

III

These studies offer a basis for understanding more clearly what it is that different types of groups expect from government and under what circumstances they are likely to be satisfied or restive about what is forthcoming. Two broad patterns of group interest activity vis à vis public regulatory policy are evidently identifiable on the basis of these various modes of observing the social scene. The two patterns may be summarized in the following shorthand fashion:

(1) Pattern A: a relatively high degree of organization—rational, cognitive procedures—precise information—an effective interest in specifically identified, tangible resources—a favorably perceived strategic position with respect to reference groups—relatively small numbers.

(2) Pattern B: shared interest in improvement of status through protest activity—an unfavorably perceived strategic position with respect to reference groups—distorted, stereotyped, inexact information and perception—response to symbols connoting suppression of threats—relative ineffectiveness in securing tangible resources through political activity—little organization for purposeful action—quiescence —relatively large numbers.

It is very likely misleading to assume that some of these observations can be regarded as causes or consequences of others. That they often occur together is both a more accurate observation and more significant. It is also evident that each of the patterns is realized in different degrees at different times.

While political scientists and students of organizational theory have gone far toward a sophisticated description and analysis of Pattern A, there is far less agreement and precision in describing and analyzing Pattern B and in explaining how it intermeshes with Pattern A.

The most common explanation of the relative inability of large numbers of people to realize their economic aspirations in public policy is in terms of invisibility. The explanation is usually implicit rather than explicit, but it evidently assumes that public regulatory policy facilitating the exploitation of resources by knowledgeable organized groups (usually the "regulated") at the expense of taxpayers, consumers, or other unorganized groups is possible only because the latter do not know it is happening. What is invisible to them does not arouse interest or political sanctions.

On a superficial level of explanation this assumption is no doubt valid. But it is an example of the danger to the social scientist of failure to inquire transactionally: of assuming, in this instance, (1) that an answer to a questioner, or a questionnaire, about what an individual "knows" of a regulatory policy at any point in time is in any sense equivalent to specification of a group political interest; and (2) that the sum of many individual knowings (or not-knowings) as reported to a questioner is a *cause* of effective (or ineffective) organization, rather than a consequence of it, or simply a concomitant phase of the same environment. If one is interested in policy formation, what count are the assumptions of legislators and administrators about the determinants of future political disaffection and political sanctions. Observable political behavior, as well as psychological findings, reveals something of these assumptions.

There is, in fact, persuasive evidence of the reality of a political interest, defined in this way, in continuing assurances of protection against economic forces understood as powerful and threatening. The most relevant evidence lies in the continuing utility of old political issues in campaigns. Monopoly and economic concentration, anti-trust policy, public utility regulation, banking controls, and curbs on management and labor are themes that party professionals regard as good for votes in one campaign after another, and doubtless with good reason. They know that these are areas in which concern is easily stirred. In evaluating allegations that the public has lost "interest" in these policies the politician has only to ask himself how much apathy would remain if an effort were made formally to repeal the anti-trust, public utility, banking, or labor laws. The answers and the point become clear at once.

The laws may be repealed in effect by administrative policy, budgetary starvation, or other little publicized means; but the laws as symbols must stand because they satisfy interests that are very strong indeed: interests that politicians fear will be expressed actively if a large number of voters are led to believe that their shield against a threat has been removed.

More than that, it is only as symbols of this sort that these statutes have utility to most of the voters. If they function as reassurances that threats in the economic environment are under control, their indirect effect is to permit greater exploitation of tangible resources by the organized groups concerned than would be possible if the legal symbols were absent. Those who are deprived become defenders of the very system of law which permits the exploiters of resources to act effectively.

To say this is not to assume that everyone objectively affected by a policy is simply quiescent rather than apathetic or even completely unaware of the issue. It is to say that those who are potentially able and willing to apply political sanctions constitute the politically significant group. It is to suggest as well that incumbent or aspiring congressmen are less concerned with individual constituents' familiarity or unfamiliarity with an issue as of any given moment than with the possibility that the interest of a substantial number of them *could* be aroused and organized if he should cast a potentially unpopular vote on a bill or if a change in their economic situations should occur. The shrewder and more effective politicians probably appreciate intuitively the validity of the psychological finding noted earlier: that where public understanding is vague and information rare, interests in reassurance will be all the more potent and all the more susceptible to manipulation by political symbols.

The groups that succeed in using official agencies as instrumentalities to gain the resources they want are invariably organized so as to procure and analyze pertinent information and then act rationally. Most voters affected by the regulatory policy are certain on the other hand to secure distorted information, inadequate for intelligent planning of tactics or strategy.

We have already noted that it is one of the demonstrable functions of symbolization that it induces a feeling of well-being: the resolution of tension. Not only is this a major function of widely publicized regulatory statutes, but it is also a major function of their administration. Some of the most widely publicized administrative activities can most confidently be expected to convey a misleading sense of well-being to the onlooker because they suggest vigorous activity while in fact signifying inactivity or protection of the "regulated."

One form this phenomenon takes is noisy attacks on trivia. The Federal Trade Commission, for example, has long been noted for its hit-and-miss attacks on many relatively small firms involved in deceptive advertising or unfair trade practices while it continues to overlook much of the really significant activity it is ostensibly established to regulate: monopoly, interlocking directorates, and so on.[31]

Another form it takes is prolonged, repeated, well-publicized attention to a significant problem which is never solved. An excellent example is the approach of the FCC to surveillance of program content in general and to discussions of public issues on the air in particular. In the postwar period we have had the Blue Book, the Mayflower Policy, the abolition of the Mayflower Policy, and the announcement of a substitute policy; but the radio or television licensee is in practice perfectly free, as he has been all along, to editorialize, with or without opportunity for opposing views to be heard, or to eschew serious discussions of public affairs entirely.

The most obvious kinds of dissemination of symbolic satisfactions are to be found in administrative dicta accompanying decisions and orders, in press releases, and in annual reports. It is as common here as in labor arbitration to "give the rhetoric to one side and the decision to the other." Nowhere does the FCC wax so emphatic in emphasizing public service responsibility, for example, as in decisions permitting greater concentration of control in an area, condoning license transfers at inflated prices, refusing to impose sanctions for flagrantly sacrificing program quality to profits, and so on.[32]

The integral connection is apparent between symbolic satisfaction of the disorganized, on the one hand, and the success of the organized, on the other, in using governmental instrumentalities as aids in securing the tangible resources they claim.

Public policy may usefully be understood as the resultant of the interplay among groups.[33] But the political and socio-psychological processes discussed here mean that groups which would otherwise present claims upon resources may be rendered quiescent instead by their success in securing nontangible values. Far from representing an obstacle to organized producers and sellers, they become defenders of the very system of law which permits the organized to pursue their interests effectively, at the expense of the disorganized or unorganized.

Thurman Arnold has pointed out how the anti-trust laws perform precisely this function:

The actual result of the antitrust laws was to promote the growth of great industrial organizations by deflecting the attack on them into purely moral and ceremonial channels . . . every scheme for direct control broke to pieces on the great protective rock of the antitrust laws. . . .

The antitrust laws remained as a most important symbol. Whenever anyone demanded practical regulation, they formed an effective moral obstacle, since all the liberals would answer with a demand that the antitrust laws be enforced. Men like Senator Borah founded political careers on the continuance of such crusades, which were entirely futile but enormously picturesque, and which paid big dividends in terms of personal prestige.[34]

Arnold's subsequent career as Chief of the Anti-trust Division of the Department of Justice did as much to prove his point as his writings. For a five-year period he instilled unprecedented vigor into the Division, and his efforts were widely publicized. He thereby unquestionably made the laws a more important symbol of the protection of the public; but despite his impressive intentions and talents, monopoly, concentration of capital, and restraint of trade were not seriously threatened or affected.

This is not to suggest that signs or symbols in themselves have any magical force as narcotics. They are, rather, the only means by which groups not in a position to analyze a complex situation rationally may adjust themselves to it, through stereotypization, oversimplification, and reassurance.

There have, of course, been many instances of effective administration and enforcement of regulatory statutes. In each such instance it will be found that organized groups have had an informed interest in effective administration. Sometimes the existence of these groups is explicable as a holdover from the campaign for legislative enactment of the basic statute; and often the initial administrative appointees are informed, dedicated adherents of these interests. They are thus in a position to secure pertinent data and to act strategically, helping furnish "organization" to the groups they represent. Sometimes the resources involved are such that there is organization on both sides; or the more effective organization may be on the "reform" side. The securities exchange legislation is an illuminating example, for after Richard Whitney's conviction for embezzlement key officials of the New York Stock Exchange recognized their own interest in supporting controls over less scrupulous elements. This interest configuration doubtless explains the relative popularity of the SEC both with regulated groups and with organized liberal groups.

IV

The evidence considered here suggests that we can make an encouraging start toward defining the conditions in which myth and symbolic reassurance become key elements in the governmental process. The conditions[35] are present in substantial degree in many policy areas other than business regulation. They may well be maximal in the foreign policy area, and a similar approach to the study of foreign policy formation would doubtless be revealing.

Because the requisite conditions are always present in some degree, every instance of policy formulation involves a "mix" of symbolic effect and rational reflection of interests in resources, though one or the other phenomenon may be dominant in any particular case. One type of mix is exemplified by such governmental programs outside the business regulation field as public education and social security. There can be no doubt that these programs do confer important tangible benefits upon a very wide public, very much as they promise to do. They do so for the reasons suggested earlier. Business organizations, labor organizations, teachers' organizations, and other organized groups benefit from these programs and have historically served to focus public attention upon the resources to be gained or lost. Their task has been all the easier because the techniques for achieving the benefits are fairly readily recognizable.

But the financing of these same programs involves public policies of a different order. Here the symbol of "free" education and other benefits, the complexity of the revenue and administrative structure, and the absence of organization have facilitated the emergence of highly regressive payroll, property, and head taxes as the major sources of revenue. Thus, business organizations, which by and large support the public schools that provide their trained personnel and the social security programs that minimize the costs of industrial pensions, pay relatively little for these services; while the direct beneficiaries of the "free" programs pay a relatively high proportion of the costs. Careful analysis of the "mix" in particular programs should prove illuminating.

If the conditions facilitating symbolic reassurance are correctly specified, there is reason to question some common assumptions about strategic variables in policy formulation and reason also to devise some more imaginative models in designing research in this area. The theory discussed here suggests, for example, a tie between the emergence of conditions promoting interests in symbolic reassurance and widened freedom of policy maneuver for those attempting to assert leadership over the affected group. It implies that the number of adherents of a political interest may have more to do with whether the political benefit offered is tangible or symbolic than with the quantity or quality of tangible resources allocated. It suggests that the factors that explain voting behavior can be quite different from the factors that explain resource allocations through government. The fact that large numbers of people are objectively affected by a governmental program may actually serve in some contexts to weaken their capacity to exert a political claim upon tangible values.

A number of recent writers, to take another example, have suggested that it is the "independence" of the independent regulatory commissions which chiefly accounts for their tendency to become tools of the groups they regulate. The hypotheses suggested here apply to regulatory programs administered in cabinet departments as well; and their operation is discernible in some of these programs when the specified conditions are present. The Grazing Service and the Anti-trust Division are examples.

In terms of research design, the implications of the analysis probably lie chiefly in the direction of emphasizing an integral tie of political behavior to underlying and extensive social interaction. Analysts of political dynamics must have a theory of relevance; but the directly relevant may run farther afield than has sometimes been assumed. Political activities of all kinds require the most exhaustive scrutiny to ascertain whether their chief function is symbolic or substantive. The "what" of Lasswell's famous definition of politics is a complex universe in itself.

NOTES

1. Harold Lasswell is a major exception, and some of his contributions will be noted.

2. E. Pendleton Herring, *Public Administration and the Public Interest* (New York: McGraw-Hill, 1936), p. 213; Avery Leiserson, *Administrative Regulation: A Study in Representation of Interests* (Chicago: University of Chicago Press, 1942), p. 14: David Truman, *The Governmental Process* (New York: John Wiley, 1951), chap. 5.; Marver Bernstein, *Regulating Business by Independent Commissions* (Princeton, N.J.: Princeton University Press, 1955), chap. 3.

3. Emmette S. Redford, *Administration of National Economic Control* (New York: Macmillan Co., 1952), pp. 385–86; Bernstein, *Regulating Business.*

4. In addition to the statements in these analytical treatments of the administrative process, evidence for the proposition that regulatory statutes often fail to have their promised consequences in terms of resource allocation are found in general studies of government regulation of business and in empirical research on particular statutes. As an example of the former see Clair Wilcox, *Public Policies Toward Business* (Chicago: Richard Irwin, 1955). As examples of the latter see Frederic Meyers, *'Right to Work' in Practice* (New York: Fund for the Republic, 1959); Walton Hamilton and Irene Till, *Antitrust in Action*, TNEC Monograph 16 (Washington: GPO, 1940).

5. Redford, *Administration of National Economic Control,* p. 383. Similar explanations appear in Herring, *Public Administration and the Public Interest*, p. 227, and Bernstein, *Regulating Business*, pp. 82–83. Some writers have briefly suggested more rigorous explanations, consistent with the hypotheses discussed in this paper, though they do not consider the possible role of interests in symbolic reassurance. Thus Truman calls attention to organizational factors, emphasizing the ineffectiveness of interest groups "whose interactions on the basis of the interest are not sufficiently frequent or stabilized to produce an intervening organization and whose multiple memberships, on the same account, are a constant threat to the strength of the claim." Truman, *Governmental Process*, p. 441. Multiple group memberships are, of course, characteristic of individuals in all organizations, stable and unstable; and "infrequent interactions" is a phenomenon that itself calls for explanation if a common interest is recognized. Bernstein refers to the "undramatic nature" of adminis-

tration and to the assumption that the administrative agency will protect the public.

6. *Cf.* the discussion of meaning in George Herbert Mead, *Mind, Self and Society* (Chicago: University of Chicago Press, 1934), pp. 78–79.

7. Truman, *Governmental Process*, pp. 439–46; Earl Latham, *The Group Basis of Politics* (Ithaca: Cornell University Press, 1952), chap. 1.

8. The writer has explored this effect in labor legislation in "Interest Representation and Labor Law Administration," *Labor Law Journal* 9 (1958): 218–26.

9. Evidence for these propositions is contained in the writer's study of congressional representation, still not completed or published. See also Lewis A. Dexter, "Candidates Must Make the Issues and Give Them Meaning," *Public Opinion Quarterly* 10 (1955–56): 408–14.

10. Randolph E. Paul, "Erosion of the Tax Base and Rate Structure," in Joint Committee on the Economic Report, *Federal Tax Policy for Economic Growth and Stability*, 84th Cong., 1st sess., 1955. pp. 123–38.

11. Harold Lasswell, *Psychopathology and Politics* (Chicago: University of Chicago Press, 1930), pp. 184, 185.

12. Herbert Fensterheim, "The Influence of Value Systems on the Perception of People," *Journal of Abnormal and Social Psychology* 48 (1953): 93. Fensterheim cites the following studies in support of the proposition: David Krech and Richard S. Crutchfield, *Theory and Problems of Social Psychology* (New York: McGraw-Hill, 1948); A. S. Luchins, "An Evaluation of Some Current Criticisms of Gestalt Psychological Work on Perception," *Psychological Review* 58 (1951): 69–95; J. S. Bruner, "One Kind of Perception: A Reply to Professor Luchins," *Psychological Review* 58 (1951): 306–12; and the chapters by Bruner, Frenkel-Brunswik, and Klein in Robert R. Blake and Glenn V. Ramsey, *Perception: An Approach to Personality* (New York: Ronald Press, 1951). See also Charles Osgood, Percy Tannenbaum, and George Suci, *The Measurement of Meaning* (Urbana, Ill.: University of Illinois Press, 1957).

13. Among the leading general and experimental studies dealing with the phenomenon are: M. Rokeach, "Generalized Mental Rigidity as a Factor in Ethnocentrism," *Journal of Abnormal and Social Psychology* 43 (1948): 259–77; R. R. Canning and J. M. Baker, "Effect of the Group on Authoritarian and Non-authoritarian Persons," *American Journal of Sociology* 64 (1959): 579–81; A. H. Maslow, "The Authoritarian Character Structure," *Journal of Social Psychology* 18 (1943): 403; T. W. Adorno et al., *The Authoritarian Personality* (New York: Harper & Brothers, 1950); Gerhart Saenger, *The Psychology of Prejudice* (New York: Harper & Brothers, 1953), pp. 123–38; Erich Fromm, *Escape from Freedom* (New York: Rinehart & Co., 1941); Robert King Merton, *Mass Persuasion* (New York: Harper & Brothers, 1950).

14. Else Frenkel-Brunswik, "Interaction of Psychological and Sociological Factors in Political Behavior," *American Political Science Review* 46 (1952): 44–65.

15. Adorno et al., *Authoritarian Personality*.

16. Leon Festinger, Henry Riecken, and Stanley Shachter, *When Prophecy Fails* (Minneapolis: University of Minnesota Press, 1956).

17. Adorno et al., *Authoritarian Personality*, p. 665.

18. Albert Salomon, "Symbols and Images in the Constitution of Society," in L. Bryson, L. Finkelstein, H. Hoagland and R. M. MacIver, eds., *Symbols and Society* (New York: Cooper Square, 1955), p. 110.

19. Lasswell, *Psychopathology and Politics*, p. 195.

20. Chester I. Barnard, *The Functions of the Executive* (Cambridge, Mass.: Harvard University Press, 1938), p. 226.

21. Charles Morris, *Signs, Language and Behavior* (New York: Prentice-Hall, 1946), pp. 210–11.

22. Kenneth Burke, *A Grammar of Motives* (New York: Prentice-Hall, 1945), p. 393.

23. Ibid., p. 362.

24. Mead, *Mind, Self, and Society*; Ernst Cassirer, *An Essay on Man* (New Haven, Conn.: Yale University Press, 1944).

25. See James G. March and Herbert A. Simon, *Organizations* (New York: John Wiley, 1958), pp. 65–81, and studies cited there.

26. See, e.g., Murray Edelman, "Causes of Fluctuations in Popular Support for the Italian Communist Party since 1946," *Journal of Politics* 20 (1958): 547–50; Arthur M. Ross, *Trade Union Wage Policy* (Berkeley and Los Angeles: University of California Press, 1948).

27. Adorno et al., *Authoritarian Personality*, p. 655.

28. Alfred R. Lindesmith and Anselm L. Strauss, *Social Psychology* (New York: Rinehart & Co., 1956), pp. 253–55. For a report of another psychological experiment demonstrating that attitudes are a function of group norms, see I. Sarnoff, D. Katz, and C. McClintock, "Attitude-Change Procedures and Motivating Patterns," in Daniel Katz et al., eds., *Public Opinion and Propaganda* (New York: Rinehart & Co., 1954), pp. 308–9; also Festinger et al., *When Prophecy Fails*.

29. Paul F. Lazarsfeld, Bernard Berelson and Hazel Gaudet, *The People's Choice* (New York: Columbia University Press, 1944). p. 83. For an account of an experiment reaching the same conclusion see Seymour Martin Lipset, "Opinion Formation in a Crisis Situation," *Public Opinion Quarterly* 17 (1953): 20–46.

30. Mead, *Mind, Self, and Society*, p. 78.

31. Cf. Wilcox, *Public Policies Toward Business*, pp. 281, 252–55.

32. Many examples may be found in the writer's study entitled *The Licensing of Radio Services in the United States, 1927 to 1947* (Urbana, Ill.: University of Illinois Press, 1950).

33. For discussions of the utility of this view to social scientists, see Arthur F. Bentley, *The Process of Government* (1908; reprint ed., New York: The Principia Press, 1949); Truman, *Governmental Process*. But cf. Stanley Rothman, "Systematic Political Theory," *American Political Science Review* 54 (March 1960): 15–23.

34. *The Folklore of Capitalism* (New Haven: Yale University Press, 1937), pp. 212, 215, 216.

35. They are listed above under "Pattern B."

RADICAL ACTION COOPERATIVE
The GAP Between Social Science and Social Reality

> While one who sings with his tongue on fire
> Gargles in the rat race choir
> Bent out of shape by society's pliers
> Cares not to come up any higher
> But rather get you down in the hole
> That he's in
> But I mean no harm, nor put fault
> On anyone who lives in a vault
> But it's all right Ma, if I can't please him.
> —Bob Dylan

Affluence of What?

The problems in our society do not lie primarily in discrete minority groups. They are rather a part of the fabric that makes up the daily lives of us all. We, blacks and whites, upper, middle, and lower classes together, are starving in the midst of an America of affluence. Every aspect of our lives is impoverished—physical and emotional and spiritual. The separation of the many aspects of our lives has caused the dissected bits to wither away. The commodity system has taken over and objectified us. We are treated as objects, and our lives themselves have become a commodity. We are passive consumers, consuming the artificial and inauthentic products of our economy and insanely trying to satisfy artificially created needs. The necessity to create such artificial needs reveals the fantastic absurdity of the system. "Work for a car to go to work." The sales agents constantly try to convince us that our personal attractiveness and self-concepts are no more than the sum of the commodities we have collected. "Modern man consumes himself out of existence. His face is something to put makeup on (as in the expression, 'put on your face'); his body is to put clothes on; his feet to put shoes on. Otherwise there are no face, body, and feet. His body as a whole is no more than a vehicle for commodities." (RAC statement "Life, Not Survival") Our daily lives are really daily death, sacrificing our desires and creativity, constantly molding our lives such that others will think of us in a good light—we become "dead bait" for a life of subjection, dependence, the pursuit of artificial desires, alienated choices and stultified existence. The grand result is either pursuit of boredom or escapism from that world of boredom.

Source: The Human Factor (November 1968): 32–36. Reprinted by permission.

Ivory Towers Made of Margarine

All individuals have the choice either to challenge their passivity or to resign themselves to impotence. But social scientists in particular may see most clearly the necessity for such a choice. By virtue of their position, they should be most able to see the depth of poverty in daily life. However, as intellectuals, they are so alienated in their ivory towers that they fail to see *themselves* among the poor. Having a blind faith in the specialized activities of their professions, social scientists tend to assume that the everyday life of man is not a concern of theirs.

Daily Life—Death by Dissection

For the social scientist, daily life is that residue of reality that has not been classified and categorized. It is in fact the domain where specialists such as they have no role. Even the most "brilliant" specialist is inept and impotent when it comes to many problems of everyday life, falling back on habitual solutions or calling in other specialists (e.g., the psychoanalyst).

This is alarming when we realize that in reality daily life is the measure of everything. The quality of our everyday lives indeed conditions what we are as human beings. Specializations, as they exist now, are rendered valueless by isolation from one's daily life, from which comes the aura of mystification about them. Yet, no individual scientist, student, or professional can measure the value of his work in terms of his own niche or specialized set of rules. Rather, he must constantly relate back to his everyday life. Thus, specialization should exist in osmosis with everyday life. This is not to suggest that the residue (read, "core") of life now ignored by social scientists should become the object of a new specialty, "daily life," for that is an impossibility. Instead, the distinction between specialties and daily life should be obliterated.

The Castrated Scientific Observer

The social scientist at present clings to his role as a describer of reality, leaving evaluative decisions to other specialists, such as the politicians or businessmen. He claims to be uninvolved, detached, passive, "objective." This attitude is a dangerous one for him, as it leaves him powerless to make decisions about changing his own life, and secondly, it means that both the specialty and his life are ghettos unto themselves. His life is something other than his work.

Furthermore, due to over-specialization, the constant influx of knowledge and the failure to translate that knowledge—modern society is now understood through a number of specialized fragments which are uncommunicable. The domain where questions can be asked in a unitary manner is outside of those—in the realm of everyday life, which is, at the same time, the domain of ignorance. Scientists atomize aspects of behavior and have no models which deal with day-to-day behavior in other than a fragmentary way. In the same way, society atomizes people as separate consumers and suppresses meaningful communication between them. Both the political and the cultural spheres are isolated from daily life. Politics is restricted to two minutes in a voting booth every couple of years, and culture is consumed in a few hours on the weekend. The greater part of daily life is both de-culturated and de-politicized. Just look around at the streets, buildings, cars, and interior decorations.

The Sterilization Process for Clean-cut Americans

Herein lies precisely the poverty of daily life. This objectified culture, commodity culture, sold to us in neat, discrete packages, is dead culture. Its death begins in our families and schools where we are taught (or teach) that culture comes from without ourselves, rather than developed from within, from our own creative potentials. We are taught to dissect our minds from our bodies, distinguish between work and play, act out in schizophrenic fashion innumerable roles, repress curiosity and spontaneity. We are taught not to criticize daily life, and the hostility often engendered by such "personal" criticism when it is made, reveals the mystification of that realm of life. The result is passive and unquestioning acceptance of the impoverishment of daily life.

Through Criticism to Creation

Not to criticize daily life is only to prolong its impoverishment. This mistake is made not only by status-quo oriented social scientists but also by potential revolutionaries. They downgrade the significance of daily life just because it is so impoverished and underdeveloped. Criticism is thwarted, moreover, by both the mystification of daily life and the restrictions imposed on behavior by "law and order." These are difficult to transcend. Yet, if we can recognize the poverty of everyday life, we can begin to consider its possibilities. We emerge from the dim tunnel of present life into the multidimensional world of the possible.

Unfortunately, these possibilities are perceived by most people as unattainable, due to the "cost" they would exact in terms of the securities of social acceptance and material abundance now offered us. Their reaction is one of "sour grapes."

> While them that defend what they cannot see
> With a killer's pride, security
> It blows the mind most bitterly
> —Bob Dylan

Stop Reading; Start Looking

Those who set out seriously to criticize daily life must be prepared to modify their own lives. Study of daily life, without explicitly aiming to modify it, is in vain. In this realm, the realm of life, one cannot profess to be "detatched" or "just an observer."

What everything depends on is the level at which one asks the questions: How do I live? Am I satisfied? One must be able to answer such questions by himself, and avoid being impressed with the claims of ads that attribute "happiness" to the existence of God, Pepsi-Cola and the Democratic Party, or that attribute "masculinity" or "femininity" to acquisition of the latest model sports car or mouthwash.

Take-off

Daily life should not be a ghetto. Its borders should be ever-expanding to include all spheres of life, ever organizing new possibilities. Creative activity should be liberated for finding ways to fulfill real needs to develop the individual, rather than directed to produce artificial needs for the benefit of the commodity system and to grind out artificial studies describing in repetitive detail impoverished fragments of other men's lives.

Think! What are the possibilities? How can we control the quality of our own lives? How can we go about making history, rather than being ruled by it? Society defines "wasted time" as time spent outside of production and consumption, but real wasted time is time spent working at what one doesn't enjoy to earn prefabricated and empty leisure time, the means of consumption, etc.—all is daily passivity manufactured and controlled by the commodity system.

Follow Through

It is necessary to think in terms of revolution, noting that the so-called Soviet revolution was a sell-out, because the quality of the everyday lives of Russians has not changed for the better any more than in the U.S. On the contrary, Russians are equally enslaved in an alienating commodity system. In fact, the two systems are rapidly converging into bureaucratic, objectified, commodity-oriented capitalism. We do not wish to promote any more such coup d'états (new faces running the same old system) as the Communists manufacture. We can do far more, for the new revolution benefits both from the mistakes of the old Left and from the modern technological base which the utopian socialists have lacked.

The revolution in daily life will create conditions in which resistance to change will be broken down, the present will dominate the past, the creative side of man will dominate the routine. Daily life will be "busy being born," never static, constantly in revolutionary growth. Individuals will be free to create situations in which new possibilities can be realized, as opposed to the perpetuation of the existing situation by the present rulers.

This new revolutionary movement is not a cultural avant-garde movement (where culture is the whole of artistic and other ways in which society defines itself to itself) nor is it a revolutionary party according to the traditional model. This culture and this politics is worn out. The revolutionary transformation of daily life must be *now*, in our daily lives, and therefore requires a new type of revolutionary organization. The taking of our lives into our own hands signifies our readiness to start making history. Simultaneously, the transformation will ring the knell on all independent specializations: specialized artistic expression, specialized politics, and specialized social science.

Social scientist, your choice is between perpetuating the sterility of your field and your life in isolation of one another and uniting the two in creative revolution!

Part Two

Mythical Roots of Property and Power in the American Politics of Everyday Life

The preceding selections have shown how the absence of a critical perspective in the everyday world of the general public relates to the lack of an adequate basis for genuine political action. We have seen that major social and political problems can partly be traced to missing or weak concepts of self- and historical interpretation, for example, ideas of "class," "violence," and "intellectuals." But we have also related this political submissiveness of the mass public to elitist policies to political rhetoric manipulating appeals to public interests in order, security, regulation, and so on. Thus mainstream ideology as a system of cultural hegemony has a dual function in American politics. First, it renders political action by the mass of the people difficult because it prevents the development of images, concepts, and theories necessary to guide such action. Second, it provides a rhetoric of justification which makes it seem as if the political action taken by the elite is in such perfect harmony with the interests and goals of the people that direct political action by them is unnecessary.

This section examines historically the convergent flow of political and economic currents of the mainstream ideology. Ralph Miliband is emphasizing one aspect of their interconnection when he observes in *The State in Capitalist Society,*

> nationalism has been a powerful force in sustaining capitalist regimes; the schools have been an important channel for its dissemination and for the internalization of values associated with it.[1] [He also notes the strong emphasis given to the "free enterprise" ideology in American schools.]

Some of the most perceptive and prescient insights into the continuing interrelations of economic and political thinking are expressed in the 1904 study of *The Theory of Business Enterprise,* by Thorstein Veblen. In the first se-

---

1. Ralph Miliband, *The State in Capitalist Society* (New York: Basic Books, 1969), p. 244.

lection in part 2, Veblen locates the political dominance of business enterprise in the cultural sentiments connected historically with patriotism and property.

Henry Ford was born during the Civil War, a few years after Veblen's birth, and died in 1947, eighteen years after Veblen's death. The selection by Sigmund Diamond focuses on the American newspaper image of Ford's life, especially at the time of his death. Diamond points out that the "entrepreneur was linked to community by the common attributes of humanity and by principles of motivation which guided his activities in the direction of service to all; enterprise was linked to nation by identification with patriotism and historical tradition."

This uncritical, business-oriented patriotism of the "press industrialists"[2] is illuminated in the Veblen and Diamond selections, which present historical insights into the way the press invests the economic system with patriotic sentiments such as love and loyalty for country. Diamond sees in the identification of business enterprise with patriotism "the clue to the realization of the new and broader consensus" that became conspicuously evident in the decade after Ford's death. One study of business ideology in the mid-1960s noted that "an unusual ideological consensus prevails and claims at least the acquiescence, if not the enthusiasm, of previously hostile groups."[3] Around the same time, many social scientists were naively confusing this ideological consensus with what they called the "end of ideology!"

The selections from Hugh Duncan discuss the "religion of money" and the "deification of the businessman." The question arises: "What is the *ideological* role of money in business power?" Psychologist William Domhoff, best known for his studies of power structures in the United States, offers a few concepts which help us develop a general perspective. Domhoff views money as a "fantasy institution" which links the dominant elites and the mass public. The common man's "money hunger" and dreams of financial success tend to create support for capitalism based on the myths that business enterprise is open to talent and hard work, and that the ultimate aim in life is to spend money. Understanding the mythical function of money deepens Veblen's view of American society as a class structure muting politically "*decisive* class conflict" and contributes to our grasp of processes working to the detriment of American radicalism.[4] The psychological power of financial mythology helps to explain some of the difficulties American radicals have had in trying to swim against the mainstream ideological currents and institutional channels of this society.

2. Robert Sherrill, *Why They Call it Politics* (New York: Harcourt Brace Jovanovich, 1972), p. 243 ff.
3. Robert Heilbroner, "The View From the Top: Reflections on a Changing Business Ideology," in *The Business Establishment*, ed. Earl F. Cheit (New York: John Wiley, 1964), p. 2.
4. Gabriel Kolko, "The Decline of American Radicalism in the Twentieth Century," *Studies on the Left* 6 (September–October 1966): 17–18.

Domhoff suggests that the original magical-sacred functions of money, as "worked" by the shamans and priest-kings of other types of societies, have been taken over by modern capitalists and their professional functionaries and integrated into the rational-economic apparatus of the socioeconomic system.[5] Veblen wrote in 1904 that nowhere else "has the sacredness of pecuniary obligations so permeated the common sense of the community, and nowhere does pecuniary obligation come so near being the only form of obligation that has the unqualified sanction of current common sense." But Veblen also notes the *"uncertain* allegiance" of some groups with little property to elite conceptions of law and order. In retrospect, it seems that Veblen had an almost mystical faith in the capacity of the "discipline of the machine" to promote a critical consciousness among the mass of people. Yet Veblen was a keen student of the ways in which "money talks" and of its role in the processes of social integration.

Both the Henry and Ewen essays present a general theory of the development of the "Commodity Self" (the human being defined as consumer). The commodity self links advertising with the religion of money, because advertising defines success within the community as a function of consuming. Stuart Ewen, pursuing advertising's changing role in the development of industrial capitalism, enlarges our view of the problems with which the elites and their functionaries have had to cope in their attempts at domination. In reading Henry and Ewen, we can comprehend the extent to which the metaphysical principles of law and order discussed by Veblen have been applied in new, dynamic versions to the entire society on a daily basis through advertising. The troublesome "discipline of daily life," which Veblen assumed might provide the basis for an ideology critique, has been blunted by the consumer myths projected by advertising. This is evident in Hugh Duncan's discussion of "spending as prayer" in the American Christmas and in the infusion of money with sacred social values in the so-called American way of death. In these domains of everyday life we discover some mythical roots of property and power on which the dominant politico-economic system stands.

Stuart Ewen's article bears particular relation to the other selections. In the discussion of Ford and Filene, Ewen shows how advertising became a vital element in the strategy of the new mass production, providing an "ideological bridge" across the uneven landscape of sociocultural diversity and division. Advertising becomes a way of producing standardized, obedient consumers who can be sold by the constant penetration of their daily life. Ewen documents the advertising ideology, showing how it relates to the mainstream and to the institutions which both generate it and to some extent get their power from it.

Advertising's philosophers (or ideologues) have tended to view it as a

---

5. G. William Domhoff, "Historical Materialism, Culture Determinism, and the Origin of the Ruling Classes," *The Psychoanalytic Review* 56 (1969): 271–87.

process of "civilization." However, such rhetoric obscures the way advertising tends to make monetary success the measure of human worth. In the philosophy of advertising one becomes a full human being through the purchase of commodities produced by large corporations. Fundamental political concepts such as freedom and equality are repackaged to support the endless quest for privatized and standardized consumer "satisfactions." Duncan writes: "American discussion over freedom soon becomes a discussion of freedom to earn and (more recently) to spend." A recent presidential candidate worried aloud about whether our national quest for the good life had turned into a race for the goods life—he lost twice. But moralistic condemnations of materialism are the regular fare of both our politicians and our preachers. The actual intent of policies in a political system such as ours is hard to follow. Kenneth Burke illustrates the point when he notes that sometimes "we" as a nation "advance funds to foreign countries from which 'we' as private corporations receive this money back in payment for exports"; by this "ambiguity of identification, as a *nation* we become 'idealists' while some of our *nationals* are involved in transactions that are, to say the least, quite realistic."[6]

What is visible to the critical eye in such transactions is the corporate ideal in the new liberal state. The individualistic moral claims of corporate liberalism tend to conceal for many people the real importance of the liberal state in social control and economic planning. Corporate liberal ideology in the age of the multinational corporation helps to hide the roots of current problems at both international and national levels. A unified humanity as the collective subject of a rational, democratic economic and political program was never an ideal seriously aimed at by corporate liberalism. But while American generosity and innocence are not entirely mythical notions, the abuse and distortion of our moral tradition will continue to be concealed from the public as long as we do not have a critical theory of the American technocorporate state and its powerful role in the world economy and political destiny of other peoples. The general trend of recent years has been that our "national politics has become a competition for images or between images, rather than between ideals," according to a conservative historian.[7] Public opinion has, in a sense, become an image which can be packaged and programmed and to which particular expressions are supposed to conform. Daniel Boorstin's discussion of the "search for self-fulfilling prophecies" recalls the logic (revealed in the Pentagon Papers) of planning *both* the Vietnam policy *and* the public response. The rise of a narrow, irresponsible executive-military elite and its fundamental lack of public accountability has been dramatized in the Vietnam War. The constitutional problem posed is merely one

6. Kenneth Burke, "Responsiblities of National Greatness," *The Nation* (17 July 1967): 50.
7. Daniel Boorstin, *The Image* (New York: Harper & Row, 1964), p. 249. See also pp. 185, 238. On the significance of the Pentagon Papers, see Hannah Arendt, *Crises of the Republic* (New York: Harcourt Brace Jovanovich, 1972).

important aspect of the larger crisis of legitimacy of the political system which has already been discussed. We have seen in the preceding selections how official liberal rhetoric and ideological obfuscation contribute to the confused relationship between thought and action reflected in the contradictions and inconsistencies of mainstream politics. We attempt now to uncover and probe some of the mythical roots of property and power that have fed both the contemporary politics of images and the penetration of everyday life by a technocorporate ideology masking new forms of domination.

THORSTEIN VEBLEN

Business Principles in Law and Politics

Popular welfare is bound up with the conduct of business; because industry is managed for business ends, and also because there prevails throughout modern communities a settled habit of rating the means of livelihood and the amenities of life in pecuniary terms. But apart from their effect in controlling the terms of livelihood from day to day, these principles are also in great measure decisive in the larger affairs of life, both for the individual in his civil relations and for the community at large in its political concerns. Modern (civilized) institutions rest, in great part, on business principles. This is the meaning, as applied to the modern situation, of the current phrases about the Economic Interpretation of History, or the Materialistic Theory of History.

Because of this settled habit of seeing all the conjunctures of life from the business point of view, in terms of profit and loss, the management of the affairs of the community at large falls by common consent into the hands of business men and is guided by business considerations. Hence modern politics is business politics, even apart from the sinister application of the phrase to what is invidiously called corrupt politics. This is true both of foreign and domestic policy. Legislation, police surveillance, the administration of justice, the military and diplomatic service, all are chiefly concerned with business relations, pecuniary interests, and they have little more than an incidental bearing on other human interests. All this apparatus is also charged with the protection of life and personal liberty, but its work in this bearing has much of a pecuniary color.

Source: Reprinted by permission of Charles Scribner's Sons from *The Theory of Business Enterprise* by Thorstein Veblen. Copyright 1904 Charles Scribner's Sons; renewal copyright 1932 Ann Bevans and Becky Veblen.

Legislation and legal decisions are based on the dogma of Natural Liberty. This is peculiarly true as regards the English-speaking peoples, the foundation of whose jurisprudence is the common law, and it holds true in an especial degree of America. In other European communities the sway of natural-rights preconceptions is not so unmitigated, but even with them there is a visibly growing predilection for the natural-rights standpoint in all matters touching business relations. The dogma of natural liberty is peculiarly conducive to an expeditious business traffic and peculiarly consonant with the habits of thought which necessarily prevail in any business community.

The current body of natural-rights preconceptions antedates the modern business situation. The scheme of natural rights grew up and found secure lodgement in the common sense of the community, as well as with its lawgivers and courts, under the discipline of the small industry and petty trade ("domestic industry") whose development culminated in the eighteenth century.[1] In industrial matters the efficient and autonomous factor in the days of the small industry was the individual workman, his personal force, dexterity, and diligence; similarly in the petty trade of the precapitalistic English situation the decisive factor was the discretion and sagacity of the small merchant and the petty employer, who stood in direct personal relations with their customers and their employees. In so far as trade and industry was not restrained by conventional regulations, statutory or customary, both trade and industry was in effect an open field of free competition, in which man met man on a somewhat equable footing. While the competitors were not on a footing of material equality, the industrial system was sufficiently loose-jointed, of a sufficiently diffuse growth, to make competition effective in the absence of mandatory restrictions. The like will hold of the business organization associated with the small industry. Both trade and industry were matters of personal efficiency rather than comprehensively organized processes of an impersonal character.[2]

Natural rights, as they found their way into the conceptions of law and equity, were in effect the assumed equal rights of men so situated on a plane of at least constructive equality that the individuals concerned would be left in a position of effectively free choice if conventional restrictions were done away. The organization was not, mechanically, a close-knit one, in the sense that the concatenation of industrial processes or of business transactions was not rigorous either in point of time relations or of the quantity and character of the output or the work. Neither were the place, pace, circumstances, means, or hours of work closely determined for the workman or his employer by mechanical circumstances of the industrial process or of the market. The standardization of life under the old regime was of a conventional character, not of a mechanical kind such as is visible in the more recent development. And this conventional standardization was gradually losing force.

The movement of opinion on natural-rights ground converged to an insistence on the system of natural liberty, so called. But this insistence on natural liberty did not contemplate the abrogation of all conventional prescription. "The simple and obvious system of natural liberty" meant freedom from restraint on any other prescriptive ground than that afforded by the rights of ownership. In its economic bearing the system of natural liberty meant a system of free pecuniary contract. "Liberty does not mean license"; which in economic terms would be transcribed, "The natural freedom of the individual must not traverse the prescriptive rights of property." Property rights being included among natural rights, they had the indefeasibility which attaches to natural rights. Natural liberty prescribes freedom to buy and sell, limited only by the equal freedom of others to buy and sell; with the obvious corollary that there must be no interference with others' buying and selling, except by means of buying and selling.

This principle of natural (pecuniary) liberty has found its most unmitigated acceptance in America, and has here taken the firmest hold on the legal mind. Nowhere else has the sacredness of pecuniary obligations so permeated the common sense of the community, and nowhere does pecuniary obligation come so near being the only form of obligation that has the unqualified sanction of current common sense. Here, as nowhere else, do obligations and claims of the most diverse kinds, domestic, social, and civil, tend to take the pecuniary form and admit of being fully discharged on a monetary valuation. To a greater extent than elsewhere public esteem is awarded to artists, actors, preachers, writers, scientists, officials, in some rough proportion to the sums paid for their work.

American civil rights have taken an extreme form, with relatively great stress on the inviolability of pecuniary relations, due to the peculiar circumstances under which the American community has grown up. The pioneers, especially in that North Atlantic seaboard community that has been chiefly effective in shaping American traditions, brought with them a somewhat high-wrought variant of the English preconception in favor of individual discretion, and this tradition they put in practice under circumstances peculiarly favorable to a bold development. They brought little of the remnants of that prescriptive code that once bound the handicraft system, and the conditions of life in the colonies did not foster a new growth of conventional regulations circumscribing private initiative. America is the native habitat of the self-made man, and the self-made man is a pecuniary organism.[3]

Presently, when occasion arose, the metaphysics of natural liberty, pecuniary and other, was embodied in set form in constitutional enactments. It is therefore involved in a more authentic form and with more incisive force in the legal structure of this community than in that of any other. Freedom of contract is the fundamental tenet of the legal creed, so to speak, inviolable and inalienable; and within the province of law and equity no one has competence to penetrate behind this first premise or to question the merits of the natural-rights metaphysics on which it rests. The only principle (attested habit of thought) which may contest its primacy in civil matters is a vague "general welfare" clause; and even this can effectively contest its claims only under exceptional circumstances. Under the application of any general welfare clause the presumption is and always must be that the principle of free contract be left intact so far as the circumstances of the case permit. The citizen may not be deprived of life, liberty, or property without due process of law, and the due process proceeds on the premise that property rights are inviolable. In its bearing upon the economic relations between individuals this comes to mean, in effect, not only that one individual or group of individuals may not legally bring any other than pecuniary pressure to bear upon another individual or group, but also that pecuniary pressure cannot be barred.

Now, through gradual change of the economic situation, this conventional principle of unmitigated and inalienable freedom of contract began to grow obsolete from about the time when it was fairly installed; obsolescent, of course, not in point of law, but in point of fact. Since about the time when this new conventional standardization of the scheme of economic life in terms of free contract reached its mature development, in the eighteenth century,[4] a new standardizing force, that of the machine process, has invaded the field. The standardization and the constraint of the system of machine industry differs from what went before it in that it has had no conventional recognition, no metaphysical authentication. It has not become a legal fact. Therefore it neither needs nor can be taken account of by the legal mind. It is a new fact which fits into the framework neither of the ancient system of prescriptive usage nor of the later system of free personal initiative. It does not exist de jure, but only de facto. Belonging neither to the defunct system nor to the current legal system, since it neither constitutes nor traverses a "natural right," it is, as within the cognizance of the law, nonexistent. It is, perhaps, actual, with a gross, material actuality; but it is not real, with a legal, metaphysically competent reality. Such coercion as it may exert, or as may be exercised through its means, therefore, is, in point of legal reality, no coercion.

Where physical impossibility to fulfill the terms of a contract arises out of the concatenation of industrial processes, this physical impossibility may be pleaded as invalidating the terms of the contract. But the pecuniary pressure of price or subsistence which the sequence and interdependence of industrial processes may bring to bear has no standing as such in law or equity; it can reach the cognizance of the law only indirectly, through gross defection of one of the contracting parties, in those cases where the pressure is severe enough to result in insolvency, sickness, or death. The material necessities of a group of workmen or consumers, enforced by the specialization and concatenation of industrial processes, is, therefore, not competent to set aside, or indeed to qualify, the natural freedom of the owners of these processes to let work go on or not, as the outlook for profits may decide. Profits is a business proposition, livelihood is not.[5]

Under the current de facto standardization of economic life enforced by the machine industry, it may frequently happen that an individual or a group, e.g., of workmen, has not a de facto power of free contract. A given workman's livelihood can perhaps, practically, be found only on acceptance of one specific contract offered, perhaps not at all. But the coercion which in this way bears upon his choice through the standardization of industrial procedure is neither assault and battery nor breach of contract, and it is, therefore, not repugnant to the principles of natural liberty. Through controlling the processes of industry in which alone, practically, given workmen can find their livelihood, the owners of these processes may bring pecuniary pressure to bear upon the choice of the workmen; but since the rights of property which enforce such pressure are not repugnant to the principles of natural liberty, neither is such pecuniary pressure repugnant to the law—the case is therefore outside the scope of the law. The converse case, where the workmen take similar advantage of their employers to bring them to terms, is similarly outside the scope of the common law—supposing, of course, that there has in neither case been a surrender of individual liberty, a breach of contract, theft, a resort to violence, or threats of violence. So long as there is no overt attempt on life, liberty of the person, or the liberty to buy and sell, the law cannot intervene, unless it be in a precautionary way to prevent prospective violation of personal or property rights.

The "natural," conventional freedom of contract is sacred and inalienable. De facto freedom of choice is a matter about which the law and the courts are not competent to inquire. By force of the concatenation of industrial processes and the dependence of men's comfort or subsistence upon the orderly working of these processes, the exercise of the rights of ownership in the interests of business may traverse the de facto necessities of a group or class; it may even traverse the needs of the community at large, as, e.g., in the conceivable case of an advisedly

instituted coal famine; but since these necessities, of comfort or of livelihood, cannot be formulated in terms of the natural freedom of contract,
they can, in the nature of the case, give rise to no cognizable grievance
and find no legal remedy.

The discrepancy between law and fact in the matter of industrial
freedom has had repeated illustration in the court decisions on disputes
between bodies of workmen and their employers or owners. These decisions commonly fall out in favor of the employers or owners; that is to
say, they go to uphold property rights and the rights of free contract. The
courts have been somewhat broadly taken to task by a certain class of observers for alleged partiality to the owners' side in this class of litigation.
It has also been pointed out by fault-finders that the higher courts decide,
on the whole, more uniformly in favor of the employer-owner than the
lower ones, and especially more so than the juries in those cases where juries have found occasion to pass on the law of the case. The like is true as
regards suits for damages arising out of injuries sustained by workmen,
and so involving the question of the employer's liability. Even a casual
scrutiny of the decisions, however, will show that in most cases the decision of the court, whether on the merits of the case or on the constitu-
tionality of the legal provisions involved,[6] is well grounded on the
metaphysical basis of natural liberty. That is to say in other words, the
decisions will be found on the side of the maintenance of fundamental law
and order, "law and order" having, of course, reference to the inalienable rights of ownership and contract. As should fairly be expected,
the higher courts, who are presumably in more intimate touch with the
principles of jurisprudence, being more arduously trained and more
thoroughly grounded in the law at the same time that they have also presumably a larger endowment of legal acumen—these higher courts
speak more unequivocally for the metaphysical principles and apply
them with a surer and firmer touch. In the view of these higher adepts of
the law, free contract is so inalienable a natural right of man that not
even a statutory enactment will enable a workman to forego its exercise
and its responsibility. By metaphysical necessity its exercise attaches to
the individual so indefeasibly that it cannot constitutionally be delegated
to collective action, whether legislative or corporate.[7] This extreme consequence of the principle of natural liberty has at times aroused in-
dignation in the vulgar; but their grasp of legal principles is at fault. The
more closely the logical sequence is followed up, the more convincingly
does the legitimacy of such a decision stand out.

In comparing the decisions of the higher courts with those of the
lower they contrast most signally with the decisions rendered by juries in
the lower tribunals. While this contrast has a significance in another connection, it casts no shadow on the legality of the decisions of the courts of

higher instance. The juries, in great measure, speak for the untrained sympathies of the vulgar, which are a matter somewhat apart from the foundations of law and order.[8]

Popular sentiment, then, does not at all uniformly bear out these decisions of the courts in disputes between property rights and naked mankind, especially not in the more rigorous enforcement of the principle of free contract. This discrepancy serves to show that the vulgar, the laity, from whose numbers the juries are drawn, have not an adequate sense of the principles that lie at the root of the law; which may be due in part to their not realizing how essential a foundation of law, order, and common welfare these principles of natural liberty are. The visible disparity in the distribution of property may make those classes who have little property envious of the wealthy members, and so make them lose interest in the maintenance of the rights of property. But apart from this, the discipline of daily life, from which the common-sense notions of the vulgar are in good part derived, is no longer in full accord with the natural-rights conceptions handed down from the eighteenth century. In other words, the conceptions of natural rights on which the common law rests embody a technically competent formulation of the deliverances of that body of common sense which was inculcated by the discipline of everyday life in the eighteenth century, before the advent of the current situation; whereas the discipline of everyday life under the current technological and business situation inculcates a body of common-sense views somewhat at variance with the received natural-rights notions.

There is apparently something of a divergence between the received notions on this head and the deliverances of latter-day common sense. The divergence is neither well defined nor consistent. The latter-day attitude toward questions of the kind involved is vague, chiefly negative or critical, and apparently fluctuating; but after all there is a somewhat persistent divergence, which may even be said to have a systematic character, so far as it goes. It runs in the direction of a (partial and vacillating) disavowal or distrust of the metaphysics of free contract, and even of natural liberty generally. This uncertainty of allegiance to the received foundations of law and order prevails in unequal degrees among the various classes of the community, being apparently largest and most outspoken among the workmen of the industrial town, and being, on the whole, less noticeable among the propertied and professional classes and the rural population. The peculiar class distribution of this disintegration of received convictions, as well as its connection with modern industrial conditions, will be taken up again presently in another connection.

The state, that is to say, the government, was once an organization for the control of affairs in the interest of princely or dynastic ends. In internal affairs statecraft was occupied with questions of the dynastic succession, the endeavors and intrigues of the political magnates, fiscal administration directed to finding adequate support for the princely power, and the like. In external politics the objective end was dynastic prestige and security, military success, and the like. Such is still in part the end of political endeavor in those countries, as, e.g., Germany, Austria, or Italy, where the transition to a constitutional government has not been completed. But since the advent of constitutional government and parliamentary representation, business ends have taken the lead of dynastic ends in statecraft, very much in the same measure as the transition to constitutional methods has been effectually carried through. A constitutional government is a business government. It is particularly through the business expedient of parliamentary voting on the budget that any constitutional executive, e.g., is kept within constitutional bounds; and the budget is voted with a main view to its expediency for business ends. The expediency of business enterprise is not questioned, whereas the expediency of an increase of princely power and dignity, with the incidental costs, may be questioned.

Modern governmental policies, looking as they do to the furthering of business interests as their chief care, are of a "mercantile" complexion. They aim to foster trade, as did the mercantile policies of the sixteenth and seventeenth centuries, although since "trade" has come to include much else than foreign commerce, the modern policies look to business in the more comprehensive sense which the term now necessarily has. But these modern mercantile policies, with their tariffs, treaties, interstate commerce regulations, and maxims prohibiting all "restraint of trade," are after all not of the same nature as the mercantile policies of the old French and German statesmen, which they superficially resemble. The old "mercantile system," as it prevailed on the continent of Europe, was conceived in the interest of the prince, the furthering of commercial advantage being a means to princely power and dignity.[9] The modern mercantilism under constitutional rule, on the other hand, looks to the prince or to the government as a means to the end of commercial gain. With the transition to constitutional rule and methods, the discretion and autonomy in the case has passed from the hands of the prince into those of the business men, and the interests of the business men have superseded those of the crown.

Representative government means, chiefly, representation of business interests. The government commonly works in the interest of the business men with a fairly consistent singleness of purpose. And in its solicitude for the business men's interests it is borne out by current public sentiment, for there is a naive, unquestioning persuasion abroad among the body of the people to the effect that, in some occult way, the material interests of the populace coincide with the pecuniary interests of those business men who live within the scope of the same set of governmental contrivances. This persuasion is an article of popular metaphysics, in that it rests on an uncritically assumed solidarity of interests, rather than on an insight into the relation of business enterprise to the material welfare of those classes who are not primarily business men. This persuasion is particularly secure among the more conservative portion of the community, the business men, superior and subordinate, together with the professional classes, as contrasted with those vulgar portions of the community who are tainted with socialistic or anarchistic notions. But since the conservative element comprises the citizens of substance and weight, and indeed the effective majority of law-abiding citizens, it follows that, with the sanction of the great body of the people, even including those who have no pecuniary interests to serve in the matter, constitutional government has, in the main, become a department of the business organization and is guided by the advice of the business men. The government has, of course, much else to do besides administering the general affairs of the business community; but in most of its work, even in what is not ostensibly directed to business ends, it is under the surveillance of the business interests. It seldom happens, if at all, that the government of a civilized nation will persist in a course of action detrimental or not ostensibly subservient to the interests of the more conspicuous body of the community's business men. The degree in which a government fails to adapt its policy to these business exigencies is the measure of its senility.

The ground of sentiment on which rests the popular approval of a government for business ends may be summed up under two heads: patriotism and property. Both of these terms stand for institutional facts that have come down out of a past which differed substantially from the present situation. The substance of both is of the nature of unreasoning sentiment, in the sense that both are insisted on as a matter of course, as self-legitimating grounds of action which, it is felt, not only give expedient rules of conduct, but admit of no question as to their ulterior consequences or their value for the life-purposes of the community. The former of these fundamental institutional habits of thought (perhaps better, habits of mind) runs back to the discipline of early barbarism, through the feudal days of fealty to the earlier days of clan life and clannish animosity. It has therefore the deep-rooted strength given by an extremely protracted discipline of predation and servitude. Under modern conditions it is to be rated as essentially an institutional survival, so ingrained in the populace as to make any appeal to it secure of a response irrespective of the material merits of the contention in whose behalf the appeal is made.[10]

By force of this happy knack of clannish fancy the common man is enabled to feel that he has some sort of metaphysical share in the gains which accrue to the business men who are citizens of the same "commonwealth"; so that whatever policy furthers the commercial gains of those business men whose domicile is within the national boundaries is felt to be beneficial to all the rest of the population.[11]

The second institutional support of business politics, viz., property, is similarly an outgrowth of the discipline of the past, and similarly, though perhaps in a less degree, out of touch with the discipline of the more recent cultural situation. In the form in which it prevails in the current popular animus, the principle of ownership comes down from the days of handicraft industry and petty trade, as pointed out above. As it is of less ancient and less unbroken descent, so it seems also to be a less secure cultural heritage than the sense of patriotic solidarity. It says that the ownership of property is the material foundation of human wellbeing, and that this natural right of ownership is sacred, after the manner in which individual life, and more especially national life, is sacred. The habits of life and thought inculcated by joint work under the manorial system and by joint rules under the handicraft system have apparently contributed much to the notion of a solidarity of economic interests, having given the notion such a degree of consistency as has enabled it to persist in the face of a visible discrepancy of interests in later, capitalistic times. Under this current, business regime, business gains are the basis of individual wealth, and the (pseudo) notion of joint acquisition has taken the place of the manorial notion of joint work. The institutional animus of ownership, as it took shape under the discipline of early modern handicraft, awards the ownership of property to the workman who has produced it. By a dialectical conversion of the terms, this metaphysical dictum is made to fit the circumstances of later competitive business by construing acquisition of property to mean production of wealth; so that a business man is looked upon as the putative producer of whatever wealth he acquires. By force of this sophistication the acquisition of property by any person is held to be, not only expedient for the owner, but meritorious as an action serving the common good. Failure to bargain shrewdly or to accumulate more goods than one has produced by the work of one's own hands is looked upon with a feeling of annoyance, as a neglect, not only of opportunity, but of duty. The pecuniary conscience commonly does not, of course, go to quixotic lengths in a public-spirited insistence on everybody's acquiring more than an aliquot part of the aggregate wealth on hand, but it is felt that he best serves the common good who, other things equal, diverts the larger share of the aggregate wealth to his own possession. His acquiring a defensible title to it makes him the putative producer of it.

The natural-rights basis of ownership is by this paralogism preserved intact, and the common man is enabled to feel that the business men in the community add to the aggregate wealth at least as much as they acquire a title to; and the successful business men are at least as well persuaded that such is their relation to the aggregate wealth and to the material well-being of the community at large. So that both the business men whose gains are sought to be enhanced by business politics and the populace by whose means the business gains are secured work together in good faith toward a well-advised business end—the accumulation of wealth in the hands of those men who are skilled in pecuniary matters.[12]

The manner in which business interests work out in government policy may be shown by following up their bearing upon one phase of this policy. An extreme expression of business politics, and at the same time a characteristic trait of the higher levels of national life in Christendom, is the current policy of war and armaments. Modern business is competitive, emulative, and the direction of business enterprise is in the hands of men who are single-minded in their competitive conduct of affairs. They neither are inclined, nor will business competition permit them, to neglect or overlook any expedient that may further their own advantage or hinder the advantage of their rivals. Under the modern situation, as it has taken shape since the industrial revolution,[13] business competition has become international, covering the range of what is called the world market. In this international competition the machinery and policy of the state are in a peculiar degree drawn into the service of the larger business interests; so that, both in commerce and industrial enterprise, the business men of one nation are pitted against those of another and swing the forces of the state, legislative, diplomatic, and military, against one another in the strategic game of pecuniary advantage. The business interests domiciled within the scope of a given government fall into a loose organization in the form of what might be called a tacit ring or syndicate, proceeding on a general understanding that they will stand together as against outside business interests. The nearest approach to an explicit plan and organization of such a business ring is the modern political party, with its platform, tacit and avowed. Parties differ in their detail aims, but those parties that have more than a transient existence and superficial effect stand for different lines of business policy, agreeing all the while in so far that they all aim to further what they each claim to be the best, largest, most enduring business interests of the community. The ring[14] of business interests which secures the broadest approval from popular sentiment is, under constitutional methods, put in charge of the government establishment. This popular approval may be secured on the ground of a sound business platform or (in part) on some ground extraneous to business policy proper, such as a wave of national animosity, a popular candidate, a large grain crop, etc. But the only secure basis of an enduring party tenure of the government machinery is a business policy which falls in with the interests or the prejudices of the effective majority.

In international competition the ultima ratio is, as ever, warlike force, whether the issue be between princes of the grace of God or princes of ownership. It is a favorite maxim of modern politics that trade follows the flag. This is the business man's valuation of national policy and of the ends of national life. So stated, the maxim probably inverts the sequence of facts, but it is none the less a fair expression of the close relation there is between business endeavor and the modern military policies. Diplomacy, if it is to be effective for whatever end, must be backed by a show of force and of a readiness to use it. The definitive argument of those who speak for armaments (in England and America) is that the maintenance of business interests requires the backing of arms. On the continent of Europe this argument commonly comes second, while patriotic fancy and animosity take first place.

Armaments serve trade not only in the making of general terms of purchase and sale between the business men of civilized countries, but they are similarly useful in extending and maintaining business enterprise and privileges in the outlying regions of the earth. The advanced nations of Christendom are proselyters, and there are certain valuable perquisites that come to the business men of those proselyting nations who advance the frontiers of the pecuniary culture among the backward populations. There is commonly a handsome margin of profit in doing business with these, pecuniarily unregenerate, populations, particularly when the traffic is adequately backed with force. But, also commonly, these peoples do not enter willingly into lasting business relations with civilized mankind. It is therefore necessary, for the purposes of trade and culture, that they be firmly held up to such civilized rules of conduct as will make trade easy and lucrative. To this end armament is indispensable.

But in the portioning out of the trade perquisites that fall to the proselyters any business community is in danger of being overreached by alien civilizing powers. No recourse but force is finally available in disputes of this kind, in which the aim of the disputants is to take advantage of one another as far as they can. A warlike front is therefore necessary, and armaments and warlike demonstrations have come to be a part of the regular apparatus of business, so far as business is concerned with the world market.

In so far as it is guided by the exigencies of trade, the objective end of warlike endeavor is the peace and security necessary to an orderly development of business. International business relations, it is well said, make for peace; in the sense, of course, that they enforce the pacification of recalcitrant barbarians and lead to contention between civilized nations for a revision of the peace terms. When a modern government goes to war for trade purposes, it does so with a view to reestablishing peace on terms more lucrative to its business men.[15]

The above inquiry into the nature and causes of the wars of nations has resulted in little else than a recital of commonplaces; the facts and their connection are matters of common notoriety, and probably no one would hazard a question of the slight and obvious inferences drawn in the course of the recital. The excuse for this discursive review of the motives and aims of a war policy is that it gives a basis for an outlook on the present and immediate future of business enterprise.

The experience of continental Europe in the matter of armaments during the last half-century, and of all the greater nations during the last two decades, argues that when warlike emulation between states of somewhat comparable force has once got under way it assumes a cumulative character; so that a scale of expenditure for armaments which would at the outset have seemed absurdly impossible comes presently to be accepted as a matter of course. Hitherto the cumulative augmentation of war expenditures and of war animus shows no sign of slackening. One after another, the states that have offered some show of peaceable inclinations have been drawn into the international game of competitive armaments, as they have one after another become ambitious to push the enterprises of their business men in the international markets. An armament is serviceable only if it is relatively large; its absolute magnitude is a matter of no particular consequence for competitive politics. It is its comparative size that counts. Hence the greater the several armaments, the greater the political need of greater armaments, and the prompter the resentment of injuries and the livelier the felt need of offending and of taking offense. A progressively larger proportion of the nation's forces are withdrawn from industry and devoted to warlike ends. In this cumulative diversion of effort to warlike ends a point is presently reached beyond which the question of armament is no longer, What amount of warlike expenditure is needed to extend or maintain business traffic? but rather, What amount will the nation's resources bear? But the progression does not stop at that point; witness the case of Italy, France, and Germany, where the war drain has visibly impaired the industrial efficiency of the several nations concerned, but where the burden still goes on growing, with no stopping place in sight. England and, more particularly, America are not so near exhaustion, because they have larger resources to draw on as well as a culture and a population more efficient for industrial work. But there is no evident reason why these two should not likewise enter on a policy of emulative exhaustion, and so sacrifice their aggregate industrial and business interest to the furtherance of the "great game."

The question may suggest itself, Why should not the business community, who have a large discretion in international politics and whose aggregate gains are cut into by excessive war expenditures, call a halt when the critical point is reached? There is more than one reason for their failure to do so. War and preoccupation with warlike enterprise breed a warlike animus in the community, as well as a habit of arbitrary, autocratic rule on the part of those in authority and an unquestioning, enthusiastic subservience on the part of the subjects. National animosity and national pride demand more and more of military standing, at the same time that the growing official class needs increasing emoluments and a larger field of employment and display. The cultural effects of the discipline of warfare and armament are much the same whether it is undertaken for dynastic or for business ends; in either case it takes on a dynastic complexion and breeds the temperament, ideals, and institutional habits proper to a dynastic system of politics. The farther it goes the more it comes to make use of business interests as a means rather than an end, as, e.g., in modern Germany, France, and Italy, and in the continental states of the sixteenth and seventeenth centuries. The crown, court, bureaucracy, military establishment, and nobility, under whatever designations, gradually come to their own again in such a situation, and affairs again come to turn on questions of the maintenance and dignity of these superior elements of the population. The objective end of protracted warlike endeavor necessarily shifts from business advantage to dynastic ascendancy and courtly honor. Business interests fall to the position of fiscal ways and means, and business traffic becomes subservient to higher ends, with a fair chance of ultimate exhaustion or collapse through the bankruptcy of the state.[16]

Business enterprise is an individual matter, not a collective one. So long as the individual business man sees a proximate gain for himself in meeting the demands for war funds and materials to maintain the courtly and official establishments that go with military politics, it is not in the nature of the business man to draw back. It is always his profits, not his livelihood, that is involved; the question which touches his profits is the relative gainfulness of alternative lines of investment open to him. So long as the pecuniary inducements held out by the state, in bidding for funds or supplies, overbalance the inducements offered by alternative lines of employment, the business men will supply these demands, regardless of what the ulterior substantial outcome of such a course may be in the end. Funds and business enterprise are now of so pronounced an international or cosmopolitan character that any business man may, even without fully appreciating the fact, lend his aid to the fisc of a hostile power as readily as to a friendly power or to the home government; whereby an equable and comprehensive exhaustion of the several communities involved in the concert of nations is greatly facilitated. Barring accidents and untoward cultural agencies from outside of politics, business, or religion, there is nothing in the logic of the modern situation that should stop the cumulative war expenditures short of industrial collapse and consequent national bankruptcy, such as terminated the carnival of war and politics that ran its course on the continent in the sixteenth and seventeenth centuries.

NOTES

1. Cf. William Ashley, *Economic History and Theory* (1893), bk. 2., especially chap. 3.

2. Cf. Thorstein Veblen, *The Theory of Business Enterprise,* chap. 4.

3. Cf. William Ashley, "The Economic Atmosphere of America," in *Surveys, Historic and Economic,* pp. 405 ff.

4. This date is true for England. For America the discipline favorable to the growth of the natural-liberty dogma lasted nearly a century longer. In America the new, modern, technological and business era can scarcely be said to have set in in good vigor until the period of the Civil War. Hence, with a longer and later training, the preconceptions of natural liberty are fresher and more tenacious in America. For the continental peoples the case is different again. With them the modern technological and business situation is of approximately the same date as in America, but their training up to the date of the transition to the modern situation was in a much less degree a training in individual initiative, free scattered industry, and petty trade. The continental peoples for the most part made a somewhat abrupt transition after the middle of the nineteenth century from a stale and dilapidated system of guild and feudalistic prescriptions to the (for them) exotic system of modern technology and business principles.

5. Under the system of handicraft and petty trade the converse was true. Livelihood was the fundamental norm of business regulations; profits had but a secondary standing, if any.

6. E.g., as to employer's liability for accidents or unsanitary premises, the safeguarding of machinery, age limit of laborers or hour limit of working time, etc.

7. E.g., where a workman's accepting employment on machinery which is not safeguarded as the law requires is construed as an exercise of the indefeasible right of free contract on his part, which thereby exempts the employer from liability for eventual accidents.

In point of legal principle the reluctance to allow or recognize limited liability in joint stock companies, in the English practice prior to the Companies Acts, was of much the same nature as the current reluctance to allow an alienation or abridgment of a workman's individual responsibility for the terms of his employment and the consequences following from it. It was felt that a pecuniary liability was a personal matter, of which the person was not competent to divest himself under that system of mutual rights and duties in which the members of the community were bound together. Impersonal, collective, and limited liability won its way, as against the system of natural liberty, in this field by sheer force of business expediency. In a conflict of principles between the main proposition and one of its corollaries, the corollary won because the facts had outgrown the primary implication of the main proposition.

8. The common law is of course a formulation of the deliverances of common sense on the points which it touches. But common law, as well as common sense, being a formulation of habits of thought, is necessarily an outgrowth of past rather than of present circumstances—in this case the circumstances of the eighteenth century—whereas the sympathies of the vulgar, as they appear in jury decisions, are largely the outcome of those modern experiences that are at increasing variance with the foundations of the common law.

It may be remarked by the way that, while the charge of partiality or corruption, often heard as against these higher tribunals, may in a few scattering instances be founded, that is after all not much to the point as regards practical consequences. The greater number of the courts, indeed virtually the entire judiciary, are no doubt above substantial suspicion in the premises. And after all, if they were not incorruptible—if the common run of the tribunals were corruptly working in the interest of the employers or owners—that need not seriously affect the outcome as regards the general tenor of the decisions handed down. If they are corrupt or biased, they will decide in favor of the owners, who can afford to pay, and they will be under the necessity of finding plausible reasons in law for so doing. Such reason can be found only in the metaphysical natural rights basis of the law; and if it can be found by the help of such legal ratiocination, then it is a valid ground of decision, that being the peculiar merit of metaphysical grounds of decision. On the other hand, if the court is a "learned, upright judge," he will look for the grounds of decision in the same place and find them in the same shape. Necessarily so, since the point in dispute is almost invariably a question of the legal rights of property as against the material requirements of comfort or of livelihood; and the rights of property are the foundation of modern law and order, while the requirements of comfort or livelihood passed out of the scope of the law on the abrogation of the outworn system of mandatory prescriptions governing industrial and trade relations in early modern times. Since the disputes in question rarely if ever arise out of a breach of contract on the part of the employer-owner, the decision can ordinarily, in the nature of the case, not go against him, inasmuch as the foundation of economic law and order is the freedom and inviolability of pecuniary contracts. It should, in fact, be nearly a matter of indifference to the "popular" side of this class of litigation whether the courts are corrupt or not. The question has little else than a speculative interest. In the nature of the case the owner alone has, ordinarily, any standing in court. All of which argues that there are probably very few courts that are in any degree corrupt or biased, so far as touches litigation of this class. Efforts to corrupt them would be a work of supererogation, besides being immoral.

9. This is not true in nearly the same degree for the mercantile policies of England, even in early modern times. In English policy, under the inchoate constitutional system of the mercantilist era, the ulterior (avowed) end is always the (business) advantage of the "commonwealth." The prince comes in rather as second than as first claimant on the solicitude of the mercantilist statesman.

10. The line of descent of the preconception of patriotism or chauvinism, as it finds expression in this lively sense of pecuniary solidarity, may be outlined as follows: Under the clan (gentile or tribal) system out of which the West European peoples passed into the regime of feudal Christendom, a given group stood together in a union of offense and defense, warlike and economic, on the basis of a putative blood relationship. When the manor or the (essentially servile) mark came to replace the clan group as the economic and civil unit, the bond of putative blood relationship persisted in a slightly modified form and force, the incidence of the sense of solidarity, the "consciousness of kind," then shifting to the new group unit, with allegiance centering on the feudal head of the group, instead of, as formerly, on the senior line of putative descent. When the state came forward in medieval and early modern times and took over the powers and prerogatives of the head of the manor of the feudal lord, it took over also the incidence of this sense of allegiance, and the sense of solidarity came to cover the larger group of the nation which had succeeded to the autonomy of the manor. Where the line of institutional descent runs through the industrial town, with guild, handicraft, and local government, the transient features of the growth are superficially different but in effect much the same. The discipline of warfare, which kept up the practice of joint action and had the appearance of joint enterprise, served to keep the sense of patriotic solidarity firm and vigorous and enabled it to cover other interests as well as the princely enterprise of warfare and state-making. Wherever unbroken peace prevailed for an appreciable period, so as to affect the growth of traditions, the sense of national solidarity showed symptoms of slackening. For purposes of economic solidarity the commonwealth is conceived after the manner of an overgrown manor. It figures as such, e.g., in English mercantilist writings of the sixteenth to the eighteenth century, as well as in the patriotic trade politics of the present.

11. In passing it may be remarked that the fact of this sense of solidarity being an anachronism must not be taken as implying anything for or against the substantial merits of such a frame of mind.

12. The two complementary sentiments—patriotism and pecuniary solidarity—are found in unequal measure among the several nations of Christendom. The disparity in this respect corresponds roughly with a disparity in past national experience. The continental peoples, e.g., have, on the whole, a readier and fuller, more unequivocal, patriotic conviction, as they have also had a longer, more severe, and later discipline in the fealty that goes with a system of dynastic warfare and graded servitude; whereas the English-speaking peoples are animated with a more secure conviction that money value is the chief end of serious endeavor and that business solvency is the final attribute of manhood. But in

either case the outcome is the primacy of business in the counsels of nations, and its empire is none the less secure for its resting more on one or the other of these two supports.

13. For England the last half of the eighteenth century, for continental Europe and America the last half of the nineteenth. In colonial commerce the date for both England and the continent is much earlier.

14. "Ring" is here used as a designation of this loose organization of business interests for the guidance of policy, without implying criticism of the ring or of its aims and methods.

15. Armaments and large military and naval establishments have also a secondary attraction, of a more intimate kind, for enterprising business men, in that they afford opportunities for transactions of a peculiarly lucrative character. One of the parties (the government official) concerned in such transactions has less than the usual incentive to drive a close bargain. His own private gain and loss is not immediately involved, so that he is less given to petty huckstering and close surveillance of the execution of the contracts made. What adds force to this consideration is the fact that military and naval establishments habitually are what the vulgar would call corrupt. The pecuniary interest of the officials does not coincide with that of the establishment. There is an appreciable "margin of error" which a sagacious business man may turn to account.

The great business interests are the more inclined to look kindly on an extension of warlike enterprise and armaments, since the pecuniary advantages inure to them, while the pecuniary burden falls chiefly on the rest of the community. It is, to say the least, highly improbable that the business gains which accrue from a well-conducted foreign policy ever, in modern times, equal the cost at which they are secured; but that consideration scarcely enters, since the costs are not paid out of business gains, but out of the industry of the rest of the people. The people, however, are animated with an uncritical persuasion that they have some sort of a residuary share in these gains, and that this residuary share in some manner exceeds the whole of the gains secured.

16. Cf. John A. Hobson, *Imperialism,* pt. 1. chap. 7, pt. 2, chaps. 1 and 7.

SIGMUND DIAMOND

The Reputation of Henry Ford

In 1923, Arthur H. Vandenberg, editor and publisher of the Grand Rapids *Herald,* sharpened his pen to prick the rapidly swelling "Henry Ford for President" bubble. "Ford has to his debit," the editor wrote, "more erratic interviews on public questions, more dubious quotations, more blandly boasted ignorance of American history and American

Source: Reprinted by permission of the publishers from Sigmund Diamond, *The Reputation of the American Businessman* (Cambridge, Mass.: Harvard University Press, 1955). Copyright 1955, by the President and Fellows of Harvard College.

experience, more political nonsense, more dangerous propaganda, than any other dependable citizen that we have ever known."[1]

On April 9, 1947, the same Arthur H. Vandenberg, now senior United States Senator from Michigan, rose on the floor of the Senate to appraise the automobile manufacturer once again. "Mr. Ford's death," the senator said,

ends one of the most thrilling and greatest careers in the life of this country. It is the vivid epitome of what one man can do for himself and for his fellow men under our system of American freedoms. Through his own irresistible genius and courage he not only rose from humble obscurity to fame and fortune, but he also founded a new national economy of mass production which blessed his hundreds of thousands of employees with his wages and his millions of customers with low prices. He has probably had as great an impact on his times as if he had been a President of the United States. With it all, he continued always to be a modest, kindly, gentle friend with a constant interest in the welfare of his country and of his fellow men.[2]

The passage of time and the emergence of new issues led others besides Senator Vandenberg to reconsider earlier judgments and to focus upon criteria which, however unimportant they appeared in an earlier day, seemed now to be those upon which appraisals should be based. Shortly after Henry Ford had taken the witness stand in 1919 during his lawsuit against the Chicago *Tribune,* the New York *Times* commented tersely: "Mr. Ford has been submitted to a severe examination of his intellectual qualities. He has not received a pass degree."[3]

But in 1947 it was not Ford's "intellectual qualities" which concerned the *Times.* That he incarnated the opportunities in which American society abounded, that his had been a life of service, that he embodied the simple virtues—these were the bases on which the new evaluation was erected:

To a peculiar degree he was the embodiment of America in the era of industrial revolution . . . It was the American success story . . . His was a single-minded devotion to the fundamentals as he saw them: hard work, the simple virtues, self-reliance, the good earth. He profited by providing what was new, but also he treasured that which was bygone . . . He built "for the great multitude," and they were, both directly and by accident, the great beneficiaries of Henry Ford, master mechanic.

For all the doubts which Senator Vandenberg and the New York *Times* had expressed concerning various facets of Henry Ford's career, neither, of course, had been antagonistic to his business activities, and it required no great sleight-of-hand on the occasion of his death to convert early doubt into present praise. But in 1947 not only former skeptics but former enemies found common ground on which to stand in sanctioning what had once been a target of attack. Ten years earlier, on May 26, 1937, several members of the United Automobile Workers of America, the CIO union attempting to organize the employees of the Ford Motor Company, were attacked by the Ford Service Department while distributing leaflets at the gates of the River Rouge plant in Dearborn, Michigan. But in April, 1947, Walter P. Reuther, now president of the UAW-CIO and one of those who had been most severely mauled in the earlier attempt at organization, issued on behalf of his fellow union officers a laudatory statement concerning the automobile manufacturer. And for the president of UAW-CIO Local 600, the union which bargains for the employees of the River Rouge plant, there was no place for enmity based on memories of an earlier day. Writing in *Ford Facts*, he said:

> The greatest tribute that could be paid to Mr. Ford is that his roots were firmly imbedded in the soil of his birth—the banks of the River Rouge. From humble beginnings on a farm . . . he welded together a vast industrial empire . . . without leaving the banks of the River Rouge. His friends and his neighbors were important to him. No absentee ownership on the banks of the River Rouge for him! Part of his greatness arose from his willingness to pioneer. Like his rugged forbears, he was never afraid to venture forth into uncharted seas. He recognized that increased purchasing power in the hands of the workers meant more contented workers and a greater potential market—a greater America . . . His mistakes were never mistakes of the heart.

What, then, were the criteria the application of which resulted in an evaluation of the automobile entrepreneur in which the area of approval was wide enough to encompass even the leaders of groups which hitherto had remained outside the consensus of acquiescence?

Henry Ford "was a benefactor of mankind. Simplicity was the keystone of his life," Republican Congressman George Dondero of Michigan said in the first of six speeches delivered by members of the United States Congress on the occasion of Ford's death:

> Born of humble parents, and with meagre education, he rose from obscurity to build the greatest industrial empire of his time . . . The poor man should never forget him. He provided transportation for him at a cost within his reach. The laboring man should never forget him. He doubled his wages voluntarily. Henry Ford and his family have been manufacturing cars, not because they needed bread but to provide employment for those who needed it.[5]

For Democrat as well as for Republican, service had been the major characteristic of Ford's life. "Henry Ford was a practical idealist who believed in helping his fellow man to help himself," Representative John Dingell asserted. "How well he succeeded can be judged by the prosperity of hundreds of thousands of his workers, associates and coordinated industries . . . As Henry Ford grew and prospered so did everyone who worked and associated with him."[6]

Other congressmen embellished the portrait. Republican Edith Nourse Rogers of Massachusetts was not concerned with Ford's business career. "He bought the historic Wayside Inn at Sudbury," she told her colleagues. "He was tremendously interested in all the old traditions of the country. He was interested in art in all its forms. The Ford Sunday symphony orchestra is heard by millions . . . He had some of the finest cattle in the United States. He made splendid contributions to agriculture."[7] Conservative Democrat John Rankin of Mississippi asked different questions of Ford's career but nevertheless came to a similar conclusion: "If it had not been for Henry Ford," he prophesied retroactively, "the average American would not be able to ride in an automobile today. There is one thing characteristically American about Henry Ford's life . . . simplicity . . ."[8]

Henry Ford as a man for whom principle prevailed over profit, for whom sevice to humanity was the fundamental law of conduct, rooted in the traditions of his country, exemplifying its opportunities, and governed by sentiments of warmth and friendship for his fellow man— this was the portrait of Ford presented by those congressmen who chose to discuss the matter. Whether or not the portrait corresponded in every detail to reality, it was one which both reflected and yet reconciled important conflicts in the society in which Ford had lived. The veneration of goodness and the rewarding of success, while always approved in the abstract, nevertheless created serious problems when applied to concrete cases; for always there had been those who insisted that the good were not always rewarded and that the successful were not always good. But in the case of Ford there could be no such problem. He had helped himself because he had helped others—not because he needed bread but because he wanted to provide bread for others had he manufactured automobiles, the congressman had said and so, for the idealists, the problem was solved because there was no problem. For those less concerned with resolving apparent paradoxes but inclined rather to accept situations as they found them, the answer was no less satisfactory. Henry Ford had proved it was possible neither to be so self-seeking as to be branded inhuman nor so good as to be condemned to poverty.

Once the portrait of the entrepreneur had been drawn, it remained only to sketch in the background in such a way as to suggest that, without the appropriate setting, the painting would be meaningless. Republican Senator Albert W. Hawkes of New Jersey and radio commentator Samuel B. Pettengill jointly undertook that responsibility. "Henry Ford's life," Senator Hawkes asserted, ". . . sounds almost like a review of the opportunities open to all people under the American system of free men. Mr. Ford benefited humanity by giving them an opportunity to benefit themselves through honest effort, work, and thrift."

For the instruction of his colleagues, Senator Hawkes read the radio address which Samuel Pettengill had delivered on April 20, 1947:

Abraham Lincoln and Ford mean America throughout the world—log cabin to White House—machine shop to industrial empire. Henry Ford and the other automobile manufacturers who, like him, have developed and applied mass production methods represent the American system at its best. They show what competitive individual enterprise can do—and I stress the word competitive . . .

Has big Government, and the cost and the waste of Government, made it impossible for America to ever have another Henry Ford? . . . Contrary to the teaching of Communist professors that "one man's gain is the other man's loss," he demonstrated on a world scale that it is possible to make more money, pay higher wages, and reduce costs all at once and at the same time—investor, worker, and consumer all gaining and no one losing by the process. The secret of this miracle of economics is high production per man-hour, which brings costs down . . . The best manager of a machine is the man who owns it; if he takes pride in his job. This is the miracle of America. It is hard to see any limit to thi progress . . . if . . . If we don't lose the magic formula in a struggle between cla and class; if investor, and manager and worker all play fair with each other . But even the magic formula cannot work except under a government friendly achievement, a government that protects a man in the fruit of his toil. Great a was, I firmly believe Henry Ford would be a name scarcely known beyond county limits of his home, if he had not lived under the protection of the Co tution of the United States . . . Ford's career was possible only in an Am .. with constitutional government and competitive free enterprise unhampered by confiscatory taxation of able men—as it was when he was born.

These, concluded the speaker, were "big facts that tie in with the argument as to whether communism, socialism, or the individual enterprise system is best for America—and the world."[9]

Never before had the identity of business enterprise and the entrepreneur with the symbols of nationalism been so explicit, and in that explicitness of identity lies the clue to the realization of the new and broader consensus. If the entrepreneur, like Abraham Lincoln, "represented the American system at its best," if competitive free enterprise and constitutional government were interchangeable parts of the same mechanism, and if—as the speaker said—these "big facts . . . tie in with the argument as to whether communism, socialism, or the individual enterprise system is best for America," then to deny the identities or to evaluate Ford differently was to court the risk of being considered antagonistic not only to business enterprise but to the nation itself, at a time when its very existence seemed to be challenged and when the conception of loyalty was being increasingly invoked as the acid test of all political and economic pronouncements. The equation of business enterprise and patriotism was not one which was derived for the first time on the occasion of the death of Henry Ford. It appeared at least as early as the time of Commodore Vanderbilt; with the discussion of J. P. Morgan it received a new impetus; and it had been utilized by Ford himself. From 1937 to 1941 he had sought to protect himself against union organization by describing the CIO as "un-American," as a Russian importation; and in November, 1941, when Ford employees in Canada were preparing to elect their bargaining representative, he had asked them to remember that the UAW-CIO was an "American" importation and to vote against the union out of loyalty to the "Canadian way."[10]

The congressmen who lauded Ford's simplicity, emphasized his career of service, and insisted that all he represented was the very essence of that which the country was mobilizing to defend were speaking, of course, to a relatively limited audience. But through the news and editorial columns of the daily press, which deviated hardly at all from the appraisal of the congressmen, the American public was saturated with obituaries which, though they purported to examine Ford's career, subordinated discussion of the man to praise for what he was alleged to symbolize.

"Only America could have produced the kind of man he was," wrote the Grand Rapids *Herald* of Ford:

> Only in America could he have revolutionized a civilization and built a powerful empire of such vast extent. For he was both the product and the exponent of the free enterprise system functioning at its best in a democratic atmosphere . . . Mr. Ford's eighty-three years give us a vivid, bright example of the opportunity America offered in his lifetime and still offers to a man with the foresight, the unswerving purpose and the indefatigable energy to grasp it . . . Thus in one man, with his foibles as his wisdom, is summed up the opportunity and the spirit of America.

Other newspapers were equally convinced that the essential clue to an understanding of the entrepreneur's career lay not in his character but in the nature of the time and place in which he had lived. "Henry Ford . . . was distinctly a product of America. In no other land and no other age could just such a career have been enacted and such a personality have flourished," the Atlanta *Journal* stated. "The times were ripe and the country of free enterprise and individual initiative was favorable to talents like his." He was, that newspaper concluded, "one among many in the long tradition of pioneering characters and inventive minds whom America has brought forth and who have made America in turn."

"In some areas of the world Henry Ford would not have been permitted to have carried out his ideas. He would have been refused a permit," one newspaper stated. But in America things were different. "Since this nation's infant days, men have climbed to marvelous heights of success on the ladder of opportunity fashioned by the American system. Like many others, the name of Henry Ford will endure as an eminent example." His was "the story of a Michigan farm boy who went to work at $2.50 a week . . . Henry Ford went on to achievement in after years which gave him world renown and gave to the world more of the benefits which constantly flow from the exercise of courage and genius under the American economic system. Henry Ford's career stands as an illustration of the American way of life at work." Newspaper after newspaper from every corner of the land reiterated the argument of the reciprocal relationship between the man and his environment—the nation had made possible the career, and the career had benefited the nation. "America gave Henry Ford his opportunity . . . Only in a free society can there be a Henry Ford; only in a free society can the productive, imaginative, able person produce for society what his own mind and courage dictate." He was, indeed, "the embodiment and example of the freedom of opportunity and enterprise that is America."[11]

That it was the quality of freedom in the American environment that had produced Henry Ford all newspapers agreed, but the precise nature of that freedom was somewhat obscure. In some analyses it seemed to refer to political institutions; in others, to that particular set of economic relationships which had become known as "free enterprise"; and in still others both concepts of freedom were so merged as to create the impression that they were, indeed, identical. None expressed the mingling of concepts so eloquently nor so clearly revealed its usefulness for the purpose of strengthening the traditional forms of enterprise than did editor William Griffin of the New York *Enquirer*. Ford's

. . . record serves to emphasize, at a crucial period in our country's history, the superiority of the American system of free government and free opportunity, as an instrumentality for the protection of the liberties and rights of the individual and of the masses, and the promotion of their well-being, over every other system known to man in the past or in the present . . . Wealth was not his by inheritance, but genuine Americanism was . . . Because long and toilsome hours did not dismay him, because he was self-reliant and farsighted, and because he was animated by the Americanism which he learned at home and at school, Henry Ford in time conferred upon his countrymen and his country benefits beyond the capacity of human calculation . . . The great American whose death our country now mourns did not receive an expensive education, with the taxpayers footing the bill. He left school when he was 16, not to dodge work and have a good time, but to busy himself as an employe in a Detroit machine shop. Those were the horse-and-buggy days before the philosophy of maximum pay for minimum effort began to wreak such horror in our national life. Henry Ford was a self-reliant individualist. Life in his parental home was American. The education he received was an American education, not the type of instruction so prevalent in our land today, when so many young Americans are the victims of an educational system that destroys patriotism and self-initiative, leads boys and girls to believe that the world owes them a living, and saddles the hard-pressed taxpayers with a burden that is of no benefit to anyone but on the contrary maintains a system which is a national destroyer . . . No country save America could have produced a success story even approaching that of Henry Ford. Ours is the task and the duty of guaranteeing that this land shall not become the victim of the totalitarian philosophies that have enslaved the Old World and are threatening to enslave the New. Henry Ford will live in history as one of America's foremost patriots and one of the greatest benefactors of mankind.

Was it free America which had produced Henry Ford, or was it free enterprise? The newspapers obviated the necessity of making a choice by presenting the two as if they were in fact one. "By utilizing the American system of free enterprise, he started from financial zero and built up during his lifetime the greatest private fortune the world has ever known," the Burlington *Free Press* editorialized. Henry Ford, stated the Charlotte *Observer* in an editorial which equated nation and economic system,

has been the living symbol of everything that we mean by American private enterprise—its initiative, its daring, its urge to achievement, its freedom from hidebound tradition and taboo, its incomparable rewards in both material and spiritual satisfaction for work well done, and, above all, its opportunity. The superiority of our system over all others was never better exemplified than in the life of this man, who demonstrated that in this land of ours humble birth is no barrier to greatness, that genius can win recognition in a ramshackle garage, that a man's capacity for attainment is limited only by his own shortcomings . . . His life was a practical demonstration that the impossible collectivist ideal of equal distribution has been attained least of all in the collectivist countries; the nearest approach to it has been made by American private enterprise.

"With the system of free enterprise we embrace in this country, more" great entrepreneurs "will follow" Ford. But "if ever the time comes when" individual initiative and private enterprise will be lost, then "it will be time for America to close up shop and call it a day."[12]

If that which was responsible for Ford's career was, however expressed, something in the American environment, then surely the career itself, capped as it was with extraordinary success, was American in a special sense.

"Mr. Ford's life story," one paper commented, "tells us that there is no limit in America to what a man can accomplish, and that it is possible to rise to the top and still walk unaffected with one's fellowmen." There could "be no better illustration of the old slogan that 'America is another word for opportunity.' " The success he had achieved was not at all unusual; indeed, "Ford may be rated as a typical American, in that he demonstrated in a monumental way the heights to which American opportunity can lead. In no other land could he have achieved the tremendous results that he did."[13]

Indeed in every aspect of his life, private as well as public, Ford was authentically American. A "man of simple tastes and of peace," he was "quite the antithesis of the Krupps or the Kruegers, his counterparts on the European continent." His qualities of "individualism . . . self-confidence . . . inventiveness, pliability and industry" were not uniquely his own, but those "of America." He was "a great American," and like "great Americans," he had been "simple and human." Americanism permeated his very being. "Like the many-sided Franklin and the versatile Jefferson, Henry Ford was, in accord with one of America's more picturesque traditions, a man of many facets. His active interests ranged from world peace and reforestation to dietary reform and folk dancing."

"There was something very earthy and American about Mr. Ford. His hobbies, expensive though some of them were, were also wholesome and much in the American tradition"; and no one had done as much to keep that tradition alive, for he had been "greatly interested in early American culture and in the perpetuation of the ideals and the virtues that have made America great." His "American saga" had been "many chaptered." His career, of course, was thoroughly in the American tradition. But there was another chapter "for the father—an immigrant out of Ireland"; and above all there was the chapter "for the widow who mourns," whom he had married "59 years ago," and who had been "his helpmate . . . his inspiration. Such long loyalty and constancy—that's American, too!" Surely this was a man who had "built himself into the history" of his country.[14]

On the basis of such evidence, the conclusion reached by the press was logical and appropriate. Henry Ford had been "an inspiration to Americans in this and future generations" and a "symbol of the United States," of "individualistic American drive," of "American productive genius and of America itself." His were "the qualities the nation must more and more appreciate for they" were "the qualities which forged the greatness of this nation, and the qualities which alone will keep it great."[15]

If this was discussion of an entrepreneur, no less was it discussion of the setting in which that entrepreneur had acted and, more precisely, discussion which held setting to be of greater consequence than agent in accounting for the nature of an entrepreneurial career. Never before had interest focused so sharply on entrepreneurial setting rather than entrepreneurial character, and never before had the defenders of business

enterprise disclosed such sensitivity to problems relating to the fundamental economic structure of society. Indeed, recognition that they were
concerned with such problems and that the real importance of Ford's
career lay in the light it shed on the merits of competing economic
systems was frankly avowed.

"You political and economic theorists," asked the Portland *Oregonian*, "you proponents of the isms, you critics of the American way of
life who believe that democracy is in decay, where are the Fords and the
Edisons of your school? Where are your Lincolns? It is more than mere
coincidence that the story of Henry Ford, inventor and industrialist, is
essentially an American story."

"The rise of Mr. Ford, a one-time obscure farm youth, to the
position which he occupied in the industrial world," the Lansing *State
Journal* observed, "is one of the most effective lessons the world had ever
had in the virtue of the American system of free individual enterprise. At
a time when that system is under attack from some quarters it is of the
greatest importance that there be reflection upon what an obscure farm
youth was able to accomplish with the opportunities which were open to
him under a system which made it possible for him to use his individual
ideas . . . Had he operated under a system which did not permit freedom
of individual enterprise he might have remained in obscurity." If
"freedom of individual enterprise" was the basic element of the system
which had produced Ford, and if that system was characteristically
American, then those who advocated alterations in it were not only guilty
of tampering with the material prosperity of the nation but of injecting
"alien poisons" into the American environment. Those who called for the
"replacement" of this system "by more and more government control,
through such alien governmental forms as communism"; the "cheap
political demagogues" and the "communist infested CIO local union"
which controlled his plant; "the collectivists and the left of center planners"; "the Judas fringe of the left"; the advocates of the "alien economic and political sophisms that, having failed to create, would attempt
by force, casuistry and deceit to pervert our democratic processes to
their own gain"—only such persons as these could be found among the
opponents of Ford, the press argued, because, by definition, only advocates of alien ideologies could oppose him. Ford had succeeded because
he was "untouched by the precocity of decadent foreign doctrines" and
because he was "the personification of strong Americanism." "If there is
a defense for a free economy, nothing speaks louder than the deeds of
Henry Ford." In this lay his triumph and significance, that the "whole
career of Henry Ford presents a glamorous testimonial for the American
system . . . the achievements of the elder Ford will intrigue young Americans so long as our free enterprise system endures."[16]

If Henry Ford's career was a testimonial to the environment which had shaped it, it was, in another sense, a testimonial to business enterprise itself; for, so at least the newspapers argued, service to humanity was the real product of the Ford factories as it was of all industry. Nor, indeed, could it be otherwise; for mass production, with which Ford was so closely identified, was, in the view of the press, to be considered less a technological aspect of the process of manufacture than an instrumentality for the elevation of standards of living. The fundamental result of mass production was to "put the motor car within the reach of the common people," to give "the lesser man not only an instrument for a freer, wider life, but . . . the purchasing power to enjoy the better things of living," to lighten "men's labor, improve their efficiency, their wages and their living standards." Appraised in terms of the results wrought by his work—"increased national wealth, conveniece in travel, progress in the making and distribution of useful articles of commerce, rational philanthropy, and patriotism"—there could be no dissent from the double verdict that Ford's "enterprises enriched his country and the world at large in spiritual and cultural as well as in material ways" and that "not mass production alone" but "mass service to all was the sparkplug that made the Ford ideal click."[17]

"He conceived that his own prosperity lay in that of others," wrote the Detroit *News*. "To place in the reach of the greatest number of people a useful product which would lift the whole level of living was, therefore, a purpose to which he committed a boundless originality and inexhaustible energy." That he had succeeded in his purpose was abundantly evident in every aspect of American life. "He released his countrymen and people everywhere from the older restrictions of locality . . . With the new freedom of movement and thinking came a new, more commodious freshness of the spirit." His "initiative and daring raised directly and indirectly the wages of millions and his mass-production methods . . . lifted living standards, comforts and conveniences to a new 'high.' " He increased the strength and prosperity of the nation. His "genius meant the making of jobs in a big industry and the building of a business which directly and indirectly contributed tremendous pay rolls of employment as well as taxes to the American economic system." His automobiles "probably accomplished more than any other agency in the past hundred years in increasing unity between city and country," for they "brought within easy range of rural families markets and recreational and cultural advantages."[18]

"Although Henry Ford showed no sentimentalism in business," the *Arkansas Gazette* concluded approvingly, "his policies were humanitarian in their results, as well as practical." He had raised the "living standard of the common people of America"—his achievement gave him "a sort of immortality," the immortality "that is reserved for those who dream and toil for humanity's sake."

In that conclusion the Negro newspaper, the Chicago *Defender*, concurred. Ford had been "an industrial genius at the service of society." But other Negro newspapers exhibited greater interest in more concrete demonstrations of the automobile manufacturer's humanity. He had befriended the noted Negro scientist, George Washington Carver, and his "high wages and revolutionary assemply line production" acted as a powerful magnet to draw Negro migrants from the "farm-bound South." Above all he had not refused to hire Negroes in his factories. "There would be no need for an FEPC if all employers took a page from the Ford book. In his passing, we have lost a real friend," mourned the *Afro-American*. This was high praise indeed for Henry Ford, but it was not praise from which enterprise in general could derive much satisfaction; for the Negro press applauded Ford not because he typified standard business practice but because, in their view, he had departed from it.

So far as Ford himself was concerned, however, editorial opinion was virtually unanimous in holding not only that the consequences of his acts were of widespread public benefit, but that consideration of public service was the compelling motive which dictated his acts and decisions. One of the cardinal principles of classical economics was, of course, the compatibility of private striving and public welfare, but the two had been linked in such a way as to make the latter dependent on the former. In the economic theory of the newspaper editors, however, there was no place for explicit avowal of private striving. Service had replaced profit as a basic category of entrepreneurial motivation. "The acquisition of a personal fortune counted for little with Henry Ford," wrote the Galveston *Daily News*. "He was not by nature a moneymaker." On the contrary, his "mind was dominated by constructive motives, the desire to invent and to invent in such a way as to lessen human labor." The very ideas which made of Ford "one of the greatest benefactors of his day" stemmed from "his love for his fellows with whose struggles he sympathized and for whose betterment he worked, his own wealth being incidental to his performance." That this was so the Ford Motor Company itself revealed. "The impression has somehow gotten abroad that Henry Ford is in the automobile business," the Company had said. "It isn't true. Mr. Ford shoots about fifteen hundred cars out of the back door of his factory every day just to get rid of them. They are the byproducts of his real business, which is the making of men . . . Mr. Ford's business is the making of men, and he manufactures automobiles on the side to defray the expenses of his main business."[19]

Indeed, the money Ford had made was really a reward both for the risks he undertook and the benefits he conferred. "He and those who lent him money took all the risks of possible, even probable, failure," the New York *Daily Mirror* states. His "vast personal fortune" was a "reward for the billions upon billions that have been made for those who have been associated with him, either as management or labor, or connected with other concerns that have profited by his production methods; and for his contribution to the happiness of the so-called 'common man.' " But in either case, whether construed as reward for risk or as reward for service, his fortune was only "a by-product," "only incidental," merely "nominal," and considerably less than the value of his "services to . . . country and to mankind." Not "by exploitation of labor and financial finagling" had he made his fortune, but by concerning himself with "the general welfare of his country and of the world." There was, in this example of the relationship of private wealth and public service, a profound lesson in political economy:

> It is individuals who have big ideas, not nations . . . It is individuals who have the drive, the patience, the persistence, to put big ideas into effect, not nations . . . If, in the process, the individual acquires a great fortune and great power, that is not necessarily worse than the acquisition of greater resources and power through the domination of government. It can be better, and often is, because government is still left to help keep the individual from getting too far offside, whereas the man who dominates a government is often beyond anyone's reach.[20]

Not even the high eminence which Ford had attained, however, placed him "beyond anyone's reach," and the fact that—as most of the press agreed—he had begun the climb to that eminence from a position no higher than that occupied by most men served less to emphasize his exceptional qualities than to place him squarely amidst the general body of his fellow men. A few newspapers, to be sure, felt that Ford's climb up the ladder of success had begun at a rung somewhere higher than at the bottom. His father, said the Chicago *Journal of Commerce*, had been "well-to-do," and the Detroit *Free Press* was even more favorably impressed with his father's economic status: "At the time of Henry's birth, his father had prospered until he held 240 acres of land. He was a progressive man. He owned and operated the latest and best of farm machinery of that day." But most editors chose not to quibble over the exact elevation at which Ford had begun his climb; the fact of his ascent and the eminence which he ultimately attained were the matters to be emphasized. "The saga of Henry Ford's rise from farm boy to the world's richest man, head of a billion-dollar company," said the New York *Daily News*, reverting to a time-honored theme, "reads like one of the novels of Horatio Alger who was one of Ford's favorite authors." His was a "life story more strange and wonderful than any spinner of tales ever dared put into words. Even the bare details . . . still seem incredible. If they had not happened before our very eyes we could not believe in the farm boy turned mechanic, inventor, racing car driver, motor manufacturer, head of one of the greatest industrial empires in the world. Yet it is all true." He "was the King Midas of all time," compared to whom "Croesus . . . was a piker"; but he had started the trek which led to such wealth "as a $2.50 a week mechanic." In this, as in all else, Ford's career was "traditionally American," for it was the "realization of the American dream" and he had written still another chapter in the history of a "country famed for its astounding episodes of the 'rags to riches' variety."[21]

In all of his undertakings, concluded the editor of the New York *Enquirer*, "Ford was a big business man with a big heart, a big understanding and sympathy with his fellow man, a big regard for the rights and advancement of his employes, a big eagerness to serve the masses, a big contempt for the detractors of the American way of life, a big faith in America and a big confidence in her future." But though big in the things that required bigness, the press argued, he was no different from his countrymen in those areas of life in which true qualities of humanity were likely to manifest themselves.

"With all of his vast wealth and his world wide prestige," said the Atlanta *Journal*, "Mr. Ford remained the simplest of men, a good neighbor, a loved companion to those who knew him, with never a tinge of ostentation . . ." "Mr. Ford was a good man and his tastes, regardless of his ability to have anything money could buy, remained modest." He loved automobile and boat racing, skating, and baseball. "Henry Ford's identity with sports was more than sufficient to humanize him," said the Detroit *News*. To the very end of his life he remained "a family man," with "strong family loyalties," and he "often said, in his latter years, that his chief aim in life was to provide happiness for his wife." But his family was not the only recipient of his kindness. "Henry Ford was the kind of man who was so worried about the chance of accident in the 1936 500-mile Speedway race that he insured all drivers and mechanics," the Indianapolis *Star* revealed. This was a demonstration, "in a practical way," of his advocacy of the Golden Rule; "he believed in it, he preached it— and within limits—he practiced it." He was, in short, "a down-to-earth human being," "a humble, God-fearing, eminently respectable and wholesome citizen."[22]

To these qualities of plainness and humanity, James Kilgallen, a columnist of the Hearst newspapers, devoted his attention:

One of the greatest things about Henry Ford was his simplicity. He was a plain, easy-to-know man, the kind you'd run into if you suddenly dropped into the village barbershop. True, he was a multi-millionaire but he never talked to you in dollars and cents. In fact, he often traveled around without a dime in his pocket.

There was no pretense about him, nothing of the "phony," no consciousness of the fact that he was a man of note whom many regarded with awe.

In Ford's personality, Kilgallen concluded, all facets of the American character were revealed and in him each American could find something of himself. "To me, Henry Ford was like . . . Tom Dewey, Jim Farley, Peggy Hopkins Joyce, Eddie Rickenbacker, 'Peaches' Browning and others who were sure-fire Page 1 copy . . . He was just plain Henry Ford. In a word, he was democratic." Reporter Robert J. Casey captured still another aspect of the man's character. The people of Detroit, he said, "spoke of his affection for children and linked him with legends like that of St. Francis and the birds." In the face of such evidence, could anyone deny that "he was fundamentally a man of the people?"[23]

But the riches which Ford had attained were more than those of the monetary variety. He had accumulated, as well, a great store of experience and wisdom. "It wasn't mechanical ability alone" that characterized him; his "other impelling and powerful" characteristics— "faith" in himself, "his distinguishing quality of intellect," his "hard, common sense," "his disposition to set impossible objectives and then achieve them," his "fierce individualism"—were applied with distinction in nonbusiness as well as in business activities. His was a career, therefore, "that had many facets. He was an ardent pacifist, a prohibitionist, deeply interested in sociology and in the development of agriculture as an adjunct to industry." He was "a humanitarian"; he "developed antiquarian interests" and was "a patron of American folkways"; and, "something of a philosopher," his thought was that of "a shrewd, kindly sage." If "as an individual" he exhibited "all sorts of misjudgments and prejudices," they were simply those which "he shared with the rest of us"; and besides, "if he exposed himself to ridicule by some of the convictions he expressed and the causes he espoused, more often than not his critics came to agree that he had been right."[24] Nowhere was this better illustrated than in the field of science. Once he had told a reporter:

I believe that the smallest particle of matter—call it an atom or an ion or what you like—is intelligent. I don't know much about atoms and the like, but I feel sure that they know what they are doing—and why. They swarm all around us. If a man is working his level best to do what he believes is right, these invisible elements pitch in and help him. If he is doing what he knows is wrong, they will work just as hard against him.

And the critics scoffed. But "today," wrote the Detroit *News*, "scientists are coming close to Henry Ford's concept in their belief that inherent spirituality is a basic function of all matter."

Since Ford remained a man of the people despite the towering heights he had attained, he was, in the view of the press, eminently qualified to impart to his countrymen the wisdom which had served him so successfully. In presenting Ford's views to the public the press was offering more than simply an interior view of the man; it was also, in effect, advising its readers that the policies which the automobile manufacturer had found serviceable in coping with problems were in the public domain and would be of equal utility to all. The practice of presenting Ford's views to the public was hardly new. For years journalists had quoted Ford's opinions on all manner of problems, and as early as 1923 a booklet had been published containing 365—one for each day of the year—of the auto maker's aphorisms.[25] What was new was the content of the aphorisms which the press chose to print on the occasion of Ford's death. There was available in the public record a body of statements by Ford on almost every conceivable subject:

I cannot conceive how we tolerate hunger and poverty when they grow solely out of bad management.

It is not necessary for people to love one another in order to work together. In a factory the sole object of everybody should be to get the work done and get paid for it.

It is pretty well understood that a man in the Ford plant works.

Wars are manufactured by war campaigns along definite lines. First the people are worked upon, their suspicions are aroused. All you need are a few agents with some cleverness and no conscience working through a press whose interests are bound up with those who benefit by war. Then the "overt act" will soon appear.

The paramount right is the right to work.[26]

It's a good thing the recovery is prolonged. Otherwise the people wouldn't profit by the idleness.[27]

The nations of Europe could come together more easily if it were not for their capitalistic governments.

A certain stream of nasty Orientalism has been observed in this country to be affecting our literature, our amusements, our social conduct and our business standards. It is traceable to one racial source. Whether this impress is to be changed or not is wholly in the hands of the Jews themselves.[28]

The cow must go.[29]

Successful persons often say that opportunities are just as plentiful as they ever were, but they don't tell you what they are, where to find them, or how to use them . . . They deal in glittering generalities that mean nothing.[30]

Maxims such as these were not, however, those which were quoted by the press at the time of Ford's death. Rather did the press select from the general body of available material those aphorisms which conformed more closely to the image of Ford it had chosen to present:

Competition is the great teacher.

It is all one to me if a man comes from Sing Sing or Harvard. We hire a man, not his history.

I am in business not to make money as money, but to do many things which I believe are of public benefit.

I have tried to live as my mother would have wanted me to.

History as sometimes written is mostly bunk. But history that you can see is of great value.

I am not interested in money but in the things of which money is merely a symbol.

The only right use for money is to capitalize industry. One might give it away but giving it away doesn't do any good.

Gold is the most useless of all things.

Profits are a public trust.

Endowment is an opiate to imagination, a drug to initiative . . . One of the greatest curses of the country today is the habit of endowing this and endowing that.[31]

It was to this Henry Ford whom the nation's leaders from every area of activity joined to pay tribute in an unprecedented display of mourning. "He typified the best in American enterprise . . . He contributed directly and by example to our high living standards," said Alfred P. Sloan, chairman of the board of the General Motors corporation. "A great man and a wonderful example of American civilization and opportunity," proclaimed Mayor Edward Kelly of Chicago. "He was a genius in many respects and an example of what continuous and hard work may do for ambitious Americans." To his friend Harvey S. Firestone, Ford "exemplified the virtues of hard work, vision and service which made this country great, and sought to preserve these virtues through his philanthropy so that the human, simple, pioneering spirit of America might be perpetuated." Ford's former associate William S. Knudsen expressed the verdict and the wish of all: "He will be remembered forever . . . for the things he has done and the beautiful example of his personal life. May God bless him and give him the reward he has so richly earned."[32]

But more than the great and the near-great exhibited their sorrow at Ford's death. It was, the Detroit *Free Press* suggested, entirely appropriate that the funeral of the man to whom "service was the watchword, profits . . . a byproduct," the man who "took the burdens off the backs of men and made the machine the slave of man," should not be a private service but a vast public display of appreciation and affection. The members of the Michigan legislature paused "in commemoration of the passing of a great man"; Governor Kim Sigler ordered all flags on state buildings to fly at half-staff until the funeral; the Detroit common council "directed that a large portrait of Ford, draped in mourning colors, be displayed on the front of the city hall for thirty days, and that mourning posters be displayed on buses"; the mayor of Dearborn proclaimed thirty days of official mourning; all Ford plants were ordered to shut down on the day of the funeral and in all automobile plants in Michigan preparations were made to stop fast-moving assembly lines for one minute of mourning; Ford dealers throughout the nation closed their establishments the afternoon of April 10; and all automobile traffic in the city of Detroit was observed to come to a complete halt as Ford's body was lowered into the grave. George W. Mason, president of the Automobile Manufacturers Association, said that "about seven million workers probably would take part in the demonstration of sympathy."[33]

For two full days before the funeral, countless numbers of persons—thirty thousand, according to the Montgomery *Advertiser*; seventy-five thousand, according to the New York *Times*—filed past Ford's bier. What mattered was not the number of those who came to pay him tribute—in any case that was large—but the social groups from which they came. "Factory workers and business men rub shoulders in a silent procession," said a reporter at the scene, because with Ford "both groups had something in common." So, indeed, did all mankind—the corporation executive who saw in Ford the model of successful enterprise, the worker and the farmer who saw in him the model of aspiration and benevolence, even the "bridal couples" who would "miss his smile" and the sad old lady, Miss Mae Tabor, his schoolmate, who "was heard to whisper, 'Good-by, Henry. You were such a good boy.' " It was for all of these that Dean Kirk B. O'Ferrall spoke as he laid Henry Ford's body down to its final rest: "I speak to you of Mr. Ford's simple personal tastes and habits and his humility; his devotion to his home and his belief in everlasting life. I doubt whether any man of great wealth ever gave more away without the knowledge of the world and his fellows generally."[34]

Rarely before had the nation's daily press so nearly approached unanimity in its evaluation of the work and character of an entrepreneur. Occasionally, of course, evidence was presented which did not quite conform to the almost universally presented description of the man. For the editorial writers of the Detroit *Free Press*, Ford "never lost the kindly touch of genuine friendship. He found joy in mixing among his fellows and would spend a day with some mechanic who did not accept him in awe, but respected him as a fellow mechanic." That conclusion stood, although reporters of the *Free Press*, interviewing long-time employees of the Ford Motor Company, found one mechanic with thirty-two years of service who could not "recall ever speaking to Mr. Ford"; and another with thirty-one years of service who "told how Mr. Ford used to walk through the Highland Park plant, watch carefully the work of the men at their machines and then pass on without speaking." The same newspaper revealed that George W. Frazier, patternmaker of the first Ford car, who was buried only two days after Henry Ford, had been deprived of his pass permitting him access to Ford property fifteen years earlier, and never "thought of asking for another, although he often wanted to renew friendship with Mr. Ford. He simply stopped going."

Significantly, even the few organs among the daily press which looked askance at Ford confined their remarks largely to his nonbusiness activities. For columnist Kenesaw Mountain Landis II of the Chicago *Sun*, "Ford democratized the automobile, distributed undreamed wealth to the nation and built the greatest private empire in the world"; and for that he deserved credit and appreciation. It was "his opinions . . . in matters of philosophy, history, sociology and morals" that earned him ridicule. Max Lerner, writing in the newspaper *PM*, drew a sharp distinction between "Ford's racist and reactionary views" and "his achievements as a technician and an industrialist." As to the latter, "mass-production, standardization, high-speed belt-line, high wages, large volume" were his accomplishments. As to the former, "his mind" was "a jungle of fear and ignorance and prejudice in social affairs." "Henry Ford is dead but the stew of hate churned by his long-defunct newspaper the Dearborn *Independent* still fouls up the atmosphere," that newspaper commented. "Only last week, the Council Against Intolerance in America received a letter from a Ford Motor Co. official, regretting that the *International Jew* was in circulation again, under the sponsorship of Gerald L. K. Smith." The conclusion of the *New Republic* was cut from the same pattern: "The mechanical genius which could conceive the Ford assembly line could never quite figure out that a man's dignity is not measured with calipers." The *Christian Century* felt that what had made Ford "one of the most appealing figures in the America of his time" was "the simplicity of his public character and way of life . . . his venturesome adoption of the principles of high wages and low prices, his interest in the social rehabilitation of men who served prison terms . . . his encouragement of technical education for boys." But "he did not understand . . . much of the world," became "involved in blunders and senseless tyrannies and even outright injustices," and because of "the power which his enormous wealth gave him" became surrounded by "men with warped or reactionary purposes who studied how to use him for their own ends."

With the commercial press approximating virtual unanimity in its reaction to Ford, ideas that differed sharply from the portrait it presented—including opposition to his business activities, dissent from the laudatory accounts of his personal character and nonbusiness activities, and denial that all Americans felt a sense of loss at Ford's death—became restricted largely to those newspapers representing political groups which openly expressed their hostility to capitalism and to that decreasing number of trade union papers which still remained under the influence of anticapitalist thought.

Missing from the columns of the Communist *Daily People's World* were the usual pictures of Ford giving slices of his birthday cake to children in Dearborn, or relaxing around a campfire with his friends Thomas A. Edison and Harvey Firestone, or standing at the side of his wife and smiling shyly at the first Ford car. Instead, that newspaper decorated its obituary of "The Paragon of Free Enterprise" with a picture of Ford receiving the Grand Cross of the German Eagle from German consuls Earl Kapp and Fritz Heiler at Detroit in 1938 on his seventy-fifth birthday. "Ford was philosopher all right," said the *People's World.* "But his philosophy was hardly original. It was written down in Hitler's Mein Kampf. Ford was a bigoted and active anti-Semite. He was an early admirer of Nazism. He financed almost every fascist movement in America." As to the vaunted efficiency of his assembly line, "thousands of workers were consumed by its relentless speed-up, used up in their youth and dumped on the scrapheap of humanity." This was no servant of mankind; "to the people of Detroit, Dearborn, and Highland Park, who built his empire, the Ford name meant police terror, anti-labor activity, anti-Semitism, discrimination against Negroes, and reaction in politics." Nor, indeed, could it have meant anything else, for Ford in reality was but "a symbol . . . of the American economic royalist who makes the vaunted 'free enterprise' system an instrument of social and political domination." Writers of the *New Masses,* applying similar criteria of evaluation, stressed aspects of Ford's career which were held to be inevitable consequences of the system which produced him. For them, the memorable events—and the ones on which ultimate appraisals should be based—were those associated with the shooting of four demonstrators at the "Ford Hunger March" of 1932; the beating of union organizers in Dearborn in 1937; the conclusion of National Labor Relations Board Trial Examiner Robert N. Denham that members of the Ford Service Department were "most brutal, vicious and conscienceless thugs"; the hectic pace of the assembly line, geared "to get the maximum work and profit out of each individual"; the "good money" Ford made "out of both world wars . . . despite his professed pacifism"; "Ford's anti-Jewish prejudice"; and "the Hitler medal" he had been awarded. Had such a man won for himself a place in the hearts of his countrymen? "Henry Ford could never buy from his workers and the people the affection and loyalty the union commands."

"The newspapers and his paid sycophants are singing weird tales about this two billion dollar tycoon and his spending on 'charity,' " the Chicago *Fighting Worker* asserted. "Everything is done to gloss over the fact that Henry Ford was merely another capitalist brigand, who made his fortune out of the sweat of Ford workers' brows." Why had not the daily press discussed his "anti-labor gangsters, private detectives and . . . involved system of spying on labor"; his "notorious anti-Semitism" and "support of Fascism"; his "brutal speed-up"? "Judge Capitalism by Its No. 1 Hero!" adjured the *Weekly People*. Such activities were manifestations of a disease rooted in the structure of society, not in the individual, and the remedy must be equally comprehensive. "The working class . . . will remember Henry Ford and vow to end the system that can give rise to such people," provided only that they "awaken and organize their economic powers."

Expressing their ideas in language less acid that that of the radical political parties, a few trade union newspapers—some still influenced by radical thought, others simply reflecting opinion in the plant—evaluated Ford in such a way as to indicate that less than universal approbation existed at the lower levels of the social structure. "Under the veil of decent regard for the dead," said the Federated Press news service, "there was little mourning for the individualistic anti-union auto maker in the Detroit area. At UAW-CIO headquarters the privately expressed sentiment harked back to the long years when Ford stamped out or tried to stamp out unionism with thugs and goons under his crony Harry Bennett. In barbershops envy and resentment overtopped expressions of esteem." Had Detroit automobile traffic really stopped—as the daily press had said—at 2:30 P.M. on the day of the funeral? "No motorists in Detroit's central district were observed to do so, except out of respect for red lights." And did the shutting down of automobile assembly lines throughout Michigan really prove the existence of warm sympathy and respect for Ford? Writing in the *Dodge Main News*, official organ of Dodge Local 3, UAW-CIO, shopworker Frank Stawski, correspondent of the Body Unit section, observed: "I was asked to put this item in the unit column. There was a pause for Henry Ford, yet on Good Friday we did not pause. God commandeth his love toward us, in that, while we were yet sinners, Christ died for us." For the daily press, consideration of Henry Ford's career had led to the conclusion that free enterprise must be maintained; but Frank Stawski, reflecting on Ford's career and focusing his attention upon speed-up and layoffs, concluded: "That is one of the main reasons why we must have a union, to protect our jobs."The "Shop News and Views" editor of the UAW-CIO *Local 599 Headlight,* newspaper of the Buick shopworkers in Flint, Michigan, cast doubt, indeed, on the degree to which even automobile industry management felt sorrow at the death of Ford.

The tribute paid to Old Henry, the King of all auto tycoons, was meant to be a publicity gag . . . The public probably thinks that dear old G.M. [rivals for market] are not deadly enemies when it comes to respect for each other. Thursday, after we went to work, they placed the notice [to stop work for one minute at 2:30 P.M.] on the bulletin boards not at 6:00 A.M., on the time clocks. Not at any time did our Bosses ask us to pause at 2:30 P.M. Also no whistle was blown. I point this incident out to you, not that Henry was kind to labor, but to the fact that this man did more to promote mass production which G.M. copied. Their tribute was a farce. Just a publicity gag of the lowest type . . . More than likely if we had paused, we would have been slapped around with a reprimand . . . I would be ashamed to print what some of our supervision said when asked why we did not pause . . . Just a lot of hot wind looking for a place to cool its heels.

And was the closing down of Ford plants throughout the country on the day of the funeral to be considered as a day of mourning—as the daily press termed it—or as a "compulsory workless day"?

"We urge you to correct this gross blunder," said the Reverend Donald Harrington, minister of New York's Community Church and national chairman of the Workers Defense League, in a telegram to Henry Ford II. "Depriving your employes of pay for the day's mourning for your grandfather does not constitute a memorial to him which you would want your workers to remember."[35]

Exactly what Ford workers would remember about their employer no one could state with certainly, but that in all probability it would not be identical with that which the daily press felt to be memorable was made clear by the editorial which appeared in the Ford workers' own newspaper, *Ford Facts:*

Henry Ford placed his reliance primarily on individuals like himself rather than on government or social action. As the foremost exponent of assembly line mass production, he revolutionized industry and with it society. Thus he did as much as any man to bring into being a world in which his own intense individualism no longer provided an adequate answer to the burning problems of either society or the individual . . . Ford's individualism brought into being its opposite—the need of collective action and thinking, of cooperation on a far-reaching scale . . . The world which he leaves behind calls for new qualities and new values.

Like the daily press, the newspaper of Ford's employees gave credit to the man for his industrial innovations. But from the conclusion that those accomplishments testified to the need for maintaining what the press called "individualism" it sharply dissented; and in that dissent lay the hint of an alternative morality and economy.

But not all, even of the labor newspapers, discussed Ford's accomplishments in the light of alternative economic systems. For the most part they applied to the appraisal of Ford criteria similar to those used by the daily press, and from similar criteria emerged similar conclusions. "Neither the saga of American industrial progress nor our rise to hitherto unknown standards of living and comfort can be understood without Henry Ford. In his own, admittedly individualistic way he did more to promote the workers' welfare than a great many men who pride themselves on their sympathies for labor," the *International Molders' Journal* said. Speed-up, opposition to unions, anti-Semitism—discussion of such issues was no more prominent in this sector of the labor press than it was in the daily press. Weighed against "the great benefits that have accrued . . . through his genius and energy," his "personal eccentricities" were as nothing. That his method of "assembly line production . . . revolutionized the nation"; that he had "held each worker is entitled to a living wage"; that his triumph was a demonstration that "democracy, being the right way of life, can recruit its leaders at the grass roots"—these were the important conclusions to be derived from a study of Ford's life.[36]

In praise of Ford both labor leaders and antilabor spokesmen united, and the common ground of their admiration for him was broad enough to support mutually exclusive reasons for approbation. The officers of the Michigan State CIO Council, for example, applauded Ford for the fact that he "was one of the first industrialists to recognize the CIO as an organization here to stay by accepting collective bargaining."[37] But one southern newspaper, the Augusta *Chronicle,* praised him because, the "essence of rugged individualism, he remained to the last an economic and political conservative and never became reconciled to trade unions even after recognizing them . . . If there is a defense for a free economy, nothing speaks louder than the deeds of Henry Ford." Both, no doubt, would have agreed with the statement of the Buffalo *Catholic Labor Observer* that "the death of Henry Ford focuses the attention of world industry and world labor on America's success in the field of mass production. Nowhere else are so many useful products of the teamwork of labor and management so available to so large a number of well-paid men and women"—for in that statement was recognition and approval of a mutuality of interest between "labor and management." To the degree that that mutuality of interest was affirmed by leaders of the labor movement—and certainly such statements were elicited to a greater extent by discussion of Henry Ford than of any other American entrepreneur—the leaders of business enterprise were assured that they would continue to function in a climate of security.

The journals of industry, of course, spared few adjectives in their portrayal of Ford as a "Courageous, far-seeing pioneer—Giant of Industry—Genius of Production—Master Craftsman in many fields—Humanitarian—A man whose life story is written in the minds of all people, whose life work benefited all mankind." To be sure, such journals felt, to a greater degree than was the case with the daily press, that while Ford "had an uncanny knack for doing the right thing and saying the right thing when it came to building motor cars," he had "a similar uncanny knack for doing just the opposite when it came to public utterances and activities in world affairs." Even that, however, had its advantages: "In the long run his own embarrassment probably was counterbalanced by the valuable publicity accruing to the company." But regarding his accomplishments in industry, his influence on society, and his contributions to human welfare, there could be no doubt. Certainly his services "cannot and should not be forgotten until time has erased the last remnants of western civilization."

"Thorough and untiring in his methods," vividly imaginative in the generation of ideas and forceful in their application, he succeeded in manufacturing a product "within the reach of everyone"; if that was "good business policy" which resulted in "a tremendous fortune" for him, it was also "a very unselfish attitude" which "promoted the welfare of mankind." No wonder then, that "workmen in overalls and fashionably dressed business executives" alike respected and loved him. They loved him because he had served them and because his life was an exemplification not only of "the creativeness of mind and the energy of our nation," but of "those enduring qualities and the high purpose . . . the simplicity and vigor" which represent "America in its finest tradition." He was, in this sense, a product of his country, but he had been one of its creators as well: "Henry Ford's favorite philosopher, Ralph Waldo Emerson, has said that great institutions are but the elongated shadow of a man. If this is true in any case it was true in the case of Ford."[38]

The magazines of public opinion agreed with the organs of industry. Through watching Ford, claimed *Time,* "two generations" of persons the world over "caught a glimpse—however distorted—of U.S. capitalism's great adventure." And great indeed had that adventure been. "The real Industrial Revolution of our day—the one which Henry Ford led and symbolized—was not a technological one, was not based on this or that machine, this or that technique, but on the hierarchical co-ordination of human efforts which mass production realizes in its purest form." Economist Peter Drucker gave Ford full credit for unsurpassed "success in technology and economics," but felt that he had failed "to solve the problems of the new industrial system." If the relatively few readers of *Harper's Magazine* were given the impression that in that sense at least Ford's life had been a failure, the millions of readers of *Life* were given no reason to qualify their approval. "The philosopher's case against Ford," that magazine asserted testily, "is that he . . . cast up economic and social problems for which he could discover no acceptable solution. But why expect him to? His apologia, if one is required, is the American standard of living, the power of machines that made it possible for this nation in two world wars to escape the frightful human toll of the war of hordes. The rest is up to the philosophers."

Other magazines, less modest, donned the philosopher's garb which *Life* had forsworn and inquired into the real meaning of Ford's life.

"Henry Ford was as American as Pike's Peak," wrote Ira E. Bennett in the *National Republic:*

> It was only in a giant land of free men that he could have developed himself and his work . . . The USA offered opportunity to a free man to develop the gifts which God bestowed upon him. The result was an astounding phenomenon of production on a continental scale, and that application of revolutionary processes that have spread benefits to all mankind, including the enemies who would destroy such free enterprise . . . Any Russian, Communist or otherwise, who should try to follow the path blazed by Henry Ford would be slaughtered as soon as the NKVD could amass the damning evidence of his individualism . . . When the New Deal was in its poisonous heyday Henry Ford refused to comply with its impudent demands. He detected the inherent baseness and un-Americanism of the NRA and its defeatist "blue eagle" of industrial servitude to bureaucracy . . . He could have been a billionaire thrice over if he had been eager to make money. But he did not crave wealth. He used money as a tool or necessary adjunct of operations . . . A free country enabled him to acquire this money-tool . . . No greedy state-tyranny snatched away in taxes the money that freely flowed toward Henry Ford in payment for his enterprise . . . He saw the dangers of communism in 1917 . . . Until his last breath he resisted the encroachments of communism in whatever guise it assumed . . . Is it true that the US is now committed to a tax policy that will forever destroy the possibility of developing private enterprise on a scale like Henry Ford's achievement? Is it possible that a new theory of government is killing individual enterprise by preventing it from accumulating and using capital as a tool of industry? Some observers think so . . . The conflict between Americanism and communism sharpens the point of the argument in favor of individual freedom, including freedom to use money for industrial development. Let the showdown come—the sooner the better.[39]

In identifying Henry Ford with the "free enterprise system," in identifying "free enterprise" with Americanism, and in regarding Ford's career as proof of the superiority of that system over all others, the *National Republic* was simply stating what the vast majority of the written media of public opinion had already in large measure affirmed. Not only Ford himself, but the economic system of which he was held to be the proudest product, was granted the high sanction of patriotism. More powerful support the press could hardly have offered; and it was as if in recognition of this that *Ford Times*—official house organ of the Ford Motor Company—felt no apparent need to make an original contribution to the discussion, as the Standard Oil Company had done when Rockefeller had died, but instead contented itself with quoting what

others—political figures, industrialists, labor leaders, and the press—had
said. . . .

Certainly the American press was virtually unanimous in presenting
Ford in such a way as to elicit the widest possible approval both for
himself and for the economic system which he was held to represent. The
methods by which this was accomplished consisted largely of a series of
statements which tended to identify both Ford and that economic system
with service to the needs of the people and with those cultural values
which were the objects of deepest loyalty and affection and which were
held to be in gravest danger.

So far as Ford himself was concerned, discussion of his role as a
businessman was hardly more important than discussion of the nonbusiness phases of his life. That he had had an amazingly successful
business career, that this success had been based on the combination of
personal abilities and a society which rewarded possession of such
abilities, and that his business activities—while profitable to himself—
were important primarily because of the effect they had in raising the
standard of living—all of this was, of course, emphatically affirmed. But
no less emphasized was the fact that Ford was more than a businessman.
He had been patriot, sportsman, philanthropist, scientist, philosopher,
sociologist, reformer, economist, teacher, historian, and, above all, a
simple homebody. That a few, reading the accounts of Ford's career at
the time of his death, might have discerned contradictions in the roles
imputed to him was doubtless of less significance than the fact that a
great many could find in those accounts such a range of gratifications as
to make possible the eliciting of a favorable response.

And gratifications enough there were.

For the multitudes who already felt that a career such as Ford's was
one of social utility and whose system of values sanctioned such
activities, the portrayal of Ford by the press was gilt for the lily. Not all,
however, felt so firmly that such careers were socially useful, that the
success attained by Ford or other great entrepreneurs was to be attributed solely to their ability, that opportunities for advancement were
distributed equally throughout the social structure, that they owed
"honor and service" to the economic organization of which Ford was a
part, or even, indeed, that it was desirable to show devotion to a society in
which upward progress—even if based on superior abilities—was
measured in terms of added income received at each rung of the ladder.
When the victory is always to the swift, the slow grow weary of perpetual
defeat and may begin to argue either that no one ought to race for bread
and butter or that the rules of the contest are unfair and in need of
change.[40] The majority of large businessmen may believe that ability—
without qualification—is at the root of economic success and give no

place to "pull" or "luck," but only a minority of unskilled workers believes so. Every successive penetration downward into the social structure reveals an increasing number of persons who deny that success is a function of ability and that opportunity is distributed equally.[41]

In this gap between economic reality and acceptance by all of that reality lurked the danger to business enterprise and to the sense of common purpose vital to the functioning of society.[42] To bridge this gap by informing the American people of the new significance of the entrepreneur in the changing conditions of American life was the achievement of the press. From the praise which the press bestowed upon Ford those who had attained even a moderate degree of economic success could take comfort, for they had a convincing demonstration that their activities were appreciated and that the system which maintained and encouraged those activities was being staunchly defended. But satisfactions could be derived by others as well. Henry Ford had indeed been a hero, but a special kind of hero. He had been, the press insisted, a hero in spite of himself, a man who would have liked nothing better than to be simply father and husband in his own house.

How was it possible to resent his superior position? Had he not remained unspoiled despite his success; had he not abundantly demonstrated that he was made of the same clay as others; had he not shown solicitude for the welfare of those who had not even the slightest claim on him? And had he not, moreover, constantly emphasized that success was not a proper goal for mankind; that he personally had not followed its siren song; and that the only true goal was that of service to one's fellows? From this even the unsuccessful could draw assurance, for they had it from the mouth of Ford himself that not wealth, but virtue, counted. By this standard, so the unsuccessful might infer, who could say that the successful were really worthy and the unsuccessful unworthy? And so far as Ford himself was concerned, if it was position in the hierarchy of virtue, not in that of economic status, which really counted, and if Ford's position in the former was at the apex, then who could deny that he deserved the tributes he received? Judge not the man of business by his balance sheets, the press admonished its readers, for by that standard what would be the verdict as to you? Judge him as ye would wish to be judged—by a higher standard of accounting, the standard of morality.[43] This was, to be sure, emphasis upon the personal qualities of the entrepreneur, but it was not emphasis upon those qualities which had characterized discussion of early nineteenth-century entrepreneurs. Then the press had been concerned with stressing those aspects of character and personality which made of the entrepreneur a unique individual, which set him apart from his fellows. Now the press stressed less those qualities which helped account for his success than those which he had in common with all others, those which drew him into and made him part of the great mass of mankind.

Nor was this the only difference between early and late newspaper discussion of great entrepreneurs. Gone was the early implication that the entrepreneur was a free-swinging individual, unaffected by considerations of time and place and circumstance and restricted only by the potentialities of his own character. The unique qualities of American social and economic organization were given full, even lavish, credit as conditions without which entrepreneurial success was an impossibility. Only in America did opportunity exist and only in America was entrepreneurial talent recognized and nourished. But the argument did not work in reverse. Society could be expected to do no more than to interpose no obstacles in the path of success; it could not guarantee success. Failure remained a function of the individual for which society was not accountable. No less an authority than John D. Rockefeller had stated one side of the case:

. . . the failures which a man makes in his life are due almost always to some defect in his personality, some weakness of body, or mind, or character, will, or temperament. The only way to overcome these failings is to build up his personality from within, so that he, by virtue of what is within him, may overcome the weakness which was the cause of his failure. It is only those efforts the man himself puts forth that can really help him . . . It is my belief that the principal cause for the economic differences between people is their difference in personality, and that it is only as we can assist in the wider distribution of those qualities which go to make up a strong personality that we can assist in the wider distribution of wealth.[44]

Nowhere, at the time of Ford's death, was the special relationship between entrepreneur and system, success and failure better expressed than in the Grand Forks *Herald:* " 'American System' Made Ford's Rise Possible"—this was the title of the editorial. But—and this was the concluding sentence of the same editorial—"Not everyone can hope to become a Ford, for his was a rare combination of vision, mechanical ability, and perseverance."

The effect of such an explanation, of course, was to allow the economic system to be included in a consensus of approval, by making it responsible for permitting success, and yet at the same time to exclude it from the arena of potential controversy, by making the individual responsible for failure.[45]

But in still another way did the press clothe business enterprise in a coat of armor that had the magical property of warding off blows even before they were struck. By identifying enterprise with the nation itself, the press was able to invest the one with the qualities of the other, to enlist in the cause of an economic system the patriotic sentiments of love and loyalty usually associated with defense of the nation.[46]

In one sense, this was an effort to influence the thought of individual men—and therefore their action—by the use of a symbol which embodied widely held concepts of morality, tradition, religion, and patriotism, with the ultimate end of attaining a social order in which, in part through the acceptance of that symbol, all groups would participate harmoniously and act in the manner that had come to be expected of them.[47] "When you affect the economic thought of the people, you automatically affect their political thought,"[48] said one spokesman of the business community, and the press had at its disposal powerful weapons for the affecting of both. Not the least powerful of those weapons was the virtual monopoly of the daily press in the purveying of ideas. Who beside a scattered handful of radical and trade union papers expressed a dissenting opinion?[49]

As to the majority opinion, it performed two basic functions. In the first place, the nature of the newspaper discussion of Ford was such as to encourage emulation and win acceptance because, in Water Lippmann's phrase, the drama of his career was presented as having originated in a setting realistic enough to make identification possible and as having terminated in a setting romantic enough to be desirable, but not so romantic as to be inconceivable.[50] In the second place, the nature of the relationship that was alleged to exist between career and system was such as to permit the system to become the object of approval while insulating it from criticism. The system was responsible for the success of the successful; it was not responsible for the failure of the failures.

The judgment of the trade union editor—"Great riches may or may not have turned Henry Ford's head. But they surely reached the heads of the editorial writers"[51]—was too harsh. Modern journalism "tended to speak the language of corporate business instead of that of the little fellow . . . not because it is corrupt and venal but because it is itself a big business, a powerful institution with its interest vested in conservative economics."[52]

That journalism did, indeed, "speak the language of corporate business" is quite clear.

For years those who sought to interpret business enterprise to the public had shown increasing sensitivity not only to attacks on individual entrepreneurs but on the system of enterprise itself. Reviewing the history of corporate public relations in the thirtieth anniversary issue of his magazine, B. C. Forbes recalled that in the very first month of its publication he had asked: "Is it to be Democracy or Socialism?" and that in almost every succeeding issue he had hammered at the theme that unless it could be "so consistently and convincingly demonstrated to the people of humble social status that their attitude toward business and toward business men" should "be one of respect and esteem . . . the present economic order, cannot, to my mind, last." The cure for "economic illiteracy"—then as now—lay in proof to the public that the "basis of modern business is Service," and demonstration of that proof called for "the most energetic efforts of every agency in the land capable of reaching the public: daily and weekly newspapers and other periodicals, owners of radio stations, educational institutions from primary schools to universities, commercial banks and savings banks, as well as all other financial organizations, insurance companies, stock exchanges and all their members, manufacturers, distributors, retailers, chambers of commerce, trade associations, every enlightened, responsible citizen."[53] Businessmen were alarmed that "the US working class" might be "entirely losing faith in capitalism's ability to maintain employment, let alone guarantee prosperity and avoid wars"; that increasing leisure for "the worker" gave him "more time to think up grievances, more inclination to listen to agitators"; and in that frame of mind even the use of the term "workshop" by the League of Women Voters was evidence of the use of "revolutionary idiom." Attacks on business enterprise and concern lest its environment be altered led businessmen to the conclusion that explanations attuned to the needs of the times were required if the public's faith in business were to be maintained and "a whole nation's economic virtue" protected.[54]

But how was this to be accomplished? James Young, of the National Advertising Council, gave a general answer when he stated, "Advertising techniques effectively employed can more powerfully influence social action than any other means of communication."[55] The reply of the public relations director of the General Foods Corporation, far more specific, revealed the degree to which presentation of Ford by the press conformed to the pattern of presentation preferred by business enterprise itself:

I am convinced that this process of identifying business with the great goals of the human race, the great but simple goals, is all that can maintain today's free corporate system. We have achieved mass production . . . and nowhere have achieved mass serenity of the peoples of this land. Instead we have only contributed to their growing frustration, their decreasing stability, their reduced happiness . . . Let us never for one moment give up our magnificent technologies. But do let us use our every power to identify the owners and managers of those technologies with the simple goals—better education for everybody's children, better health and nutrition, better housing, better opportunities based on ability, more security for the aged and infirm, more respect for the opinion of any man who has opinions.[56]

"The employer organizes the forces of production. He is the natural

leader of his workmen," said the National Association of Manufacturers, and "should bring to bear constantly upon them influences for
right thinking and action for loyalty to the common enterprise."[57] And
how was the employer to do this? By taking "his place alongside of home,
and school, and church" as the Ford Motor Company had done when it
presented its employees with a list of publications it would be pleased to
have them read; by revealing—again as the Ford Motor Company had
done in the case of Henry Ford—that "the guiding SPIRIT OF SERVICE,"
not profit, is the motive of enterprise; by showing that in all essential
respects employer was like employee.[58] The General Motors Corporation illustrated these principles admirably in the definition of a businessman which it presented in the magazine it publishes for its employees:

> A businessman is one who invests his money in an enterprise which gives em-
> ployment and provides a regular income to himself and others.
> For example, a man paid by GM to drive a truck is an employe. If he saves
> enough money to start his own trucking business, He's a Businessman.
> Although the truck driver is now a businessman, he is pretty much the same
> fellow as when employed by GM. He looks the same and has the same friends.
> True, his responsibilities are very much greater . . . but otherwise he is no
> different personally than he was before.[59]

In such fashion, too, had Henry Ford been presented by the daily
press—different from others only in that he was an employer, which was
not such a difference after all.

Nor was this the only parallel in discussion of business enterprise between the daily press and corporation press. No less than the former did
the latter identify business enterprise with the nation itself. In the lexicon
of corporation house organ editors, "the American system" and "the
competitive system" were one and the same, and criticism of the one,
which meant criticism of the other, was therefore "alien."

"It belongs to all of us," said Uncle Sam pointing to a map of the
United States labeled "B US INESS"; and in defense of what that map
symbolized, the General Motors Corporation told its employees: "Of
course, there are faults in the American system. Our society is made up
of millions of people, none of whom is perfect, so our system cannot be
perfect. But our system can be improved, and without changing its
form."[60]

In writing their obituaries of Henry Ford, therefore, the daily newspapers were defining the role of the entrepreneur in a manner parallel to
that utilized by enterprise itself. In the performance of that task,
presentation of factual detail was of less importance · than pronouncement of judgment. Years before, Mark Twain, seeing the distinction between the two, offered to pay for the privilege of editing his
own obituary:

Of necessity, an Obituary is a thing which cannot be so judiciously edited by any hand as by that of the subject of it. In such a case it is not the Facts that are of chief importance, but the light which the obituarist shall throw upon them, the meanings which he shall dress them in, the conclusions which he shall draw from them, and the judgments which he shall deliver upon them. The Verdicts, you understand . . . not their Facts, but their Verdicts.[61]

With respect to Henry Ford, the verdict of the press was as clear as it was decisive. In his life the American people might see dramatic confirmation of two fundamental precepts: entrepreneur was linked to community by the common attributes of humanity and by principles of motivation which guided his activities in the direction of service to all; enterprise was linked to nation by identification with patriotism and historical tradition. At no time, at least not since the death of Stephen Girard in 1831, were American entrepreneurs given more reason to feel that their activities were thoroughly in accord with national aspirations. In 1947, to be sure, the entrepreneur did not mean to the American people what he had meant in 1831. Emphasis upon personal uniqueness and, with it, the belief that character determines fate had largely disappeared; but they had disappeared because the new conditions of American society imposed new requirements and gave opportunity for new meanings to be seen in the lives of businessmen. Absent was the uniqueness of the entrepreneur, but present was identification with his fellows; absent was the implication that entrepreneurial qualities were everywhere and always applicable, but present was the understanding that entrepreneur and social system were inseparable. The entrepreneur had, indeed, "built himself into the history" of his country.[62]

NOTES

1. Quoted in Keith Theodore Sward, *The Legend of Henry Ford* (New York and Toronto: Rinehart & Co., 1948), p. 127.

2. *Congressional Record,* 10 April 1947, pt.93:3277.

3. Quoted in Sward, *Henry Ford,* p. 106.

4. Sward, *Henry Ford,* pp. 389–96.

5. U.S., Congress, House, *Congressional Record,* 9 April 1947, pt.93:3243.

6. Ibid., p. 3248.

7. Ibid., p. 3246.

8. Ibid., p. 3250.

9. Senate, *Appendix to the Congressional Record,* 25 July 1947, pt.93:A 3830–31.

10. Detroit *News,* 10 November 1941; Anonymous pamphlet, *Henry Ford Swims the Red Sea* (Indianapolis, 1941), *passim.*

11. Butte *Standard,* 8 April 1947; Mobile *Register,* 9 April 1947; New York

Daily Mirror, 9 April 1947; Baltimore *News-Post,* 10 April 1947; Indianapolis *News,* 8 April 1947.

12. Sioux City *Journal,* 9 April 1947; Mobile *Register,* 9 April 1947.

13. Reno *Nevada State Journal,* 10 April 1947; Portsmouth *Press Herald,* 9 April 1947; Manchester *New Hampshire Morning Union,* 9 April 1947.

14. Indianapolis *News,* 8 April 1947; Indianapolis *Star,* 9 April 1947; Rochester *Democrat and Chronicle,* 8, 9 April 1947; Boston *Herald,* 9 April 1947; Harrisburg *Patriot,* 9 April 1947; Houston *Post,* 9 April 1947; Memphis *Commercial Appeal,* 9 April 1947.

15. Mobile *Register,* 9 April 1947; Cincinnati *Enquirer,* 9 April 1947; New York *Herald Tribune,* 8 April 1947.

16. Harrisburg *Patriot,* 9 April 1947; Grand Forks *Herald,* 8 April 1947; Santa Fe *New Mexican,* 10 April 1947; Augusta *Kennebec Journal,* 9 April 1947; San Francisco *Examiner,* 9 April 1947; Augusta *Chronicle,* 9 April 1947; Topeka *Daily Capital,* 9 April 1947.

17. Sioux City *Journal,* 9 April 1947; Boston *Post,* 9 April 1947; Denver *Rocky Mountain News,* 9 April 1947; Washington *Star,* 8 April 1947; Denver *Post,* 9 April 1947.

18. New Orleans *Times-Picayune,* 9 April 1947; Milwaukee *Journal,* 9 April 1947; San Francisco *Examiner,* 9 April 1947; Tucson *Daily Citizen,* 10 April 1947.

19. Manchester *New Hampshire Morning Union,* 9 April 1947; Buffalo *Evening News,* 8 April 1947; *The Ford Idea in Education* (Detroit, 1917), p. 3.

20. Washington *Daily News,* 9 April 1947; Grand Forks *Herald,* 9 April 1947; Grand Rapids *Herald,* 9 April 1947; Boise *Idaho Statesman,*9 April 1947; Concord *Daily Monitor,* 9 April 1947.

21. Tucson *Daily Citizen,* 8 April 1947; Washington *Daily News,* 8 April 1947; Wilmington *Journal-Every Evening,* 8 April 1947; New Orleans *Item,* 9 April 1947; Augusta *Kennebec Journal,* 9 April 1947; Brooklyn *Eagle,* 8 April 1947.

22. Columbia *State,* 9 April 1947; Norfolk *Virginian-Pilot,* 9 April 1947; Atlanta *Constitution,* 9 April 1947; Indianapolis *Star,* 9 April 1947; Bismarck *Tribune,* 9 April 1947; Sioux City *Journal,* 9 April 1947; Butte *Montana Standard,* 8 April 1947.

23. Chicago *Herald-American,* 9, 10 April 1947; San Francisco *Examiner,* 9 April 1947.

24. Chicago *Herald-American,* 11 April 1947; Jacksonville *Florida Times-Union,* 9 April 1947; Little Rock *Arkansas Democrat,* 9 April 1947; Reno *Evening Gazette,* 8 April 1947; Newark *Evening News,* 8 April 1947; Birmingham *News,* 8 April 1947; Portland *Press Herald,* 9 April 1947; New York *Times,* 8 April 1947; Baltimore *Sun,* 9 April 1947; Wilmington *Journal-Every Evening,* 8 April 1947.

25. Henry Ford, *365 of Henry Ford's Sayings* (New York: The League-for-a-living, 1923).

26. Ibid., pp. 2, 7, 20–21, 28.

27. Detroit *Free Press,* 7 September 1930.

28. Ford, *Ford's Sayings,* pp. 40, 41.

29. Detroit *Times,* 27 July 1936.

30. Dearborn *Independent,* 1919, quoted in Sward, *Henry Ford,* p. 145.

31. New York *World-Telegram,* 8 April 1947; Grand Rapids *Herald,* 9 April 1947; Atlanta *Journal,* 8 April 1947; Chicago *Sun,* 9 April 1947; Los Angeles *Times,* 8 April 1947; Portland *Oregonian,* 9 April 1947.

32. Los Angeles *Times,* 9 April 1947; Phoenix *Arizona Republic,* 9 April 1947; Chicago *Herald-American,* 8 April 1947; New York *Times,* 9 April 1947; Baltimore *Sun,* 9 April 1947.

33. Lansing *State Journal,* 9 April 1947; Washington *Post,* 9 April 1947; Montgomery *Advertiser,* 10 April 1947; New York *Times,* 9 April 1947.

34. Detroit *Free Press,* 9 April 1947; Mobile *Register,* 11 April 1947.

35. Workers Defense League News Service Press Release, New York, 30 April 1947. Local 600, UAW-CIO, filed a grievance against the Ford Motor Company charging that because of the layoff on the day of Ford's funeral employees who worked on Saturday of that week were deprived of the time-and-one-half pay they would have received if they had worked a normal forty-hour week. The umpire decided against the union and pointed out that the company was arranging "to provide a premium day's work for all employees to make up for their lost earnings that week." *The Umpire, Ford Motor Co. and UAW-CIO,* Case No. 4690, Opinion A-242, 15 May 1947.

36. Long Beach *Labor News,* 18 April 1947; North Hollywood *American Aeronaut,* 18 April 1947; Washington *Machinist,* 17 April 1947; Washington *Labor,* 12 April 1947.

37. The statement that Ford was "one of the first industrialists to recognize the CIO" is contrary to the facts. The General Motors Corporation recognized the UAW-CIO in February, 1937; Chrysler, shortly thereafter; and Ford—the last automobile company to recognize the union—not until June 21, 1941.

38. *Automotive and Aviation Industries,* 15 April 1947, p. 17; *Steel,* 14 April 1947, pp. 73–74; *American Machinist,* 24 April 1947, p. 75; *Iron Age,* 17 April 1947, pp. 74–76.

39. In relation to the statement that Ford "saw the dangers of communism" as early as 1917, it should be pointed out that he also saw no contradiction between anticommunism and economic aid to Russia. He accepted his first contract from Russia—for $75,000,000—in the early 1920s, and throughout the next two decades exported automobiles, tractors, heavy machinery—even an entire rubber-tire plant—and trained Russian technicians in his factories. While the Ford Motor Company was denouncing the so-called "Ford Hunger March" of March 7, 1932, at its River Rouge plant, as a "Red rising," a large group of Russian engineers—who were being trained in Ford production methods in return for $30,000,000—were within the plant. William C. Richards, *The Last Billionaire Henry Ford* (New York and London: Charles Scribner's Sons, 1948), pp. 224, 345–47; Sward, *Henry Ford,* p. 242.

40. Charles Horton Cooley, *Human Nature and The Social Order* (New York: Charles Scribner's Sons, 1922), pp. 310–11; Thomas Humphrey Marshall, *Citizenship and Social Class* (Cambridge, England, 1950), pp. 125–27.

41. R. Centers, "Attitude and Belief in Relation to Occupational Stratification," *Journal of Social Psychology* 27 (1928): 168–73.

42. Robert S. Lynd, *Knowledge for What?* (Princeton, N.J.: Princeton University Press, 1939), p. 81.

43. For a discussion, though relating to a different medium of communication, of the social consequences of presenting a public figure in terms of multiple roles, see Robert King Merton, *Mass Persuasion: The Social Psychology of a War Bond Drive* (New York: Harper & Brothers, 1950), pp. 143–71. See also Robert King Merton, *Social Theory and Social Structure* (Glencoe, Ill.: Free Press, 1958), pp. 131–32; Lowenthal, "Biographies," in Paul F. Lazarsfeld and Frank Stanton, *Radio Research 1942–43* (New York: Duell, Sloan and Pearce, 1944), pp. 513–48; Clyde Kluckhohn, *Mirror for Man* (New York: McGraw-Hill, 1949), p. 233.

44. John D. Rockefeller, *Random Reminiscences of Men and Events* (New York: Doubleday, Doran, 1933), pp. 153–54.

45. Merton, *Mass Persuasion*, p. 153; Merton, *Social Theory*, pp. 130–31.

46. For a discussion of the identification of nation and economic system, see Merle Curti, *Roots of American Loyalty* (New York: Columbia University Press, 1946), pp. 235, 240; Robert Green McCloskey, *American Conservatism in an Age of Enterprise* (Cambridge, Mass: Harvard University Press, 1951), pp. 131–32.

47. George Sawyer Pettee, *The Process of Revolution* (New York: Harper & Brothers, 1937), pp. 42–43; J. A. R. Pimlott, *Public Relations and American Democracy* (Princeton, N.J.: Princeton University Press, 1951), pp. 238, 243; Robert Staughton Lynd, preface, in R. A. Brady, *Business as a System of Power* (New York: Columbia University Press, 1943), pp. xii–xiv.

48. J. B. Sheridan, director, Missouri Committee on Public Utility Information, quoted in A. M. Lee, "Power-Seekers," in Alvin Ward Gouldner, ed., *Studies in Leadership* (New York: Harper & Brothers, 1950), p. 672.

49. For a discussion of the importance of "monopoly" presentation by the press, see J. T. Klapper, "Mass Media and the Engineering of Consent," *The American Scholar* 17 (1948): 427; Merton, *Mass Persuasion*, p. 171.

50. Walter Lippmann, *Public Opinion* (New York: Macmillan Co., 1922), p. 166.

51. *Union Reporter*, May 1947.

52. Herbert Brucker, *Freedom of Information* (New York: Macmillan Co., 1949), p. 69.

53. B. C. Forbes, "Industry Missing Fire on Public Relations," *Forbes Magazine*, May 1, 1947, pp. 19–20, 37.

54. S. Mangan, "State of the Nation," *Fortune* 28 (1943): 262; M. Dodge, "Labor," *Public Relations Journal* 2 (1946): 4, 6; Lucille Cardin Crain and Ann Burrows Hamilton, *Packaged Thinking for Women* (New York: National Industrial Conference Board, 1948), p. 16. For a discussion of the history of corporate public relations and its objectives, see L. A. Sussman, "The Personnel and Ideology of Public Relations," *Public Opinion Quarterly* 12 (1948–49): 697–708.

55. Quoted in "Advertising and Public Relations," *The Oil Forum*, June 1947, p. 147.

56. W. H. Chase, "Human Relations—Key To A New Era," *Journal of Communication* 1 (1951): 14–15.

57. *Proceedings of the 28th Annual Meeting of the National Association of Manufacturers,* Open Shop Report (n.p., 1923), pp. 156–59.

58. Carl F. Braun, *Management and Leadership* (Alhambra, California: C. F. Braun, 1948), pp. 21–22, 24. The list prepared by the Ford Motor Company was as follows: "All Ford publications, including Dearborn *Independent;* all Ford biographies; auto trade publications; farm publications; *Administration, Advertising and Selling, American Magazine, Business Philosopher, Forbes Magazine, Printers' Ink, Sales Management, System, Success* (Marden's); *Scientific American, Science and Invention, Popular Science, Popular Mechanics; Correct English: How to Use It; Saturday Evening Post, Collier's, Cosmopolitan, Current Opinion, Hearst's International, Literary Digest, McClure's, National Geographic;* Alexander Hamilton Institute course, LaSalle Extension University course, Sheldon School course; Newspapers; Spencer's *First Principles,* Emerson's *Essays,"* Don C. Prentiss, *Ford Products and their Sale: A Manual for Ford Salesmen and Dealers in Six Books* (Detroit: Ford Motor Co., 1923), bk. 5, pp. 563–65. See also bk. 6, p. 641.

59. *GM Folks,* September 1947.

60. Ibid. December 1948. See also ibid., October 1948, November 1948; *Corning Glass Works Gaffer,* March 1947. For a discussion of the way in which corporation-sponsored radio programs and motion pictures similarly identify the businessman with all men and enterprise with the nation, see R. Arnheim, "The World of the Daytime Serial," in Lazarsfeld and Stanton, *Radio Yearbook,* pp. 34–85, and A. Sturmthal and A. Curtis, "Program Analyzer Tests of Two Educational Films," in ibid., pp. 485–06

61. "Amended Obituaries," in *The Writings of Mark Twain,* deluxe ed. (Hartford, 1899–1907), pp. 231–32.

62. Memphis *Commercial Appeal,* 9 April 1947.

HUGH DALZIEL DUNCAN
The Social Mystifications of Money

The Shift from the Puritan Ethic of Earning to an Ethic of Spending

Money has reached transcendence in our society through freeing spending, as well as earning, from religious and social inhibitions. Symbols of exchange are now treated as symbols of all human relations. We deduce freedom itself from a free market, because we believe that

Source: From Hugh Dalziel Duncan, *Communication and Social Order* (Totowa, N.J.: The Bedminster Press, 1962). Copyright 1962 The Bedminster Press, Inc. Reprinted by permission.

such a market supplies the conditions in which a free social act could occur. American discussion over freedom soon becomes a discussion of
freedom to earn and (more recently) to spend. God's laws as well as
nature's laws, formerly considered the grounds for freedom, have been
replaced by market laws (the law of supply and demand, the iron law of
profit, etc.). Money is no longer thought of as a means, a medium of exchange, but as a means to social integration. We do not use money to
produce, distribute, and consume more goods and services, but to
"develop the community."

We make more money because we believe that money will produce
unlimited good. The promise of American life is not an increased, but an
ever increasing, standard of living. What we have now is more than we
had in the past and is but a promise of what is to come. The past is killed
through style (annual and seasonal models). The present is infused with a
future which is at once orgiastic, spiritual, and infinite. No material want
need be denied ourselves or others, because such satisfactions are but a
way to other satisfactions. It is our "right" to spend as we see fit—so
long as we spend on the market. It is "unjust" to prevent the Negro from
spending. Adolescents (and even children) have a "right" to spend their
own money, and, indeed, are coached in how to do so in advertisements
of all kinds. We need not think beyond our individual prosperity, because
as we prosper the community prospers. And if the community prospers,
it is a sign that God loves us. Thus making and spending money is really
an act of service, a community satisfaction.

Our commercial magicians and priests of consumption[1] do not urge
us to buy things because they will last. On the contrary, it is being merely
a step closer to buying another thing, a promise of an infinitely expanding
future of bigger and better things, that moves us to buy. *Hierarchal usefulness,* not function or utility, determines our purchases. Even the
foreign car which is "made to last" is soon traded in for a new model.
The power of style in America derives from its power to communicate to
others, and at the same time to ourselves, that we can spend freely and
frequently. We are urged to spend before we earn, not after, by the same
bankers who in the days of the Puritan ethic exhorted us to abhor debt.
We work to pay off debts for houses, cars, and clothes which we have already used, and to go into debt for more things and services (but much
more often for things) we do not have. Pecuniary propriety does not
allow us to be satisfied with what we have. Obsolescence becomes a standard of value. We are only worth what we spend, and our discontent with
what we have is but a mark of ambition to spend more, for as we spend
we enhance our stature in the community. The individual who spends up-
holds prosperity, just as the industrialist who spends on new machinery,
or the politician who builds new roads, develops "community resources."

NOTE

1. The growing school of Madison Avenue apologists hold that successful advertising adds a new value to a product. A lipstick may be sold at Woolworth's under one name and in a department store under another, nationally advertised name. Almost any teenage girl will prefer the latter, if she can afford to pay the difference. Wearing the Woolworth brand, she feels her ordinary self; wearing the other, which has been successfully advertised as a magic recipe for glamor, she feels a beauty. The new value added here is expense. What the girl is saying is, "The more expensive I look (or smell), the more desirable I become."

HUGH DALZIEL DUNCAN

Money as a Form of Transcendence in American Life

Spending as Prayer: The American Christmas

If America has done much to form symbols of equality into transcendent symbols of social order, and thus added to the hierarchal lore of modern society, it has also created other characteristic forms in the "spiritualization" of money in both religion and art. We see this most clearly in the celebration of Christmas. The commercial exploitation of the Nativity in America began about 1890. By 1920 merchants and advertising agencies recognized the commercial potentialities of holy days; by 1930 their studied exploitation became part of our business life. In 1950, December sales ranged from 11 to nearly 23 per cent of the year's sales.[1] Merchants open the "Christmas shopping season" on the Monday after Thanksgiving (also celebrated by great spending on food and liquor). Carols, both sacred and secular, blare through business streets. Everything from garbage cans to automobiles are advertised under headings describing the "joy of Christmas" as the "spirit of giving." Nativity scenes appear in advertisements for every kind of commodity, under captions of "peace on earth, good will to men."

The traditional English "Father Christmas" and the German St. Nicholas and Knect Rupprecht, who symbolized the gaiety and feasting of Christmas Eve, were transformed into gift bringers. After 1890 gifts which had been made by hand and selected with great care[2] were sup-

Source: From Hugh Dalziel Duncan, *Communication and Social Order* (Totowa, N.J.: The Bedminster Press, 1962). Copyright 1962 The Bedminster Press, Inc. Reprinted by permission.

planted by purchased gifts, lavishly wrapped and sent by mail. The master of revels, Santa Claus, became a patron of children and the family. Older folk customs of setting off firecrackers, shooting guns, convivial drinking, and gay song died out.[3] Christmas is now a family celebration centering around a gift-laden tree. Women buy and prepare most of the gifts. Even in stores where men wrap and prepare merchandise for mailing and delivery throughout the year, women are hired as gift wrappers for the Christmas season. Santa, once a Falstaffian knight or a kindly father, now takes on a soft androgynous body. He is fat, jolly, old, no longer masculine but maternal. At Christmas time woman herself is transformed. Erotic, romantic, and occupational roles must be replaced by maternal and familial images in December advertising. This strengthens other festive images of the American Christmas Madonna who gives, not her breast, but gifts bought for money.

The older personal and intimate gift of home-baked bread or a knitted scarf had little money value. It was a gift of time, an indication of thought and concern for the other. As we take such a gift we know that the giver thought of us and tried to create something for us, and for us alone. But the purchased gift is a thing, an object whose only radiance comes from its price. As with any priced thing, it cannot have any intrinsic value. It can even be exchanged for something else and, indeed, exchange services are a necessary part of Christmas shopping. Thus the symbol of money has replaced the older folk symbol of fellowship created in preparing gifts, reveling together, and the sacred Christian celebration of the Nativity as a fellowship and brotherhood in Christ.[4]

The older, folk Christmas revels, so repugnant to the Puritans and banished from the home by the ascendency of mother and child, have been revived in business life. Work slackens, time for shopping is allowed, vacations and holidays are given, a Christmas bonus is distributed, and (since the end of the Second World War) office parties are held. These parties revived the older American custom among male workers of drinking and joking together on the job throughout the day before Christmas. The office party temporarily banishes distinctions of rank, furnishes unlimited amounts of alcohol, encourages song, jokes, pranks, and sex play. As the popular press describes it:

On one night or another just before Christmas the lights burn late in many American business houses. The occasion is that great leveler, the office Christmas party, an antidote for formality which ranks between a few discreet cocktails and a free-for-all fight. Then all business barriers collapse; executives unbend; the office clown finds a sympathetic audience. This is the only time the pretty file clerk gets kissed in public and the homely one gets kissed at all.[5]

Individual, institutional, and familial gifts are matched by community-wide collection and distribution of money. Millions of dollars are collected and given to the sick, the unfortunate, and the poor. Local welfare agencies, service clubs, churches, the Red Cross, the Salvation Army, the Tuberculosis Association, the American Legion, and Veterans of Foreign Wars send gifts to prisons, jails, mental institutions, convalescent homes, and orphan homes. Newspapers publish appeals for gifts for bed-ridden children, children whose families are killed, or families whose homes are destroyed by fire. Often these "orgies of Christmas generosity" actually run counter to the planned aid program of social work agencies. Hospital patients must give away many of their gifts because they are useless, duplications of what they already have, or highly perishable. Some social welfare agencies refuse such help on the ground that citizens of a free community should not be given gifts but money or help with their family affairs.

Spending and Death

The infusion of money with sacred social values can also be seen in our funeral practices. Few funerals are conducted now in homes, yet as late as 1910, most families insisted on bringing their dead from hospitals, or wherever death occurred, to the house as soon as possible. Funeral parlors were used by those who had no home of their own, or had no friends or relatives willing to offer them their homes. The body was laid out by the bereaved or by friends in the neighborhood experienced in handling the dead. Washed, dressed in the best or favorite suit or dress, the body was moved to the parlor where it was put on view even before the casket arrived. Friends visited the bereaved home as soon as news of the death reached them; members of the family seated themselves in the living room to receive condolences. Each caller tiptoed into the parlor to see the corpse. The kitchen was soon piled high with cakes, pies, and meats brought by friends and neighbors. Services at the home were long, solemn, and sad. The mystery of death was a promise of eternal life. Where it was believed that life was essentially tragic and sinful, death was welcomed as a release from suffering and guilt.

By 1900, funeral homes were already advertising their "homelike rooms" and "elegant parlors."[6] The funeral chapel was mentioned discreetly by only 10 per cent of advertisers in 1925; but in 1950 the funeral chapel had become a standard part of nearly all urban and many town and village funeral homes. Funeral "artists," working from a photograph of the deceased, restored the corpse to an appearance of health and life. Powder, rouge, lipstick, mascara, and other beauty aids are used to fit the body for the elegance of the casket and its floral backdrop.[7] The custom of sitting with the dead and holding night-long wakes is no longer thought proper to the "routine of modern funeral home operations," for now the funeral ceremony is held in the funeral home, as well as in the church.

Funeral homes of the 1960s, unlike those of 1880, do not emphasize the "parlor" and do not stress "hominess." They are built around the chapel, which is modern in design, air-conditioned throughout, equipped with the latest in livery equipment (including limousines), and luxuriously appointed rooms that look out over beautifully landscaped grounds. In these modern funeral homes, we are assured, everything moves smoothly with a "reserved elegance." And as the undertakers' advertisement goes on to say: "All this costs no more than an ordinary funeral."[8] The architecture of funeral homes varies widely, from Early Colonial to "modern." But whatever the style, the building must be imposing, accessible to transportation, highly public, and kept in good order. Funeral homes are community showpieces, a fitting background for the funeral director who tends to think of himself as a person who carries out his vocation in surroundings that are scrupulously neat, sanitary, dignified, and even beautiful.

The "elegant reserve" and "dignity" of the funeral home is not created through ageless and traditional forms. The archaic forms of "conspicuous waste" which Veblen found so characteristic of devout observances in 1890, and which characterized the old family mansion taken over as a funeral home, are now replaced by funeral homes which are "the most modern in all America." The crude coffin of Colonial times and the pine box of pioneer days have been replaced by ornate caskets. Casket styles are changing more rapidly each year. "A funeral director who would buy a hundred caskets in 1910 would hesitate to stock a quarter that many ten years later, and five years later might consider ten caskets a precarious inventory."[9] The undertaker, now a mortician, mortuary consultant, funeral counselor, or more generally, a funeral director, no longer takes the corpse wrapped in a shroud to a graveyard in a hearse. He takes the patient in a funeral-car or casket coach dressed in a slumber-robe, from the reposing-room to a memorial park, a Garden of Memories, or a Forest Lawn. Here there is no ground burial, but mausoleum entombment in pretentious and costly tombs and every conceivable style from Gothic to modern.

Death, like birth, has been made salable and, thus, subject to the mystery of money. We now bury our dead "in style." Obsolescence in products and services necessary to decent burial of the dead is a matter of style, not decay. "Long before rolling stock wears out it becomes obsolete, and long before funeral homes actually begin to look shabby many funeral directors feel the urge to redecorate."[10] We submit to the rising costs of funerals because we believe there is a direct connection between the money spent on the funeral and the respect given to the dead. In this moment of symbolic transformation quantity becomes *quality* as the social mystery of money fastens its spell upon us.

But it is a mistake to think of the pecuniary expression of Christmas and of death simply as "secularization." Death has lost none of its mystery or power. The clerk who spends several hundred dollars (which he must borrow and pay back in small installments) on his father's funeral is not "secularizing" funeral rites. Funerals have shifted from churches and homes to commercial funeral homes because spending money in itself has become a way of showing respect, and now in our time, of showing reverence. The indigent family which sinks further into debt to provide an expensive funeral is practicing mortification. Such spending is a penance, a self-punishment. For, in going into debt the debtor pledges many future hours of work to his creditor. And he does it in such a highly public fashion that his good name will be greatly threatened if he does not pay.[11]

We are accustomed to think of asceticism and rituals of renunciation as sacred.[12] But as theologians themselves tell us, Christ's law of mortification implies something more than mere self-restraint. It implies the use of what Jeremy Taylor calls "rudeness" against oneself. Christian temperance implies the control of appetite at those points where its demands are most importunate and difficult to resist. The aim of the temperate Christian is *positive,* not negative. He aims not merely at the subjugation of greed but at the cultivation of moral and spiritual power. He makes circumstances subservient to his spiritual progress and "passes through them upwards and onwards to God." Possession of money means (to those under the spell of money) that we struggled against temptation to sloth. Going into debt to bury our dead is a pledge to meet and fight such temptation again. For in the supernatural as well as the social realm, risk-taking brings us glory. Willingness to take risks is our grasp of faith, and thus in a system of hierarchy based on money, risk brings glory so long as it is money risk.

The Deification of the Businessman

The religion of money reached its apogee around 1925, when Calvin Coolidge, our President, told us: "The business of America is business." By 1929 big businessmen were leaders of the nation. A religion of money, replete with saints (and sinners), developed. Business hagiography became a popular and profitable literary genre. It was written in the spirit of Babcock who declared that "Business is religion, and religion is business."[13] Both political parties turned to businessmen for leaders. The Democratic National Chairman was also a Chairman of General Motors. The words of a Morgan partner were often given more publicity than those of the President or the Secretary of State. Faith in Wall Street ran deep. Money, the new symbol of life, was beyond danger because it was "self-regulating."

The most widely read nonfiction book of 1925, *The Man Nobody Knows: A Discovery of the Real Jesus* by Bruce Barton, a leading advertising agent, makes literal use of money as a symbol of God, and propounds the gospel of service through earning and spending money. The Bible is translated into business terminology.

Great progress will be made when we rid ourselves of the idea that there is a difference between *work* and *religious work*. We have been taught that a man's daily business activities are selfish, and that only the time which he devotes to church meetings and social service activities is consecrated. Ask any ten people what Jesus meant by his "Father's business," and nine of them will answer "preaching." To interpret the words in this narrow sense is to lose the real significance of his life. It was not to preach that he came into the world; nor to teach; nor to heal. These are all departments of his Father's business, but the business itself is far larger, more inclusive. . . . The race must be fed and clothed and housed and transported, as well as preached to, and taught and healed. Thus *all* business is his Father's business. All work is worship; all useful service, prayer.[14]

Barton links business with religion, explains religion by business, and then uses business terms as religious terms. In the first chapter Jesus becomes an "executive," in the second he is an "outdoor" man, a "he-man," not the "sallow-faced, thin-lipped, so-called spiritual type," in the third Jesus is discovered to be a "good mixer," "the friendliest man who ever lived, yet one who has been shut off by a black wall of theological tradition." In Chapter Four we find that Jesus was the Great Advertiser. "We speak of the law of 'supply and demand' but the words have got turned around. Elias Howe invented the sewing machine, but it nearly rusted away before American women could be persuaded to use it. With anything which is not a basic necessity the supply always precedes the demand. . . . Assuredly there was no demand for a new religion; the world was already oversupplied." But as we study Jesus' teachings, "worthy of the attentive study of any sales manager," we find him using parables—"the most powerful advertisements of all times." The secret of Jesus' success was his recognition that "all good advertising is news." Jesus would have made many great headlines, as a paraphrase of his actions in modern newspaper copy style shows. "If he were to live again, in these modern days, he would find a way to advertise by his service, not merely by his sermons. One thing is certain: he would not neglect the market-place. Few of his sermons were delivered in synagogues. For the most part he was in the crowded places, the Temple

Court, the city squares, the centers where goods were bought and sold."[15]

But the "present day market-place is the newspaper and the magazine. Printed columns are the modern thoroughfares; published advertisements are the cross-roads where the sellers and the buyers meet." If Jesus lived today he "would be a national advertiser . . . as he was the great advertiser of his own day." For when all is said and done, Jesus was "the founder of modern business," for did not Jesus make it plain when he said, "wist ye not that I must be about my father's business?" that he "thought of his life as *business*." For modern business, like Jesus, serves mankind. "We are great because of our service." "Service is what we are here for," manufacturers exclaim. They call it the "spirit of modern business"; they suppose, most of them, that it is something very new. But Jesus preached it more than nineteen hundred years ago, as the words and deeds of modern business saints such as George W. Perkins, Henry Ford, Theodore N. Vail, and the partners of J. P. Morgan and Company prove.[16]

NOTES

1. In his study, *The American Christmas* (New York: Macmillan Co., 1954), James H. Barnett gives the following figures: building materials 7 percent of year's total; department stores 14.8; drugstores 11; eating and drinking places 8.9; family and other apparel 15; general merchandise 14.5; jewelry 22.7; liquor 15; men's clothing and furnishings 16; women's apparel and accessories 13.1. If sales were constant, each month would account for approximately 8.3 of the annual total.

2. A "boughten" gift was thought vulgar or common unless given by a bachelor or someone who could not make his own.

3. These elements were revived in the "office party" in the business community.

4. Merchants seek to counter the impersonality of the purchased gift by offering a wide range of gifts. Concern for the other is indicated by gifts that are in good style and wrapped with elegance and care. Indications of diligent and careful shopping are supposed to personalize the gift. Shopping aids and guides, elaborate check lists of gifts classified according to age, relationship, or sex are given us. It is even possible to order by phone. The impersonality of this is recognized by merchants who list such services as "*Personalized* Shopping Service" and who refer constantly to "a good old-fashioned Christmas."

5. *Life*, 27 December 1948. Quoted from Barnett, *American Christmas*, p. 140.

6. I have followed the descriptions given by Robert W. Habenstein and William M. Lamers in their *History of American Funeral Directing* (Milwaukee, Wis.: Buflin Printers, 1955).

7. Evelyn Waugh, in his novel *The Loved One,* satirizes the art of "restoration" in American funerals.

8. Such advertising is common in classified telephone directories.

9. Habenstein and Lamers, *American Funeral Directing,* p. 547.

10. Ibid., p. 583.

11. Habenstein reports that most funeral directors write off only about 2 percent of their income to bad debt losses.

12. We forget that austerity, like consumption, may become highly conspicuous. Thus we hear from India that outward or conspicuous austerity has become a "political imperative." The glorification of asceticism creates many incongruities in a nation struggling for a place among world powers devoted to production of goods and services.

13. This identification is still very strong in the accounts of success given to the press by businessmen. Great wealth is a "trust," businessmen are "stewards" of wealth who must lead pious, Christian lives of devotion to the community. Businessmen of all faiths use this Puritan stereotype.

14. Bruce Barton, *The Man Nobody Knows: A Discovery of the Real Jesus* (Indianapolis: Bobbs-Merrill, 1924), pp. 179–80. Barton's italics. Emerson foresaw this in 1860 when he wrote in *The Conduct of Life* that "the gods of the cannibals will be a cannibal, of the crusaders a crusader; and of the merchants a merchant."

15. Ibid., p. 138.

16. The "gospel of service" is discussed in chapter six of *The Man Nobody Knows,* where Jesus is described as "The Founder of Modern Business."

JULES HENRY

Advertising as a Philosophical System

Advertising is an expression of an irrational economy that has depended for survival on a fantastically high standard of living incorporated into the American mind as a moral imperative. Yet a moral imperative cannot of itself give direction; there must be some institution or agency to constantly direct and redirect the mind and emotions to it. This function is served for the high-rising living standard by advertising which, day and night, with increasing pressure reminds us of what there is to buy; and if money accumulates for one instant in our bank accounts, advertising reminds us that it must be spent and tells us how to do it. As a quasi-moral institution advertising, like any other basic cultural institution anywhere, must have a philosophy and a method of thinking. The purpose of this

Source: From *Culture Against Man,* by Jules Henry. Copyright © 1963 by Random House, Inc. Reprinted by permission of the publisher.

chapter is to demonstrate the character of advertising thought, and to show how it relates to other aspects of our culture. In order to make this relationship manifest at the outset I have dubbed this method of thought *pecuniary philosophy.*

The Problem

Since the problem of truth is central to all philosophy, the reader is asked to ask himself, while perusing the following advertising, "Is it literally true that . . . ."

. . . everybody's talking about the new *Starfire* [automobile]?

. . . *Alpine* cigarettes "put the men in menthol smoking"?

. . . a woman in *Distinction* foundations is so beautiful that all other women want to kill her?

. . . *Hudson's Bay Scotch* "is scotch for the men among men"?

. . . if one buys clothes at Whitehouse and Hardy his wardrobe will have "the confident look of a totally well-dressed man"?

. . . *Old Spice* accessories are "the finest grooming aides a man can use"?

. . . *7 Crown* whiskey "holds within its icy depths a world of summertime"?

. . . "A man needs *Jockey* support" because *Jockey* briefs "give a man the feeling of security and protection he needs"?

. . . one will "get the smoothest, safest ride of your life on tires of *Butyl*"?

. . . the new *Pal Premium Injector* blade "takes the friction out of shaving" because it "rides on liquid ball bearings"?

. . . *Pango Peach* color by Revlon comes "from east of the sun . . . west of the moon where each tomorrow dawns" . . . is "succulent on your lips" and "sizzling on your finger tips (And on your toes, goodness knows)" and so will be one's "adventure in paradise"?

. . . if a woman gives in to her "divine restlessness" and paints up her eyelids with *The Look* her eyes will become "jungle green . . . glittery gold . . . flirty eyes, tiger eyes"?

. . . a "new ingredient" in *Max Factor Toiletries* "separates the men from the boys"?

. . . when the Confederate General Basil Duke arrived in New York at the end of the Civil War *"Old Crow* [whiskey] quite naturally would be served"?

. . . *Bayer* aspirin provides "the fastest, most gentle to the stomach relief you can get from pain"?

Are these statements, bits of advertising copy, true or false? Are they merely "harmless exaggeration or puffing"[1] as the Federal Trade Commission calls it? Are they simply para-poetic hyperboles—exotic fruits of Madison Avenue creativity? Perhaps they are fragments of a new language, expressing a revolutionary pecuniary truth that derives authority from a phantasmic advertising universe. In the following pages I try to get some clarity on this difficult and murky matter by teasing out of the language of advertising some of the components of pecuniary philosophy I perceive there.

Pecuniary Pseudo-Truth. No sane American would think that literally everybody is "talking about the new *Starfire*," that Alpine cigarettes literally "put the men in menthol smoking" or that a woman wearing a *Distinction* foundation garment becomes so beautiful that her sisters literally want to kill her. Since he will not take these burblings literally, he will not call them lies, even though they are all manifestly untrue. Ergo, a new kind of truth has emerged—*pecuniary pseudo-truth*—which may be defined as a false statement made as if it were true, but not intended to be believed. No proof is offered for a pecuniary pseudo-truth, and no one looks for it. Its proof is that it sells merchandise; if it does not, it is false.

Para-Poetic Hyperbole. 7 *Crown* whiskey's fantasies of icy depths, Revlon's rhapsodies on *Pango Peach, The Look's* word pictures of alluring eyes, and similar poesies are called parapoetic hyperbole because they are something like poetry, with high-flown figures of speech, though they are not poetry. Note, however, that they are also pecuniary pseudo-truths because nobody is expected to believe them.

Pecuniary Logic. When we read the advertisements for *Butyl* and *Old Crow* it begins to look as if *Butyl* and *Old Crow* really *want* us to believe, for they try to prove that what they say is true. *Butyl,* for example, asserts that "major tire marketers . . . are now bringing you tires made of this remarkable material"; and *Old Crow* says that the reason it "would quite naturally be served" to General Duke in New York was because he "esteemed it 'the most famous [whiskey] ever made in Kentucky.' " When one is asked to accept the literal message of a product on the basis of shadowy evidence, I dub it *pecuniary logic.* In other words, pecuniary logic is a proof that is not a proof but is intended to be so for commercial purposes.

There is nothing basically novel in pecuniary logic, for most people use it at times in their everyday life. What business has done is adopt one of the commoner elements of folk thought and use it for selling products to people who think this way all the time. This kind of thinking—which accepts proof that is not proof—is an *essential* intellectual factor in our economy, for if people were careful thinkers it would be difficult to sell anything. From this it follows that in order for our economy to continue in its present form people must learn to be fuzzy-minded and impulsive, for if they were clear-headed and deliberate they would rarely put their hands in their pockets; or if they did, they would leave them there. If we were all logicians the economy could not survive, and herein lies a terrifying paradox, for *in order to exist economically as we are we must try by might and main to remain stupid. . . .*

Pecuniary Truth

Most people are not obsessive truth-seekers; they do not yearn to get to the bottom of things; they are willing to let absurd or merely ambiguous statements pass. And this undemandingness that does not insist that the world stand up and prove that it is real, this air of relaxed wooly-mindedness, is a necessary condition for the development of the revolutionary mode of thought herein called *pecuniary philosophy*. The relaxed attitude toward veracity (or mendacity, depending on the point of view) and its complement, pecuniary philosophy, are important to the American economy, for they make possible an enormous amount of selling that could not otherwise take place.

Every culture creates philosophy out of its own needs, and ours has produced traditional philosophies based on truths verifiable by some primordial objective or supernatural criteria, and another, pecuniary philosophy, derived from an irrational need to sell. The heart of truth in our traditional philosophies was God or His equivalent, such as an identifiable empirical reality. The heart of truth in pecuniary philosophy is contained in the following three postulates:

> Truth is what sells.
> Truth is what you want people to believe.
> Truth is that which is not legally false.

The first two postulates are clear, but the third probably requires a little explaining and a good example. A report in *Science* on the marketing practices of the *Encyclopaedia Britannica* is just what we need at this point.

One of the tasks of the Federal Trade Commission, according to the Encyclopaedia Britannica, is to order business organizations to stop using deceptive advertising when such organizations are found to be so engaged. A few weeks ago Encyclopaedia Britannica, Inc., was ordered by the Federal Trade

Commission to stop using advertising that misrepresents its regular prices as reduced prices available for a limited time only. . . .

Some of the company's sales practices are ingenious. The FTC shows, for example, how the prospective customer, once he has gained the impression that he is being offered the Encyclopaedia and accessories at reduced prices, is led to believe that the purported reduced prices are good only for a limited time. This is done by two kinds of statements, each one being true enough if regarded separately.

The first kind of statement, which appears in written material, says such things as "This offer is necessarily subject to withdrawal without notice."[2]

Science explains that the second kind of statement is made by the salesman when he applies pressure to the prospective customer by telling him he will not return. The Federal Trade Commission, in enjoining the *Encyclopaedia Britannica* from using this kind of sales technique, argued that the first statement plus the second created the impression in the customer's mind that if he does not buy now he will lose the opportunity to buy at what he has been given to think is a reduced price. Actually, *Science* points out, it is not a reduced price, for the price has not changed since 1949. Since it is literally true that a business has the right to raise prices without advance notice, the *Britannica* advertisement is not legally false, even though it reads like a warning that prices will go up soon. I have coined the term *legally innocent prevarication* to cover all statements which, though not legally untrue, misrepresent by implication. . . .

Pecuniary Philosophy as a Total System

Every culture produces, in an unbelievably appropriate and rigid way, a philosophy that fits its needs like a glove. Pecuniary philosophy is a total system, embracing, like some great classical school, not only a metaphysics and morality, but also a psychology, a biology, a history, a poetics, and so on. It has also a theory of birth and death—the birth and death of products. Fundamentally what pecuniary philosophy does is place the product in its proper perspective in our culture, for the product and its attached claim are considered central, while the inert consumer, or rather his head (box) is placed where it belongs—in secondary or, perhaps, merely adventitious position. Consumers are necessary to the existence and evolution of products; consumers (like air and water) are the environment in which products (in a way similar to plants and animals) evolve and have their being; and just as deprivation of air and water causes plants and animals to die, so loss of consumers causes the death of products.

Thus advertising rests on a total system of thought and pursues ends that are fundamentally at odds with the traditional academic philosophies of our culture. And because it is at odds with these philosophies and their old-fashioned morality, it is vulnerable to attack from them. On the other hand, however, the contribution pecuniary philosophy makes to our economy is so great that in spite of the fact that it flies in the face of orthodoxy, it needs to be defended. This is accomplished, in great part, through starving the agencies of Government that have been specifically established to supervise it. In 1960, for example, Congress appropriated only $33 million for the Federal Trade Commission, the Federal Communications Commission, and the Food and Drug Administration—about three-tenths of 1 percent of what was spent for advertising that year. . . .

I shall use the term *monetization* where cultural factors not usually thought of as entering the processes of production and sale are used to make money. Another example of monetization would be the exploitation of women's feeling that they have nothing to offer but allure, for this transmutes feelings of inadequacy into cash.

Monetization

Since values like love, truth, the sacredness of high office, God, the Bible, motherhood, generosity, solicitude for others, and so on are the foundation of Western culture, anything that weakens or distorts them shakes traditional life. The traditional values are part of traditional philosophy, but pecuniary philosophy, far from being at odds with them appears to embrace them with fervor. This is the embrace of a grizzly bear, for as it embraces the traditional values pecuniary philosophy chokes them to death. The specific choking mechanism is *monetization.*

Let us consider the following advertisement for a popular women's magazine: Against a black sky covering almost an entire page in the *New York Times* of June 2, 1960 is chalked the following from the New Testament: "Children, love ye one another." Below, the advertising copy tells us that *McCall's* magazine will carry in its next issue parables from five faiths, and that

Such spiritual splendor, such profound mystical insight, seem perfectly at home in the pages of *McCall's,* where the editorial approach is all-inclusive, universal, matching the infinite variety of today's existence.

Guilt by association is familiar enough to the American people through the work of various sedulous agencies of Government. *McCall's,* however, has discovered its opposite—*glory* by association, or, in the language of this work, pecuniary transfiguration. Since "spiritual splendor" and "mystical insight" are traits of holy books, and since examples of these are printed in *McCall's,* it is by that fact a kind of holy book. This is what I mean by the use of values for pecuniary purposes; this is value distortion through monetization.

Consider now the following report from the *New York Times,* July 27, 1961:

> It is understood that President Kennedy for the first time has authorized the use of his name and photograph in an advertisement.
>
> The ad will be one of a series of institutional advertisements run in behalf of the magazine industry. The President's picture will appear together with a statement discussing the role of magazines in American life.
>
> An element of controversy has surrounded the use of President Kennedy's name and photograph in advertising. Last week the National Better Business Bureau criticized the unauthorized use of the President's name and likeness and warned that White House policy forbade such practices. The bureau noted such items as a "Kennedy Special" fish stew, J.F.K. rocking chairs and so forth.

The reason certain forms of logic are abandoned is not because they are wrong, but rather because they have proved inadequate to new problems and new knowledge. The old logics cannot make distinctions that must now be made, or they make distinctions that are no longer necessary. In the *Times* article we perceive such a situation, for obviously practitioners of pecuniary logic have somehow used the President's name inappropriately in naming a fish stew after him. Consider the following imaginary slogans:

> John F. Kennedy, President of the United States, endorses the American way of life.
>
> John F. Kennedy, President of the United States, endorses our fish stew.
>
> John F. Kennedy, President of the United States, endorses American magazines.

One can see instantly that endorsement of the American way of life by the President would make one feel comfortable, whereas presidential endorsement of fish stew would cause one to feel vaguely unhappy and perhaps a little sick. The third statement might merely stimulate a little wonder that the President could do anything so brash. However, if magazines can be linked by pecuniary transfiguration to a basic value like "the American way of life," then it becomes reasonable to bring in the President. Herein lies the genius of the Madison Avenue logicians—the wave of the future—for though in the present case they have avoided the worst pitfalls of pecuniary logic, they have remained true to its spirit. The failure of pecuniary logic in the fish stew case lies in its inability to make a distinction between something of high cultural value ("the American way of life") and something of little or no cultural value (fish stew). This failure can be referred to the inadequacy of the basic premise, "anything that sells a product is right." In the present instance the premise was not right because it brought pecuniary thinking into collision with tradition as embodied in the Better Business Bureau. The magazine men were smarter.

Consider now the following imaginary brands:

> "George Washington" Corn Chowder.
> "Abe Lincoln" Blackstrap Molasses.

The reader will not very likely take offense at either of these because (a) Washington and Lincoln are dead; (b) corn chowder and blackstrap molasses have a primordial, earthy, American atmosphere about them. The fish, however, is a deprecated, rather low-caste animal in American culture, in spite of the enamoured pursuit of it by millions of weekend fishermen. Furthermore, though *fried* fish has higher status, fish *stew* sounds plebian and even hateful to many people. One can now begin to understand the instinctive revulsion of the BBB to attachment of the President's name to fish stew. Fundamentally it has nothing to do with the monetization of a national symbol. Basically BBB recoiled at the degradation of the symbol through association with fish, and at the connection of a *living* president with a commercial product. (It would not be so bad if he were dead.)

Though Americans have traditionally shown little respect for public office, some men, like the Founding Fathers and Abraham Lincoln, have become almost sacred, and their memories are still rallying points for the forces of traditional ethics in American life. Hence their names and likenesses, *downgraded,* perhaps, are yet useful for advertising many things, from banks to whiskey. This being the case, we can surmise that the reason we do not protest the use, for pecuniary purposes, of passages from the New Testament, or the widespread monetization of values is because *traditional values are losing the respect and the allegiance of the people,* even though Madison Avenue can still transmute into cash what residues of veneration they yet evoke. An important social function of the Franklin, Lincoln, and Washington sagas is to make Americans ready to patronize any institution or buy any product bearing their names. One might say, "Sell a kid on the cherry tree and you can sell him cherries the rest of his life."

In their wars of survival pecuniary adversaries will use anything for ammunition—space, time, the President, the Holy Bible, and all the traditional values. Monetization waters down values, wears them out by slow attrition, makes them banal and, in the long run, helps Americans to become indifferent to them and even cynical. Thus the competitive struggle forces the corruption of values. . . .

Advertising, Consumption Autarchy, and the Self

Consumption autarchy is the term I have coined for the condition in which a country consumes all it produces. In 1960 the United States exported 4 percent of its gross national product.[3] This closeness to consumption autarchy is made necessary by the low purchasing power of much of the rest of the world and by reduction to a mere trickle of exports to the communist countries. Thus advertising's extreme behavior is inseparably connected with the *world* consumption pattern and fear-ridden international relations.

Advertising methods are related also, however, to a first tenet of American business: profits must increase without limit. Given consumption autarchy and the tenet of limitless increase, only the wooly-minded consumer, trained to insatiability, can put the tenet into effect; and advertising alone can excite him to the heroic deeds of consumption necessary to make of the tenet a concrete reality.

In the background of all of this is the collective Self of the American people which has been educated to put the high-rising living standard in the place of true Self-realization. Consumption autarchy, the drive toward higher profits, and alienation from Self are the factors that account for advertising. To ignore these while considering America's problems of production, consumption, and advertising is to ignore the ocean while studying the tides.

Configuration and Subculture. Unique to the so-called high cultures of the world is their capacity to constantly generate within their vast bellies subcultures which, while having some connection with the archetypal, the so-called great or traditional culture, are somehow remote from it and encapsulated. Members of these subcultures talk mostly to one another, receiving in this way constant reassurance that their perceptions of the world are the only correct ones and coming to take for granted that the whole culture is as they see it. What has frustrated the efforts of social scientists to analyze the United States as a configuration, as a unitary system of ideas and activities, is the fact that it has so many apparently separate subcultures. Yet they are all connected with and depend on one another and on the fundamental orientations of the American configuration—toward private property, the high-rising standard of living, competition, achievement, and security. Thus the *stupefied* TV audience is the natural and necessary complement to the *alert* advertiser; and the merchants of *confusion* on Madison Avenue are a necessary complement to hard-pressed industry, pursuing economically *rational* ends. The *dubious modes of thought* of pecuniary philosophy integrate with the *undemandingness toward truth* characteristic of American folk, and their desire for a higher living standard makes them susceptible to the advertising that assails them with increasing pressure to raise it. And so it goes. The *survival anxiety* among products and claims is matched by the worker's *worry* about his job. He *passively awaits* the turn of the system—whether it will support him or let him drift—while industry and advertising collaborate in a fierce survival *fight* for markets. The worker measures his fluctuating *security* in terms of the steadiness of his job, advertising in terms of the *steadiness* of its billings: worker employment seems no more fickle and *uncertain* than advertising accounts, as they *shift around* from one agency to another. . . .

NOTES

1. An expression used by the Federal Trade Commission in dismissing a complaint against a company for using extreme methods in its advertising.
2. *Science,* 14 July 1961.
3. United States Department of Commerce, World Trade Information Service. *Statistical Reports.* Part 3, No. 60–30. September 1960, 4.1 percent, the actual figure given by the Department of Commerce, includes military supplies and equipment and other forms of foreign aid.

STUART EWEN

Advertising as Social Production: Selling the System

> Mass reproduction is aided especially by the reproduction of masses. . . . the masses are brought face to face with themselves.—Walter Benjamin

Proletarianization, meaning that process by which human life is implicated in the universe of bourgeois production, has always been a cultural "offering." Karl Marx initiated his argument for a critique of culture from the conceptual touchstone of proletarianization; as the mode of culture itself, the process of proletarianization stood at the heart of his understanding of modern history. Marx argued further, in pursuit of his radical understanding, that a critique of culture was inextricably bound up in the revolutionary perception of civil society. Concomitant with any "stage of development of [the] material powers of production," Marx wrote in his "Preface to a Critique of Political Economy,"

Source: Reprinted, with deletions and revisions, from Stuart Ewen, "Advertising as Social Production," *Radical America* 3 (May–June 1969): 42–56. Reprinted by permission of *Radical America* and the author.

specific and corresponding social formations and relations of production would arise. Thus it would appear that to focus historical attention on the study of *social production*—that is, on the specific means and consequences of the process of proletarianization (the transvaluation of "use-value" into "exchange value")—could hardly qualify as a methodological innovation, since Marx long ago both located and formulated its primacy. Yet few contemporary studies of emerging industrial culture deal seriously with the problem of perception as a social formation; a notable exception is E. P. Thompson's brilliant social history of the clock, *"Time, Work-discipline, and Industrial Capitalism,"*[1] which views the emergence of industrial capitalism as a world-historic shock that beyond being a significant change in the "material powers of production," required its participants to assume a critically altered perception of time—of reality. Thompson concludes his essay with the instructive though implicit admonition that "there is no such thing as economic growth which is not, at the same time, growth or change of a culture; the growth of social consciousness."

The emergence of bourgeois social production meant the creation of a *social life style* over and above a work style prescribed by the conditions of the job. While the history of nineteenth-century social production and proletarianization seems largely informed by the boundaries of work, it should be viewed more radically as informed by that *social style.* Corresponding to a definite, and in our terms primitive, arrangement of the material forces of production, the social style seems precluded by the work style only when one fails to view the nature of work as exigent to a specific level of social production. To view proletarianization in early industrial America solely as the creation of "workers" in the most colloquial sense (i.e., people to work in factories) ignores the social mode of the system. In short, the most significant aspect of capital was that it historically defined the limitations of all social bonds within its expanding arena of influence. In the early period of accumulation, its social definition is perhaps most clearly located in the factory relations between capitalist and worker, yet to isolate the work style as the sole mode of proletarianization in the nineteenth century is as deceptive as the work of bourgeois "culture critics"; work which takes issue with the character of consumption culture, branding it anomalous, while accepting the "positive" integrity of our social institutions and the tenets of our political economy. Both the conceptual isolation of the work style and the writings of bourgeois culture critics extricate particular aspects of social capitalism from their *totality.*

Contemporary proletarianization extends far beyond the creation of workers to man the productive machinery of industry. Although the proletarianization of nineteenth-century capitalism was—as it continued

to be—a process of habituation to a *social style,* its limits were narrower
and its focus less specific than the proletarianization of contemporary
capitalism. The nature of the productive machinery and its capacity to
produce (and have its products consumed) meant a very privatized and
work oriented proletarianization—a privatized level of social production.
"Worker" indicated "wheelhorse." The number of hours spent on the
job; the introduction of a "clock-time" oriented work day; the imposition
of a routinized moderation and thrift that was bent on making an
essentially non-industrial work force "socially responsible"; and the
ideological *embourgeoisment* of religious and other cultural institutions
were the often self-conscious attempts on the part of an industrial
bourgeoisie to educate people to production. These aspects of industrial
life must be seen as attempts not to create fourteen hour-per-day
workers, but proletarian men and women.

The development of a more highly technologized capitalism
promised to disengage vast numbers of "wheelhorse" proletarians from
their previous social role. In the process of producing vast quantities—
"mass" numbers—of goods for consumption, it necessarily altered the
character, although not the substance of their proletarianization.
Character and *substance* have often been confused and fused in the
description of the "beneficial" *choices, freedoms, leisures,* and *affluence*
that have been "attained" by the modern industrial worker. Such
"gains" are generally regarded as having elevated the contemporary
"mass" above its previous proletarian status.

Yet the maintenance of the notion "mass" should give pause to such
sanguinity. *Choice, freedom, leisure,* and *affluence* can not be viewed as
transhistoric absolutes in the context of corporate capitalism, but rather
as the *historic* demarcations of the elements of *proletariat*—those
aspects of *social style* which commit the proletariat to, rather than extricate it from, serving the continual fiscal needs of bourgeois society. An
appraisal of the quality and direction of *choice* reveals its link of commitment to the counter-human consumer market. Apparent disen-
gagement from proletarian life represents its opposite: a further involvement in that life. *That which appears to be is not.*

Consumption, likewise, is not what it appears to be. Though
generally considered (and ideologically defined) as increasingly
expanding *time off from production,* leisure time consumption is rather a
modern social-economic formation that, like factory discipline, commits
our TIME, our LIVES, to the maintenance of the ascendant bourgeois
class. Sebastian de Grazia pointed out the fatal contradictions of our
leisure and the substance of (alienated and deferred) pleasure when he
cryptically noted that "consumption gobbles time up alive."[2]

During the 1920s the creation of an advanced advertising bureaucracy was an attempt to put culture to more efficient work for capitalism. While in the minds of both capital and labor, early industrial proletarianization was closely associated with the productive plant and its disciplines, the intensified use of cultural apparati (media) in the proletarianizing process tended to obfuscate that association. While the ad industry was bureaucratically linked to the industrial machinery, its products were capitalistic *art forms* which publicly ignored any bourgeois complicity except insofar as their message implored people to consume. The advertising industry's ability to perform such an obfuscation was deliberate and historical; historical in that advanced technological art forms were increasingly conducive to camouflaging their source. Walter Benjamin has noted that as technologically reproduced art is designed for prolific exhibition, the notion of authenticity—the sense of there being *an original*—is lost.[3] The essential element in each work of mechanically reproduced art is its immediacy, its every showing, rather than its ability to be located absolutely "in time and space." The consumer, confronted with a commercial advertisement, views but an off print, not the economic-cultural apparatus from which it is generated and his own life in relation to that apparatus. As such, he has only his own critical abilities with which to draw connections between "art" and its source. As the social style of technological corporatism, and art forms themselves, represent a continual assault on that ability to critique—attempting, as Herbert Marcuse would have it, to absorb all opposition—that critical ability itself may be domesticated; the "connection" between art and source reduced to a pacified epigram of modern life.

It was this sense of immediacy, the apparent lack of source, which gave advertising its particular value as an efficient productive tool. Advertising was a way of projecting the necessitated values and activities of the system which broke from the traditional context of proletarianization, and correlated these values and activities to an ideological notion of pleasure. The "performance principle" (to borrow from Marcuse's *Eros and Civilization*) which capitalism demanded, was appealingly cloaked in the garb of the "play/pleasure principle" which capitalism denied.

It is with these concepts in mind that the following is presented.

I

In 1910, Henry Ford instituted the "line production system" for "maximum production economy" in his Highland Park (Mich.) plant.[4] The innovation, though in many ways unsophisticated, and hardly educated as to its own implications, was the beginning of a momentous transformation in America's capacity to produce. In quantitative terms, the change was staggering. On the 1910 line, the time required to assemble a chassis was twelve hours and twenty-eight minutes. "By spring of 1914, the Highland Park plant was turning out over 1000 vehicles a day, and the average labor time for assembling a chassis had dropped to one hour and thirty-three minutes."[5]

Mass production was a way of making production more economical. Through his use of the assembly line, Ford was able to utilize "expensive, single-purpose" machinery, along with quickly trained, "single-purpose" workmen to make a single-model, inexpensive automobile at a rate which, with increasing sophistication, continued to dwarf not only the production levels of pre-massified industry, but the output of less refined mass production systems.[6]

By the 1920s, interest in and employment of the industrial potential of mass production extended far beyond the automobile industry. In recognition of such industrial developments, the United States Special Census of 1921 and 1923 offered a study of productive capacity[7] which was one of the first general discussions of its kind.[8] Consumer goods manufacturers increasingly recognized that mass production and mass distribution were "necessary" steps toward survival in a competitive market. Edward Filene, of the Boston department store family, and a businessman founder of the consumer union movement, recognized and articulated the competitive compulsion of mass production; competition, said Filene, ". . . will compel us to Fordize American business and industry."[9]

And yet, what Filene and others meant by "Fordizing" American industry transcended the myopic vision of Henry Ford. While Ford stubbornly held to the notion that ". . . the work and the work *alone* controls us,"[10] others in the automobile industry,[11] and (for our purposes) more importantly, ideologues of mass industry outside of the auto industry, viewed the strategy of production in broad social terms. Before mass production, industries had produced for a limited consumer market. With a burgeoning capacity to produce, industry promised to become distended in comparison to traditional non-proletarian markets and conventional buying habits. While traditional markets had been viewed as a distinct and dependable receptacle for consumer goods, "scientific" production promised to make the conventional notion of "consumer" anachronistic.[12]

The mechanism of mass production could not function unless markets became more dynamic, growing horizontally (nationally), vertically (into social classes not previously among the consumers), and ideologically. "Ideological" growth refers to the needs of a mass industrial capitalism to produce, change, or habituate men into responding to the demands of the productive machinery. The corollary to a freely growing system of goods production was a "systematic, nationwide plan to endow the masses with more buying power," a freely growing system of consumer production.[13] The modern mass producer could not depend upon an elite market to respond to his productive capacity. From a dependence upon local markets or localized markets scattered nationally,[14] the manufacturer was forced to "count on the whole United States if he [was] going to manufacture a large enough quantity of goods to reduce the cost to the point where he [could] compete with other manufacturers of the same goods,"[15] and subsequently distribute his mass-produced ware more efficiently and profitably. He was required to create an ideological bridge across traditional social gaps; section, taste, need, and class, which could congeal prejudices in his favor.

Considering the quantitative possibilities of mass production, the question of "national markets" became one of qualitatively changing the nature of the American buying public. In response to the exigencies of the productive system of the twentieth century excessiveness replaced thrift as a social value. It became imperative to invest the laborer with a financial power and a psychic desire to consume.

By the end of the depression of 1921, "productive machinery was so effective that even more so than before much greater markets were absolutely necessary than those provided by the existing public buying power."[16] As the question of expanding old and creating new markets became a function in the massification of industry, foresighted businessmen began to see themselves as social producers. It was a necessity for them to organize their businesses not merely around the production of goods, but around the creation of a buying public, men and markets correlative to such goods production. "The changes that we shall be obliged to make in production," noted Filene, "will lead to pretty thorough overhauling of our machinery and methods of distribution, and, in the end, both the quantity and quality of consumption will be dictated by them."[17] As the "twentieth-century industrialist realized to a greater extent than did his predecessors, that he must understand the living world contained by his factory,"[18] so too did he realize that he must understand, and manipulate, as part of his productive apparatus, the total world occupied by his workers. The necessity to "influence human conduct," the knowledge that goods production meant social production, gave some businessmen's rhetoric a revealing idiom; they spoke of "human conduct" or the "consumer's dollar" as industrial discoveries, or as more valuable to manufacturing "than the uses of electricity or steel."[19] Within an ideal of a "scientifically" managed industry raw materials and consumers were both viewed as malleable. They both would have to be shaped by the demands of the production line, pecuniary interests, and the increasingly managerial tools of capital.

As capitalism became increasingly characterized by mass production and the subsequent need for mass distribution, traditional expedients for the real or attempted manipulation of labor were transformed. While the nineteenth-century industrialist coerced labor, both on and off the job, to be the "wheelhorse" of industry, modernizing capitalism sought to change "wheelhorse" to "worker," and "worker" to "consumer," on and off the job.[20]

To the worker on the job within modernizing industries, the movement toward mass production had severely changed the character of his labor. The modern manufacturing plant culminated a trend of industrialism which made him a decreasingly "significant" unit of production. "The man who had been the more or less creative maker of the whole of an article became the tender of a machine that made only one small part of the article."[21] The time required to teach the worker the "adept performance" of his "operation on assembly work" was a matter of a few hours.[22] This development had significant repercussions both in terms of the way in which a laborer viewed his proletarian status, and in terms of the manufacturer's need to mass distribute the mountainous fruits of mass production. The two phenomena merged in the redefinition of that proletarian status. While mass production defined labor's work in terms of monotony, and rationalized his product to a fragment, some businessmen spoke of "economic freedom" or "industrial democracy"[23] as the blessing promised the worker by modern production methods. Yet the "freedom" and "democracy" offered by mass industry stopped short of a freedom to define the uses, or to rearrange the relationships, of production. "The industrial democracy I am discussing," Filene assured those who might fear its anticapitalist implications, "has nothing to do with the Cubist politics of class revolution."[24] What was meant, rather, was that modern industrial production required that workers be free to "cultivate themselves" among the uncontestable fruits of the new industrial cornucopia.

The endowment of the masses with "industrial democracy" was seen as a complex and involving process. Their traditional role in capitalism had afforded them neither the cash nor the conviction to be so "democratized." It was imperative that the worker, "desire(s) a larger share in the mental and spiritual satisfactions of the property of his daily job much more than *a larger share in the management of the enterprise which furnishes that job.*"[25]

Not only was this alleged democracy designed to define the modern worker as a smoothly running unit of industrial production, but it also tended to define protest and proletarian unrest in terms of the desire to consume, making it also profitable. By protesting for the right to be better consumers, the aspirations of labor would be profitably coordinated with the aspirations of capital. Such convictions implicitly attempted to divest protest of its anticapitalist content. Modern labor protest should have no basis in class antagonism.[26]

By the twenties, the ideological vanguard of the business community saw the need to endow the masses with what economic historian Norman Ware has called the money, commodity, and psychic wages (satisfactions), correlative and responsive to the route of industrial capitalism.[27] A major part of this endowment was the movement toward objective conditions which would make mass consumption feasible: higher wages and shorter hours. Giving official credence to such visions, Herbert Hoover noted that "High wages [are the] very essence of great production."[28] In 1923, Julius Barnes, president of the U.S. Chamber of Commerce, spoke of the need to *prevent* the overconcentration of wealth, which threatened the development of a "broad purchasing market necessary to absorb our production."[29] Certainly the movement to higher wages preceded the twenties but it is mainly in the literature of the twenties (and later) that this is linked to a general strategy to consumerize the worker. As early as 1914, Henry Ford had instituted the five dollar work day wage, but his innovation coexisted with a nineteenth-century Protestant value system which the worker was expected to maintain.[30] This system significantly clashed with the "economic freedom" that, out of necessity, attempted to subvert the moderation earlier valued for the masses.

The question of shorter hours was also tantamount to offering labor the "chance" to expand the consumer market. And yet, "chance," as "industrial democracy," and as "economic freedom" were subterfuges, in so much as these alleged freedoms and choices meant a transformed version of capitalism's incessant need to mold a work force in its own image. "As modern industry [was] geared to mass production, time out for mass consumption becomes as much a necessity as time in for production."[31] The shortening of hours was seen as a qualitative as well as quantitative change in the worker's life, without significantly altering his relation to power over the uses and means of production. In addition to increasing the amount of leisure, it was hoped that shorter hours would productively determine, "to some extent, the use of leisure and consumption."[32] Shorter hours and higher wages were seen as a first step in a broader offensive against notions of thrift and an attempt to habituate a national population to the exigencies of mass production. A capitalism that had previously required the worker to "live, move, and [have] his being *there on the job*"[33] was now, among some industries, trying to undo such notions and realities of "the job." Now priorities demanded that the worker spend his wages and leisure time on the consumer market. Realizing that earlier conditions had not been "favorable to such a worker's finding in, say the sector of his home the

sought-for satisfactions of forward movement and distinction," Whiting
Williams, personnel director for a steel company, and an ideologue of
"scientific" management, felt that labor had developed a "suspicion" of
such "sought-for satisfactions." Once again linking the rhetoric of
freedom to the necessities of capitalism, Filene noted that

modern workmen have learned their habits of consumption and their habits of
spending (thrift) in the school of fatigue, in a time when high prices and relatively
low wages have made it necessary to spend all the energies of the body and mind
in providing food, clothing and shelter. We have no right to be overcritical of the
way they spend a new freedom or a new prosperity until they have had as long a
training in the school of freedom.[34]

Within the vision of consumption as "school of freedom," the entry
onto the consumer market was described as a "civilizing" experience.
"Civilization" was the expanded cultural world which flowed from capitalism's broad capacity to commodify material resources. The experience of civilization was the cultural world this capacity produced.

And yet the "school of freedom" posed various problems. The
democratic terminology within which the profitable vision of consumption was posed did not reveal the social and economic realities that
threatened that vision. In terms of economic development, the financial
growth of industrial corporations averaged 286 percent between 1922
and 1929. Despite some wage hikes, and relatively shorter hours in such
industries,[35] the average manufacturing wage earner showed a wage increase of only 14 percent during this same period.[36] The discrepancy
between purchasing power and the rate of industrial growth was dealt
with in part by the significant growth of installment selling[37] that
followed the 1921 "buyer's strike."

Despite the initiation of a corporate credit system which offered
consumers supplementary money, the growth of the productive system
forced many industrial ideologues to realize the continuous need to psychically habituate men to consumption beyond the level of familiar
structural change.

II

The man with the proper imagination is able to conceive of any commodity in
such a way that it becomes an object of emotion to him and to those to whom he
imparts his picture, and hence creates desire rather than a mere feeling of
ought.[38]

Modern advertising must be seen as a direct response to the needs
of mass industrial capitalism. Second in procession after the manager of
the production line, noted Whiting Williams, "came the leader who

possessed the ability to develop and direct men's desires and demands in a way to furnish the organized mass sales required for the mass production made possible by the massed dollars."[39] Advertising, as a part of mass distribution within modernizing industries, became a major sector for business investment. Within the automobile industry, initiated by the broad and highly diversified G.M. oligopoly, distribution came to account for about one-half of that investment. Among producers of small consumer goods, the percentage of capital devoted to product proliferation was often greater.[40]

In the 1920s, advertising played an increasingly significant role in industry's attempt to develop a continually responsive consumer market. Although committed national corporations saw advertising as an invaluable integrant of critical economic planning,[41] its acceptance was hardly universal. A mass advertising industry developing in concert with the mass needs of industrial corporations was continually selling itself to industry. Between 1918 and 1923, a greater percentage of articles in the advertising trade journal, *Printers' Ink,* were devoted to ways of convincing "ancient" corporations that advertising was a given of modern industrialism, than were devoted to advertising and merchandising techniques. During the 1920s, however, advertising grew to the dimensions of a major industry. In 1918, total gross advertising revenues in General and Farm magazines was $58.5 million. By 1920 the gross had reached $129.5 million; and by 1929, $196.3 million. Such figures do not include newspaper revenues, or more significantly, direct-to-buyer advertising which still comprised a major, though declining, sector of the industry.

In an address to the American Association of Advertising Agencies (27 October 1926), Calvin Coolidge noted that the industry now required "for its maintenance, investments of great capital, the occupation of large areas of floor space, the employment of an enormous number of people."[42] As the production line had insured the efficient creation of vast quantities of consumer goods, ad men spoke of their product as "business insurance"[43] for profitable and efficient distribution of these goods. While line management tended to the process of goods production, social management—advertisers—hoped to make the cultural milieu of capitalism as efficient as line management had made production. Their task was couched in terms of a secular religion for which the advertisers sought adherents. Calvin Coolidge, applauding their secular clericism, noted that "advertising ministers to the spiritual side of trade."[44]

The reality of modern production dictated the creation of vast national markets. Although many corporations boasted of having attained national markets without the aid of advertising, *Printers' Ink,* the trade journal, argued that these "phantom national markets" were actually inefficient, unpredictable, and scattered aglommerations of heterogeneous local markets.[45] Advertising offered itself as a means of efficiently creating consumers and as a way of homogeneously "controlling the consumption of a product."[46] The significance of the notion of efficiency in the creation of consumers lies in the fact that the modern advertising industry, like the modern manufacturing plant, was an agent of mass social production. As Ford's assembly line utilized "expensive single-purpose machinery" to produce automobiles inexpensively and at a rate that dwarfed traditional methods, the costly machinery of advertising that Coolidge had described set out to produce consumers, likewise inexpensively and at a rate that dwarfed traditional methods. To create that body efficiently the advertising industry had to develop universal notions of *what makes people respond,* going beyond the "horse sense" psychology that had characterized the earlier industry.[47] Such general conceptions of human instinct offered to provide ways of reaching a mass audience via a universal appeal. Considering the task of having to build a mass ad industry to attend to the needs of mass production, the ad men welcomed the work of psychologists in the articulation of these general conceptions.[48]

The ideological vanguard of the business community found the social psychology of such men as Floyd Henry Allport useful in terms of developing a universal appeal to consumers.[49] Such theories seem to give an ideological cohesion to much of what one sees in the advertising of the twenties. The notion of man as the object of continual and harsh social scrutiny that underscored the argument of much of the ad texts of the decade (Part III), found at least close companionship within the psychological professions. Explicating his notion on the way in which man develops a sense of himself from infancy, Allport asserted that "our consciousness of ourselves is largely a reflection of the consciousness which others have of us. My idea of myself is rather my own idea of my neighbor's view of me."[50]

Whether or not the general conception of "self" as propounded by Floyd Henry Allport had a direct bearing on the *Weltanschauung* held by advertising in the 1920s is not clear. It was generally conceded however, that a "knowledge of people—human nature—"[51] was as necessary a constituent of social production as the line manager's knowledge of his raw materials was to goods production. While agreeing that "human nature is more difficult to control than material nature,"[52] ad men nonetheless discovered in such general notions of human self-conception useful tools for advertising, given their desire to predictably control men in order to create new habits and desires for consumer products.

Beyond the search for a general conception of human nature, ad men spoke in specific terms of "human instincts" which if properly understood could induce people "to buy a given product if it was scientifically presented. If advertising copy appealed to the right instincts, the urge to buy would surely be excited."[53] The utilitarian value or traditional notion of mechanical quality was not sufficient to move products at the necessary rate and volume required by mass production.

Such traditional appeals would not change the disposition of potential markets to consumption. Instead, it would offer each product isolatedly, not in terms of the social-economic consumerization (i.e., proletarianization) of men, but through an appeal to traditional notions of quality. The advertisers were concerned with effecting a self-conscious change in the psychic economy, which could not come about if they spent all their time talking about a product, and none talking about the "reader." The appeal to instincts was a way of "scientifically" controlling mass goods distribution. Advertising literature, following the advent of mass production methods, increasingly spoke in terms of appeals to instinct. Anticipating later implementation, by 1911, Walter Dill Scott, psychologist/author of *Influencing Men in Business*, noted that "goods offered as means of gaining social prestige make their appeals to one of the most profound of the human instincts."[54] Yet the instinct for "social prestige" as well as others of a broad "constellation"[55] of instincts were channeled into the terms of the prpoductive system. The use value of "prestige," of "beauty," of "acquisition," of "self-adornment," or of "play" was placed in the service of advertising's basic purpose—to provide effective mass distribution of products. Carl A. Naether, an ideologue of advertising for women, demonstrated how the link might be effected between "instinct" and mass sales.

An attractive girl admiring a string of costly pearls just presented to her would in no few cases make the one seeing her in an advertisement exclaim: "I wish that *I, too,* might have a set of these pearls and so enhance *my* personal appearance." Such and similar longings are merely expressions of real or fancied need for what is advertised.[56]

The creation of "fancied need" was crucial to the modern advertiser. The transcendence of traditional consumer markets and buying habits required people to buy not to satisfy their own fundamental needs, but rather, to satisfy the real, historic needs of capitalist productive machinery. Advertising was a way of making people put time and energy into what Calvin Coolidge referred to as their "education"[57] to production. The investment of time and energy in deliberation over an advertisement, as described by Scott,[58] enacted in requisite microcosm the commitment of one's total time and energy to consumption. Advertising demanded but a momentary participation in the logic of consumption.

Yet hopefully that moment would be expanded into a life style by its educational value. A given ad asked not only that an individual buy its product, but that he experience a self-conscious perspective that he had previously been socially and psychically denied. By that perspective, one was able to ameliorate social and personal frustrations through his access to the marketplace.

In the light of such notions as Allport's "social self," and other self-objectifying visions of popularity and success,[59] a new cultural logic was projected by advertising beyond the strictly pecuniary one of creating the desire to consume. The social perception was one in which people ameliorated the negative condition of social objectification through consumption, material objectification. The negative condition was portrayed as social failure derived from continual public scrutiny. The positive goal emanated from one's *modern* decision to armor himself against such scrutiny with the accumulated "benefits" of industrial production. Social responsibility and social self-preservation were being correlated to an allegedly existential decision that one made to present a mass produced public face. Man, traditionally seen as exemplary of God's perfect product, was now hardly viable in comparison with the man-made products of industrial expertise. The elevation of man's works in the cosmos which had effected the half-way covenant among New England Puritans was now being secularized into the realm of mass social production. It was felt that capitalism through an appeal to instincts—ultimately feelings of social insecurity—could habituate men to consumptive life.[60] Such social production of consumers represented a shift in the social and political priorities of the cosmos, which has most probably characterized much of the "life" of American industrial capitalism. The functional goal of national advertising was the creation of desires and habits. In tune with the need for mass distribution that accompanied the development of mass production capabilities, advertising was trying to produce in readers personal needs which would dependently fluctuate with the expanding marketplace.

Exposing an affirmative vision of capitalist production, Calvin Coolidge reassured the members of the ad industry in 1926 that "rightfully applied, it [advertising] is the method by which the desire is created for better things."[61] The nature of this desire and not, incidentally, the nature of capitalism required an unquestioning attitude towards the uses of production. The use of psychological methods, therefore, attempted to turn the consumer's critical functions away from the product and toward himself. The determining factor for buying was self-critical and ideally ignored the intrinsic worth of the product. The Lynds, in their study of *Middletown,* noted that unlike ads of a generation before, modern advertising was concentrating increasingly upon a type of copy aiming to make the reader emotionally uneasy, to bludgeon him with the fact that decent people don't live the way he does. . . . This copy points an accusing finger at the stenographer as she reads her motion picture magazine and makes her acutely conscious of her unpolished finger nails . . . and sends the housewife peering anxiously into the mirror to see if her wrinkles look like those that made Mrs. X in the advertisement "old at thirty-five" because she did not have a Leisure Hour electric washer.[62]

Advertising hoped to elicit the "instinctual" anxieties of social intercourse. Cutex Hand Preparations translated well-prepared hands as armor for success. Hoping to prepare the psyche for such an argument, they declared in crescendo

You will be amazed to find how many times in one day people glance at your nails. At each glance a judgment is made. . . . Indeed some people make a practice of basing their estimate of a new acquaintance largely upon this one detail.

Even those whose physical appearances were marketably "safe," who appeared to be "the picture of health," were warned of their natural contingencies. Listerine was offered as an agent to militate against "The Hidden Wells of Poison" that lurk and conspire against the "program[s] of pleasure" of even the most beautiful women.

The Lynds saw advertising "and other channels of increased cultural diffusion from without [as] rapidly changing habits of thought as to what things are essential to living and multiplying optional occasions for spending money."[63] The critical analysis offered by the Lynds found unwitting support in predominant advertising theory. It was recognized that in order to get people to consume and, more importantly, to keep them consuming, it was more efficient to endow man with a critical selfconsciousness in tune with the "solutions" of the marketplace, than to fragmentarily argue for products of their own merit. Writing in *Printers' Ink,* Frederick P. Anderson spoke of the industry's conscious attempt to direct man's critical faculties against himself or his environment, "to make him self-conscious about matter of course things such as enlarged nose pores, bad breath. . . ."[64]

In mass advertising, the consciousness of a selling point was precisely the theorized "self-consciousness" of the modern consumer which had occasioned the Lynds' remarks.[65] This consumer self-consciousness was clearly identifiable with the continuous need for product proliferation that increasingly informed mass industry. Linking the theories of "self-consciousness" to the exigencies of capitalism, one writer in *Printers' Ink* commented that "advertising helps to keep the masses dissatisfied with their mode of life, discontented with *ugly things* around them. Satisfied customers are not as profitable as discontented ones."[66]

III

In his sympathetic book on the *History and Development of Advertising,* Frank Presbrey articulated the conception of a predictable, buying, national population in proud and patriotic terms. "To National Advertising," noted Presbrey, "has recently been attributed most of the growth of a national homogeneity in our people, a uniformity of ideas which, despite the mixture of races, is found to be greater here than in European countries whose population is made up almost wholly of people of one race and would seem to be easier to nationalize in all respects."[67] Presbrey's conception of "national homogeneity" was a translucent reference to what Calvin Coolidge saw as "the enormous capacity for consumption of all kinds of commodities which characterizes our country."[68]

The idea that advertising was producing a homogeneous national character was described within the trade as a "civilizing influence comparable in its cultural effects to those of other great epoch-making developments in history."[69] Yet not all of the conceptions of advertising were expressed in such epic and transhistorical terminology. Sensitive to the political and economic context of such notions as "civilizing," "national homogeneity," and "capacity for consumption," William Allen White bridged the gap between "civilization" and civil society, noting that modern advertising was particularly a formation of advanced capitalist production. Aiming his critique at internal and external "revolutionist" threats to capitalism, White turned contemporary conceptions of revolution on their head. Reasserting the efficacy of the American Revolutionary tradition, he argued that advertising men were the true "revolutionists." Juxtaposing the consumer market to revolution of a socialistic variety, White presented a satirical political strategy to halt the "golden quest" for consumer goods. "I would cut out the advertising and fill the editorial and news pages with material supplied by communists and reds. That would stop buying—distribution of things. It would bring an impasse in civilization, which would immediately begin to decay."[70] Identifying ad men with the integrity and survival of the American heritage, White numbered advertising among our sacred cultural institutions.

Through advertising then, consumption took on a clearly cultural tone. Within governmental and business rhetoric, consumption assumed an ideological veil of nationalism and democratic lingo. The mass "American type," which defied unity on the bases of common ethnicity, language, class, or literature, was ostensibly born out of common desires—mass responses to the demands of capitalist production. Mass industry required a corresponding mass man, cryptically named him "Civilized American," and implicated his national heritage in the marketplace. By defining himself and his desires in terms of the good of capitalist production, the worker would implicitly accept the foundations of modern industrial life. By transforming the notion of "class" into "mass," business hoped to create a massified "individual" who could locate his needs and frustrations in terms of the consumption of goods rather than the quality and content of his life (work).

Advertisements aimed at transforming pockets of resistance contained the double purpose of sales and "civilization." Resistance to the universal type appeals to modern advertising was often dealt with in racial or national terms. In an article dealing with immigrant readers of the domestic foreign language press, a writer in *Printers' Ink* noted that these *less American* elements of the population had not yet been sophisticated to the methods of modern advertising. While other Americans were portrayed as responding to appeals to universal instinct, the author noted that "Swedes and Germans . . . study the most minute detail of anything they consider buying."[71] It was felt that a particular form of advertising had to be developed to temporarily accommodate immigrant and other defined resistance to nationalization. While it was suggested that for immediate sales ads could be written offering extensive proof of a product's intrinsic worth, other forms of advertising assumed the task of the "democratization" which Edward Filene had exalted. "Antidote advertising" and other, less theoretical tactics were designed to repudiate antique beliefs which had no place in *the social style* of modern industrial life. Often, such ads were geared to make people ashamed of their origins and, consequently, the habits and practices that betrayed them as alien. The Sherwin Cody School of English advertised that a less than perfect mastery of the language was *just* cause for social ostracism. "If someone you met for the first time made . . . mistakes in English . . . what would you think of him? Would he inspire your respect? Would you be inclined to make a friend of him? Would you care to introduce him to others as a close friend of yours?"[72] Rather than arguing that a knowledge of the language would be helpful in conversation and effective communication, the ad argued that being distinguishable from the fabricated national norm, a part of advertising's mythologized homogeneity, was a justification for social failure.

In an attempt to massify men's consumption in step with the requirements of the productive machinery, advertising increasingly offered mass-produced solutions to "instinctive" strivings, as well as to the ills of mass society itself. If it was industrial capitalism around which crowded cities were being built, and which had spawned much of the danger to health, the frustration, the loneliness and the insecurity of modern industrial life, the advertising of the period denied complicity. Rather, the logic of contemporaneous advertising read: one can free himself from the ills of modern life by embroiling himself in the maintenance of that life. A 1924 ad for Pompeian facial products argued that

unless you are one woman in a thousand, you must use powder and rouge. Modern living has robbed women of much of their natural color . . . taken away the conditions that once gave natural roses in the cheeks.[73]

Within such literature, the term "modern living" was an ahistorical epithet, devoid of the notion "Modern Industrial Society," and rent with visions of the benefits of civilization which had emerged, one would think, quite apart from the social conditions and relations to which these "benefits" therapeutically addressed themselves. On the printed page, modern living was defined as "heated houses, easy transportation, and the conveniences of the household." To the reader it may have meant something considerably different: light-starved housing, industrial pollution, lack of nutrition, boredom. In either sense, modern life offered the same sallow skin and called for a solution through consumption. Within such advertisements, business called for a transformation of the critique of bourgeois society to an implicit commitment to that society.

The reality of modern goods production and distribution called for a dependable mass of consumers. The advertising which attempted to create that mass often did so by playing upon the fears and frustrations evoked by mass society. Within a massifying culture, the ads offered mass-produced visions of individualism by which people could extricate themselves from the mass. While on the level of ideological consciousness, people were being offered commoditized individuality, on the level of the marketplace their acceptance of that individuality meant an entrenchment within the dependable mass of consumers that advertising was attempting to build. The rationale was simple. If a person was unhappy within mass industrial society, advertising was attempting to put that unhappiness to work in the name of that society.

In terms of the self-conscious use of language by advertisers, the idea was to "hitch" concepts and feelings which were familiar to readers and link them to a new and profitable context,[74] the marketplace. In an attempt to boost mass sales of soap, the Cleanliness Institute, a cryptic front group for the soap and glycerine producers' association, pushed soap as a "Kit for Climbers" (social, no doubt). The illustration was a multitudinous mountain of men, each climbing over one another to reach the summit. At the top of this indistinguishable mass stood one figure, his arms outstretched toward the sun, whose rays spelled out the words

"Heart's Desire." The ad cautioned that "in any path of life, that long way to the top is hard enough—so make the going easier with soap and water." In an attempt to build a responsive mass market, the Cleanliness Institute appealed to what they must have known was a major dissatisfaction with the reality of mass life. Their solution was a sort of mass pseudo-demassification.

A good deal of drug and toilet goods advertising made more specific references to the quality of industrial life. Appealing to dissatisfaction and insecurities around the job, certain advertisements not only offered their products as a kind of job insurance, but intimated that through the use of their products one might become a business success, the capitalist notion of individual "self-" fulfillment.

Listerine, whose ads had taken the word "halitosis" out of the inner reaches of the dictionary and placed it on "stage, screen and in the home," offered this anecdote:

He was conscious that something stood between him and greater business success—between him and greater popularity. Some subtle something he couldn't lay his hands on . . . Finally, one day, it dawned on him . . . the truth that his friends had been too delicate to mention.

When a critical understanding of modern production might have helped many to understand what actually stood "between them and greater business success," this ad attempted to focus man's critique against himself—how his body has kept him from happiness. Within the world view of a society which was increasingly divorcing men from any notion of craft, or from any definable sort of product, it was also logical that "you couldn't blame a man for firing an employee with halitosis to hire one without it." The contingency of a man's job was offered a non-violent, apolitical solution. It offered man as the victim of himself, the fruits of mass production as his savior. Ads constantly hammered away at everything that was his own; his bodily functions, his self-esteem, and offered something of theirs as a socially more effective substitute.

In addition to the attempt on the part of advertising to habituate men to buying as a solution to the particular realities of a growing industrial society, ad men presented products as means to what they viewed as instinctual ends. Speaking often to women,[75] ads offered daintiness, beauty, romance, grace, security, and husbands through the use of certain products. Traditional advertising had conceived of these "ideals" as integrants of a Protestant notion of thrift and moderation. The dainty woman, a pillar of sense and temperance within the home, had been characterized as physically divorced from the marketplace not to mention her self. Increasingly, within the texts of ads in the twenties, these desires are fulfilled on the marketplace. Thrift no longer cohabitates with daintiness, but threatens to prevent it. Positing goals such as marriage, romance, social grace, etc., ads begin telling women that through the consumption of their products, those goals could be reached. Within the rhetoric of these ads, the accumulation of various products, each for a separate objectified portion of the body, was equated with the means to success. Correlative to Allport's vision of "social self," advertising offered the next best thing to people who were unhappy or could be convinced that they were unhappy about their lives, a *commodity self;* an appropriate popular, successful conglomeration of mass-produced breath, hair, teeth, skin, and feet. Each portion of the body was to be viewed critically, as a *potential* bauble in a successful assemblage. Woodbury's soap was offered as a perfect treatment for the "newly important face of Smart Today"; another product promised to keep teeth white. "A flashing smile is worth more than a good sized bank account. It wins friends." After she has used Caro Cocoanut Oil Shampoo, a dashing gentleman informs the lady, "I'm crazy about your hair. *It's* the most beautiful of any here tonight." Within the vision offered by such ads, not only was social grace and success attainable, but also defined through the use of specific products. You don't make friends, your commoditized smile "wins" them; your embellished hair, and not you, is beautiful. "Smart today" required one to compete on a social marketplace, though it would be gone tomorrow, yielding its momentary, though cataclysmic, importance to a newly profitable "smart today." As the ads intimated that anything natural about the consumer was worthless or deplorable and tried to make him schizophrenically self-conscious of that notion, they offered weapons by which even people with bad breath, enlarged nose pores, corned feet and other such maladies could eclipse themselves and "succeed."

As notions of failure were to be perceived within a style of self-denigrating paranoia, notions of success were likewise portrayed in purely self-involved terms. Though the victorious heroines of cosmetic advertisements always got their man, they did so out of a commodity defined *self-fetishization* which made that man and themselves almost irrelevant to the quality of their victory. Their romantic triumphs were ultimately commercially defined versions of the auto-erotic ones of Alban Berg's prostitute, *Lulu,* who declares that "When I looked at myself in the mirror I wished I were a man—a man married to me."

During the twenties, civil society was increasingly characterized by mass industrial production. In an attempt to implicate men and women within the efficient process of production, advertising built a vision of culture which bound old notions of "civilization" to the new realities of civil society. In what was viewed as their instinctual search for traditional ideals, people were offered a vision of *civilized man* which was transvaluated in terms of the pecuniary exigencies of society. Within a society that defined real life in terms of the monotonous insecurities of mass production, advertising attempted to create an alternative organization of life, which would serve to channel man's desires for self, for social success, for leisure, away from himself and his works, and toward a commoditized acceptance of "civilization."

NOTES

1. E. P. Thompson, "Time, Work-discipline, and Industrial Capitalism." *Past & Present*, no. 38 (December 1967).

2. Sebastian de Grazia, *Of Time, Work and Leisure* (New York: Doubleday, 1962), p. 211.

3. Walter Benjamin, "The Work of Art in the Age of Mechanical Reproduction," in *Illuminations* (New York: Schocken Books, 1968). This essay originally appeared in the *Zeitschrift fur Sozialforschung* 1 (1936).

4. Alfred Dupont Chandler, *Giant Enterprise* (New York: Harcourt Brace, 1964), p. 29. Chandler is citing the "Federal Trade Commission Report on the Motor Vehicle Industry."

5. Ibid., p. 26.

6. ". . . during a period of eighteen years commencing in 1908, Ford Motor Company manufactured and offered for sale only one basic model of passenger automobile . . . This was the (black) Model T." See Ibid., pp. 27, 37.

7. Harold Loeb, *National Survey of Potential Product Capacity* (New York: Viking Press, 1935), p. 3.

8. This may be seen as a response to a combination of things. Aside from the fact of proliferating mass production methods, the 1921 depression/"buyers' strike" served as an impetus to this study.

9. Edward A Filene, *The Way Out* (Garden City, N.Y.: Doubleday, Page, 1925), p. 93.

10. Chandler, *Giant Enterprise,* p. 143.

11. Notably Alfred P. Sloan of General Motors. Sloan saw productive strategy in broad social terms. His biography, *My Life With General Motors,* gives an account of these early developments.

12. Loeb, *Potential Product Capacity,* p. xv. In regard to "the capacity of the nation to produce goods and services. If full advantage were taken of existing resources, man power, and knowledge . . . every new invention, every improved method, every advance in management technique, will increase the final quantitative estimate." Such a question would be answered by "a running inventory of our approach to perfection rather than a research into existing capacity as determined by production."

The survey considered such a potential too open-ended to effect meaningful speculation.

13. Edward A. Filene, "The Consumer's Dollar," *John Day Pamphlets* 41 (1934): 13.

14. *Printers' Ink* (hereafter, *P.I.*) 124, no. 12, p. 180. As the trade journal for the ad industry dating back into the nineteenth-century, *Printers' Ink* is an invaluable source for any research in this field.

15. Ernest Elmo Calkins, *Business, the Civilizer* (Boston: Little, Brown, 1928), p. 10.

16. Filene "The Consumer's Dollar," p. 29.

17. Filene, *The Way Out*, p. 50.

18. Loren Baritz, *The Servants of Power* (Middletown, Conn: Wesleyan University Press, 1960), p. 15.

19. Whiting Williams, *Mainsprings of Men* (New York: Charles Scribner's Sons, 1923), p. 297.

20. Whiting Williams, *What's on the Worker's Mind* (New York: Charles Scribner's Sons, 1920), p. 317.

21. Filene, *The Way Out*, p. 62–3.

22. Williams, *Mainsprings of Men*, p. 51.

23. Filene, *The Way Out*, p. 127.

24. Ibid., p. 137.

25. Williams, *Mainsprings of Men*, p. 127.

26. By the 1920s, wide-spread elements of the union movement had accepted such an ideology. Among others, William English Walling of the Labor Progressives, dissolved the class struggle in one fell swoop. Almost paraphrasing the ideologues of scientifically planned capitalism, he felt that "to bring labor to the maximum productivity, the American labor movement believes, requires new organization and policies in the administration of industry." Walling, *American Labor and American Democracy* (New York: Harper & Brothers, 1926), p. 233.

Walling spoke of *labor* and *consumer* as interrelated aspects of the total life of the American worker. His concern for consumer rights reflected the ideology of progressive capital no less than did the writings of Edward Filene, who although he had one foot in the 'consumer category,' placed his other on the side of financial power rather than in the monotony of factory life.

27. Norman Ware, *Labor in Modern Industrial Society* (Boston: D. C. Heath, 1935), p. 88.

28. Walling, *American Labor*, p. 212.

29. Ibid.

30. In an attempt to assure that his workers carried on a "moderate" life off the job, Ford developed a *Sociological Department*, staffed by thirty investigators who were "empowered to go into the workers' homes to make sure that no one was drinking too much, that everyone's sex life was without blemish, that leisure time was profitably spent, that no boarders were taken in, that houses were clean and neat." Baritz, *Servants of Power*, p. 33.

31. Ware, *Labor in Modern Industrial Society*, p. 101.

32. Ibid., p. 94.

33. Williams, *What's on the Worker's Mind*, p. 299.

34. Filene, *The Way Out*, p. 202.

35. Ware, *Labor in Modern Industrial Society*, p. 95. According to Ware's studies, union manufacturing labor averaged 40–48 hours per week. Non-union

labor in similar industries averaged 50 hours per week; while labor in more traditional areas, mills, shops, were working 48–60 hours per week.

36. Ibid., pp. 16–17.

37. Robert S. Lynd, "The People as Consumers," in *Recent Social Trends: Report of the President's Research Committee on Social Trends* (1933), I: 862. Such credit buying was initiated primarily in the automobile industry, with the General Motors Acceptance Corporation (GMAC).

38. Walter Dill Scott, *Influencing Men in Business* (1911) rev. ed. enlarged by Delton T. Howard (New York: Ronald Press, 1928), p. 133.

39. Williams, *What's on the Worker's Mind*, p. 317.

40. "In some lines, such as whiskey and milk, distribution cost is from four to ten times the cost of the production." Chandler, *Giant Enterprise*, p. 157.

41. Harry Tipper et al., *Advertising: Its Principles and Practice* (New York: Ronald Press, 1921), pp. 16–18. See also, Alvin Hunsicker "Stabilizing Profits Through Advertising," *P.I.* 124, no. 13, p. 81.

42. Frank Spencer Presbrey, *The History and Development of Advertising* (Garden City, N.Y.: Doubleday, Doran, 1929), p. 620.

43. Calkins, *Business*, p. 236.

44. Presbrey, *History and Development of Advertising*, p. 625.

45. *P.I.* 124, no. 12, p. 180.

46. Ibid. 124, no. 5, p. 152.

47. Baritz, *Servants of Power*, p. 27.

48. Ibid., p. 26.

49. Williams, *Mainsprings of Men*.

50. Floyd Henry Allport, *Social Psychology* (Boston: Houghton Mifflin, 1924), p. 325.

51. Calkins, *Business*, p. 123.

52. Scott, *Influencing Men*, p. 3.

53. Baritz, *Servants* p. 26.

54. Scott, *Influencing Men*, p. 132.

55. Baritz, *Servants*, p. 26.

56. Carl A. Naether, *Advertising to Women* (New York: Prentice-Hall, 1928), p. 97.

57. "When we stop to consider the part which advertising plays in the modern life of production and trade, we see that basically it is that of education . . . it makes new thoughts, new desires and new actions." Presbrey, *History and Development*, p. 620.

58. Scott, *Influencing Men*, p. 43.

59. "Physical or sex attraction . . . other things being equal, qualities which make one pleasing to look at or to caress render their possessor popular to many and loved by not a few." Allport, *Social Psychology*, p. 365.

60. Not incidental to this direct appeal to the consumer's self image, advertisers argued that "heavy expenditures for consumer advertising by a manufacturer . . . (might) induce merchants to favor him with orders." Harold Maynard et al., *Principles of Marketing* (New York: Ronald Press, 1927), p. 439.

61. Presbrey, *History and Development*, p. 622.

62. Robert and Helen Lynd, *Middletown* (New York: Harcourt Brace, 1929), p. 82.

63. Ibid., pp. 81–2.

64. *P.I.* 136, no. 8, p. 130.

65. In "The People as Consumers," Robert Lynd further characterized the advertising of products of mass technology in terms of the questions of "uniformity" and the nature of the modern capitalist market place.

"Technological uniformity and complexity . . . tends to remove further the complex of characteristics blanketed by a brand name from the sorts of empirical comparisons that were more often possible a generation ago. . . . There is a ceaseless quest for what advertising men call 'million dollar ideas' . . . to disguise commodities still further by identifying them with cryptic characteristics." *Recent Social Trends,* I: 876–7.

66. *P.I.* 150, no. 6, p. 163.

67. Presbrey, *History and Development,* p. 613.

68. Ibid., p. 622.

69. Ibid., p. 608.

70. Ibid., p. 610.

71. *P.I.* 140, no. 5, p. 108.

72. See Presbrey, 'Illustrated Appendix,' *History and Development.*

73. The *Ladies Home Journal,* May 1924, p. 161.

74. *P.I.* 133, no. 2, p. 196.

75. Carl Albert Naether noted that "Women buy 80–90 percent of all things in general use in daily life." The breakdown of this generalization specified: 90 percent of the dry goods, 87 percent of the raw and market foods, 67 percent of the automobiles, 48 percent of the drugs, etc. Naether, *Advertising to Women,* p. 4, citing figures from Hollingworth, *Advertising and Selling* (New York: D. Appleton, 1913).

Part Three

The American Dream and the Democratic Mirage: the Facts of Anti-development

The United States is not an "affluent society" in which poverty is only a marginal, "special" problem. Furthermore, by comparison with similar societies, the United States has a poorly developed social welfare system. In fact, some economic and political analysts question whether the United States has a genuine welfare state. There is evidence indicating that it is better described as a sort of *private* welfare state. (See the selections by Thernstrom, Ross, and the Winston-Salem editorialist reprinted below.) Nevertheless, in the United States there is a large, vocal minority that has not reconciled itself to the existence of any kind of welfare state, and advocacy of state intervention is often treated as a "socialist" conspiracy.

The capitalist or business community is not at all agreed upon the corporate liberal approach to social reform and what is called social responsibility. For example, many small businessmen espouse or are attracted to laissez faire economic conceptions. Indeed, there is evidence, alluded to in part 1, that the remnants of an old individualistic liberal tradition persist to inhibit collective economic and political awareness and action among a variety of socioeconomic groups. The essay by T. B. Bottomore provides an important historical overview of the factors retarding the development of a working-class movement with influential ideas of "class interest, and of socialism as an alternative form of society." The cultural distortion (through the hegemonic apparatus) of the perception of social conflict, mobility, and equality continues in part through the persistence of a traditional ideology, whose objective foundations have been largely destroyed.

This cultural or ideological backwardness is a fundamental aspect of what Denis Goulet calls "anti-development." Development, for Goulet, "has three goals: optimum life-sustenance, esteem and freedom." Failing to attain the latter two goals the United States ranks as "possibly the most under-developed society in the world." This is reflected in the widespread inability to raise or formulate basic questions about the quality of life in society, the relation between goods and the good, and human control over change processes. Many people do not have anything approaching a viable, critical perspective on technocorporate society that, by placing their values and goals in a wider context, would permit basic questions to be raised in a politically effective way. Yet they are not able to ignore the social and economic conditions that impinge on their lives and, therefore, have an anxious awareness of the extent to which the American dream is a democratic mirage. But the disquieting facts of antidevelopment (in the area of ecological performance, for example), while they seem to add up to something important, are seldom focused in a general perspective of political significance and action. This also defines what might be regarded as a fundamental failure of the American New Left: the incapacity to establish a theoretically coherent movement for radical change. Young radical activists have publicized the facts of antidevelopment in area after area but have failed to promote critical consciousness of the interrelations of so-called social reform problems.

One of the trends defined in part 2 is clarified further by Goulet's essay. He writes that economic abundance, modern institutions, and technological efficiency are means to the good life: "But in the U.S.A. they have become ends in themselves and genuine ends are treated as means." Thus alternative community values that might suggest a different constitution of the technological/economic order are obscured. By and large, social rationality (the critical reflection on values) has been collapsed into technological rationality (the calculative logic appropriate to choosing among merely technological means). So it has been plausible, as the editor of *Manas* puts it, "for planners to argue that if everybody has a fair share of goods, the subjective need to act in one's own behalf can be satisfied by careful economic planning and equitable manipulation. In this way, the historically typical use men have made of their freedom is assumed to be the freedom itself."[1] Goulet maintains that this obsession with measurable results leads to the glorification of experts "who do things better, faster, or more efficiently than the untrained" (so it is assumed).

This tendency relates to Bruce Johnson's claim, in the last selection, that a *conservative* "fear of democracy," so long a part of the liberal tradition, has become a dominant motif of the "new liberalism." Yet ironically some elements of the new corporate liberalism, which has done so much to stabilize and buttress the dominant socioeconomic system, are widely regarded as a *radical* attack on the very foundations of the system. The extent of bias against the comparatively meager welfare measures for the poor is astonishing in light of the diverse forms of "welfare" for the nonpoor that go unrecognized as such (for example, farm price supports and export subsidies). The Winston-Salem editorial and the selection by Leonard Ross indicate the

1. "The Classical Questions," *Manas* 20 (6 September 1967): 7–8.

mythical nature of the assumption that welfare liberalism has been a great "leveling" force. Ross reveals the meager egalitarian achievements of reform liberalism, while Goulet and Johnson suggest that liberal reform in this century may have done little more than rationalize the basic operations of the mainstream of our culture. American reform liberals fail to see this, perhaps because they have enjoyed a tremendous sense of intellectual and moral superiority in opposing what is, compared to similar societies, an unusually large and culturally backward right wing. They have generally believed Arthur Schlesinger, Jr.'s, assertion that "liberalism in America has been ordinarily the movement on the part of the other sections of society to restrain the power of the business community." As socialist historian James Weinstein says in his attack on this view, "false consciousness of the nature of American liberalism has been one of the most powerful ideological weapons that American capitalism has had in maintaining its hegemony."[2]

Bruce Johnson's article clarifies a major dimension of this false consciousness through the concept of "internal stratification," by which he means a general tendency for the "pluralistic representation of the upper sector of various groupings" to involve simultaneously the neglect (combined with efforts at social control) of their bottom sectors. For example, how much do corporate directors represent small stockholders or labor-union leaders represent rank-and-file workers? Johnson does not deny that this new corporate liberal order has a pluralistic dimension but he does deny that "such decentralization of power as exists in America is a *democratic* phenomenon." This "internal stratification" is not limited to the middle classes, old and new. For example, among farmers there has developed a split between a highly productive elite of big farmers and a much less productive mass of small farmers. The large, commercial farmers, who make up less than 15 percent of the farm population, receive better than 60 percent of farm subsidies. "Labor, a group expected to rise in size and power as industrialization proceeds, has been internally stratified along skill lines." At the same time, the range of decisions by administrative experts has been enlarged at the expense of party politics. The new corporate liberal order has involved the development of an array of elite-based power structures which by various means have acquired control over major areas of public policy. (See, in this regard, the works listed in the bibliography by Theodore Lowi, Grant McConnell, and E. E. Schattschneider.) Thus, it is a pluralistic illusion to believe that the surrender of public authority to a larger number of private hands results in democracy. The American pattern of bureaucratic politics catering to small, narrow constituencies—given great impetus by Franklin Roosevelt's New Deal—represents neither "national planning" nor "participatory democracy." In fact, Bruce Johnson's "new liberalism" may not be as "new" as he seems to think.

---

2. James Weinstein, *The Corporate Ideal in the Liberal State, 1900–1918* (Boston: Beacon Press, 1968), pp. xi–xii.

Johnson's historical analysis of the problem of elitism in American liberal society clarifies further elite strategies and techniques of domination in the contemporary politics of everyday life discussed in the preceding selections. Mainstream politics has historically been chiefly a matter of interelite conflict in which non-elites have alternately tasted a few crumbs or felt the crunch when they seemed to get out of line. Today, non-elites continue to be offered the "American dream" in the rhetoric of equality and symbolic reassurance which, by mobilizing political bias and official violence against radical democratic change, helps assure that they get only the democratic mirage.

T. B. BOTTOMORE

The Persistence of Ideology

It was in the general acceptance of an egalitarian ideology, which still persists in some degree, that the USA differed most remarkably from the European societies in the nineteenth century. In America, there was no established system of feudal ranks, no historical memory of an aristocratic order of society hierarchy. The American war of independence indeed was an important influence upon the European revolutions against the *ancien régime*. In the USA, in contrast with the European countries, the ownership of property was quite widely diffused in the early part of the nineteenth century, and some 80 percent of the working population (excluding the Negro slaves) owned the means of production with which they worked. America was, predominantly, a society of small farmers, small traders, and small businessmen; the closest approach there has been to a "property-owing democracy." Of course, disparities of wealth existed, but they were not so extreme as in Europe, and they did not give rise, except in some of the southern states, to disparities of social rank comparable with those in the still aristocratic and oligarchical European societies. De Tocqueville saw in the USA the prime example of a tendency toward equality in modern societies; a society in which, as he wrote: "Great wealth tends to disappear, the number of small fortunes to increase."

The sense of belonging to a society of equals was enhanced by the possibility of easy movement in the still rudimentary hierarchy of wealth. America was the "land of opportunity," a vast, unexplored, and unexploited country in which it was always possible, or seemed possible, to escape from economic want or subjection by moving to a new place, acquiring land or some other property, and adding to it by personal effort and talent.

A century and a half of economic change has destroyed most of the foundations upon which the egalitarian ideology rested. The society made up of small property-owners and independent producers began to be undermined soon after the Civil War. The 1880s and 1890s, a period in which industry grew rapidly and modern communications were vastly expanded, saw the "closing of the frontier," the emergence of the first industrial and financial trusts, and a considerable growth of inequalities of wealth. Class divisions began to appear more clearly, and to resemble more closely those in the European societies, and they were more openly asserted. The conscious emergence of an upper class was signalled by the establishment of the Social Register (the guide to the new American "aristocracy"), and by the foundation of exclusive boarding schools and country clubs; and wealth and social position came increasingly to be transmitted through family connections. At the same time the working class became more strongly organized in trade unions and political associations, and from the 1890s to the 1930s there were numerous attempts, though without any lasting success, to bring these associations together in a broad socialist movement.

The changes in the economic system can be documented clearly from the statistics of occupations. Early in the nineteenth century 80 percent of the employed white population were independent (self-employed) producers; by 1870 only 41 percent were self-employed, and by 1940 only 18 percent. In the words of C. Wright Mills:

Over the last hundred years, the United States has been transformed from a nation of small capitalists into a nation of hired employees; but the ideology suitable for the nation of small capitalists persists, as if that small-propertied world were still a going concern.[1]

There are several reasons for the persistence of this inapt ideology, apart from the inertia which characterizes social doctrines in general. One is that the concentration of property ownership was not accompanied by any sudden expansion of the working class, or by any decline in the level of living. The industrial workers formed 28 percent of the population in 1870, and 31 percent in 1940; and wage-earners as a whole made up 53 percent of the population in 1870, and 57 percent in 1940. During the same period, however, the proportion of salaried employees in the population increased very rapidly, from 7 percent to 25 percent; and this expansion of the new white-collar middle classes made possible a new kind of social mobility, in place of that which had been achieved earlier by the settlement of fresh lands.

Again, the concentration of wealth and income in a few hands seems never to have proceeded so far in America as in many European countries; and the gilded age of spectacular fortunes in the midst of widespread poverty lasted for a relatively short time. As in other industrial countries, there has been a persistent effort to redistribute wealth and income in the USA through progressive taxation, estate duties, and taxes on capital gains. Since the war, the continued economic expansion, rising levels of living, and the steady growth of the middle classes have had their effect upon the class structure in the same way as in other countries, but in a more conspicuous fashion. And whilst in Britain, for example, such changes have so far produced only modifications and questionings of a class system which is still extremely solid and which profoundly affects political life, in America they have brought instead confirmation of an inherited ideology of "classlessness" and have practically extinguished the tentative class consciousness which found expression in the politics of the 1930s.

This divergence is not to be explained by a higher rate of social mobility in the USA in recent times, nor by a more rapid progress in the redistribution of wealth and income. Several studies have indicated that the USA does not have a rate of mobility significantly higher than that of some other industrial societies, in which class consciousness is nevertheless much more intense.[2] This is the case, at least, when the broad movement from manual to non-manual strata into the elites does seem to be greater in the USA than in most other countries;[3] but even so, it has not been very considerable at any time during the present century. William Miller has shown that even in the first decade of the century successful businessmen had not generally risen from the lower strata of society, but had come for the most part from old established families in the business and professional strata.[4] Similarly, a very thorough study of social classes in Philadelphia has revealed that the leading positions in the economic system are occupied predominantly by individuals from the established upper-class families.[5]

The idea that a steady reduction of income inequalities has been proceeding during the present century is strongly contested, just as a similar view is contested in Britain. In the case of the USA the contention rests largely upon the statistical studies of national income by Simon Kuznets;[6] but as Gabriel Kolko has recently pointed out,[7] the relevant part of these studies deals only with the wealthiest 5 percent of the population, and does not examine the changes which have taken place in the income of the other groups in the population. Kolko's own calculations, based upon studies of personal incomes before taxation by the National Industrial Conference Board (for 1910–1937) and by the Survey Research Center (for 1941–1959) indicate that between 1910 and 1959 the share in national income of the top income-tenths declined only slightly (and has fluctuated around 30 percent in the past decade), while the shares of the second and third income-tenths actually increased and the shares of the two poorest income-tenths declined sharply (from 8.3 percent of national income to only 4 percent). Kolko also observes, as Tit-

muss has done in his study of the same question in Britain, that calculations based upon declarations of pretax income necessarily leave out of
account various forms of real income which benefit mainly the upper
class and thus increase inequality.

It may be argued, then, that it is the traditional conception of
American society as highly mobile rather than any exceptional degree of
mobility at the present time, and the general increase in prosperity
(though with a good deal of partially concealed poverty)[8] rather than any
strong movement towards greater economic equality, which play the
main part in weakening class consciousness. But there have also been
other factors at work, especially in inhibiting the development of a
working class movement in which the ideas of class interest, and of socialism as an alternative form of society, would have a major influence.
Among these factors, the situation of the Negroes and the successive
waves of immigration are particularly important. The Negroes have
formed a distinctive American proletariat, with the lowest incomes, the
most menial and subservient tasks, and the lowest social prestige (in part
because of their slave origins) of any group in American society. The existence of this large, relatively homogeneous, easily identifiable, and exploited group has meant that every white American, even the lowest paid
laborer, possesses a certain social prestige which raises him, at least in his
own view, above the level of a proletarian. Immigration has worked in the
same way to raise the social position of the ordinary American worker,
since many groups of immigrants (the latest being the Puerto Ricans)
entered the lowest levels of the occupational hierarchy, and made it
possible for those already established to advance themselves. But neither
the Negroes, nor any immigrant group, have formed a proletariat in the
sense that they have challenged the established order of society. And so,
although the present vigorous struggle of the Negroes to gain full economic, civil, and political rights may be likened to early class conflicts in
Europe so far as these were concerned with the right to vote, with labor
legislation, and with social reform, it differs entirely from these conflicts
insofar as it aims exclusively at winning acceptance in the existing society
and accepts the predominant values of the society. The success of the
struggles waged by Negroes and other ethnic minorities, however, would
diminish the importance of ethnic divisions in American society, and one
result might be the appearance of more sharply differentiated social
classes and a greater awareness of class interests.

NOTES

1. C. Wright Mills, *White Collar: The American Middle Classes* (New
York: Oxford University Press, 1951), p. 34.

2. See especially, Seymour Martin Lipset and Reinhard Bendix, *Social Mobility in Industrial Society* (Berkeley: University of California Press, 1959).

3. S. M. Miller, "Comparative Social Mobility," *Current Sociology* 9, no. 1 (1960): 58.

4. "American Historians and the Business Elite," in William Miller, ed., *Men in Business,* new ed. (New York: Harper & Row. 1962).

5. E. Digby Baltzell, *An American Business Aristocracy,* new ed. (New York: Collier Books, 1962).

6. See especially his *Shares of Upper Income Groups in Income and Savings* (Princeton, N.J.: National Bureau of Economic Research, 1952).

7. Gabriel Kolko, *Wealth and Power in America,* rev. ed. (New York: Frederick A. Praeger, 1964).

8. See, on the extent of poverty, Gunnar Myrdal, *Challenge to Affluence* (New York: Pantheon Books, 1963), chap. 4, and Michael Harrington, *The Other America* (New York: Penguin Books, 1962). The latter book makes plain that poverty is widespread, but as in Britain it is concentrated in particular sections of the population—here among the old, ethnic minorities, and workers in such regions as the Appalachians—and so often tends to go unrecognized.

WINSTON-SALEM *SUNDAY JOURNAL AND SENTINEL*

Who's On Welfare?

Two basic problems face the Nixon administration in its efforts to reform public welfare: The sheer cost and difficulty of overhauling such a complicated apparatus as the welfare system, and the reluctance of Congress to accept sweeping changes in the system. Traditionally, Congress has preferred to nibble at problems rather than cure them. It doesn't like being confronted, as it may be in this case, with an entirely new method of doing things.

But whatever Mr. Nixon proposes in the way of reforms, he will have to deal with a third problem as well: The problem of public hostility toward the whole process of giving unemployed or helpless people a fixed amount of cash each month. Americans are not a callous lot. They are willing to see public money used to feed and house poor people. But their sufferance grows short. Welfare costs and welfare scandals are increasing all across the country, and patience with the system as well as the recipients is wearing thin.

This attitude is understandable. In a nation that places supreme im-

Source: Winston-Salem, North Carolina, *Sunday Journal and Sentinel,* 16 March 1969. Reprinted by permission.

portance on work and achievement, those who neither work nor achieve are viewed, at best, with sympathetic contempt. "The public trough" is what we customarily call the welfare system—a "dole" system taking care of the needy as well as many who are just plain lazy.

But the truth of the matter is hidden much deeper than this attitude goes. For the truth is that we are a welfare nation—period. Not just poor people, not just the lame and the halt, the helpless and the unemployed, but most of us, in some measure and to some degree, enjoy the fruits of public welfare. We are a people who seem to believe that every man is entitled to his share of the public dole—every man, that is, but the poor man. And it is at this point that we begin indulging in a bit of hypocrisy.

Farmers, for example, are paid quite a bit more public welfare money, per capita, than most poor people on the welfare rolls. Some farmers are paid *not* to grow certain crops; others are paid to grow *only* certain crops. Price supports guarantee a minimal profit for the farmer—and at least a dozen other programs in the Department of Agriculture are there to make sure he is taken care of. If the farmer happens to be rich, he receives even more welfare money than the poor farmer. This might seem strange, at first glance, but it makes a kind of peculiarly American sense when you think about it.

We see this subsidy system as a way of restoring a proper and equitable economic balance among growers, distributors, and consumers. But it is actually a system of relief. It is a way of giving the farmer something to live on in exchange for limited activity—in many cases, no activity at all—on his part.

Should we then call the farmer a "lazy, good-for-nothing bum"?

A more complicated form of indirect welfare is the money the federal government loses on middle-class housing. The tax codes allow deductions for interest paid on home mortgages and deduction of property taxes, as well as accelerated depreciation schedules for owners of apartment buildings.

Last year, according to a housing report issued by the Johnson administration, these special subsidies for the middle class cost the government $3.7 billion. During the same period, by contrast, only $1.08 billion was spent on public housing for low-income families.

And what about the transportation industry—the public subsidies given aircraft companies and American-flag vessels, the vast reserves of public land that have been given to the railroads? What about the extensive use of our public roads by the trucking companies? Highway maintenance is an expensive undertaking; and no trucking firm is ever able to reimburse state and federal governments to the extent of road damage caused by loaded trucks.

What about manufacturing companies engaged in defense work?

There are many companies absolutely dependent on defense contracts; in a free market place, they wouldn't survive at all. Moreover, they produce nothing of any real social or lasting economic value through this defense work—even though they absorb a great deal more public money than our social welfare programs.

And yet they are reputable, respected, and altogether acceptable companies in the public's eye, even though they feed heaviest of all at the public trough.

What about the veteran, with his free treatment in government hospitals for so-called service-connected disabilities, his GI Bill, his subsidized insurance policy, his pension. Does this country—does any country—really owe veterans something special for defending it? Americans think so and we prove it by giving the veteran a full range of subsidies and grants for his welfare.

What about the stockholder who takes advantage of loopholes in our tax laws or those with large incomes who pay no taxes at all? Are they bums? Varmints? Worthless welfare recipients? Well, they certainly aren't worthless, but they are welfare recipients—as much a part of the public dole as the poorest family man in East Winston.

What about special tax write-offs for industry? What about the mineral depletion allowances? What, really is the difference between reimbursing an oil man for a well that *might* go dry sometime in the future and reimbursing a poor man because he can't find a job? The difference, we would suggest, is in the mind.

Certainly, there are many things wrong with the public welfare system. Too many able-bodied men are on the rolls; and the provisions for dependent children have never adequately solved the problem of illegitimacy.

But just as much is wrong with our more respectable dole systems—our loophole-ridden tax codes, our welfare subsidies to individuals and corporations, our welfare support of the transportation industry and the sick Merchant Marine and the airlines and the railroads and the stockholders and the oil men.

All of these welfare systems are in need of reform. But it is the poor man's system that needs it most urgently. He is the man we must reach—or, if not him, then his children. And this can't be done so long as the public and the Congress continue to think of the problem as something unique in American society. As Prof. Charles Reich of Harvard puts it: "There is a law for the poor and a law for the rest of us. Receipt of government aid by the poor carries a stigma, whereas receipt of government aid by the rest of the economy has been made into a virtue."

It may be time, then, to end hypocrisy, to begin thinking of the public welfare system as a program that must be put right and made to serve the interests of the recipients, not the prejudices of non-recipients or the vagaries of a bureaucracy.

This system may well be a dismal weight around the taxpayers' neck, but so, for that matter, is the Department of Defense *and* the individual who earns his income through stocks *and* the farmer who is paid to plant and not to plant *and* the trucking company that devastates our highways *and* the broadcaster who uses the public channels for his own profitable business *and* the companies that use special mailing privileges for their merchandise *and* the veteran who may have spent his tenure of duty driving a six-by-six truck at Ft. Jackson, S.C.—but who shares the veterans' gravy train with combat veterans—*and* the scientist or scholar who gets a free research ride.

All of these Americans, to one degree or another, feed at the public trough—not just the poor man or the crippled man.

For it is, after all, a mighty big trough; and if we start looking around at the customers there, we might begin to see the problem in a different light.

LEONARD ROSS

The Myth That Things Are Getting Better

Rich Man, Poor Man
by Herman P. Miller.
Crowell, 305 pp.,
$8.95; $3.95 (paper)

Two myths about the distribution of income comforted liberals during the 1950s. They believed that incomes were becoming steadily more equal, and that government spending programs uniformly accelerated that trend. Frederick Lewis Allen spoke for a self-satisfied New Deal generation when he said that "we had brought about a virtually automatic redistribution of income from the well-to-do to the less well-to-do"[1] through the mechanism of the welfare state.

As the fifties ended the first myth began to give way to evidence. Income distribution, it appeared, had barely changed since the war. The changes that did occur were at the expense of the poorest as well as the

Source: Excerpt from Leonard Ross, "The Myth That Things Are Getting Better," *New York Review of Books* 17 (August 12, 1971): 7–9. Reprinted with permission from *The New York Review of Books.* Copyright © 1971 The New York Review, Inc.

richest parts of the population, yielding a slight bulge around the middle classes. In 1947, the poorest 20 percent of the nation's families shared only 5.1 percent of the nation's income; by 1960, they had to make do with 4.9 percent.[2] Between 1947 and 1960, the percentage of families earning less than one-half the median income—a good relative measure of poverty—increased from 18.9 percent to 20.3 percent.[3]

As liberals began to acknowledge the persistence of inequality in the private economy, they redoubled their faith in spending by "the public sector." John Kenneth Galbraith's 1958 book, *The Affluent Society,* summed up the postwar liberal strategy. Galbraith argued that inequality could not be attacked directly through a stiffer income tax. Most Americans, he observed, were too prosperous to care very much about soaking the rich. Thus equality had faded as a political issue. It could be approached only indirectly, through a general expansion of public spending. The poor, Galbraith argued, "would be among the first beneficiaries of [government spending on] education, health, housing and other services. . . ." Admittedly, an enlarged public sector would support itself in major part through regressive taxation, for example by hiking sales taxes. But that was no objection:

> It will be argued that some people are still very poor. The sales tax, unlike the income tax, weighs heavily on the small consumption of such individuals. But if the income tax is unavailable or in service to other ends, the only alternative is to sacrifice social balance [between public and private spending]. . . . The modern liberal rallies to protect the poor from the taxes which, in the next generation, would help eliminate poverty.[4]

Galbraith's ideology made virtuous what liberal politicians had already found necessary: a program which did not rely principally on the defunct Roosevelt coalition based on labor and the ethnic minorities. The defeat of national health insurance and the emasculation of public housing had by 1952 ended hope for a second New Deal. Liberals could succeed only with new measures and new partners. Within a few years the transition was accomplished. Labor and the academic liberals joined with downtown business interests in sponsoring urban renewal; with auto manufacturers and highway contractors in supporting vast road projects; with suburban legislators in promoting state-supported higher education.

But the result was not a redistribution of income. Galbraith had assumed that a basically middle-class electorate could be hoodwinked into supporting a measure of equality through public spending that it would never endorse directly. If anything, the outcome was the reverse. The new public programs built homes and roads for the middle class, provided college education for the upper middle class, and lavished private aviation facilities on the rich. The poor were placed at the wrong end of a bulldozer. Only in the mid-sixties, with the proclamation of the War on Poverty, was any new measure of redistribution even attempted. But its scope has been minor and, in significant part, rescinded. In the meantime, regressive sales and social security taxes have been growing; the income tax during the fifties was "progressive"–i.e., it imposed larger proportionate burdens as income rose—only to a minute degree, and this has now been largely eroded.[5]

Precise statistics have become available on only some of these questions. They confirm the durability of inequality in the private economy and the primarily passive role of the public sector, except for compulsory education and subsistence welfare for the very poor. H. P. Miller's book, *Rich Man, Poor Man,* shows that the distribution of income among classes was even less mobile from 1957 to 1968 than in the previous decade. There was a shift along racial lines—the relative income of non-whites increased from 51 percent of the white median in 1958 to 63 percent in 1968. But much of this change was due to black migration from the low-wage South and from rural to urban areas, not to waning discrimination or better education. The real gains from such higher income in wretched city ghettos is debatable to say the least. A more detailed study by J. Gwartney has found, moreover, that, within particular regions, non-white males have made *no* relative progress during the entire 1947 to 1969 period, although there were substantial gains for non-white females.[6]

Gwartney shows that changes in relative education have actually worked *against* non-whites since World War II. The jobs requiring the most education show the greatest racial disparities in income; thus, as both races become better educated, the comparative situation of blacks tends to deteriorate. This effect has been offset somewhat by faster educational progress for non-whites. But even if blacks were suddenly to receive the same amount of schooling as whites, gross income differentials would persist. H. P. Miller quotes 1960 census figures showing that "the average non-white with four years of college could expect to earn less over a lifetime than the white who did not get beyond the eighth grade."

Taxes have hardly any effect on the relative distribution of income. The progressive rates of the income tax are offset by well-known loopholes, more respectable but equally regressive benefits (e.g., the deductibility of mortgage payments), and regressive social security taxes. The over-all burden of federal taxes is roughly proportional to income for all but the affluent.[7] State and local taxes are sharply regressive for the very poor and roughly proportional for everyone else.[8] The net impact is a small gain for the middle classes at the expense of the extremes.

The tax system is not, and has never been, a vehicle for significant redistribution.

Government spending does accomplish some redistribution, though in a far more limited way than liberals have imagined. The basic distinction is between straight payments which transfer money directly from the government—such as welfare and social security—and government programs designed to provide specific goods and services, such as schools, housing, and transportation. Transfer payments are indispensable aids for the very poor—families earning under $2,000 a year in 1965 received more from government transfers than from all other sources. But transfers barely affect the distribution of income for the highest-earning 85 percent of the population. . . . .

NOTES

1. Frederick Lewis Allen, *The Big Change* (New York: Harper & Brothers, 1952), p. 286.

2. S. M. Miller and Pamela Roby, *The Future of Inequality* (New York: Basic Books, 1970), p. 38.

3. Ibid., p. 36.

4. John Kenneth Galbraith, *The Affluent Society* (Boston: Houghton Mifflin, 1958), pp. 245, 247.

5. See Joseph Pechman, "The Rich, the Poor and the Taxes They Pay," *The Public Interest,* November 1969, p. 27.

6. J. Gwartney, "Changes in the Non-white/White Income Ratio, 1939–67," *American Economic Review* 60 (December 1970): 872.

7. Pechman, "The Rich, the Poor," p. 32.

8. Ibid., p. 33.

STEPHAN THERNSTROM

The Myth of American Affluence

In 1958 John Kenneth Galbraith, as his publishers tell us, "added a new phrase to our language" by declaring that ours was an "affluent society." Median family income in the United States then was less than $4,000 per year. Soon after, the Eisenhower recession gave way to the Kennedy and Johnson boom, eight years which comprised the most dramatic and sus-

Source: Commentary 48 (October 1969): 74–78. Reprinted from *Commentary,* by permission; Copyright © 1969 by the American Jewish Committee.

tained economic spurt in the country's history. A newly-revised edition of *The Affluent Society* has recently appeared, at a time when the annual earnings of the average American family have almost reached the $8,000 mark. After taking inflation into account and putting the figures into constant dollars, we find that the real income of the ordinary citizen has risen fully 85 percent in little more than a decade. If we were affluent in 1958, by now we must be Rockefellers all.

But how many Americans *feel* so very affluent? Why have what Galbraith dismissed as "the obsolete and contrived preoccupations associated with the assumption of poverty" not vanished altogether in a world "where the ordinary individual has access to amenities—foods, entertainment, personal transportation, and plumbing—in which not even the rich rejoiced a century ago"? If *The Affluent Society* "has changed the basic economic attitudes of our age," as the ad-men would have it, has it changed them for the better? I think not. The myth of American affluence has become the new conventional wisdom, and it constitutes a formidable obstacle to understanding our present condition.

Let it be said immediately that my concern here is not with Galbraith's analysis per se, but rather with the implications of the concept of affluence to which he gave currency. Ideas filter into the public consciousness in strange and distorted ways, and the element of distortion in the filtration process may have been particularly large in the case of *The Affluent Society*. What seemed to be the central point of the book was a sound one—that there was an appalling lack of "social balance" in the American economy, a glaring and indefensible disparity between the opulence of the private sector and the starvation level at which the public sector was forced to operate. Ours is a society in which "automobiles have an importance greater than the roads on which they are driven. We welcome expansion of telephone services as improving the general well-being but accept curtailment of postal services as signifying necessary economy. We set great store by the increase in private wealth but regret the added outlays for the police force by which it is protected. Vacuum cleaners to insure clean houses are praiseworthy and essential in our standard of living. Street cleaners to insure clean streets are an unfortunate expense. . . . Alcohol, comic books, and mouthwash all bask under the superior reputation of the market"; not so schools, judges, and municipal swimming pools.

This imbalance, Galbraith noted, worked to the special disadvantage of people in the lower income brackets, who were least able to afford substitutes for public services in the private market. America should make a determined effort to right the balance and to deal with the social needs the private market left unmet, an effort mindful of the fact that contemporary poverty was a structural problem which would not disappear with the application of traditional Keynesian remedies designed to maximize employment and output.

Something was very much wrong with American economic and social arrangements; a major new effort to intervene in the private economy to promote social justice was essential: such seemed to be the policy conclusions that were to be drawn from *The Affluent Society*. Thus it was that Galbraith's book came to be paired with Michael Harrington's *The Other America* as an influence which alerted President Kennedy to the problems of the poor and led him to initiate the planning that culminated in the Economic Opportunity Act of 1964.

If the overt message of *The Affluent Society* was reformist, however, the real thrust of the book seemed to be at odds with the policy conclusions. What was most original and influential about Galbraith's work was his emphasis upon the remarkable material prosperity of the ordinary American citizen. The myth of American affluence which Galbraith helped to create mirrored the dominant political and social tendencies of the Age of Eisenhower. Whatever the author's intent, the book directed attention away from the economic deprivation which was still commonplace in the United States and provided the well-to-do with an intellectually respectable vantage point from which to criticize the materialistic strivings of the vulgar masses rather than the American social order itself. In recent years the mythology has undergone significant modification, with the rediscovery of poverty and the deepening racial crisis. Yet the assumption of affluence dies hard. It continues to influence popular perceptions of the nature of our society, and impedes the formation of political alignments which might bring about constructive social change.

In its original, pristine version, vintage 1950s, the myth of affluence held quite simply that poverty was no longer to be found in the United States. Some people had more money than others, to be sure, but even those with least of all were not too badly off. It was thought that the New Deal, supplemented by some mopping-up Fair Deal measures, had quite adequately taken care of the "one third of a nation" whose misery had attracted attention in the depression years. Presumably there had been a fundamental, some said revolutionary, shift toward greater equality of income distribution; presumably there was now a smoothly-functioning network of social services available to all as a matter of right. And there was new confidence in the productive potential of the private economy, ardent discussions of the wonders of "people's capitalism" and "the 20th-century capitalist revolution."

That Republican speechwriters believed all this is not surprising. But the mood was far more widespread. Symptomatic was Arthur Schlesinger, Jr.'s announcement that the successes of the Roosevelt and Truman years had been so complete as to render outmoded "quantitative liberalism," a liberalism concerned with such grubby, old-fashioned, and easily-measured matters as wage rates, unemployment levels, and the number of substandard housing units. With all these issues nicely resolved already, the task of liberalism was to turn to Higher Things, and to advance programs aimed at improving the quality of American Life.

The Affluent Society bears the marks of this cultural climate, and indeed was a prime source of the new perspective. This despite the later effect the book is supposed to have had in opening John Kennedy's eyes to the existence of poverty (the authority who notes this influence, incidentally, is none other than Arthur Schlesinger, Jr., who discovered through the experience of the 1960s that "quantitative liberalism" was not so outmoded after all), and despite Galbraith's efforts in the new edition to make his discussion of poverty seem a good deal more prescient than in fact it was.

What is striking about the treatment of poverty in the 1958 edition of the book is how belatedly it came—in the twenty-third chapter—and how minor a problem Galbraith thought it to be. In so affluent a society, he remarked casually, poverty was not "a universal or massive affliction," but "more nearly an afterthought." Only one American family in thirteen had annual incomes of less than a thousand dollars, which he apparently deemed a reasonable boundary between poverty and affluence. Economic deprivation was not widespread, but instead was confined to two special categories of persons. There was "case poverty," which could be attributed to some quality peculiar to the individual or family involved—mental deficiency, bad health, excessive procreation, etc.—and there was "insular poverty," afflicting large groups of people inhabiting an especially unfavorable environment, such as the urban slum or the declining rural area. Galbraith did express concern over the unfortunate plight of this small minority of low-income families, and he noted that *general* advances in the Gross National Product would do very little to ameliorate structural poverty of this type. But it is doubtful indeed that this brief discussion, which assumed that only the 8 percent of families with incomes below the $1,000 line were poor, and emphasized the special characteristics of those unhappy few, could have shocked any of the book's readers into new awareness of the shame of continued poverty in the midst of affluence.

Whether or not poverty in America as of 1958 was a mere "afterthought," Galbraith's consideration of the matter certainly seemed an afterthought. It would not be unfair, though perhaps unkind, to say that Galbraith and those who read him approvingly were far more distressed by the vulgar barbecue pits, television sets, and tailfins of the vast majority than by the sufferings of what they took to be a tiny minority. Conspicuous consumption, not economic deprivation, was the real villain. This was an affluent society, and Galbraith defined an affluent society as one in which the productive machinery churned out such vast quantities of goods that there was an enormous surplus left over after the "real" needs of its members were satisfied. New needs, "artificial" needs, thus had to be created to absorb the surplus: "many of the desires of the individual are no longer even evident to him" until they are "synthesized, elaborated, and nurtured by advertising and salesmanship."

Obviously there is some truth in this. The economic "needs" of Americans today and of the aborigines of New Guinea differ in kind, clearly, and it could be said that those of the latter are more "natural" (though primitive peoples too have their conspicuous consumption). All our economic desires are culturally conditioned, and deliberate attempts to shape and manipulate them through the media doubtless have their effect.

But it is not very illuminating, I think, to judge the behavior of American consumers against a standard derived from an image of man in a state of nature. It can provide a base for a lively and witty polemic, as was the case with Galbraith and his great predecessor, Thorstein Veblen, but a polemic which too easily can be converted to snobbish and self-serving ends, as happened with the myth of affluence. Galbraith's root conception—that the bulk of consumer desires in an advanced industrial society are socially created—derives squarely from Veblen, though in his brief discussion of Veblen, Galbraith curiously fails to note the influence.

Veblen was a genuine Puritan, whose profound distaste for the American way of spending stemmed from the mores of the strict Minnesota Norwegian subsistence farming community in which he was raised. And Galbraith, too, is something of an ascetic, perhaps because he too was a farm boy (unlikely though that seems today), and comes from another strict ethnic minority, the Canadian Scotch. Both men imbibed a stern ethical code with their mother's milk, and cast a cold eye on the gross, corpulent, consumer society in which they found themselves. Americans have too much, Americans have it too easy: these were the moral premises which underlay their pungent critiques. I find their conception of the good life rather too Spartan for my tastes, and believe that the validity of their economic analyses depends upon the validity of those moral premises. Still, Veblen and Galbraith came by their views honestly and adhered to them consistently.

What is troubling is the way in which Galbraith's attack upon the affluent society was picked up by those who did not have a similarly consistent moral position. The myth of American affluence became a weapon with which people who had attained a considerable measure of wealth expressed their scorn for those who had less and spent it vulgarly. Asceticism is one thing; asceticism *for others* something else. The notion that the ordinary American had more than enough income to meet his "real" needs but was being brainwashed by Madison Avenue to believe he needed costly and ugly inessentials—a mauve and cerise air-conditioned, power-steered, and power-braked automobile was Galbraith's example— became an article of faith in cultivated circles in the Age of Eisenhower. Often the loudest complaints against tailfins were voiced by people whose own Spartan mode of transportation was a Porsche. It was somewhat less anomalous to hear this from a VW owner, but not much less when he commonly took three-month rather than three-week vacations, and used what he saved on the VW to indulge in a sailboat or estate-bottled wine. I prefer VW's and sailboats myself (though I would like a Porsche even more), but I find it hard to view the choice as evidence of my moral superiority.

When *The Affluent Society* was first published there were very few Americans who lived in truly Asiatic poverty, crammed eight or ten to a room in houses without clean water and modern plumbing, subsisting on rice or potatoes, with infant mortality rates of 400-500 per 1,000 and a life expectancy of twenty years or so. Poverty in the absolute subsistence sense was virtually, though not entirely, obliterated; the "real" needs of even the poorest were being satisfied. But the distinction between "real" and "artificial" needs was irrelevant and unreal. In 1958, 60 percent of all families and unrelated individuals in the United States earned less than $6,000, and more than a third took in less than $4,000. The top 20 percent of income earners, meanwhile, were raking in nearly half of the total, with 20 percent of it going to the richest 5 percent. The needs of the bottom 60 percent were surely as "real" as the needs of those on the top, a good deal more real in the sense that the people on the bottom had a far harder time making ends meet. The myth of affluence encouraged the complacent illusion that poverty had been eliminated and that unequal distribution of income was no longer a problem. The problem was rather that the masses were lusting after the bread and circuses devised by the ad-men. Few of those who mouthed the clichés about American affluence felt *themselves* to be blessed with excessive income. The assumption was that others were not sufficiently spiritual to make proper use of their undue affluence.

The 50s now seem far behind us, their social thought about as remote from our present concerns as that of the Jazz Age. Nothing is heard any longer about the need to substitute "qualitative" for "quantitative" liberalism, and poverty is the subject of endless discussion (if not much action). *The Affluent Society,* in its current incarnation, has smoothly adjusted to the changed intellectual climate. The reference in the 1958 edition to poverty as an afterthought in a country "with a weekly industrial wage of eighty dollars and a $3,960 median family income," has been deleted. The 1969 edition declares that in a country "with a weekly industrial wage of $110 and a $7,974 median family income, [poverty] can no longer be presented as a universal or massive affliction." Industrial wages have risen nearly 40 percent and median family income doubled (with prices up only 16 percent). Nevertheless poverty seems to have become more an obsession than an afterthought. Alice and the Red Queen would appreciate the logic of this.

The change is for the better, despite my mocking reference to Alice, for in dealing with poverty in a society like ours it is necessary to run very fast merely to stand still. Galbraith, and Americans generally, have slowly come to realize that in an advanced industrial society poverty is a *relative,* not an absolute, matter. A family earning $2,900 a year, a little below the current poverty line established by the federal government, would have been quite well-off by the standards of 1900, even after adjustments to take into account the lower price level. Even in 1929 they would have been fairly prosperous; well over half of the population earned under $3,000 (in 1962 dollars) then. But this is no consolation at all, for their needs have been shaped in this society today. There is no divinely-ordained standard of adequacy for housing, diet, medical care, education, entertainment, etc. What feels adequate is inescapably dependent upon what is available to others in the society.

There is no better evidence of this than the long series of efforts, dating back to the late 19th century in the United States, to establish coldly objective minimum subsistence budgets for families. Numerous attempts were made to specify an absolute minimum figure necessary for the satisfaction of "real" needs, uncontaminated by changing societal assumptions about what was possible. Had these attempts succeeded, they would necessarily have revealed steady progress toward the elimination of poverty, given the dramatic growth of the Gross National Product over time and the absence of increased inequality in income distribution. But they disclosed nothing of the sort, for the estimates of the absolute minimum income required for bare subsistence crept steadily upward, in close correspondence with the rising GNP. Indeed, there was a striking tendency for the minimum subsistence figure at any point to approximate closely one half of the median family income.

Yet if a new awareness of the economic plight of the bottom quarter or so of the income distribution pyramid has developed in recent years— the notion that virtually all Americans are affluent enough to satisfy their "real" needs with plenty left over for foolish luxuries is heard no more—

an element of the myth of affluence is still very much with us. This is the myth of the affluent worker and the trade-union Establishment. For the assumption of the 50s that the ordinary citizen was prosperous, indeed too prosperous for his own good, we have substituted a view that is little more sophisticated. There are the very poor, the underclass (erroneously thought to be composed mainly of blacks), and there are the affluent, the latter including even the most menial white-collar employees and organized blue-collar workers. Some of the affluent—upper-middle-class liberals—understand that it is the duty of the rich to help the poor, and are happy to do so, especially when it can be accomplished by measures which, like "community control," have no effect on the rich themselves. The organized working class, however, and the lumpen-bourgeoisie remain stubbornly oblivious of their duty and selfishly attached to their privileges—the new Mustang, the two-family dwelling in Queens. They "indulge themselves" in annoying and unnecessary strikes, and display an unaccountable responsiveness to the Mario Procaccinos, even the George Wallaces, abroad in the land. These presumably are people without serious economic problems, but they lack the grace to behave with the political highmindedness appropriate to their station.

It is not my purpose, I need hardly say, to defend the choice of a Procaccino, a Louise Day Hicks, a George Wallace. But it is very important to understand why their supporters feel as they do—an understanding which the trade-union baiting so fashionable in some quarters today makes very difficult. The concept of relative deprivation cannot be introduced to demonstrate the poverty of those earning less than $3,000 and then dropped in favor of an absolute standard when considering the position of people a rung or two higher up the economic ladder, so that the carpenter or factory worker supporting a famiiy of five on $6,000 or $7,000 a year is suddenly seen as an established fat cat with more money than he knows what to do with. It is common in upper-middle-class circles to bemoan the outrageous wages commanded by skilled workers, so much so that the plumber problem has become the servant problem of our time. But the median earnings of skilled craftsmen employed full-time in the United States in 1966, the most recent year for which data are available, were only $6,981, a princely income only to those who have never attempted to live on it. It is hardly surprising that people scraping by on the wages provided by most unionized blue-collar or menial white-collar jobs feel embittered when they encounter the assumption that poverty shades into comfortable affluence at the $3,000 or $4,000 line, or the equally common belief that economic deprivation in this society is confined largely to Negroes. Nor is it surprising that many are fearful, rigidly defensive, and punitive about the blacks who seem to threaten them, with the support of upper-middle-class liberals.

There may indeed be genuine conflicts of interest between the underclass, and the middle mass of organized workers and lower white-collar employees. The racism of many of the craft unions, for example, stems from a scarcity psychology which has been confirmed by cruel experience. It will take more than the radical's wishful thinking about a coalition of progressive forces to bring such an alignment into existence, and I have no magical new formula to unveil here. But I would insist on both moral and political grounds that intellectuals on the Left must broaden their concern, to embrace not only the very poor but those who, through painful struggle, have inched a short rung or two up the slippery ladder of success. If the upper working class and lower middle class conceive of themselves as "forgotten men," and ally themselves with Nixon or worse, it is hard to see where the political muscle necessary for constructive social change can come from.

The fundamental domestic problem of American society is inequality, inequality in wealth, political power, and social privilege, and more than an underclass of 20 or 25 percent of the population suffers from that inequality. Future efforts to eliminate poverty, if they are to be morally sound and politically viable, must be part of a larger effort to eliminate the major sources of inequality in our affluent, stratified society.

DENIS A. GOULET

The United States: A Case of Anti-Development

Americans enjoy the greatest prosperity ever known to man. Understandably, therefore, they consider the United States to be the world's most developed country. By contrast, underdevelopment conjures a vision of starving millions in India, frightful slums in Rio, a life expectancy of thirty-four years in rural Africa. More than half of mankind are chronically poor and diseased, their chances for improvement slim because a brutalizing culture of poverty mires them in ignorance and inertia. Ordinary men and experts alike view development as a crucible through which all societies must pass. If successful, they will emerge purified: modern, affluent, and efficient.

Social critics acknowledge the existence of poverty areas in our land, and disadvantaged minorities excluded from the mainstream of affluence. But these are seen as minor flaws in a society judged basically

Source: Motive 30 (January 1970): 6–13. Copyright by Denis A. Goulet. Reprinted by permission.

sound. According to usual indicators, can anyone doubt that the United States is highly developed? Its industry is productive, its population literate, its wealth diversified, its technology advanced, and its values modern.

Nevertheless, America's development is not genuine. It is anti-development, a glossy counterfeit of the real thing. We delude ourselves by using the wrong yardstick to measure progress. Our assumption is that prosperous societies are advanced. But development means more than freeways choked with cars, television in every home, or soaring national production. What economists tally as national wealth is often mere waste or caters to men's fanciful needs for baubles. But the evidence shows that plentiful goods cannot substitute for the good life. The standard American image of development frustrates those who place their hopes in it. Although it is exported to the world under the label "progress," this image is unrealistic, narrow, and oppressive.

If the good life simply meant abundance, development would consist in using technology to multiply dynamic economies. Investment capital in the right place, plus expert advisors to run things and train replacements, plus education to get "backward" people to desire modern life would suffice to eliminate world poverty. But this formula has not worked; we keep discovering new factors in the development equation. Capital and technicians won't do the job without good institutions. Yet these cannot thrive unless people hold certain values which, in turn, may threaten culture's very foundations. To illustrate, factory workers in undeveloped lands often practice absenteeism when salaries are increased. Instead of working longer to earn more, they work less to have more time to enjoy what they already have.

Development goes beyond economics, politics, and technology. It raises basic questions about the quality of life in society, the relation between goods and the good, and human control over change processes. Control is the key since change takes place everywhere and always. Can men harness these processes to their goals? An image of development centered on affluence cannot cope with the structural problems of backwardness: legitimacy, incentives, meaning, identity, determinism, and freedom. Abundance is no solution because development raises new issues about the meaning of life in developed and nondeveloped societies.

A narrow view of development assures that prosperity determines whether society is advanced or backward. Yet Toynbee found that technological progress usually announces a civilization's decline. There is no reason to consider America's wealthy businessmen or sophisticated technicians more developed than Sahara Bedouins or Greek sheepherders. And why should a bright American youngster who answers quiz program questions be deemed more educated than the illiterate fisherman's son in Brazil who has studied the sea, the land, and his people, through legends about the benevolent sea-goddess *Imanja,* or the redoubtable *Oxumare?* Because our standards of comparison are ethnocentric, we disdain informal knowledge whose contribution to a "liberal" education exceeds that provided by trivial facts.

Ethnocentrism leads rich societies to fashion a vocabulary which exalts their achievements while downgrading those of others. Such cultural imperalism does not escape the notice of Blacks in Watts, peasants in China or tin-miners in Bolivia. Upon first visiting New York, Le Corbusier remarked that skyscrapers were greater than the architects who built them. Thus with economic development: a towering edifice of production has been erected by puny men with no wisdom to match their science. When French engineer Le Play was asked last century what was the most precious commodity to come out of the mines, he replied: "Miners." Not gold, silver, copper, or coal—but men! This lesson is ignored by "developed" societies, for whom the important thing is profits, not enhanced human beings. Dutch poet Laurens Van Der Post compares the behavior of "civilized" Western countries, in their dealings with Africa, to that of a one-eyed giant. The good eye is technology— efficient and marvelous in its results but voraciously destructive of men. Missing is the eye of wisdom, to nurture contemplation, love of life, joy, creativity, and the strength to face death serenely.

Technology must not be allowed to control men. Consequently, me- dieval Chinese restricted gun-powder to firecrackers on holidays, a sin- gularly uneconomic use. Many "undeveloped" societies are poor because they have concentrated on progressing in spheres other than eco- nomics. Nevertheless, we need not romanticize or overlook their ap- palling poverty, their indulgence toward slavery, superstition, and caste systems. Gandhi condemned misery as a special kind of hell and urged that India's sacred cows be transformed into edible proteins instead of remaining as parasites on a starving land. *The choice is not between de- velopment and underdevelopment, but between qualitatively different patterns of development.*

Traditional societies are no longer free not to develop. Their popu- lation grows rapidly and demands new goods and services. Production must be boosted simply to avoid famine. And this means using technology. Moreover, there is no way to keep out foreign influences: products, tourists, ideas, or technology. Consequently, *how* development is achieved is more important than *what* benefits are obtained by de- velopment. But developed nations have not successfully controlled the processes which bring prosperity. Development American style stresses the benefits of development to the detriment of human control over the means by which these are obtained. In a word, it is too narrow.

This concept of development is also oppressive. It rewards those who are economically aggressive while stigmatizing those who value cooperation. Where competition for profit is the governing principle, and not solely a regulative mechanism of economic life, men enter the "rat-race" as upon a treadmill leading to success. To paraphrase Vance Packard, the American system subliminally persuades men to seek status, climb pyramids, and make waste in an unrelentingly competitive spirit. Yet competition among unequals breeds domination in the strong and servility in the weak. Galbraith is sad because this country has not created a "compassionate" society and Paul Goodman denounces it, not because it mistreats men, but because it makes them irrelevant. Advertisers honor America's personalist myth by addressing each customer as a very special *You*. Yet this is done in such a manipulative way that the *You* is stripped of all content apart from a man's functions as consumer, producer, voter, bearer of arms, and agent of increasingly meaningless gestures.

A second pattern of oppression fosters elitism. Preoccupation with measurable results leads a society to glorify experts who do things better, faster, or more efficiently than the untrained. "Getting the job done" takes precedence over improving men while they perform tasks. Predictably, American technicians abroad distrust non-elitist models of development, whether practiced by Cuba or Tanzania.

Cybernetic experts now agree that most Americans are superfluous for purposes of production although they are still needed as consumers. Some military strategists favor using chemical gasses which *merely* kill people while leaving property intact—the logical expression of a general value underlying American life, namely, that efficiency dictates the choice of instruments. Such instrumental treatment of human values raises serious doubts about the quality of American development.

Economic abundance, modern institutions, and technological efficiency are means toward the good life. But in the U.S.A. they have become ends in themselves and genuine ends are treated as means. If telling the truth interferes with his Vietnam policy, Richard Nixon distorts facts or withholds them from the public, in the name of national security (read: political expediency). When a president cannot refute the arguments of student dissenters, he flees to a "safe" campus and lectures youth on its responsibility not to "destroy" America. Of course Mr. Nixon is no less the slave of impersonal forces than lesser citizens; he has his own very special rat-race to run.

This country has paid too high a price for its development: it has gotten pseudo-development, not authentic development. To justify this assertion one must ponder the goals of development and the manner in which these are pursued. Everett Hagen, M.I.T. economist and theorist of social change, believes the only valid motive for getting developed is to make people happier and adds that the only excuse for not getting developed is likewise to make people happier. On balance, he concludes, it is not certain whether development makes people happier than before. Hagen correctly asserts that development goals must be so broad as to apply even in cases where development is repudiated. My own view is that development has three goals: optimum life-sustenance, esteem, and freedom. This is not the place to expound the reasons for my choice. I contend, however, that America's development is spurious because it concentrates unduly on providing goods, while neglecting to enchance esteem and freedom for men. This it has done smoothly, almost imperceptibly. But the disguise is beginning to wear thin, a fact which explains the irrational response of most Americans to critiques of their values formulated by Black ideologues or campus revolutionaries. Our nation displays a pathological reluctance to debate real issues. Instead of inquiring whether detractors are correct, allowing for inflated rhetoric or exhibitionist bad taste, opinion-makers resort to *Coue*-like formulas stating that America is a healthy land and the world's most developed nation.

Behind appearances, however, men are no longer esteemed or free in this highly developed land. They enjoy the trappings of esteem if their credit is good or their votes needed and they are free to choose from a widening array of automobiles, frozen vegetables, and telephone styles. But genuine esteem is the sense that one is a being of worth on his own terms, not merely an instrument of other men's purposes. And to be free means more than release from ignorance, disease, or economic stagnation. These freedoms are but prologue to realization and plenitude. Psychologist Abraham Maslow judges the chief requirement of growth in individuals or societies to be internal freedom from deterministic outside stimuli. Judged by this criterion, the United States is possibly the most underdeveloped society in the world. Our citizens are manipulated in their desires more persistently than primitive men trapped in a rigid hierarchical society. The main lesson one Black leader learned as a boy is that "if you're nobody economically, you're nobody, period." This aphorism accurately mirrors America's values. Our cultural gold standard is bankrupt, for glitter has replaced substance. Nevertheless, more serious objections exist to the United States' love affair with its illusions. Besides suffering from alienation in abundance, our country practices oppressive foreign policy and ecological irresponsibility.

This nation's stance vis à vis underdeveloped countries is consistent with its domestic values. A society dedicated to the indiscriminate satisfaction of wasteful needs is necessarily voracious of raw materials and markets. Independently of the intentions of its economic or political agents, it will scour the world for commodities and investment opportunities. While doing so it forms alliances with native classes benefiting from this strategy. These are unlikely to coincide with groups who champion social justice or fight to abolish privilege in their own societies.

Notwithstanding its rhetoric, the United States does not seek the genuine development of the Third World. Such development would jeopardize its ability to maintain prosperity at the expense of powerless groups outside its borders as well as within them. No longer could six percent of the world's population pre-exempt fifty percent of its resources for wasteful or warlike purposes. No longer would American capital be "free" to fly where profits are to be made. No longer could political pressure bring a recalcitrant country into line because its economy has been pawned to U.S. interests. America doubtless wants development of a sort—the domesticated, tame kind which does not challenge its privilege in the world. This country points proudly to Taiwan, Greece, and South Korea as examples of successful national development aided by its funds. But as one observer notes, "U.S. aid works best in countries which are lackeys of American policy."

Ecological irresponsibility is another form of oppression. Pollution of U.S. waters may soon become irreversible and millions of people risk permanent damage to their hearing because they are subjected to sounds—from jet planes and industrial machines—far above healthy decibel counts. Thanks to our radioactive atmosphere, polluted waters, and contaminated foods, the day may come when healthy human specimens may survive only in museums created to satisfy the curiosity of affluent cripples who wonder what it was like to be normal before the world got fully "developed."

Tragic ecological harm is being wrought, not only by impatient profit-seekers but by conscientious problem-solvers as well. Behind all the hand-wringing one important truth stands out: ecological renewal is incompatible with a manipulative outlook on nature. Men in "developed" lands have grown so accustomed to bend nature's forces to their own designs that they forget to respect nature's limits. Modernizers disparage Buddhist or animist cultures, accusing them of inertia in the face of disease and malnutrition. They themselves, however, tamper with the planet's finely calibrated eco-systems beyond the point where full regeneration is possible. Our ecological performance has been so disastrous that we have no legitimate claim to call ourselves "developed."

Ultimately, America's approach to the use of goods must undergo a revolution. Large-scale voluntary austerity is indicated if Americans are to wrest a modicum of freedom from technology's cannibalistic drive to become an end in itself. More importantly, our affluent society will grow insensitive to urgent world needs unless it accepts voluntary austerity as a step toward solidarity with that portion of mankind for whom imposed austerity is the road to development.[1]

   This country needs to revise its notion of development and recognize its own pattern as anti-development. Moreover, it must allow other models of development to prosper even if these cannot be "domisticated." China scholar Michel Oksenberg has written that U.S. officials are reading the Cultural Revolution all wrong and that Mao's "folly" may prove to be an excellent measure for consolidating China's drive toward modernity.

   Should the United States observe a moratorium on spreading its expertise throughout the world until it learns a little wisdom to match its science? Should its scholars stop labelling other societies "underdeveloped" until they discover how culture-bound their own standards are? Must economic planners take lessons in ecological responsibility before teaching men how to spoil the biosphere without really trying? Perhaps.

   Such measures are utopian, of course. If the United States were prepared to admit that its "experts" are not expert at all regarding the basic value questions posed by development, it would not need to undergo a cultural revolution of its own. And scholars would not label societies "underdeveloped" if they already understood how culture-bound is their own vision. Finally, planners might suddenly find themselves unemployed if they set priorities on ecological grounds. In all three domains, the very standards of success need to be modified. Certainly the propoals just made are unrealistic; this is precisely what is wrong. They need to be made realizable. At the very least, reflection on them ought to produce a pedagogical impact on the "developed." Beyond that, however, they must be brought one step closer to feasability. For illustrative purposes, therefore, it is worth asking how this might happen. We may take a specific case: The call for a moratorium on expertise.

   Quite apart from other considerations, Parkinson's Law assures us that the United States will continue sending "experts" to underdeveloped lands. Expertise will in fact continue to be exported and a moratorium is impossible. Nevertheless, progress can begin on two fronts. First, a new pedagogy can be launched to educate technical advisors from "developed" lands. These must learn that their expertise is a purely relative superiority which gives them no warrant for tampering with values and behavior in other societies except on the latter's own terms. And these terms are the safeguard of self-respect and self-determination in recipients. Secondly, new relationships must come to exist between "experts" and the populace "helped." Development and technology must both be seen for what they truly are: mere means to the good life.

   American experts in particular must come to recognize that the United States constitutes, by and large, an example of anti-development rather than of genuine development. With recognition comes a new perspective on the relationships between "expert" and populace. Thus the expert is conditioned to perceive how poorly his own technological skills have been integrated to larger human goals within his own society. Then he begins to view other societies, not so much as "underdeveloped," but perhaps as more "civilized" or "humane" than his own. Finally, the rule of reciprocity imposes upon him the role of equal partnership in the dialogue over new syntheses to be formulated between technology and changing values.

The "expert" can adopt this stance only if he makes himself vulnerable to recipients.[2] In practice this means that his sponsoring governmental or other agency must accept new ground rules for the conduct of technical cooperation. It also means that major institutions concerned with planning, financing, technical assistance, and others must be radically overhauled. It may well be that, ultimately, the only suitable form of technical cooperation founded on reciprocity, instead of on structural dominance and dependence, is to create a world technical pool and a new international brotherhood of developers at the service of all mankind! Since we are still far removed from such sublime realism, we must for the present be content with an incremental step; not however, a mere palliative but a creative measure designed to open up new possibilities in the future. This modest step is to educate "experts" to recognize that they are not "experts" in the most fundamental value dimensions of development. More importantly, research on development, policy planning, and implementation must all be conducted in the mode of dialogue. Elitism in all three spheres needs to be countered by new and specific practices such as these now being tried in a few cultural settings.[3] Such creation is clearly a major task faced by students and practitioners of development in all societies.

The harm wrought by the transfer of expertise can be minimized by changing the structures within which experts function. What is required of experts as a first step is a moratorium on complacency, insensitivity to value dilemmas created by inter-cultural transfers, and ignorance of the insufficiency of their own models of development.

The United States is unable to cope with the world's underdevelopment. Confusion will endure until it takes a critical new look at its own "development." More important than affluence or efficiency is that men have dignity and that their lives have meaning. Americans are swept along by impersonal forces because our society appeals to a shallow material standard of success and flees reality by basking in the glory of past accomplishments or purely technological feats. It clings to the obsolete American dream. Waste is a duty in this compulsive consumer society and ends become superfluous because they interfere with the efficient deployment of means. To limit one's wants judiciously or to harness productive energies to satisfy priority needs of mankind is seen to be unpatriotic. Such attitudes would augur the end of our competitive system and of our status as a privileged nation.

Although the United States lacks standards for determining what genuine development is at home, it has spread its image of the good life to the rest of the world. What Americans call development, however, is in truth anti-development.

NOTES

1. "Material austerity (imposed or voluntary) is acceptance of privation to overcome a crisis, enhance one's future position or achieve equity in distributing goods. . . . Apart from religious considerations, *two compelling human reasons* dictate the practice of voluntary austerity in the use of material goods. The first reason involves freedom: man must free himself from manipulation of his desire mechanisms. To do so, individuals living in societies which goad them to consume compulsively should freely choose not to have certain material objects, even useful ones, which they can afford, in order to assert the primacy of their persons over the forces so powerfully organized to violate their faculties of desire. . . . A further reason exists for practicing voluntary austerity in a prosperous society: to forge a bond of solidarity with the wretched of the earth who constitute the majority of mankind. I have already referred to the dangers inherent in practicing this type of poverty, the risk of playacting. Indeed, unless it springs from inner detachment from egocentric pursuits and flowers into active respect for others, voluntary austerity is nothing other than fastidious moral masturbation."— From Denis A. Goulet, "Voluntary Austerity: The Necessary Art," *The Christian Century,* June 8, 1966, pp. 748–52.

2. The theory and practice of "vulnerability" is treated at length in Denis A. Goulet, *The Cruel Choice, An Ethical Approach to Development.* (New York: Atheneum, 1971).

3. These experiments are described in ibid.

BRUCE C. JOHNSON

The Democratic Mirage: Notes Toward a Theory of American Politics

> It took me four days
> to hitchhike from Saginaw.
> —Simon & Garfunkel

I. The Problem and Existing Approaches

Most extant sociological theories of American politics are wrongheaded. I shall defend this hyperbole at some length below, though not in every nook and cranny of the field. My concern is the resolution of what is perhaps the major problem of American politics, the contradiction between its pervasive equalitarian rhetoric and the inequalitarian social structure within which it operates. More particularly, the problem is to see and to explain the massive blocks to equalitarian political action which are inherent in American politics. Louis Hartz' work on the liberal tradition in American politics represents a partial exception to my general indictment, and his theory is the starting point for my own.

Perhaps the major axis of recent American political sociology has been the debate between the pluralists and the power elitists. Pluralists typically deal with the equalitarian rhetoric/inequalitarian reality problem by minimizing the extent of the contradiction. Their work draws heavily on Tocqueville's *Democracy in America.* Yet this would appear to be an irrelevant model, for the democratic promise Tocqueville saw in the Jacksonian era never reached fruition. There has been almost no redistribution of income in an equalitarian direction during the last century in the United States, and rather less redistribution has taken place here than in most countries of Western Europe.[1] Today, income disparities between strata in the United States are among the highest in the world.[2] It is facts such as these that lead me to regard the application of Tocqueville's pre-industrial analysis of America to our contemporary situation as an exercise in myth-making rather than as relevant social analysis.

In rejecting contemporary pluralist formulations, one need not accept such evident alternatives as power elite theory. The latter school of thought is properly attentive to the fact of elite power in the United States, but it has by no means satisfactorily explained the stability of that power, the cultural dynamics behind its maintenance. The critical question, as stated, is the equalitarian rhetoric which dominates American

Source: Berkeley Journal of Sociology 13 (1968): 104–43: Reprinted by permission of the *Berkeley Journal of Sociology* and the author.

political life. If it is not taken seriously why does it persist? If it is taken seriously, why is it not a source of political instability? The answer I would offer is that our political rhetoric is not substantively equalitarian, and that belief in it is spread unevenly (though systematically) through the American population. These two social facts are essential features of the contemporary structure of American politics, a structure which I term the "new liberalism."

The elaboration of these points into a theory will require a considerably closer look at the historical development of American politics than either pluralists or power elitists have regarded as necessary. I shall utilize a tripartite framework, one which is incidentally chronological. First, I shall analyze the establishment of the liberal unity, which was substantially complete by the time Andrew Jackson reached the Presidency. Next, I shall analyze the cracks in the liberal monolith induced by industrialization, as revealed by the political crisis America faced in the late nineteenth century. Finally, I shall analyze the negative resolution of that crisis in our time, the emergence of the new liberalism. While there is something of a dialectic in this argument, it is not one for which Marxist thought has prepared us. This is because the transcendence of liberalism was not achieved in this country. For America, liberalism is not a stage but the whole of her history.

Since neither the pluralists nor the power elitists have yet exhausted the possibilities for coherent theory inherent within their respective approaches to American politics, it may seem unjustified to move in a new direction. However, the inadequacies of these schools of thought are due less to the idiosyncrasies of work done so far than to the fundamental principles underlying each school. Pluralists are part of the American tradition of political analysis, while power elitists are part of the European one.[3] A brief defense of the usefulness of this broad dichotomy will serve to underscore the features of Hartz' work that make it new and important.

The intellectual traditions of America and Europe are quite distinct. The low level of contact between them is especially pronounced in the study of history and politics.[4] American historians have expressed little concern over the philosophy of history; they have hardly participated in such great European debates as that over historicism and positivism. Their concerns have been more "substantial," as the prominence of Frederick Turner and Charles Beard testifies. Political science in America is similarly parochial, as its preoccupation with pluralism exhibits. American pluralism descends from Madison and Hamilton, not from Figgis, Cole, and Laski. American pluralists see groups as a means of disciplining individuals (e.g., civility, cross-pressures) to provide for societal cohesion and stability; European pluralists saw groups as a means of defending the liberty of individuals against a powerful state. The liberal state is *assumed* by American pluralists, though it is not by their European counterparts. American sociology is somewhat better off than history and political science, for it has not been allowed to forget its European heritage; however, even in this discipline, we hear much of pluralism. Moreover, bodies of thought imported into American sociology from Europe do not often escape being fundamentally recast into a liberal pluralist framework.[5]

This dissimilarity between America and Europe in traditions of political analysis is ultimately due to basic differences in the political structures of the two areas. Samuel Huntington argues that American political institutions started out essentially similar to English institutions of the Tudor period, and that they have not evolved since that time (as English political institutions obviously have).[6] Louis Hartz would have it that American political institutions are liberal ones, but he agrees that they have not changed in the last three centuries.[7] The extraordinary continuity in American politics has been philosophical as well as institutional. In Europe, social change and political change have been relatively congruent; thus, new economic interests produce new political ideologies. In American politics, however, new issues arise within the framework of a received and static doctrine. In consequence, the very meanings of key political concepts in America have changed over time. Such peculiarities of American politics as these have made its internal dynamics quite different from those of European politics.

Neither of these traditions of political analysis, American or European, is adequately equipped to explain American politics. Such native bodies of thought as the frontier thesis, American pluralism, or Perlman's theory of the labor movement are cultural mirrors, projections of national myths. As such, they are ultimately exercises in subjectivity rather than explanatory tools. To this argument, it may be objected that subjectivity is a component of all social theories, since they conceptualize only part of the evidence. While true, this fact does not ordinarily cripple the explanatory power of a theory, since alternate theories exist as a check. Where (as in Europe) a variety of political ideologies contend, it is easier to see the root assumptions and limitations of any one of them. In the United States, root assumptions are never challenged, and thus never examined. It is the theoretical consensus that makes American work cripplingly subjective.

We should not be too quick to see European theories as those alternate interpretations of American politics that could bring detachment and self-awareness to American theories. It is difficult for European political theories to grasp the American experience because they are geared to societies wherein political change is fairly congruent with other kinds of social change. Tocqueville, Weber, and Marx all understood America and Europe to be basically similar, so that America was understandable in the terms which they had elaborated for the European experience. Tocqueville and Weber both saw America as further along, "ahead" of European nations in a rather linear sense.[8] To Marxists, America is behind Europe, as a case of "arrested development." Actually, the United States is neither ahead of Europe nor behind it, but on a different path entirely.

Hartz' work reflects an alertness to this fundamental contrast between American and European politics. The heart of his method is the reiteration of that contrast at many levels. Hartz does not, however, fall into the "American uniqueness" trap. Sensitive to the particular American conditions, he is also detached from them. He reproves historians of both America and Europe for failing to overcome their separated perspectives.[9] One can find fault with political scientists and political sociologists on the same grounds. The enormous growth of comparative studies which has occurred in these fields in the last fifteen years,[10] has done little to improve this state of affairs. The comparative trend has thus far consisted largely of a surge of interest in underdeveloped countries. Since little sophisticated comparative work has yet focused on the United States, the task of conquering the intellectual provincialism that has characterized studies of American politics has just begun. Hartz' work is the most substantial effort in this direction which we possess at present.

Since the argument of this paper derives in fair measure from Hartz' theory, it is appropriate to briefly examine the theory's strengths and weaknesses. Hartz has published three books; all are preoccupied with American history, though their scope widens over time. *Economic Policy and Democratic Thought* (1948) deals with Pennsylvania during the century succeeding 1776; *The Liberal Tradition in America* (1955) deals with the whole of the American Republic; and *The Founding of New Societies* (1964) deals with five "fragment societies" (including the United States) which were born in an escape from Europe.[11] While wags may project a book on the world for 1975, I believe that Hartz has expanded his frame of reference as far as he wishes to. One indication that this is so is a certain turning back which *New Societies* exhibits; in it, Hartz goes to some effort to re-work problems ill-handled in *Liberal Tradition*, such as Puritanism and the racial question.

The Liberal Tradition in America is Hartz' best-known book, though in some respects undeservedly so. It spells out the impact which America's "fixed, dogmatic liberalism" has had on her political history. Centrally, the United States has lacked both a genuinely revolutionary tradition and a genuinely reactionary one, since all political factions have based their ideologies on property. Working from the status uncertainties and other attributes of this state of affairs, one can generate a rather interesting model of American class relations. The aspects of this model which most concern me at present are the unusual elite political and economic strategies it called forth, and their devastating impact on the mass of Americans. Even our equalitarian rhetoric was eventually adapted to the maintenance of elite power. Such ideological subtleties are Hartz' forte, but his framework can be adapted to "harder" analyses as well.

Hartz' theory is not without its problems. *Liberal Tradition* displays an emphasis on the liberal presence in American life which is almost Durkheimian; liberalism becomes a "collective representation" which constrains even groups that wish to rebel. The historical record casts doubt on the existence of political unanimity at this level in the United States.[12] Moreover, this formulation possesses two formal defects: a static, determinist character and an idealist explanatory emphasis. We may be permitted to doubt that these defects are intrinsic to Hartz' theory, since his first and third books do not share them. Both of these books offer a complex and subtle analysis which credits the conflict that has attended the maintenance of the liberal "consensus" in this country,[13] and which soft pedals the strictly idealist formulations.[14] This variation from book to book seems to stem from the different levels of generality rather than from self-contradiction. This judgment, along with my basic appreciation of Hartz' viewpoint, leads me to read his work eclectically rather than to abandon it entirely.

Hartz' claim that a liberal unity has dominated and shaped American politics does not amount to a benign view of American history. In this respect, his work shares little with the consensual emphasis of authors such as Richard Hofstadter or Seymour Lipset. In fact, Hartz never uses the term "consensus," so far as I know. He remarks: "The argument over whether we should 'stress' solidarity or conflict in American politics misleads us by advancing a false set of alternatives."[15] In Hartz' eyes, the liberal tradition has not eliminated conflict and tension from our history, but simply given it peculiar form.

Accepting or rejecting in toto such a grand theory as Hartz' is not my style. To me, his importance lies in the propositions specific to given eras and problems which are generated by the overall interpretation. In the rest of this essay I will explore the application of Hartz' ideas to the problem of the stability of American politics over the course of industrialization. If a goodly number of the sub-interpretations implicit in Hartz' work were demonstrated by comparative empirical research, his overall assertion of the importance of the liberal tradition would gain enormous significance.

II. An Alternate Perspective

I am concerned here both to discount the two prevailing schools of thought on American politics and to elaborate an alternate perspective. A certain forensic symmetry could be achieved were I to approach each issue under consideration with two negative arguments and a positive one. This is not possible, for no distinctive power elitist analysis exists for nineteenth-century America. In fact, C. Wright Mills admits the rough validity of the pluralist analysis for the period up to 1886.[16] The conflict between the two schools is not fully joined until post-World War I America comes under scrutiny. Thus the negative concerns of this essay will be directed largely toward the pluralists for the nineteenth century, and will emerge in re both schools of thought only for the later period.

During the eight decades or so of industrialization in the United States (1840–1920), many popular movements arose to deal with its effects upon their followers' lives. Labor agitation is naturally the most important contributor here. In the United States, the agrarian sector of the economy was of significant size very late in industrialization, and farmers also contributed much to the popular agitation of this period. In analyzing the frustration of popular aspirations, I will draw evidence for specific points from labor and farmer movements, though to a certain extent my analysis applies to the third major protesting group of the era, the Negro populace, as well.

Popular protest over the course of industrialization was less massive and less far-reaching (especially ideologically) in America than in Western Europe generally. There is surprisingly wide academic acceptance of the view that this difference was due to the high level of opportunity in nineteenth-century America; this view extends, as noted, even to the power elitists. Actually, in all the forms in which the assertion of opportunity has been presented, it is unfounded. Before we can undertake a serious answer to the question of why farmer and worker mobilization for protest was halting and incomplete in industrializing America, we must dispose of the hardy historical myth of opportunity. It has taken four major forms over time.

The most venerable form of the opportunity myth is the frontier thesis. The essential idea is that the frontier acted as a safety valve to absorb urban discontent. The best known exponent of this theory was Frederick Turner, though it has been cited as a factor in American labor's conservatism by Marx, Trotsky, and Gunnar Myrdal as well. Recent historical studies have shown the safety valve idea to be unfounded, since it took considerable skill and cash to go west and to succeed there in the nineteenth century.[17] Those members of the working class who did go west were in all likelihood not discontented laborers, but well-off skilled workmen. The unskilled who migrated from a given city were likely to remain part of the general urban labor market. Thus, if the safety valve had had any effect on the course of American labor history, it should have been to help radicalize the labor movement.

The second major form of the opportunity myth is the economic abundance thesis. The argument is that America's great natural resources and rapid economic expansion created a high standard of living, which in turn meant that subordinate classes in this country were relatively satisfied with their position. Note that this argument is distinct from the argument that social mobility has been high in the United States. The abundance thesis has been offered by Myrdal and Seymour Lipset: David Potter is perhaps its best known exponent.[18] The first objection which may be made to it is that the material well-being of American workers and farmers over time has been exaggerated. Second, the hypothesis is conceptually inadequate. The argument that a high standard of living disposes a labor movement against radicalism is based on the notion that absolute rather than relative deprivation is the primary source of labor radicalism. This notion is not borne out by the facts, at least in the developed countries. In Sweden, for instance, a high standard of living coexists with a labor movement considerably more radical than the American one.

The most popular expression of the opportunity myth in America has been the stress on social mobility. This stress has presented itself in two specific hypotheses: occupational mobility and property mobility; these are the third and fourth forms of the opportunity myth. The occupational mobility argument has been made by Myrdal, Werner Sombart, and many others. It holds that in America many workers could rise in the economic and social structure, or at least that proportionately more could do so here than could in Europe. And if class relations were not fixed, there was no impetus to class action, or to collective action generally, for social rewards.

The belief that occupational mobility is, or has been, higher in the United States than in European countries has been discredited by recent research. Seymour Lipset and Reinhard Bendix' 1959 study, *Social Mobility in Industrial Society*, carefully reviewed available evidence and concluded that "the overall pattern of social mobility appears to be much the same in the industrial societies of various Western countries."[19] One problem with their case was that data was not available for the period prior to 1900. In 1964, Thernstrom published a detailed study of social mobility in nineteenth-century Newburyport, Massachusetts.[20] His conclusion was that occupational mobility was no easier for American laborers in the late nineteenth century than in the twentieth; if anything, it had been harder to come by in the past.

Thernstrom has made an ingenious attempt to save the opportunity myth by arguing the salience for American workers of *property* mobility. He argues that the ability of workers to buy small homes and to accumulate savings, while remaining workers, was immensely meaningful to them. In a context of low expectations, this low-level social mobility seems to have been sufficient verification of the mobility ethic for the average worker. Actually, Thernstrom's tables considerably overstate the level of property mobility of workers.[21] In addition, Thernstrom's own findings lead one to believe that such property holding as did exist among workers was not a form of upward mobility at all. It seems to have been a pecuniary pattern of a defensive rather than an ambitious stripe. Savings were used to weather hard times rather than to get ahead. Immigrants (who were disproportionate savers) often sent money to the old country, to support relatives there or to bring them to the United States. The price of having funds available for this gesture was typically a bare subsistence existence and the early withdrawal of children from (mobility-aiding) school into jobs.

In sum, the general emphasis upon absence of mass grievances in industrializing America, on the existence of individual loopholes which gave workers and farmers little reason to protest, fails to convince.[22] Actually, there was a considerable discrepancy in this period between the relatively high level of popular grievances and the minimal protest which they engendered. The liberal society concept offers an excellent framework for analysis of this discrepancy. We can get a purchase on the particular processes involved by examining a recurrent crisis phenomenon of American politics, the moralistic binge.

The phrase "moralistic binge" refers to the intolerant crusades supporting various absolutes in which Americans periodically engage. These absolutes include abolitionism, temperance, nativism, and anti-Communism. What is the genesis of such moralistic binges? Pluralists would have it that they emerge from the breakdown of independent group life among non-elites. The explanation has some plausibility, for moralistic binges have been more widespread in the nineteenth century than in the twentieth, and it has only been since the turn of the century that significant "group life" has emerged in the United States.[23] However, participatory activity as a whole has probably declined in America in this century; there has been an enormous rise in social apathy. Political apathy will be discussed more fully below; what is relevant for the understanding of moralistic binges is the growth of cultural quiescence in our time. Puritanism supplied much of the fervor necessary for moralistic binges; the Great Awakening and the Great Revival (of the early eighteenth and early nineteenth centuries, respectively) were prototypical binges. The late nineteenth century growth of "mind cure" religions which made no demands on society was a reaction against Puritanism; in this century, this "other-directed" mode has spread beyond religion to other spheres of social life as well.[24]

Reference to Puritanism helps us explain not only the incidence of moralistic binges, but also the functions they perform. Hartz has argued that being a "fragment society" poses enormous problems of self-definition.[25] Based in migration to an empty continent, these societies had no past to offer them a national identity. The identity which did emerge was necessarily fragile, a fact which inspired rigid overreactions to developments which threatened the fragment. The Puritan colonies faced this problem, as did the liberal society which succeeded it. The fact that French Canada, another fragment society, has experienced similar moralistic binges shows that it is not any particularly Puritan intolerance that is involved here. The analogue of the fragment society's problem of self-definition for groups within that society is the problem of status. Status is a far more important social issue in a fragment society than in a European one, for status positions are not clearly defined or differentiated from one another. In this situation, moralistic binges are an appropriate means for resolving status ambiguities; their relevance to this end is one reason they have recurred over time.

Joseph Gusfield argues correctly that status politics has proven no less rational than class politics in American history: "Far from being a pointless interruption of the American political system, [the politics of status goals] has exemplified one of its characteristic processes."[26] However, within this context, Gusfield reaffirms the common distinction between class and status politics. Actually, status politics (at least in the form of moralistic binges) has not been an alternative to class politics in the United States, but a crisis version of that politics. Business elites have capitalized upon the petty bourgeois unease behind most moralistic binges to contain movements which challenged elite dominance. This was true of the free silver craze and the 1919 Red Scare, for instance. Even abolitionism served to divert attention from conditions in the factories owned by abolitionists.[27] In sum, moralistic binges have not represented the breakdown of normal social action in this country so much as its exaggerated fulfillment. Moralistic binges do not threaten the American social order, as pluralists argue, but sustain it.

These remarks point out a critical defect in pluralist analysis. I do not refer to the common charge that pluralists fail to appreciate the extent to which political and economic power are concentrated in the United States. If pluralism could explain any political configuration, it could explain that one. There is more amiss with pluralism than an empirical implication: its very conception of power is inadequate. The idea of social pluralism, as applied to the United States, has usually featured two central propositions.[28] First, social life consists of a series of distinct power centers whose interaction provides a rough mutual balancing. This idea comes from Madison, who believed that checks and balances upon fully mobilized social forces could stabilize a political situation. Realizing that this Madisonian premise is a fallacy, contemporary pluralists have added a second proposition designed to show that mobilization is actually incomplete. This is the notion that people's lives consist of a number of distinct spheres (so that, for instance, union membership does not influence a worker's life off the job). This proposition, however, is no less mechanistic than the first; in either its Madisonian or its contemporary form, pluralism fails to grasp the more subtle aspects of power and of the ways in which it becomes concentrated or dispersed, stabilized or relocated, in society. In America, these subtleties consist in fair measure of the ideological and cultural components of politics. Conceivably, a mechanistic conception of power could be of use in analyzing European politics, since there ideological differences mirror rather directly those wooden aspects of power upon which the pluralist conception focuses. In American politics, however, the ideological question is by no means so readily handled. Here, class confict appears in such unlikely guises as the moralistic binge; no analysis which ignores this fact is ultimately of much use in analyzing American politics.

The United States is more properly regarded as a liberal society than as a pluralist society. By liberalism, I mean that Lockian philosophy which regards the state as a night watchman concerned only with the personal security of the citizens; the constricted liberal definition of politics gives primacy to economic action in society.It is less easy to define a liberal *society*. As the American orthodoxy, liberalism has many sides, some of which this essay seeks to illuminate. The prism is the orthodoxy itself—more amorphous at some points in the American experience than others, but never entirely absent. Disraeli portrayed industrializing England as "two nations between whom there is no intercourse and no sympathy."[29] In terms of standard of living and of income distribution, the same two nations existed in industrializing America; yet this economic cleavage acquired scant political expression. America remained "one nation," with a remarkable cultural and political uniformity.

The liberal tradition persisted during and after industrialization primarily because the mass of Americans were not able to build an alternative to it, though they sought to do so. The roots of this popular inability to sustain dissent or independent action lie in the weakness of *class community* in the United States. Working class neighborhoods existed in nineteenth century America, but few of them were real communities. The importance of class community as a foundation for sustained independent action has been affirmed by many studies.[30] Kerr and Siegel found that industries are most strike-prone when workers form an undifferentiated and socially isolated mass.[31] In this situation, labor grievances quickly become collective experiences, since they are shared by nearly everyone on a worker's social horizon. Homogeneity also enhances the communication and mobilization processes inherent in redressing grievances.[32] Young, in his discussion of the British case, emphasizes more subtle aspects of class community, such as horizontal social controls and social supports and the emergence of defensive institutions.[33]

There were, to be sure, situations where class community could be found in America throughout industrialization—in geographically isolated company towns for workers, and in the crop-lien system of the post-bellum South for farmers. Yet these are limiting cases, situations where class community could hardly be prevented from developing. They but reiterate the hostility to particularistic loyalties and communities inherent in the liberal tradition. What strikes one in general is the remarkable influence over popular life exerted by elites in America. Workers and farmers have been able to develop almost no autonomous institutions. American education has been considerably more uniform across class lines than has European education. Religious institutions, when popular among workers, have been more elite-controlled in America than in Europe.[34] Even the labor union, the institution one would expect to be most nearly autonomous, has not been safe from elite penetration. Labor spies have been much more widely used by American employers than by European ones.[35] Much of the rest of this essay will be concerned to elaborate how circumstance and elite design have combined to keep class community weak in America.

The themes of my argument are offered by Hartz' answer to the question at hand, his "law of Whig compensation." He writes that the Hamiltonian Federalists, after perforce failing at the European Whig strategy of *divide et impera,* learned

the Alger mechanism of enchanting the American democrat and the 'Americanistic' mechanism of terrifying him, which was the bounty they were destined to receive for the European strategies of which they were deprived. For the defeat of Hamilton, so long as the economy boomed, they were bound to get the victory of McKinley. One might call this the great law of Whig compensation inherent in American politics. The record of its functioning takes up a large part of American history.[36]

We can use Hartz' formulation to succinctly summarize elite strategy during industrialization: early use of Alger enchantment, followed by Americanist terror when that failed. Stress should be laid upon the terror rather than the enchantment, for the law of Whig compensation worked in American history without a boom. There were seven major economic depressions in this country between the Civil War and World War I.[37] Speaking more sociologically, we can take "enchantment" as incorporation, and "terror" as legalist repression. Until around 1890, the American mass was composed largely of natives and old immigrants; ideological incorporation and the implications of American federalism kept class community (and thus insurgency) weak among them. The sudden influx after that time of the new immigrants, who possessed a fullblown class community, presented American elites with a radical new problem. Their response to this threat provides a case study in what might be called the repressive underside of American liberalism.

III. Early Industrialization:
The Liberal Enchantment Obscures Grievances

At the outset of industrialization, in the Jacksonian era, the mass of Americans was thoroughly incorporated into the liberal structure. This is an important phenomenon; it has no parallel in Europe, where the masters and the servants (Tocqueville) could easily tell one another apart. Hartz regards ideology as the mainspring of this mass incorporation, a formulation I prefer to go beyond. A brief treatment of the substantive structural bases of the liberal unity will indicate the lines which a more extensive analysis could take. I will deal with the colonial educational system and the colonial economy.

A general system of elementary education was established considerably earlier in America than in England.[38] Consequently, mass literacy was achieved here well over a century earlier than it was in England.[39] This development laid the basis for the cultural uniformity that was to develop over time. While there were nations on the continent (e.g., Denmark, Prussia) which established popular education almost as early as did America, the implications of this fact were quite different in the two situations. Bendix argues that there is an important element of national consensus in the establishment of the right to an elementary education.[40] This is so, but the consensual element was much more important in America than in Europe, where popular education did little to undercut social hierarchy. In America, *higher* education became relatively widespread far earlier than it did in Europe; it remains to this day available to but the few in much of Europe. Also, colonial education went considerably farther than did its European counterpart toward creating a uniform national language and speech; dialect remains a significant clue to class background in Europe, though not in the United States.[41] American education's search for broad uniformities bespeaks an important social fact, the atrophy of particularistic (especially class-based) communities and cultures.

While one can find, at least in the Puritan colonies, systematic attempts to create a unitary culture, this is not the main reason it emerged. Hartz' fragment analysis carries us beyond conscious intentions here. It points, first, to America's nakedness of institutions. Before Europe modernized, education had already been established as the prerogative of the church; in America, no such prior claims existed to delay or modify the development of popular education.[42] Second, the fragment analysis points to the relative uniformity of the colonists' European origins. This fact set America off from a nation like Canada, whose *dual* fragmentation became an important prop to stratification.

None of this is meant to deny that colonial America was significantly stratified. Not only did slaves and bound labor exist, but there was great status differentiation among free whites as well. However, very little internal economic conflict, of a type that would have threatened the emerging cultural unity, was generated in colonial America. The enormous labor shortage made the bargaining position of free (and even bound) labor very strong.[43] Colonial real wages ranged from 30 percent to 100 percent higher than contemporary English ones.[44] On a more general level, the sizeable subsistence sector of the colonial economy was no source of economic strife; conflicts in the market sector of the economy were largely external, since it exported staples to England.

Once the Revolution was won, this bourgeois society was free to establish its own political structure. The one that emerged reflected the sense of unity sketched above. The men who drew up the Constitution deeply feared power and conflict, and envisaged a politics free of them.[45] But this is no politics at all. These misconceptions would not have mattered a great deal, save for the fact that the Constitution was made very difficult to amend. In Europe, reform of the legal structure of politics continued to occur after more modern features (such as political parties) developed. The relatively immutable legal structure of American politics, by contrast, has become a massive anachronism.[46] During industrialization, social conflicts unanticipated by the drafters of the Constitution emerged, and American politics could not adequately adapt. The most salient aspect of the Constitution vis à vis social conflict was, ironically, one not at all discussed during the torturous debates of the summer of 1787. This was the *state by state* basis of national politics, which was created simply because it was thirteen separate colonies that were federating. This feature was later to help negate that great positive aspect of the politics of the early Republic, widespread suffrage.

We are able, then, to indicate three structural bases for the ideological incorporation of the mass of Americans by the 1830s. The first two are popular education and economic circumstance. The third is the early achievement of manhood suffrage. Possession of the vote helped make it evident to the American worker and farmer that he was the social equal of any. Was not Andrew Jackson, a self-made man and a democrat, in the White House?

As industrialization began, America took abrupt leave of this liberal utopia. The Lynn, Massachusetts shoemakers complained in 1844 that their new economic relationship with manufacturers had created distinctions "anti-republican in character, which assimilate very nearly to those that exist between the aristocracy and the laboring classes of Europe."[47] This complaint of an increase in social distance between classes had no small basis. Ware has documented the degradation of the industrial worker which occurred in the early period of industrialization, the two decades preceding the Civil War. He concludes that workers were losing ground absolutely in the 1840s and relatively in the 1850s.[48] By contrast, manufacturers were gaining enormous profits at this time; they did this by holding wages down while increasing worker productivity.[49]

The basis for the rapid pace of American industrialization had been well-laid in the eighteenth and early nineteenth centuries. American economic growth was rapid from at least 1750 onward. Economic expansion was a major theme in the social life of the colonies and the early Republic; both the Revolution and the War of 1812 were fought in its name.[50] The roots of this development are to be found partly in the ubiquity of the Protestant ethic, though the developing liberal tradition implied two more concrete facilitating conditions as well. First, popular education helped insure that the populace as a whole possessed the abilities and attitudes conducive to economic mobilization. Second, few legal reforms had to be undertaken in this early period; there were no feudal institutions that required adaptation or destruction for economic expansion to proceed.

Naturally, the liberal community could not substantively survive industrialization. The shift of scale [51] and the emergence of serious economic conflict insured this. Yet liberalism *had* pointed America toward rapid industrialization. In fact, there was an ideological dynamic in America toward maintenance of liberal unity at a certain level. On this point, note the contrasting concerns of industrializing elites in America and Europe in their quest for legitimation. The European bourgeoisie had to legitimate entrepreneurial *activity;* in this respect they were oriented toward the aristocracy. Once entrepreneurial activity was accepted, legitimation of entrepreneurial *dominance* of the lower classes was readily obtained, by a straightforward application of feudal legacies of social hierarchy. The American bourgeoisie, by contrast, had much more trouble legitimating entrepreneurial dominance than entrepreneurial activity per se. In this respect, they were oriented toward the masses rather than the (non-existent) aristocracy. American industrializing elites could discover no element in the liberal tradition with which to ideologically extricate themselves from the lower classes. They could not cast off the lower classes, as in the Poor Law Reform in England, for this would be to abandon a paternalism that never was. Their only obvious ploy was to try and sustain the ideological incorporation of the masses, to maintain the impression of unity among equals.

Within this context, there occurred at the outset of industrialization a perceptible loosening of the community ties of early liberalism. The characteristics of the wide-ranging public debate which surrounded the emergence of the legal principle of limited liability in the United States make this clear. It is instructive to note the arguments which were popularly mounted during the 1830s and 1840s against the chartering of business corporations.[52] One theme was the unjustice of forcing small enterprises to compete with large ones, with "aristocracies." Another theme was community restraint on acquisitiveness, in the form of admonitions to honest toil and the moral use of wealth; it was argued that when liability was limited, responsibility to the community would atrophy. Another theme was the public interest; the slogan went: in a monarchy, corporations limit the power of the king, and in a democracy, they limit the power of the people.

These anti-corporate arguments reveal the wide-ranging impact of the quite early acceptance of limited liability in the United States. Inequality of opportunity was established. The ground was laid for the elite irresponsibility which was to appear later. And the concept of a distinctive public interest was dissolved into a simple aggregate of private interests. These ideological redefinitions entailed a shift in the function of the state. To its task as the defender of human rights and democracy was added the role of guarantor of economic growth and power. These functions can conflict; at such times in American history, the economy has typically come before the individual. In sum, the continuity of liberalism following the onset of industrialization had a manipulative, and even cynical, quality not previously present.

The pre-industrial incorporation of the mass of Americans into the liberal framework gave business elites important ideological opportunities during the first three decades of industrialization. Some of the most critical episodes in the redefinition of fundamental social concepts occurred during this period. Such redefinition is a political phenomenon unique to fragment societies. More specifically, one of the major ideological concerns of business elites early in industrialization is to limit the influence of equalitarian rhetoric. The typical European strategy here was the assertion of counter-values of hierarchy (e.g., deference). American elites, by contrast, engaged in a kind of ideological imperialism, appropriating equalitarian rhetoric to their own ends. The redefinition of the concept of equality itself was their signal victory in this strategy.

During the first half-century of American independence, much debate and polemic took place over the meaning of equality.[53] The concept's substantive meaning (equality of condition; balanced distribution of status, income, and power) was a term in this debate, though its implications were so explosive that few eminent men cared to endorse it. Even Thomas Jefferson never talked of equality without countervailing reference to a "natural aristocracy." The political salience of equality is shown by the fate of the Federalists. Their open espousal of social hierarchy was a major cause of their political decline. Post-Federalist elites absorbed this lesson and were more circumspect in their attack on equality. By the Jacksonian era, they had gained their essential victory. Equality had lost its substantive meaning and had been redefined as "equality of opportunity." Daniel Webster was a critical figure in this emasculation of the levelling, democratic implications of the concept. The outcome of this debate over equality shows the weakness of Lipset's argument that the values of equality and achievement have continually conflicted over the course of American history.[54] Rather, by the 1830s, equality had been defined *as* achievement in this country.[55] Equality of opportunity is an inversion of substantive equality masquerading as its prerequisite; opportunity was not actually equal, and no promulgator of the new definition of equality intended it to become so.

A similar analysis could be made of other American political concepts, such as community, public, and liberty. All three lost their original meanings during early industrialization. The upshot was that the mass of Americans were denied even the skimpy conceptual resources with which they had entered industrialization. It became difficult for workers and farmers to define their opposition to elites, for the separateness of elite and mass was obscured rather than clarified by ideological developments. The pre-industrial incorporation of the American mass played a major role in their initial acquiescence before this ideological obfuscation. American farmers and workers entered industrialization with a greater faith in economic expansion than did their European counterparts. Ideologies of industriousness, efficiency, and social change were more widespread in this country at the outset of industrialization than they were in Europe.

In 1840, Orestes Brownson came forward with an all-encompassing critique of the philosophy of opportunity, of what would later emerge as the Horatio Alger ethic. His effort was ignored, because the philosophy of economic expansion had entrenched itself as the popular answer to American problems.[56] Rather more was involved here than pious optimism. The belief in expansion fundamentally colored the social analysis which popular groups made. To accept the view that one's economic position depends upon prosperity and expansion (rather than, say, upon income redistribution) is very integrative vis a vis elites, whose economic position actually does depend upon economic expansion. The form which expansionism took among farmers was speculation, which was a major agrarian activity along the expanding frontier.[57] The form which expansionism took among workers was the belief that a labor shortage was their sine qua non.[58]

The crash of 1873 dealt a severe blow to popular faith in economic expansion. At this time it became apparent to many that the redefinition of equality had concealed a fraud, that opportunity was not equal. Most workers ceased to believe that maintaining personal opportunity through a labor shortage was their major problem. Similarly, agrarian speculatory activity virtually ceased by the mid-1880s.[59] The corollary of these abandoned bourgeois hopes was a sharp upswing in social protest. In the decade following 1876, there occurred an impressive wave of labor strikes. During the 1880s, agrarian protest moved beyond the inflationary concerns appropriate to speculation, a maturation which culminated in the radical Populist platform of 1892.

At the end of World War I, after a half-century of earnest protest, American farmers and workers had very little to show for their effort. The argument presented thus far prepares us to understand the extraordinary blocks to effectiveness which this insurgent activity faced. Popular political action was virtually impossible, either inside or outside the electoral framework.[60] The mass of Americans could neither elect effective reformers nor build toward extra-legislative political action (e.g., a general strike). Let us examine these two in turn.

Electoral politics frustrates popular aspirations in the United States because its structure favors the formation of pre-electoral coalitions among economic adversaries. The distinction between pre-electoral and post-electoral political coalitions is important. Post-electoral coalitions are part of the very stuff of democratic politics, the interplay of articulate interests. Pre-electoral coalitions typically stifle this interest articulation. When economic adversaries search for a program to mutually run on, the result is often not a self-interest program, but the functional equivalent of one.[61] Such a program provides its adherents with symbols to rally around (e.g., external scapegoats), but does not provide proposals actually relevant to the economic interests of the groups involved. The commitment is to abstract rather than concrete goals.

The propensity to irrelevancy characteristic of American politics is partly due to the ideological obfuscations analyzed above. But this state of affairs could not have sustained itself through industrialization had it rested on no more than an ideological impulse. The system has been further sustained by the legal structure of American politics.[62] The federalist system erected by the Founding Fathers permits but two political parties in the long run.[63] A two-party system favors pre-electoral coalitions, while a multi-party system favors post-electoral coalitions.

Lipset argues that a two-party system is better able to resist extremist inroads on political stability than is a multi-party system.[64] This is only half true. Two-party polities readily produce right extremism, that is, intolerant movements which serve to maintain the existing distribution of social rewards. What two-party polities lack is left "extremism," that is, movements which serve to enlarge political and economic democracy. What renders Lipset's argument plausible is the fact that almost all nations with a two-party legal structure are fragment societies. In fragment societies, all political movements appear to be of the center; in particular, right movements do not have the clerical, etc. trappings of traditional European authoritarianism. Because of the overlap in these two ways of grouping nations, the party-system and fragment analyses perforce converge on this issue. In these societies, the right is favored and the left circumscribed by both the propensity to pre-electoral coalitions (party-system analysis) and by the propensity to moralistic binges (fragment analysis).

The critical feature of American federalism is the large size of the political units of national politics, viz. states. Given economic and social conflicts are much more likely to become politicized if they involve sectional antagonisms than if they do not.[65] In other words, geographically concentrated groups have a better chance for political mobilization in America than do geographically dispersed groups. This is one major reason why there was an agrarian party but no labor party in late nineteenth-century America. Both farmers and workers were faced with the same major party unresponsiveness at this time,[66] but the option of building a third party was available only to the geographically concentrated farmers.

American labor was very aware of the structural roadblocks presented by electoral politics, and after 1896, its interest in this avenue of social action declined.[67] American farmers departed from politics more flamboyantly than did labor, but they were no less stymied by American liberalism. The Populists shifted from a radical economic program in 1892 to a non-radical quasi-economic program in 1896. Free silver was a textbook moralistic binge, which united rural America (farmers with their economic adversaries, small towners) in a quixotic crusade against urban America.[68] The transformation, or deradicalization, of Populism between 1892 and 1896 can be laid directly to the weakness of class community among farmers. This can be demonstrated by a comparison of the two major wings of the Populist movement. Cotton-growing southern Populists were considerably more skeptical than were wheat-growing western Populists about free silver. The crop-lien system had created a viable class community among cotton farmers, enabling them to better resist the ideological obfuscation which free silver offered.[69]

Existing political channels were inadequate to cope with popular responses to the great disruptiveness of American industrialization. This inadequacy was so pronounced (and so beyond remedy) as to render the early achievement of manhood suffrage virtually hollow as a step toward democracy. Given these conclusions, one is led to ask why labor did not move beyond electoral politics to radical action, political or industrial.[70] The answer, as stressed above, is the absence of working-class community. The point is worth reiterating here, for late in industrialization the American business elite was given an opportunity to refine and extend its strategies for destroying class community. This opportunity was created by the new immigration.

IV. Late Industrialization: The Liberal Terror Crushes Protest

During late industrialization, the combination of rapid industrialization and agrarian resistance[71] gave an important impetus to immigration as the answer to the industrial labor supply problem. Immigrants began to arrive in noticeable numbers from Southern and Eastern Europe in the 1880s, and by 1896 these new immigrants were arriving in greater numbers than were "old" immigrants from Northern and Western Europe.[72] The new immigrants were not a factor in the Knights of Labor or in the American Railway Union.[73] However, by 1909, the new immigrants made up the majority of the industrial working class in the United States.[74] The importance of this rapid change in the composition of the American working class is hard to overemphasize.

The new immigration caused a sharp break in the American working-class tradition. The producers' philosophy represented by the Knights of Labor was forgotten almost overnight.[75] Its demise was aided by the limited organizational continuity between the two eras,[76] as well as by such simple facts as the language problem. The old immigration brought proportionately more newcomers into American society than did the new immigration,[77] but its effect on the native American working class was far less. Those elements of the old immigration which were least "American" (German, Scandinavian) tended to go into agricultural or petty bourgeois pursuits. The more "American" elements (British, Irish) were the ones which typically entered the American working class. Their influence there lay more in the reinforcement of selected existing tendencies than in the creation of whole new tendencies. Most notably, British and Irish immigrants contributed to AFL strength.[78]

The new immigrants reacted vigorously to the industrial conditions they found in America. They were the backbone of many militant and cohesive strikes during the Progressive era.[79] Strikes eased off during the war, but burst forth again in 1919, the most strike-bound year in American history.[80] Many of the features of the American labor movement during this era, particularly its level of organization and hypercritical view of employers, are to be found in the mature labor movements of other nations. But in the American case, it is the break with the past, not the evolution from it, which bears emphasizing. The critical element which the new immigrants introduced to American labor was that of working-class community. As Brody writes of the 1919 steel strike:

Strikes had the force of a communal action among immigrants. In Pueblo and elsewhere wives joined their men on the picket line. To violate the community will peculiarly disturbed the immigrant, for he identified himself, not primarily as an individual in the American manner, but as a member of a group. 'Slavish' strikers in Monessen wanted to return to work, a company spy reported, but were 'holding back for no other reason than that they would be called scabs and have a bad name among their fellow employees after the strike would be over.'[81]

This solidarity was based in ethnic culture and institutions.[82] The strength of its hold on immigrants was increased by the fact that distinctions in the work place paralleled ethnic distinctions. There was little occupational differentiation among the new immigrants, who were almost entirely unskilled workers.

The turn of the century emergence of working-class community in America should not be regarded, despite its external roots, as an entirely unexpected shift in the course of American labor development. There are grounds for believing that fairly strong working-class institutions of some type would have emerged during late industrialization in any case. This holds true even though European working-class communities and cultures have usually had venerable roots. Tradition is not the only source of working-class solidarity and militance, for traditions and ideologies must be embodied in institutions and structures to have continuing relevance. Atomization and fragmentation of the working class are characteristic features of the early industrializing period; thus the institutions of working-class solidarity which emerge during late industrialization are new in an important sense even in Europe.[83] Similarly, the early absence of strong working-class institutions in America cannot be the entire explanation for their later absence. On both sides of the Atlantic, a working-class community could be expected to emerge during later industrialization as a situational response.

American business elites reacted with great coldness to the emergence of this first serious challenge to their power. Their short-run response was ruthless repression, and their long-run response was destruction of the class community in which the challenge was based. In both cases, their weapons were supplied by the liberal tradition.

Edward Shils has argued that a major difference between American and British society is the greater *civility* that is to be found in Britain.[84] This is an apt general characterization of differences between the two countries in industrial relations. Both American and British labor historians have concluded that industrial conflict has been far more violent in the United States than in Britain.[85] Shils argues that uncivil behavior is primarily a popular characteristic, an attribute of the populistic mass of Americans. Yet American businessmen have been less civil than American workers (or farmers) have been. Most of the violence surrounding American economic conflict has been instigated by elites. The suppression of the IWW is perhaps the outstanding episode of elite violence in the industrial sphere. Most worker violence in the United States has been a desperate response to elite violence.[86] The major outbreak of violence in agrarian politics occurred in the 1890s. The community-based solidarity of the southern Populists kept them from being enchanted by that non-issue, free silver. It also led them to commit the ultimate heresy in southern politics, crossing the color line. During the 1880s and early 1890s, the Populists made a determined attempt to build an *interracial* political movement. Splitting the poor on racial lines had been a basic strategy of southern business elites, and their response to the Populist challenge was unequivocal. During the 1892 campaign in Georgia, some fifteen Negroes and several whites were killed by the Democrats and an attempt was made on Tom Watson's life; this was but the most extreme aspect of a general repression.[87] The Jim Crow tide of this era led directly to the wholesale disfranchisement of Negroes and poor whites in the South.

We should ask how this unsavory side of American business history was able to prosper in a polity not frankly authoritarian, one committed (in the schoolboy phrase) to "liberty and justice for all." Moralistic binges are part of the answer. Behind and beyond them has stood elite manipulation of the legal order to its own ends. Popular movements have faced legal restrictions in all advanced industrial nations, but in the United States these have been particularly extensively and intensively applied. Access to the legal order was for American elites both a weapon against popular movements and a smokescreen for other weapons. The level of repression thereby achieved surpassed even that imposed by Bismarck upon the German labor movement. American labor movements were penetrated and destroyed, not merely circumscribed and left to grow sub rosa, as in Europe. Legalism, as it may be called, was the distinctive American contribution to the panoply of anti-labor strategies found in developed countries. Its sources and functioning bear analyzing.

The distinctive legalism of American politics is well-known. It is reflected in such simple facts as the very high proportion of lawyers in public office in the United States relative to other countries. At the level of issues, legalism has been reflected in a continuing American disposition to see legal reform as an efficacious means of resolving social issues, as in Prohibition and Progressivism. The preeminent characteristic of legalism as a political stance is a fear of power. The whole political intent of legalistic reform movements is often to curb power. Moreover, the weak institutional devices they have proposed in order to effect the curbing display a fear of *wielding* power. At bottom, legalism seeks to end politics entirely.

Legalistic reform naturally failed to curb the power of the industrializing elites in America. In fact, it was transformed by elites into an efficient means of preserving their power. The American business world's appropriation of Progressive regulatory agencies to its own ends is by now well documented.[88] In the area of labor disputes in particular, the most striking example of this is the use of the Sherman Act of 1890 to break strikes. The Sherman Act was intended to regulate business trusts, but for forty years it was characteristically used against labor rather than against business. If this seems remarkable, consider the fact that far more use of the anti-trust laws against labor occurred after 1914 (when the Clayton Act specifically exempted unions from anti-trust prosecution) than before 1914.[89]

Throughout late industrialization, American courts not only directly used their powers to limit labor organization, but also gave legal sanction to virtually every form of employer hostility to labor.[90] The sweeping scope of the law in the hands of American business is demonstrated by the infamous labor injunction.[91] The injunction originated in English equity courts, as a device to prevent physical damage to property during pendency of a suit. It was a reasonable emergency legal device, though its potency led English courts to severely restrict its applicability. No such restraint characterized American courts when they adopted the injunction in the 1880s. They extended its scope to include intangible property as well as physical property. Consequently, in some cases American labor injunctions prohibited workers from engaging in any organizing activity whatsoever.

The single most important use of legalism against American labor occurred in the Pullman strike of 1894. This strike destroyed the American Railway Union, the first strong and effective mass labor organization to emerge in the United States.[92] One of the ARU's great strengths in the strike situation was the semi-skilled status of its members, which meant that strikebreakers could not easily be obtained.[93] In the contemporaneous gas-workers' strike in Great Britain, this same striker indispensability insured the victory of the strike.[94] However, such considerations did not deter American railroads in 1894; the injunction they obtained was the first use of the Sherman Act against labor. The contrast between the two trials which resulted from the Pullman strike shows nicely how legalism works culturally.[95] Through legal action, the railroads sought to redefine the issue at hand from social grievances to law and order. They sought to make breaking the strike look like action in the public interest. The divergent outcomes of the two trials indicate the success of this strategy. The conspiracy case was argued in social terms; the ARU nearly won it before it was dismissed. The contempt case was argued in legal terms; the ARU lost it.[96]

Elites made less use of legalism in response to agrarian protest than in response to labor protest, largely because farmers confined themselves to electoral politics. In a way, however, the agrarian episodes of legalism are more important, for they reveal that even institutionalized protest can be rendered ineffective when American elites seek to defy it. In the nineteenth century, state courts had a notorious penchant for invalidation of any significant laws passed by Populist legislatures; the Canadian CCF, a comparable movement, received far more aid and comfort from provincial governments.[97] The failure of the Non-Partisan League in North Dakota reveals that even popular control of all aspects of formal state power does not necessarily assure successful implementation of reforms.[98] During World War I, NPL representatives enacted into law a program of state ownership of the wheat farmer's key economic institutions. The 1920–21 depression financially damaged the state-owned industries and the state bank, and private bankers seized the initiative. With the cooperation of other midwestern financial interests, the solvency of the state of North Dakota was successfully questioned.[99]

American elites have been able to use the law in a manner virtually devoid of content or conceptual restraint. There are several reasons why, despite such distortions, the appeal to law is popularly successful. American patriotism, lacking most of the foci of language, custom, and ancient tradition typical of European patriotisms, has always centered around our political institutions.[100] The sacrosanctity which these institutions have gained through being the keystone of the "American way of life" has contributed to the relatively uncritical acceptance of whatever is done in their name. Moreover, state and nation are more closely linked in the United States than in other countries.[101] For instance, the roles of head of state and head of government both inhere in the office of the Presidency, though they are typically separated in European nations.[102] This makes it relatively easy to delegitimize dissent in America, for a challenge to the government can be cast as a challenge to the state. The concept of a loyal opposition (that is, loyal to the nation) is rather underdeveloped in the United States.

We have in legalism the means by which elite violence was carried out, but its ends are not entirely self-evident. Preservation of elite power was not the only end involved, for in many instances the intensity of the repression greatly overbalanced the reality of the threat which it met.[103] The existence of elite violence was no indication of a "need" to go beyond normal channels for settling industrial disputes. The crux of the matter was the elite refusal to concede that *any* normal channels existed for settling industrial disputes. No good American worker had any grievances. Hartz, writing of the early twentieth century, remarks:

While the material gap between the top and the bottom of American society was actually widened, the shattering even of the Hamiltonian distinctions of the earlier time meant that culturally it was more unified than ever. . . . An elite suspended between aristocratic frustration and bourgeois anxiety is bound to have some limitations, and one of these was that it did not always display the highest degree of responsibility. If it was 'un-American' to be feudal, why should one bother with feudal paternalism? Power, as once again Ashley saw, came to be an end in itself for the new American giant, 'his essential reward,' which gave him the feeling, as with Pullman, that a 'principle was involved' when labor unions struck.[104]

American elites sought to repress industrial conflict out of existence because of a virtual inability to legitimate their power. Forced to use the democratic rhetoric they abhorred, elites had no adequate theories of status. The Alger ethic is a tangential justification for elite power: we're rich because we worked hard. But it still reflects the fundamental fact that American liberalism does not justify stratification, but denies that it exists. The problem of false consciousness is posed much more sharply in the U.S. than in Europe, and one result has been elite irresponsibility.

Legalistic repression was not a stable long-term solution to the elite dilemma, for it only presaged further distintegration of the social fabric. The more stable solution was the destruction of those particularistic communities which did not affirm the liberal consensus. The most significant effort in this direction was the Progressive era crusade to Americanize the new immigrants.[105] Americanization demanded rather more of the new immigrants than the popular phrase "melting pot" implies.[106] Assimilation was steadily pressed upon immigrants through public schools, settlement houses, and political machines; it was also stimulated by periods of particularly virulent nativism. By defining community-based labor solidarity as foreign and unacceptable, Americanization performed a social control function for the new middle class of industrializing elites. By defining the WASP style of life as superior, Americanization performed a status function for the old middle class.[107] The processes by which these two functions, social control and status, were carried out might be called hard and soft embourgeoisement, respectively. Hard embourgeoisement was primarily the work of the business community, and soft embourgeoisement the work of women and religious institutions.

Americanization directly blocked unionization efforts in some instances. Brody concludes that the Red Scare and the accompanying wave of nativism were major elements in the defeat of the 1919 steel strike.[108] The long-term implications of Americanization were of a similar nature. Americanization resulted in a distinct weakening of the ethnic communities which the new immigrants had created in the United States. By the third generation, sanctions against aspirations to assimilation and mobility could no longer be enforced. When this occurred, ethnic communities had lost their regenerative powers. Working-class community in Europe has been far sturdier than this.[109]

This characterization of the new immigrants' communities as quickly and drastically undermined by Americanization may seem overdrawn. Many sociologists have concluded that substantial ethnic subcultures persist to this day in the United States. Yet Herbert Gans, a leading spokesman for this point of view, emphasizes that these surviving subcultures provide their members with little basis for economic or political action, and in fact hinder such action.[110] Surviving ethnic subcultures may make life meaningful for their members, but they are no longer bases for building a better life. American nativism may have wished to accomplish more than this, but what it did accomplish was quite enough. When the new immigrants lost influence over their offspring, the radical labor movement which they had built atrophied.[111]

It is entirely misleading to regard the assimilation of the new immigrants into the American way of life as a natural process or a forgone conclusion. The new immigrants did not have much choice in the matter, and comparative evidence leads one to conclude that they did not seek assimilation. Immigrants to other nations typically have retained far more of their European heritage than have American immigrants, and it is unlikely that selective migration accounts for this difference.[112] Intolerance of ethnic diversity is a prominent characteristic of fragment societies, typically expressed in restrictive immigration policies, but also in high assimilation demands upon those who do immigrate.[113] Far from being eager to assimilate, communities of new immigrants in America tended to split sharply on the issue. The more respectable sector of the community accepted it, while the working-class sector opposed it.[114] Even in the acceptance evinced by the former, we may perhaps be permitted to detect the rationalization of fate.

V. The New Liberalism

Thus the industrializing period in the United States ended as it began, with an attempt to enforce the liberal consensus among the mass of Americans. But a strict return to the social relations characteristic of the Jacksonian era was not possible. Industrialization could not fail to have a permanent impact on American political life. The agrarian movement never recovered from its turn of the century defeats, for farmers were a declining social class. Labor and corporate business, however, were permanent fixtures in American society; and the conflict between them remained to be resolved. When the resolution came, it was negative: that is, to the advantage of business. By the time business power had been thus stabilized, the main outlines of the modern American political structure had been established. This structure is fundamentally liberal, so that there is continuity of a kind from the days of Madison and Tocqueville. Yet the realignment which began to emerge after 1896, and which was stabilized during the 1920s, is distinctive enough that it should be termed a *new* liberalism.[115]

The new liberalism resembles pluralism, for it is based on the turn of the century emergence of group life in America. However, the new liberalism deviates from the pluralist model in one crucial respect. The various natural economic groupings[116] did not simply become more cohesive and organized as such; rather they split internally and became organized around that split. The split was in each case between the wealthier and poorer elements of the grouping. This is the linchpin of the new liberalism: the *internal stratification* of natural economic groupings. Internal stratification has been the usual fate of the middle class during industrialization. Yet the disparity between the old and new middle classes has probably extended further in this country than in other industrially advanced nations. For instance, American big business has largely stripped the old middle class of even its cultural role; mass culture is more prominent in this country than in others.[117] Moreover, internal stratification has emerged unexpectedly in this country in groups outside the middle class. Farmers, a group expected simply to decline in size and power as industrialization proceeds, have instead split into a highly productive elite of big farmers and an unproductive mass of small farmers. Labor, a group expected to rise in size and power as industrialization proceeds, has been internally stratified along skill lines.

Internal differentiation of this kind can be found among the agrarian and industrial masses of all developed nations, but nowhere is it so sharp as in the contemporary United States. In Europe, class community restrains the "better elements" among the mass from being co-opted. No similar restraints are operative in the United States. The processes by which an American labor elite and farmer elite came to abandon their poorer brethren and to make a separate peace with the corporate economy differed. The internal stratification of labor was a relatively circumstantial consequence of the ponderous workings of the liberal tradition. Among farmers, however, internal stratification was created by direct elite intervention. Let us examine the latter development first.

While late nineteenth-century American farmers did vary in income and economic security, there were few developments in this era which made this differentiation socially or politically important. In particular, the Alger ethic of opportunity did not so contribute. The Alger ethic divided farmers into speculators and settlers, but this differentiation did not parallel and reinforce income differences; speculators were not markedly better off than settlers. The internal stratification of American farmers was essentially created by the agricultural education movement of the Progressive era.[118] The agricultural education movement sought to persuade farmers to increase their productivity through extensive mechanization, soil improvement, and the like. The heavy capitalization involved would tie the farmer more closely to his old adversaries in the business community, bankers and merchants. Essentially, the agricultural education movement was a business-sponsored effort to economically and politically co-opt the farmer. Few farmers were amenable to change; business pressured them into giving agricultural education a full hearing with such devices as the threat to withhold credit. Those farmers already the best off were the most cooperative; thus the spread of the new farming techniques widened the existing economic differences among farmers. Today agrarian stratification is such that half the marketed farm products in the United States are produced by an eighth of the farmers.[119]

The internal stratification of American labor had its beginnings in the late nineteenth century. Among workers, unlike farmers, ideological differences of the era reinforced existing status differences. Historical evidence indicates that after the 1873 disillusionment, very few workers had any faith in the Alger ethic of opportunity, though there was some interest in it among skilled workers.[120] Actually it is questionable whether even skilled workers ever kept the Alger faith in its strict (that is, flamboyantly optimistic) form. The major ideological struggle within labor during the last quarter of the nineteenth century was over a more muted form of the liberal faith. Gomper's American Federation of Labor believed in economic expansion, not because it would make workers rich, but because it would reduce the competition for existing jobs. This was the reason why the AFL declined to risk aiding the mass organization of workers when such opportunities as the 1886 Haymarket affair and the 1894 Pullman strike presented themselves. The massive strikes of the era indicate that semi-skilled and unskilled workers had no interest in the job control strategy. They were moving away from this incorporative liberal analysis, and toward a more radical conception of labor's aims. Yet skilled workers had not entirely isolated themselves from the mass of workers below them at this time. Within the AFL, there was continuous left agitation up to the turn of the century. This agitation was strong enough to remove Gompers from the AFL presidency for one year.

The incipient skilled-unskilled split in American labor crystalized during the Progressive era. The final break was precipitated by the immigration question. The new immigrants were almost entirely unskilled workers, skilled positions being taken by native Americans and old immigrants. The usual differences between skilled and unskilled workers were exacerbated at this time by differences of language and culture. Skilled workers reacted coldly to the new immigrants' sudden appearance on the American scene. Spokesmen for craft unions invoked their labor shortage ideology to justify their opposition to immigration. These fears of job competition and wage depression were objectively unfounded, a fact that was known at the time.[121] Moreover, explicitly nativist statements were often made by craft spokesmen.[122] It was, then, both the liberal economic analysis and a generalized commitment to the American way of life (including liberal intolerance) that led skilled workers to distance themselves from unskilled workers at this time.

Most students of the American labor movement have regarded immigration as a critical factor in its history, but few have accurately interpreted its impact. It should be emphasized that it was not ethnic heterogeneity that splintered the American working class at this time, in the sense that ethnic cleavages in themselves hampered interaction and organization. Within the ranks of the unskilled, the various ethnic groups cooperated very well industrially and politically. This held true even when they literally could not understand one another.[123] Nor was it true that American unions had trouble organizing the new immigrants.[124] Established unions hardly tried to organize them, and had great success whenever they did try. The critical development was rather the failure of the (native) skilled workers to cooperate industrially with the new immigrants. Their actions made the skilled-unskilled gap a barrier which none could hurdle.[125]

Over the years, Samuel Gompers and other spokesmen for American craft unions repeatedly stated that they would help organize the mass of American workers as soon as the skilled sector was securely organized. Their intentions may have been good, but their strategy was inappropriate to this larger end. The pace of American industrialization and the ferocity of American industrial conflict meant that the time for mass organization would never be so propitious as the AFL demanded that it be. American labor had to take risks; in this context, mass organization in the Progressive era would have been a sound gamble. The enormous expansion of the Knights of Labor into the ranks of the unskilled and semi-skilled during the 1880s[126] had proven unstable, because its new members lacked a social basis for organizational tenacity. The new immigrants possessed, in ethnic community, just such a basis. In this light, the refusal of skilled workers to deal with the "un-American" new immigrants was disastrous for labor unity.

Having analyzed antecedents, let us describe the functioning of the new liberalism more explicitly.[127] Contemporary interest groups typically have a narrow constituency, the upper fraction of a given economic grouping; their goals are narrow and concrete. Both of these features are new to American society. In the nineteenth century, interest group constituencies were larger and their goals were more general. The public interest was a more relevant conception in political life then than now. Being narrowly based, group goals today are often extreme. There is little impetus to mutual checking of demands. This is because the various interest groups are not fundamentally competing with one another. They all gain from the new liberalism; losses are absorbed by the unrepresented millions at the bottom of each natural economic grouping. It is not incidental that many are left out; the system is based on their exclusion.[128]

The American elaboration of this process of internal stratification into a general principle of social life is the key to the stability of marked stratification in an ostensibly equalitarian society. The pluralistic representation of the upper sector of various groupings has enabled America to forget the bottom sectors involved. Are there reports of poor workers? Well, they have in the ALF-CIO a potential voice, should they choose to avail themselves of it. Are there reports of poor farmers? Well, they have in the American Farm Bureau Federation a potential voice, should they choose to avail themselves of it. It is conveniently assumed that the AFL-CIO and the AFBF speak for all workers and all farmers, or have the potential for doing so. Yet these organizations actually speak for a narrow upper stratum of workers and farmers. They are unlikely ever to jeopardize the gains of their narrow constituencies by reaching out to their poorer brethren.

These considerations introduce some new elements into the scholarly dispute over who rules America.[129] A strict "power elite" analysis is difficult to sustain. While it can be easily demonstrated that most social decisions are made by a few persons, it is much harder to demonstrate that the interests of these elites converge or that they are autonomous vis à vis the rest of society. It is easier to attack the pluralists on their own ground, by denying that such decentralization of power as exists in America is a democratic phenomenon. The first element in such an argument is the fact of organizational oligarchy. If America's many private associations are internally undemocratic, how can they be essential to democracy?[130] But this is not the entire point, for many private associations are as democratic as one could expect; they represent their constituencies well. These constituencies, however, are narrow and exclusive. The Tennessee Valley Authority, as interpreted by Philip Selznick, provides an excellent example of the undemocratic decentralization of power.[131]

I suggest that the question of whether the contemporary structure of power in America significantly favors any one group or class is less significant than many assume. If different pluralist groups are unequal in power and influence, this is of little consequence, for they are not playing a zero-sum game. They all win; the mass loses. For example, the AFL-CIO and big business don't fight one another; they co-exist, and mutually benefit from the plight of unorganized labor and the petty bourgeoisie. In this context, the fact that business corporations have more power than does organized labor is not the central issue. The fact that there are many power groups in the United States does not mean that they constrain one another or that they are dependent on mass support. Each member of this broadly based oligarchy ignores the wider public.

The political consequences of the new liberalism have been extensive and negative. The scope of administrative politics has been enlarged at the expense of party politics. The defect of party politics, from the standpoint of new liberals, is that it involves the mass of Americans. This makes its outcome uncertain; new liberals have found that their political goals can be more readily achieved by direct interaction with government bureaucracies. The various interest groups have established extensive contact with the relevant administrative agencies—the broadcasting industry with the FCC, the lumber industry with the Forest Service, and so on. The extent of private infiltration of public regulatory agencies is shown by the fact that few private interests object to being so regulated.[132]

Most Americans play little political role in the new liberalism. There has been a substantial increase in political apathy in the United States in the last three-quarters of a century. As Walter Burnham writes:

The late 19th-century voting universe was marked by a more complete and intensely party-oriented voting participation among the American electorate than ever before or since. . . . The 19th-century American political system, for its day, was incomparably the most thoroughly democratized of any in the world.[133]

The retreat from this achievement has been considerable. Burnham concludes that in present-day America, political apathy exists "on a scale quite unknown anywhere else in the Western world." His specific estimates for America are the following:

	Regular voters	Occasional voters	Non-voters
Late 19th-century	66	10	24
1920s	33	17	50
Present day	44	16	40

In recent decades, while American voter turnout varied from 44 percent to 60 percent, voter turnout in Britain averaged around 80 percent.[134] And in Sweden, voting participation has steadily increased over the last half-century, in stark contrast to the American trend.[135]

The distinctively high political apathy in contemporary America requires an explanation which goes beyond the causes usually adduced for political apathy, such as differential access to information and cross-pressures.[136] Such an explanation would have to deal with the additional fact that political apathy is more concentrated in lower status groups in America than it is in Western Europe.[137] Political apathy is kept high in contemporary America because this helps stabilize the new liberalism. There are two mechanisms by which this end is accomplished. First, the formal barriers to electoral participation are higher in this country than in Western Europe generally.[138] The need to meet residence requirements and to frequently re-register, and the fact that elections are held at a variety of times and invariably on a normal working day, all tend to keep people away from the polls. Second, the structure of the new liberalism helps insure that outsiders are a diverse group, sharing few substantive interests on which a political program might be built.

Some will seek to disclaim my melancholy perspective, even if they have followed me to this point, by referring to the 1930s. It will be argued that both the New Deal and the more radical activity of the depression decade represent a reinvigoration of American political life, a renewal of our democratic promise. The facts do not bear out this view. It is an error to regard the 1930s as one of the high points of protest and reform activity in American history. In the political sphere, Franklin Roosevelt's landslide election victories must be interpreted in light of the continuing political apathy. The highest voter turnout for FDR (1940) was lower than the turnout for *any* presidential election between 1840 and 1908, inclusive.[139] This is understandable if we note that the New Deal helped to establish the administrative politics which the new liberals favor. In the industrial sphere, depression developments were similarly muted.

When American mass unionization finally emerged in the 1930s, it had very limited aims. Even the Knights of Labor had possessed in "End wage slavery!" a cry more radical than anything the CIO later offered. The social philosophies of the new unionists such as Walter Reuther were little more radical than that of Gompers had been.[140] Given the objective economic distress of the era, the moderation of American labor in the 1930s was remarkable. The Great Depression probably represented a sharper economic decline for the United States than for any other nation save Germany.[141] Yet, compared to Germany and most other European nations, the United States of the 1930s was the very picture of social calm. Far less turmoil and challenge to the social order occurred in the United States than one would have expected. The roots of this anomaly lay in the earlier developments which I have analyzed.

The Wagner Act of 1935 and other reforms gave labor organizing its first effective legal protection, and helped to end the labor repression of old.[142] But, by the 1930s, labor was in little position to take advantage of this opportunity, for it had been internally stratified and socialized to an "American" way of thinking. Conflict between labor and capital was no longer open-ended. Labor was unable to translate the right to organize into substantive gains. An examination of shifts in distribution of personal income in the United States since 1929 is instructive on this point.[143] The income share of the very rich has declined, but the essential gains have been made by the middle (and especially upper middle) class, not by the mass at the lower end of the scale.

The fear of democracy which has so long been a part of American liberalism has become in this century the dominant motif of American politics, and democracy has been curbed. In the European context, liberalism was a defense of freedom. In the American context, where it was the orthodoxy, liberalism has proven to be repressive. It is not my part to be a seer and to judge how stable the new liberalism, or the liberal tradition in general, will be. However, it should be noted that the new liberalism *has* resolved the class conflict in this country, albeit negatively. American class conflict has not moved toward a positive resolution, as in Sweden, nor has it remained unresolved, as in Britain. The mass of Americans have not had, and do not have, that strong class community needed to build toward sustained dissent. Such community could in principle yet emerge, but the splits among the American dispossessed run deep. If prognosis is demanded, I would offer the opinion that the American liberal tradition is more likely to be shattered from the right than from the left. Such a denouncement would not be entirely unfitting.

NOTES

1. Kerr's statistics show virtually no change between 1929 and 1953 in the U.S. in employee compensation as a percentage of national income. The term "employee compensation" includes wages *and salaries;* thus the wage trend as such in this period may have been regressive relative to income share. Though statistics are not available for the pre-1929 U.S., Kerr concludes that employee's income share has not increased in the last century. For Great Britain, Kerr's statistics show that wage earners gained more in income share between 1870 and 1950 than did other sectors of the British population. See Clark Kerr, "Labor's Income Share and the Labor Movement," in George Taylor and Frank Pierson, eds., New Concepts in Wage Determination (New York: McGraw-Hill, 1957), pp. 260–98.

2. Seymour Martin Lipset, *The First New Nation* (Garden City, N.Y.: Anchor Books, 1967), pp. 375, 210–12.

3. In light of the great influence of Tocqueville's work upon the pluralists, the separation between American and European political theory sketched below may seem overdrawn. Actually, the very fact of this influence confirms my analysis, since Tocqueville's work has functioned in the United States less as an intellectual tool than as a social myth.

4. See Louis Wirth, "The Social Sciences," and W. Stull Holt, "Historical Scholarship," in Merle Curti, ed., *American Scholarship in the Twentieth Century* (Cambridge, Mass.: Harvard University Press, 1953), pp. 33–110; Michael Rogin, *The Intellectuals and McCarthy: The Radical Specter* (Cambridge, Mass.: M.I.T. Press, 1967), chap. 1.

5. Theories of mass society are an example of this phenomenon; see Leon Bramson, *The Political Context of Sociology* (Princeton, N.J.: Princeton University Press, 1961). One might also note that while early American sociologists were influenced by German thought, these influences were precisely that aspect of early American sociology that did not "take" in the long run.

6. Samuel Huntington, "Political Modernization: America vs. Europe," *World Politics* 18, no. 3 (April 1966): 378–414.

7. Louis Hartz, *The Liberal Tradition in America* (New York: Harcourt Brace, 1955) and Hartz, *The Founding of New Societies* (New York: Harcourt, Brace, and World, 1964), chap. 4.

8. Alexis de Tocqueville, *Democracy in America,* trans. Henry Reeve and Francis Bowen (New York: Vintage Books, 1954), vol. 1, pp. ix–x. H. Stuart Hughes, *Consciousness and Society* (New York: Vintage Books, 1961), pp. 321–22.

9. Hartz, *Founding of New Societies,* pp. 69–70.

10. Cf. Reinhard Bendix and Seymour Martin Lipset, eds., *Class, Status, and Power,* 2nd ed. (New York: Free Press, 1966), introduction.

11. In *New Societies,* Hartz wrote the overview and the chapters on the United States; others contributed other national histories. Of these, I would particularly recommend Richard Morse's essay on Latin America and Richard Rosecrance's essay on Australia. Hartz' fragmentation typology unifies the various chapters. The United States is characterized as a bourgeois fragment of

Europe. Analogously, Australia is a proletarian fragment; Latin America is a feudal fragment; Canada is a bourgeois (English) and a feudal (French) fragment; South Africa is a bourgeois (Dutch) and a proletarian (English) fragment. This typology generally works very well, although the South African and Latin American cases are somewhat problematic, for neither developed entirely on an empty continent, as did the other three fragments.

12. Hartz' discussion of political thought in the ante-bellum South is a case in point. These chapters constitute his most striking attempt to assert the ubiquity of the liberal presence in American political thought. After demonstrating that the "reactionary enlightenment" was not feudal in cast, Hartz infers that it was reluctantly liberal. However, feudalism is a straw man in this instance. Such critical southern political concepts as Calhoun's "concurrent majority" were neither feudal nor liberal, but Burkeian. Both Burke and Calhoun offered what Samuel Huntington terms a situational, or positional, conservatism. Also, this southern conservatism did not die because of an inexorable American liberal ideology, but because the South lost the war. See Samuel Huntington, "Conservatism as an Ideology," *American Political Science Review,* (June 1957,): 454–73.

13. To be sure, Hartz tries to conceal the determinism with forensic dexterity. At crucial points in *Liberal Tradition,* his phrasing is ambiguous; if something was "bound to" happen, does this mean it was likely or certain? Nevertheless, *Liberal Tradition* displays a less frank appreciation of countertrends than do the other two books.

14. While all three books offer idealist formulations, the insistence on ideology as prime mover is most unequivocal in *Liberal Tradition.* In his first book, *Economic Policy and Democratic Thought* (Cambridge, Mass.: Harvard University Press, 1948), Hartz credits economic interests as such with an independent role, and analyzes the way in which liberalism shaped their political expressions (pp. 42, 61–62, 76, 121, 129–30, 168, 297–305). In his third book, Hartz adds new explanatory variables which are unrelated to liberalism (*New Societies,* pp. 5, 20, 72, 81, 86, 94). The first of these two methods of dealing with the inadequacies of a strictly idealist analysis is the soundest, for it preserves the logical closure of the theory.

15. Hartz, *Liberal Tradition,* p. 20.

16. In *The Power Elite,* Mills omits historical considerations to a degree remarkable in one claiming to be committed to this kind of work. See C. Wright Mills, *The Power Elite* (New York: Oxford University Press, 1959), chap. 12, and Mills, *The Sociological Imagination* (New York: Grove Press, 1959), chap. 8.

17. Henry Smith, *Virgin Land* (New York: Vintage Books, 1950), chap. 20.

18. David Potter, *People of Plenty* (Chicago: University of Chicago Press, 1954).

19. Seymour Martin Lipset and Reinhard Bendix, *Social Mobility in Industrial Society* (Berkeley: University of California Press, 1959), chap. 2.

20. Stephan Thernstrom, *Poverty and Progress* (Cambridge, Mass.: Harvard University Press, 1964). See also Stephan Thernstrom, "Class and Mobility in a Nineteenth-Century City," in Bendix and Lipset, *Class, Status, and Power,* 2nd ed.

21. His table on property holdings of laboring families seems to show considerable upward movement over time. For instance, 11 percent of his families were property holders in 1850, while 53 percent of them were in 1880. Yet the early decades in his table include those who *left* Newburyport, as the later decades obviously do not. The 11 percent figure is based on 175 families, while the 53 percent figure is based on 34 families. The actual *number* of property holders is the same in each case: eighteen. The least occupationally mobile and well-off workers were much more likely to leave Newburyport than were the better-off workers. The fact the migration was selective in this way means that the actual increases over time in workers' property holdings were considerably less than Thernstrom's percentage estimates indicate. See Thernstrom, "Class and Mobility," pp. 604–5, 608.

22. Nor is it likely that *belief* in the existence of great opportunity was deeply rooted in the popular imagination. The persistence over time of such a massive misperception is a priori unlikely; the historical evidence on this point will be presented below.

23. Cf. William Appleman Williams, *The Contours of American History* (Chicago: Quadrangle Books, 1964), pp. 356–60.

24. Donald Meyer, *The Positive Thinkers* (Garden City, N.Y.: Anchor Books, 1966).

25. Hartz, *New Societies*, chap. 1.

26. Joseph Gusfield, *Symbolic Crusade* (Urbana, Ill: University of Illinois Press, 1963), especially chaps. 1 and 7.

27. One reason for suspecting the moral purity of the abolitionists is the heavy prior involvement of New England merchants in slavery, as slave *traders*. The crisis leading to the Civil War represents the most serious split within elites in our history. (Ironically, the polemics surrounding the slavery issue consisted in fair measure of northern and southern elites squabbling over which group was the worst exploiter of the masses.) The split was patched up in 1877 and in 1896, with no diminution in elite power in either region. Cf. Williams, *Contours*, pp. 98, 291.

28. For a useful summary see Clark Kerr, "Industrial Relations and the Liberal Pluralist," Proceedings of the Seventh Annual Meeting of the Industrial Relations Research Association (n.d.), pp. 1–15; also Reprint No. 80, Institute of Industrial Relations, University of California, Berkeley, 1955.

29. Asa Briggs, *The Making of Modern England* (New York: Harper Torchbooks, 1965), p. 294.

30. Class community/culture is a necessary but not sufficient condition for sustained radical action. Compare the relatively insular and ineffective working class culture in Great Britain to the politically relevant ones in Germany and Sweden.

31. Clark Kerr and Abraham Siegel, "The Interindustry Propensity to Strike—An International Comparison," in Arthur Kornhauser et al., eds., *Industrial Conflict* (New York: McGraw-Hill, 1954), pp. 189–212.

32. A number of observers have attributed importance to the distinctively high *geographic* mobility of American workers. Perlman believed that "moving on" typically entailed upward occupational mobility, a contention which Thernstrom's work refutes. The actual impact of geographic mobility upon

radical action is mixed, for it tends to radicalize attitudes at the same time that it hampers stable interaction among workers. In some situations, American workers have made great use of geographic mobility, as when Wobblies gathered for free speech fights. In others, geographic mobility hurt their efforts, as when workers left the vicinity of a strike to look for jobs elsewhere. It seems best to regard geographic mobility not as an independent factor, but as an artifact of class community. The IWW created community among its mobile followers, but in other blue collar occupational groupings (where geographic mobility is not intrinsic to the job), such mobility is probably a good indicator of the weakness of class community.

33. Nigel Young, "Prometheans or Troglodytes? The English Working Class and the Dialectics of Incorporation," *Berkeley Journal of Sociology* 12 (1967): 15–21.

34. European examples include the French worker-priest movement and English Methodism; see E. J. Hobsbawm, *Laboring Men* (Garden City, N.Y.: Anchor Books, 1967), chap. 3. Liston Pope has analyzed a typical American episode in his *Millhands and Preachers* (New Haven, Conn: Yale University Press, 1942).

35. In the late 1920s, there was about one labor spy for every seventeen union members in the United States. In Britain, labor spies were used only very early in the nineteenth century (and, interestingly, by government rather than by employers). See Irving Bernstein, *The Lean Years* (Baltimore, Md: Penguin Books, 1966), pp. 84, 149; G. D. H. Cole and Raymond Postgate, *The British People, 1746–1946* (London: Methuen, 1961), sects. 3 and 4.

36. Hartz, *Liberal Tradition,* pp. 19–20.

37. Richard Morris, ed., *Encyclopedia of American History* (New York: Harper & Brothers, 1961), pp. 536–41.

38. Ibid., p. 587; Daniel Boorstin, *The Americans* (New York: Vintage Books, 1964), pp. 169–88, 300–01; Hobsbawm, *Laboring Men,* p. 350.

39. E. P. Thompson is so chary of statistics that he declines to give an estimate for the English case, but we can infer from his discussion that perhaps half of adult Englishmen were effectively literate early in the nineteenth century. This level was achieved before 1700 in the southern and middle colonies; literacy was perhaps *never* that low in New England. See E. P. Thompson, *The Making of the English Working Class* (New York: Vintage Books, 1966), pp. 406, 648, 712–17; Morris, *Encyclopedia,* pp. 587, 590.

40. Reinhard Bendix, *Nation-Building and Citizenship* (New York: John Wiley, 1964), pp. 87–93.

41. Boorstin, *The Americans,* part 10.

42. Cf. Cole and Postgate, *British People,* pp. 362–64.

43. Most bound laborers were *voluntary* immigrants; also the terms of indenture were not always enforceable, since servants could often be induced by better offers to switch employers illegally. See Morris, *Encyclopedia,* pp. 467–69, 546–47; and Richard Morris, *Government and Labor in Early America* (New York: Harper Torchbooks, 1965).

44. Morris, *Encyclopedia,* p. 547.

45. Madison's insistence on the ubiquity of conflict in social life must be

viewed in this context; on its face it is quite unconvincing. See Hartz, *Liberal Tradition,* chap. 3.

46. Cf. Huntington, "America vs. Europe."

47. Norman Ware, *The Industrial Worker 1840–1860* (Chicago: Quadrangle Books, 1964), pp. 41–42.

48. Ibid., especially chaps. 1–4, 7.

49. Ibid., chaps. 1, 6.

50. William Appleman Williams has written a fluent interpretation of the whole of American history with economic expansion as virtually its only theme. See Williams, *Contours.*

51. The American population increased more than a third each decade from 1790 (3.9 million) to 1860 (31.4 million). Morris, *Encyclopedia,* p. 468.

52. Hartz, *Economic Policy,* pp. 19–33, 59–79, etc.

53. For several of the points in this paragraph, I am indebted to John Schaar.

54. E.g. Lipset, *First New Nation,* pp. 1–2, 115–16, 231–33, 366.

55. Cf. Ibid., p. 370: "The focus on the ideology of equal opportunity for each individual has made Americans relatively insensitive to gross inequalities of income and wealth in their country." Actually, 'some Americans' would be better phrasing; the poor are not unaware of their plight.

56. Williams, *Contours,* pp. 270–81.

57. Paul Gates, "The Role of the Land Speculator in Western Development," *The Pennsylvania Magazine of History and Biography* 66 (July 1942); 314–33.

58. This belief was the primary rationalization for the race hatred which workers expressed so savagely in the New York "draft riots" of 1863. This misnamed outburst was actually primarily anti-Negro; 1200 people died in four days, making this the worst race riot in American history. The economic expansion/labor shortage ideology also later implicated American workers in nationalism and imperialism; this tendency, which affected labor in all industrially advanced nations, was particularly pronounced in the United States.

59. See e.g., Walter Nugent, "Some Parameters of Populism" (Paper read before the American Historical Association meetings, December 1963); Stanley Parsons, "Who Were the Nebraska Populists?", *Nebraska History* 44, no. 2 (June 1963): 83–99.

60. Of popular political *behavior,* there was no dearth. This is one way of stating the critical defect of American politics: that it reduces action to behavior. See Hannah Arendt, *The Human Condition* (Garden City, N.Y.: Doubleday Anchor, 1959), and *On Revolution* (New York: Viking Press, 1963).

61. Lipset introduces this idea in his *Agrarian Socialism* (Berkeley: University of California Press, 1950), pp. 121–25, and further develops it in *Political Man* (Garden City, N.Y.: Anchor Books, 1963), chap. 5.

62. Political scientists have been more disposed to recognize the impact of formal constitutional provisions on politics than have sociologists. In fact, they have overdone the insight, which has crucial relevance only for American politics.

63. Lipset, *First New Nation,* chap. 9.

64. Ibid., pp. 352–58.

65. Cf. Ware, *Industrial Worker,* p. ix.

66. Major parties were unresponsive to popular protest throughout the last half of the nineteenth century because they were controlled by industrializing elites. This indicates the non-pluralistic character of American politics; that is, its various features (two-party structure, moralistic binges) do not hamper all groups equally, as pluralist analysis would predict.

67. The Socialist Party is only an apparent exception to this trend. The SP had an unimposing working-class base; skilled workers were not interested, and unskilled workers were consistently mistreated by the SP (see Charles Leinenweber, "The American Socialist Party and 'New' Immigrants," *Science and Society* 32, no. 1 (Winter 1968). The impressive vote totals gained by the SP during its first two decades did not bespeak organizational strength. They rather represented a personal tribute to Debs, as can be seen by the fact that the SP vote was consistently at least ten times larger than the SP membership.

68. It was free silver, not Bryan's 1896 defeat, that killed Populism. Even if Bryan had won (and he almost did), his program could not have eased the economic plight of farmers or workers. Incidentally, Bryan's "Cross of Gold" speech is a classic example of ideological obfuscation; in it he proclaimed that farmers and workers too were businessmen.

69. For a fuller discussion, see my paper, "The Transformation of Populism, 1892–1896" (M.A. thesis, Department of Sociology, University of California at Berkeley, 1967).

70. In isolated instances, it did so—viz. the IWW. This question of "what next" is less relevant for farmers, who were a declining class anyway. Still, one can point to two post-Populist agrarian organizations with radical features: the Southern Tenant Farmers Union and the National Farmers Organization.

71. Until the agricultural education movement took hold at the beginning of this century, American farmers successfully resisted the complete rationalization of commercial agriculture. Thus they significantly delayed the labor force exodus from agriculture which is typical of advanced industrialization.

72. Marcus Hansen, *The Immigrant in American History* (New York: Harper Torchbooks, 1964), pp. 150–51.

73. Marc Karson, *American Labor Unions and Politics, 1900–1918* (Boston: Beacon Press, 1965), p. 324; Almont Lindsey, *The Pullman Strike* (Chicago: Phoenix Books, 1964), p. 50.

74. Charles Leinenweber, "The American Socialist Party," p. 1.

75. This older tradition has been much criticized, and often justly. But it is worth noting that Norman Ware, Chester Destler and other American labor historians have seen great missed potential in it. Their search has been for a "native radicalism." In Hartzian terms, these historians have argued for the existence in nineteenth-century America of a democratic form of the liberal tradition which might have transcended the liberal consensus. I sympathize with these historians, and particularly with their attempt to escape the Commons-Marxist orthodoxy. However, I am not entirely convinced by their work as points made elsewhere in

this essay should make clear. The dispute over native American radicalism cannot be settled unequivocally, but its existence reminds us to avoid retrospective determinism.

76. There was carryover in the person of Debs, though his ARU had more in common with the 1910s than with the 1880s. Such completely new organizations as the IWW were very prominent in the new era.

77. Ware, *Industrial Worker*, pp. 10–11.

78. Rowland Berthoff, *British Immigrants in Industrial America* (Cambridge, Mass.: Harvard University Press, 1953), pp. 99–100; Karson, *American Labor Unions*, chap. 9.

79. Notable examples include the 1909 McKee's Rock, Pa. steel strike, the 1912 Lawrence textile strike, the 1913 Paterson silk strike, the 1907 and 1916 Mesabi iron strikes, and the nationwide 1919 steel strike. Only the first two strikes mentioned were won.

80. David Brody, *Labor in Crisis* (Philadelphia: J. B. Lippincott, 1965), p. 129.

81. Ibid., p. 157.

82. It is also of interest to note that among wheat farmers, unassimilated immigrants seem to have been disproportionately Populists. They were better farmers than native Americans and less prone to speculation; thus it is unlikely that they were enthusiastic about free silver. See James Malin, *Winter Wheat in the Golden Belt of Kansas* (Lawrence, Kansas: University of Kansas Press, 1944), p. 133; Nugent, "Some Parameters of Populism," p. 6.

83. It can be argued that rapid industrialization helps prevent creation (or re-creation) of working-class community. In Britain, slow industrialization provided for a period of class abatement (c. 1849–1870). Young has stressed the importance of this period of quiescence in the growth of English working-class institutions (see Young, "Prometheans or Troglodytes?," pp. 13–18). Bendix suggests a quite different argument of similar import. He remarks that the rise of the tertiary branch of economic production gives a pervasive influence to middle-class standards of aspiration. From this one could infer that rapid industrialization, which continually alters the occupational structure in the direction of expansion of the tertiary sector, helps block the formation of a stable working-class culture. (See Reinhard Bendix, "Social Stratification and Political Power," *American Political Science Review* 46, no 2 (June 1952): 360–61.) Comparing the American and British cases would tend to corroborate these arguments. However, we have in the Swedish case the coexistence of rapid industrialization and a flourishing working class culture.

84. Edward Shils, *The Torment of Secrecy* (Glencoe, Ill.: Free Press, 1956).

85. Bernstein, *Lean Years*, p. 204; Cole and Postgate, *British People*, pp. 481–82.

86. Schumpeter ascribes this violence not to the repression labor faced but, incredibly, to the criminal proclivities of immigrants. Joseph Schumpeter, *Capitalism, Socialism, and Democracy* (New York: Harper Torchbooks, 1962), p. 333.

87. C. Vann Woodward, "The Populist Heritage and the Intellectual," in

Woodward, *The Burden of Southern History* (New York: Vintage Books, 1960), pp. 150–51 and *Tom Watson, Agrarian Rebel* (New York: Rinehart & Co., 1938), pp. 223–40.

88. See e.g., Grant McConnell, *Private Power and American Democracy* (New York: Alfred A. Knopf, 1966).

89. Bernstein, *Lean Years*, pp. 206–15.

90. Ibid., pp. 148–49, 205.

91. Ibid., pp. 149, 195–202.

92. This shows how misleading it is to understand American labor history strictly in terms of particular organizations. The Knights of Labor, for instance, can be faulted for having poor leadership, a muddled financing system, and too benign a view of the employer. Cf. Norman Ware, *The Labor Movement in the United States* (New York: Vintage Books, 1929), pp. 80–96, 118–126. However, the ARU shared none of these defects and was also beaten.

93. Lindsey, *Pullman Strike*, p. 174.

94. Hobsbawm, *Laboring Men*, pp. 193–94.

95. Lindsey, *Pullman Strike*, chap. 12.

96. Note, too, that the conspiracy case was a jury trial, while the contempt case was not.

97. John Hicks, *The Populist Revolt* (Lincoln, Neb: University of Nebraska Press, 1961), pp. 181–85, 299–300; Lipset, *Agrarian Socialism*, chaps. 3 and 4.

98. Cf. Perry Anderson, "Origins of the Present Crisis," in The New Left Review, ed., *Towards Socialism* (London: Fontana Library, 1965), pp. 41–47.

99. Lipset, *Agrarian Socialism*, pp. 13–16.

100. Henry May, "Communism and America," *California Monthly* 73, no. 1 (October 1962): 14.

101. The linkage is closer here than in other fragment countries; cf. Hartz, *Founding of New Societies*, pp. 296–97.

102. Thus the public reaction to President Kennedy's death resembled the English reaction to the death of George VI (1952) more than it did the Australian reaction to the death of Prime Minister Holt (1968).

103. Hartz regards this imbalance as an essential feature of moralistic binges in all fragment societies (Hartz, *Founding of New Societies*, p. 13).

104. Hartz, *Liberal Tradition*, pp. 219–224.

105. New immigrants were subjected to more intense Americanization pressures than were old immigrants, largely because they posed a more significant threat to the liberal order. However, precedents for Progressive era nativism were by no means lacking.

106. Milton Gordon, *Assimilation in American Life* (New York: Oxford University Press, 1964), chaps. 4–6.

107. Cf. Gusfield, *Symbolic Crusade*.

108. Brody, *Labor in Crisis*, pp. 128–46.

109. Even today, those British youths of working-class background who get on in the world are as likely to become angry young men as marginal men.

110. Herbert Gans, *The Urban Villagers* (New York: Free Press, 1962), chaps. 12 and 13.

111. Hyman Berman, "Education for Work and Labor Solidarity: The Immigrant Miners and Radicalism on the Mesabi Range" (Manuscript, University of California at Berkeley, 1967), pp. 25–29, 61–62.

112. Hansen, *Immigrant in American History,* pp. 24–25.

113. Hartz, *Founding of New Societies,* p. 14. The comparative work on slavery suggests that Latin America should be exempted from this generalization.

114. Of course, the very fact of a split helped to break down and redirect ethnic institutions. See Berman, "Education for Work and Labor Solidarity," pp. 20–22, 31; Hansen, *Immigrant in American History,* pp. 117–19.

115. See Walter Burnham's excellent summary, "The Changing Shape of the American Political Universe," *American Political Science Review* 59, no. 1 (March 1965): 23–28.

116. By natural economic grouping, I mean any aggregate of persons who perform the same function in the organization of production—in other words, Marx' "class as such."

117. Meyer, *Positive Thinkers,* pp. 209–10.

118. Grant McConnell, *The Decline of Agrarian Democracy* (Berkeley: University of California Press, 1959), pp. 23–35, 160–65; Richard Hofstadter, *The Age of Reform* (New York: Vintage Books, 1955), pp. 124–127; Theodore Saloutos and John Hicks, *Twentieth-Century Populism* (Lincoln, Neb.: University of Nebraska Press, 1951), chap. 9.

119. V. O. Key, *Politics, Parties, and Pressure Groups,* 4th ed. (New York: Thomas Y. Crowell, 1958), p. 37.

120. Don Bremme, "The Ideology of Success and the Union Man, 1870–1893" (Manuscript, University of California at Berkeley, February 1968), 25 pp. This paper is a content analysis of eight representative American labor union journals of the period.

121. Leinenweber, "American Socialist Party," p. 3.

122. Ibid.; Brody, *Labor in Crisis,* pp. 41–43, 130–31.

123. See e.g., Berman, "Education for Work and Labor Solidarity," pp. 33–36.

124. Cf. Lipset, *First New Nation,* p. 202.

125. The IWW linked native and new immigrant elements loosely during this era, but its organization was strong only at selected crisis moments, and was soon decimated by repression.

126. Ware, *Labor Movement,* chap. 4.

127. Cf. McConnell, *Private Power and American Democracy.*

128. I hesitate to be precise about the term "many," for a continuum rather than a dichotomy is involved here. In the economic realm, one would have to include at least the 25 percent of Americans who are poor (Michael Harrington, *The Other America* [New York: Macmillian Co., 1963], appendix). In addition, the new pluralism has exacted its price from many who are getting by economically (for instance, by forcing the wife to work). Since about one-third of American wives work, this adds perhaps another one-fifth of the population to the one-fourth who are officially poor. In the political realm, at least half of the American population has been left aside by the new pluralism, if we take electoral

participation as a measure. For a more detailed discussion here, see Schaar, "Insiders and Outsiders."

129. For a succinct summary of the issues involved here, see William Kornhauser, " 'Power Elite' or 'Veto Groups'?," in Reinhard Bendix and Seymour Martin Lipset, eds., *Class, Status, and Power,* 2nd ed., pp. 210–18.

130. McConnell, *Private Power and American Democracy,* pp. 122–23.

131. Philip Selznick, *TVA and the Grass Roots* (New York: Harper Torchbooks, 1966).

132. McConnell, *Private Power and American Democracy,* pp. 284–85.

133. Burnham, "Changing Shape," pp. 22–24, 27.

134. Ibid., pp. 10–11.

135. Lipset, *Political Man,* p. 188.

136. Ibid., chap. 6. Lipset, in his encyclopedic manner, takes note of the sharp recent decline in American voter turnout. However, he drops the matter, failing to offer even an implausible explanation for it.

137. Ibid., pp. 189, 213.

138. Burnham, "Changing Shape," p. 12.

139. Ibid., pp. 10–11; Charles Sellers and Henry May, *A Synopsis of American History* (Chicago: Rand McNally, 1963), pp. 145–46.

140. Ronald Radosh, "The Corporate Ideology of American Labor Leaders from Gompers to Hillman," *Studies on the Left* 6, no. 6 (November-December 1966): 66–88.

141. Lipset, *Political Man,* p. 18.

142. American unions had been given legal protection during World War I, but after the Armistice repression renewed in earnest.

143. Lipset, *First New Nation,* p. 370.

SUPPLEMENTARY BIBLIOGRAPHY

Alex Arnett, *The Populist Movement in Georgia,* Ph.D. diss., Columbia University, 1922.

Henry Lloyd, "The Populists at St. Louis," *Review of Reviews* 14, no. 3 (September 1896): 298–303.

Chester Destler, *American Radicalism, 1865–1901,* New York: Octagon Books, 1965.

Albert Gates, "The Early Crisis of American Socialism," *The New International* 20, no. 3 (May–June 1954): 124–45.

Eric Goldman, *Rendezvous with Destiny,* New York: Vintage Books, 1956.

Charles Gulick and Melvin Bers, "Insight and Illusion in Perlman's Theory of the Labor Movement," *Industrial and Labor Relations Review* 6, no. 4 (July 1953): 510–31.

Walter Nugent, *The Tolerant Populists,* Chicago: The University of Chicago Press, 1963.

Selig Perlman, *A Theory of the Labor Movement,* New York: Augustus M. Kelley, 1949.

John Schaar, "Insiders and Outsiders," *Steps* (Published by its editors and the Free University of Berkeley, 1703 Grove St., Berkeley, California, 1967), no. 2, pp. 2–14.

Fred Shannon, *The Farmer's Last Frontier,* New York: Holt, Rinehart, & Winston, 1945.

Edward Whymper, *Scrambles Amongst the Alps,* Philadelphia: J. B. Lippincott 1871.

Chilton Williamson, *American Suffrage From Property to Democracy, 1760–1860,* Princeton, N.J.: Princeton University Press, 1960.

The Rhetoric of Equality in the Mobilization of Political Bias and Official Violence

Part Four

America's social classes have generally lacked the cultural resources to develop and articulate coherent, self-conscious images of their own long-range interests. We have examined the mythical and psychocultural dynamics of property, money, advertising, patriotism, and power each of which helps to explain the social and political dominance of business elites in the modern American experience. The American Dream has depressed critical perspectives on the democratic mirage, offering a structure of counterfeit sentiments rooted in the blurred images produced by the elite-dominated organs of society and politics. A Lockean-liberal egalitarian ideology has persisted in the face of antidevelopment, including gross inequality in wealth, political power, and social privilege. Arnold Rogow says in part 4: "Depressions, financial panics, recessions, and the prevalence of poverty amidst plenty, have never undermined the faith in America as the land of *individual* opportunity." This assumption that problems of poverty and subordination are individual problems solvable through individual efforts has been crucial to mainstream mystification and justification of the socioeconomic system of privilege and inequality.

In recent years, however, some members of the New Left and of the black community have taken significant but precarious and faltering steps in challenging this pattern of mainstream ideological hegemony. The development of black consciousness and community control based on values countering the mainstream pattern has been uneven and uncertain. Support for this process has so far been mobilized primarily in piecemeal ways. There are major obstacles to both New Left and black efforts to attain greater power, partly related to their lack of a clear ideological direction.[1]

Andrew Kopkind's analysis of the Kerner Commission Report sug-

1. See Alberto Martinelli, "In Defense of the Dialectic: Antonio Gramsci's Theory of Revolution," *Berkeley Journal of Sociology* 13 (1968): 18; and Eugene Genovese, "On Antonio Gramsci," *Studies On the Left* 7 (March–April 1967).

gests the possibilities of mainstream domination through a new corporate liberal imperialism aimed at the ghetto poor. This domestic imperialism would operate through an "economic growth" strategy of penetration of the ghetto by what has been called the social-industrial complex, not to mention the "black capitalism" sponsored by the Nixon-Agnew administration. The corporate liberal strategy is based on the premise that the big problem is "white racism," a view challenged in Paul Goodman's essay. The main elements of the corporate liberal strategy of attacking the big problem are: economic growth, education and training for "equality of opportunity," reducing discrimination in the aforementioned fields, "internal stratification" (Bruce Johnson's concept), and selective repression (for those who won't play the game by these rules). This strategy is the dominant mainstream attempt to meet the "coming test of American democracy" identified about ten years ago by Hans Morgenthau. He wrote that the "two great issues with which American democracy must come to terms—equality in freedom for the American Negro and the restoration of a meaningful economic and social order—are . . . interconnected. The former cannot be fully achieved, and might even be ultimately jeopardized, without the latter."[2] The corporate liberal strategy fails to face the latter task, which depends on a fundamental redistribution of wealth and power.

As a result, this strategy feeds (whether intentionally or not) the antidemocratic tendencies of the "revolt against social equality" which have gathered momentum since Arnold Rogow's 1957 analysis. The corporate liberal use, or at least toleration of selective, tactical repression tends to succumb to right-wing pressures toward more generalized measures of repression. But what merits careful consideration at this point is *how and why* the corporate liberal strategy is consistent with the *historical* operation of mainstream ideology as a system of cultural hegemony for business elites. This volume has stressed that hegemony is not merely a result of shrewd political behavior by business elites combined with general apathy about economic interests on the part of subordinate groups. Rather we have attempted to uncover how routine structures of meaning that underlie and guide everyday behavior are mobilized in a system of power relations and distorted communication to foster the myth of American affluence discussed by Thernstrom and the democratic mirage analyzed by Johnson.

Stephan Thernstrom indicated some of the social consequences and

2. Hans J. Morgenthau, "The Coming Test of American Democracy," *Commentary* 37 (January 1964): 63. Cf. Sidney Willhelm, *Who Needs the Negro?* (Garden City, N.Y.: Doubleday Anchor, 1971) which includes an important analysis of technological development and the Negro in American society, while concluding with a brief discussion of Morgenthau's essay. For a better understanding of corporate liberalism in twentieth-century U.S. politics, the historical studies of James Weinstein are indispensable. See the bibliographical listings at the end of this volume.

political uses of the "affluent society" concept. His concept of "relative deprivation" deserves consideration in the context of Arnold Rogow's analysis of
the revolt against social equality. As can be seen from the Schaar and Rogow
selections, the American ideology and class system set up a terrible contest
for dignity which seems especially tragic for the least economically secure
groups, white and black. It may be, too, that Rogow, while pointing out the
"hostility" of white-collar groups ("significantly attracted to Eisenhower in
1952 and 1956") toward blue-collar union groups making some improvement in economic position, does not illuminate adequately the exaggerated
notion the middle classes have of working-class gains. As some of the studies
in the part 3 bibliography indicate, while the rising New Class of professionals
and managers may have fallen on good times, this is hardly the case for blue-
collar workers and lower echelon white-collar employees.

Professor Thernstrom's remarks about "the plumber problem," "trade-
union baiting," and the myth of the "affluent worker" suggest that the revolt
against social equality works to conceal and distort actual inequality in
wealth, political power, and social privilege. The sociocultural dimension of revolt identified by Rogow apparently cuts a little higher into the social scale
than some middle-class liberals, who support the Kerner Commission's
"white racism" thesis and the corporate strategy, would allow. To put it
bluntly, the self-righteous tendency of some middle-class liberals to ridicule
this society's so-called hard hats and Archie Bunkers reveals a commitment
not only to a legalistic notion of equality but also to the capitalistic socioeconomic order of privilege and inequality it serves. Thernstrom's article
disclosed the middle-class liberal tendency to ignore inequality and to affirm
myths such as the one that recent decades have brought significant income
redistribution through new public programs (e.g., in housing, highways, and
education).

John Schaar's article, which traces the equal-opportunity doctrine
back to the individualist model of society, raises a fundamental question
about the middle-class commitment. Schaar's argument is that the popular
doctrine of "equality of opportunity" is a "cruel debasement of a genuinely
democratic understanding of equality." The true pathos of the opposition of
blue collar whites to corporate liberal programs of welfare and preferential
treatment lies in their insistence that *their sacrificial contract* with the
bourgeois-liberal individualist doctrine of equality and class society be
honored by the government.[3] The blue-collar whites do not want other down-
trodden groups to be aided by special quotas and privileges when they
themselves have been victims of the liberal-capitalist rat race. Instead of the

---

3. For an in-depth view of the "sacrificial contract," see Richard Sennett and
Jonathan Cobb, "Betrayed American Workers," *New York Review of Books* 19 (5
October 1972): 31–33.

same old egalitarian rhetoric, with its notions of enterprise and opportunity, what is needed is a "fuller conception of equality . . . one stripped of the antagonistic and privatistic overtones of the equal-opportunity principle," as John Schaar suggests. This fuller conception requires, in turn, "a broader view of politics than is afforded by the 'who gets what, when, how' perspective."

The selection by the late Paul Goodman identifies in American society "a *general* drive to dispossess, control, and ignore human beings who are useless and bothersome, whether small farmers, displaced coal miners, the aged, the alienated young, the vastly increasing number of 'insane.' And unassimilable racial minorities." Of course, Goodman did not deny the existence of white racism in American society which persists as a major dimension of cultural hegemony. But, we must relocate white racism in the larger alienating framework of what Benjamin Nelson has called the "universal otherhood of modern capitalism." Nelson has written that it "is a tragedy of moral history that the expansion of the area of the moral community has ordinarily been gained through the sacrifice of the intensity of the moral bond, or, . . . that all men have been becoming brothers by becoming equally others."[4] John Schaar's analysis shows that the pervasive American notion of "equality of opportunity" is rooted in the "universal otherhood of modern capitalism," in a society in which people are forced to compete *against* one another for self-respect. This is the historical basis of the revolt against social equality discussed below. This is the "background" which enabled Paul Goodman to avoid an *abstract* appeal to "community," while insisting that our colonialism, at home and abroad, will not be remedied without "profound institutional changes and structural changes in the economy." Perhaps only in a polity with such a large and stupid right wing could there be such difficulty in appreciating the smug conservatism of the middle-class liberal's assumption that "white racism" is the remaining major barrier to the harmonious democratic community. The ecology-oriented advertisements proclaiming that "people cause pollution, and people can stop it" and the white liberal appeals to "communication" and "community" are cut from the same corporate liberal cloth. Perhaps, as Bruce Johnson suggested, the American liberal tradition will be shattered from the right, if fundamental change is ignored much longer.

The new corporate liberalism discussed in parts 2 and 3 has generally assumed a so-called *pluralist* view of the political system. That view "is committed to the balancing of well-organized and resourceful private interests rather than to a distribution of the social product and an organization of the

---

4. Benjamin Nelson, *The Idea of Usury: From Tribal Brotherhood to Universal Otherhood* (2nd ed.; Chicago: University of Chicago Press, 1969), pp. 134–37. For the Marxist development of the related theme of alienation, see especially chaps 1 and 9 of Istvan Meszaros, *Marx's Theory of Alienation* (New York: Harper & Row, 1972).

work process permitting the creation of ennobling public roles for all that recognize man's capacity for civility."[5] In other words, supposedly pragmatic, pluralist politics cannot attack the fundamental obstacles to the development of a more communal basis for American society. To do so would involve confronting the capitalistic structure of industrial economy and the cultural apparatus of mainstream ideology. However, the questions of democratic equality and community continue to be posed in increasingly more drastic ways.

As the threat of widespread disorder has increased, academic pluralists have sought ways to reestablish the order, consensus, and stability that they assumed was achieved in the first fifteen years after the Second World War. At the same time, running contrary to the academic pluralist illusion of approaching the problem of order in strictly procedural terms, the Right presses to impose an "Americanist" solution by generalized repression if necessary. Pluralist blindness to the ideological basis and dynamics of American politics prevents comprehension of the master strategy of mainstream politics. But critics of pluralism have been able to unmask the mainstream ideology and show how supposedly neutral procedures support inequalities of wealth and power and breed loneliness rather than genuine community. Public claims against the power of private property have been overridden or deflected by the elite manipulation of patriotic sentiment through the symbols and appeals of American nationalism. Corporate liberalism can be understood more fully through the perspective of the historical interplay of American pluralism and patriotism (or nationalism). Nationalism becomes a way in which narrow elite interests in a politics of power are justified in the name of a false community. The corporate liberal strategy entails a pluralistic elite politics of power which continues to operate at the expense of broader values and goals of participation and public meaning. Rather than effective power and redistribution of wealth, the common man gets myths of national greatness. In failing to attack the authoritarian political and economic foundations of public conflicts and problems, corporate liberals foster political hysteria and super-nationalism.

When disadvantaged groups have complained politically about the biases of the pluralist balance of interests and values, they have been urged by the system's leaders to streamline their organizations for the pursuit of the "one-dimensionalized" goods the system has to offer. In other words, leaders encourage piecemeal attacks "through channels" on specific aspects of inequality and discrimination. However, a concern with the foundations of the general structure of power and inequality evokes the charge of ideological, au-

5. Darryl Baskin, "American Pluralism: Theory, Practice, and Ideology," *Journal of Politics* 32 (February 1970): 95. Cf. William Connolly, ed., *The Bias of Pluralism* (New York: Atherton Press, 1969).

thoritarian "mass politics." It must be added that this charge is commonly leveled to impugn the political identity of potential mass leaders as, for example, "communists" or "fascists." Foreign observers have often been puzzled at the political potency of the concept of the "un-American," as well as the preoccupation with "order" (sometimes spun over with cotton candy words like "confidence" and "progress") among both pluralist politicians and academicians. Critics such as Rogin, Levin, Parenti and Baskin have shown that conservative elites dominate by invoking a mainstream ideology that includes both populistic rhetoric and pluralist images. Studies by Rogin and Levin and others, building in part on Hartz's work, have demonstrated what academic pluralists have been unable to grasp: that the Red Scare and McCarthyism cannot be explained except in terms of the manipulation, by elite groups, of mainstream ideology as a system of cultural hegemony. Bruce Johnson, emphasizing the historical record of elite irresponsibility, pointed out that it has been relatively easy to delegitimize dissent by invoking the sacredness of the so-called American way of life.

John William Ward's essay makes clear the liberal-democratic capacity for repression by arguing that the idealized image of America as a land of equality, opportunity, and freedom results in the widespread inability to appreciate the repressive nature of violence employed to support the dominant structure of authority. Many people cling to the view that American violence, is "an aberration of an otherwise sound and healthy society." They fail to appreciate the *historical tendency for the elite mobilization of political bias through the American nationalist rhetoric of equality and achievement to pass over into the legitimation of official violence.* Official violence and repression have come increasingly to the forefront of public life as mainstream ideological hegemony has been challenged by relatively unfocused protest, dissent, and despair. Perhaps intellectuals share some responsibility for the triumph of despair over effective action. Professor Ward maintains that American intellectuals in general have failed to examine publicly and critically the "professed ideals of society, and to make clear the meaning of the social forces implicit in the actions of society which contradict those ideals." Kopkind and Goodman provide critical analyses of the liberal pluralist tendency to treat social ills as moral and psychological problems. This strategy, by falsifying the roots of discontent only compounds general public confusion and anxiety. To this it must be added that some social scientists are proceeding, from a tacit tradition-oriented ideological base, to develop a variety of computerized enterprises for what is called tension-management, social control, and future-planning. There may be some intimate connections between the growing futilitarianism (despair) of popular political culture and the development of technocratic ideology as a new dimension of corporate liberal strategy. However, these are questions we can only anticipate here and take up in part 5.

JOHN H. SCHAAR
Equality of Opportunity, and Beyond

I

Equality is a protean word. It is one of those political symbols—liberty and fraternity are others—into which men have poured the deepest urgings of their hearts. Every strongly held theory or conception of equality is at once a psychology, an ethic, a theory of social relations, and a vision of the good society.

Of the many conceptions of equality that have emerged over time, the one that today enjoys the most popularity is equality of opportunity. The formula has few enemies—politicians, businessmen, social theorists, and freedom marchers all approve it—and it is rarely subjected to intellectual challenge. It is as though all parties have agreed that certain other conceptions of equality, and notably the radical democratic conception, are just too troublesome to deal with because they have too many complex implications, too broad a scope perhaps, and a long history resonant of violence and revolutionary fervor. Equal opportunity, on the other hand, seems a more modest proposal. It promises that the doors to success and prosperity will be opened to us all yet does not imply that we are all equally valuable or that all men are really created equal. In short, this popular and relatively new concept escapes many of the problems and pitfalls of democratic equality and emphasizes the need for an equal opportunity among men to develop and be paid for their talents, which are of course far from being equal.

The doctrine itself is attractively simple. It asserts that each man should have equal rights and opportunities to develop his own talents and

Source: John H. Schaar, "Equality of Opportunity, and Beyond," Reprinted from *Equality: Nomos IX,* edited by J. Roland Pennock and John W. Chapman (New York: Atherton Press, 1967), pp. 228-49. Copyright © 1967 Atherton Press. Reprinted by permission of Lieber-Atherton, Incorporated.

virtues and that there should be equal rewards for equal performances. The formula does not assume the empirical equality of men. It recognizes that inequalities among men on virtually every trait or characteristic are obvious and ineradicable, and it does not oppose differential evaluations of those differences. Nor is the formula much concerned with complex chains of normative reasoning: it is practical and policy-oriented. In addition, equal opportunity is not, in principle, confined to any particular sector of life. It is held to be as applicable to politics as to law, as suitable for education as for economics. The principle is widely accepted as just and generous, and the claim is often made that application of the principle unlocks the energies necessary for social and economic progress.

Whereas this conception of equality answers or evades some questions, it raises others. Who is to decide the value of a man's talents? Are men to be measured by the commercial demand for their various abilities? And if so, what happens to the man whose special gifts are not recognized as valuable by the buying public? And most important, is the resulting inequality, based partly on natural inequalities and partly on the whims of consumers, going to bury the ideal of democratic equality, based on a philosophy of equal human worth transcending both nature and economics?

These are serious questions, and it is my intention in this essay to probe their deeper meanings, as well as to clarify some major assumptions, disclose the inner spirit, and explore some of the moral and political implications of the principle of equal opportunity.

II

The first thing to notice is that the usual formulation of the doctrine—equality of opportunity for all to develop their capacities—is rather misleading, for the fact always is that not all talents can be developed equally in any given society. Out of the great variety of human resources available to it, a given society will admire and reward some abilities more than others. Every society has a set of values, and these are arranged in a more or less tidy hierarchy. These systems of evaluation vary from society to society: soldierly qualities and virtues were highly admired and rewarded in Sparta, while poets languished. Hence, to be accurate, the equality of opportunity formula must be revised to read: equality of opportunity for all to develop those talents which are highly valued by a given people at a given time.

When put in this way, it becomes clear that commitment to the formula implies prior acceptance of an already established social-moral order. Thus, the doctrine is, indirectly, very conservative. It enlists support for the established pattern of values. It also encourages change and growth, to be sure, but mainly along the lines of tendency already apparent and approved in a given society. The doctrine is "progressive" only in the special sense that it encourages and hastens progress within a going pattern of institutions, activities, and values. It does not advance alternatives to the existing pattern. Perhaps we have here an example of those policies that Dwight D. Eisenhower and the theorists of the Republican Party characterized as the method of "dynamic conservatism."

If this argument is correct, then the present-day "radicals" who demand the fullest extension of the equal-opportunity principle to all groups within the society, and especially to Negroes and the lower classes, are really more conservative than the "conservatives" who oppose them. No policy formula is better designed to fortify the dominant institutions, values, and ends of the American social order than the formula of equality of opportunity, for it offers *everyone* a fair and equal chance to find a place within that order. In principle, it excludes no man from the system if his abilities can be put to use within the system. We have here another example of the repeated tendency of American radicals to buttress the existing framework of order even while they think they are undermining it, another example of the inability of those who see themselves as radical critics of the established system to fashion a rhetoric and to formulate ends and values that offer a genuine alternative to the system. Time after time, never more loyally than at the present, America's radicals have been her best conservatives.

Before one subscribes to the equality-of-opportunity formula, then, he should be certain that the dominant values, institutions, and goals of his society are the ones he really wants. The tone and content of much of our recent serious literature and social thought—thought that escapes the confines of the conservative-radical framework—warn that we are well on the way toward building a culture our best men will not honor. The facile formula of equal opportunity quickens that trend. It opens more and more opportunities for more and more people to contribute more and more energies toward the realization of a mass, bureaucratic, technological, privatized, materialistic, bored, and thrill-seeking, consumption-oriented society—a society of well-fed, congenial, and sybaritic monkeys surrounded by gadgets and pleasure-toys.

Secondly, it is clear that the equal-opportunity policy will increase the inequalities among men. In previous ages, when opportunities were restricted to those of the right birth and station, it is highly probable, given the fact that nature seems to delight in distributing many traits in the pattern of a normal distribution, and given the phenomenon of regression toward the mean, that many of those who enjoyed abundant opportunities to develop their talents actually lacked the native ability to benefit from their advantages. It is reasonable to suppose that many members of ascribed elites, while appearing far superior to the ruck, really were not that superior in actual attainment. Under the regime of equal opportunity, however, only those who genuinely are superior in the desired attributes will enjoy rich opportunities to develop their qualities. This would produce, within a few generations, a social system where the members of the elites really were immensely superior in ability and attainment to the masses. We should then have a condition where the natural and social aristocracies would be identical—a meritocracy, as Michael Young has called it.[1]

Furthermore, the more closely a society approaches meritocracy, the wider grows the gap in ability and achievement between the highest and the lowest social orders. This will happen because in so many fields there are such huge quantities of things to be learned before one can become certified as competent that only the keenest talents, refined and enlarged by years of devoted study and work, can make the grade.[2] We call our age scientific, and describe it further as characterized by a knowledge explosion. What these labels mean from the perspective of equalitarianism is that a handful of men possess a tremendous fund of scientific knowledge, while the rest of us are about as innocent of science as we have always been. So the gap widens: the disparity between the scientific knowledge of an Einstein and the scientific knowledge of the ordinary man of our day is greater than the disparity between a Newton and the ordinary man of his day.

Another force helps widen the gap. Ours is an age of huge, complex, and powerful organizations. Those who occupy positions of command in these structures wield enormous power over their underlings, who, in the main, have become so accustomed to their servitude that they hardly feel it for what it is. The least efficient of the liberal-social welfare states of our day, for example, enjoys a degree of easy control over the ordinary lives of its subjects far beyond the wildest ambitions of the traditional "absolute" rulers. As the commanding positions in these giant organizations come to be occupied increasingly by men who have been generously endowed by nature and, under the equal-opportunity principle, highly favored by society, the power gap between the well- and the poorly-endowed widens. The doctrine of equality of opportunity, which in its origins was a rather nervous attempt to forestall moral criticisms of a competitive and inequalitarian society while retaining the fiction of moral equality, now ironically magnifies the natural differences among men by policies based on an ostensibly equalitarian rationale. The doctrine of equal opportunity, social policies and institutions based on it, and advances in knowledge all conspire with nature to produce more and more inequality.

This opens a larger theme. We untiringly tell ourselves that the principle of equality of opportunity is a generous one. It makes no distinctions of worth among men on any of the factitious grounds, such as race, religion, or nationality, that are usually offered for such distinctions. Nor does it set artificial limits on the individual. On the contrary, it so arranges social conditions that each individual can go as high as his natural abilities will permit. Surely, nothing could be fairer or more generous.

The generosity dissolves under analysis. The doctrine of equal opportunity, followed seriously, removes the question of how men should be treated from the realm of human responsibility and returns it to "nature." What is so generous about telling a man he can go as far as his talents will take him when his talents are meager? Imagine a footrace of one mile in which ten men compete, with the rules being the same for all. Three of the competitors are forty years old, five are overweight, one has weak ankles, and the tenth is Roger Bannister. What sense does it make to say that all ten have an equal opportunity to win the race? The outcome is predetermined by nature, and nine of the competitors will call it a mockery when they are told that all have the same opportunity to win.

The cruelty of the jest, incidentally, is intensified with each increase in our ability to measure traits and talents at an early age. Someday our measuring instruments may be so keen that we will be able to predict, with high accuracy, how well a child of six or eight will do in the social race. Efficiency would dictate that we use these tools to separate the superior from the inferior, assigning the proper kinds and quantities of growth resources, such as education, to each group. The very best training and equipment that society can afford would, of course, go to those in the superior group—in order to assure equality of opportunity for the development of their talents. It would seem more generous for men themselves to take responsibility for the matter, perhaps by devising a system of handicaps to correct for the accidents of birth, or even by abandoning the competitive ethic altogether.

Three lines of defense might be raised against these criticisms of the equality-of-opportunity principle.

It might be replied, first, that I have misstated the principle of equal opportunity. Correctly stated, the principle only guarantees equal opportunity for all to *enter* the race, not to *win* it. That is certainly correct: whereas the equal-opportunity principle lets each individual "go as high as his natural abilities will permit," it does not guarantee that all will reach to the same height. Thus, the metaphor of the footrace twists the case in that it shows fools, presumably deluded by the equal-opportunity doctrine, trying to stretch hopelessly beyond their natural reach. But there is no reason to think that fat men who foolishly compete against Roger Bannister are deluded by a doctrine. They are deluded because they are fools.

These reservations are entirely proper. The metaphor of the footrace does misrepresent the case. But it was chosen because it also expresses some features of the case which are often overlooked. The equal-opportunity principle probably does excite a great many men to dreams of glory far beyond their real capabilities. Many observers of American life have pointed to the frequency of grand, bold, noble "first acts" in the drama of American life, and the scarcity of any "second acts" at all. The equal-opportunity principle, with its emphasis on success, probably does stir many men to excesses of hope for winning and despair at losing. It certainly leaves the losers with no external justification for their failures, and no amount of trying can erase the large element of cruelty from any social doctrine which does that. Cases like that of the footrace, and our growing ability to measure men's abilities, makes it clear that the equal-opportunity principle really is not very helpful to many men. Under its regime, a man with, say, an Intelligence Quotient of ninety, is given equal opportunity to go as far as his native ability will take him. That is to say, it lets him go as far as he could have gone without the aid of the doctrine—to the bottom rung of the social ladder—while it simultaneously stimulates him to want to go farther.

Secondly, it might be argued that the equality-of-opportunity principle need not be interpreted and applied, as it has been in this treatment, within a setting and under the assumptions of social competitiveness. The principle could be construed as one that encourages the individual to compete against himself, to compare what he is with what he might become. The contest takes place between one's actual and potential selves, rather than between oneself and others.

This is an interesting, and hopeful, revision of the principle. It would shift the locus of judgment from society to the individual, and it would change the criteria of judgment from social utility to personal nobility. This shift is possible, but it would require a revolution in our present ways of thinking about equality, for those ways are in fact socially oriented and utilitarian. Hence, this defense against the criticisms is really no defense at all. It is irrelevant in the strict sense that instead of meeting the specific charges it shifts the question to a different battleground. It is an alternative to the existing, operative theory, not a defense of it. In fact, the operative doctrine, with its stress on overcoming others as the path of self-validation, is one of the toughest obstacles in the way of an ethic of personal validation through self-transcendence. The operative doctrine specifies success as the test of personal worth, and by success is meant victory in the struggle against others for the prizes of wealth and status. The person who enters wholeheartedly into this contest comes to look upon himself as an object or commodity whose value is set, not by his own internal standards of worth but by the valuations others placed on the position he occupies. Thus, when the dogma of equal opportunity is effectively internalized by the individual members of a society, the result is as humanly disastrous for the winners as for the losers. The winners easily come to think of themselves as beings superior to common humanity, while the losers are almost forced to think of themselves as something less than human.

The third defense is a defense, though not a strong one. It consists in explaining that the metaphor of the footrace oversimplifies the reality that is relevant to an appraisal of the equal-opportunity principle. What actually occurs in a society is not just one kind of contest but many kinds, so that those who are not good at one thing need only look around for a different contest where they have a better chance of winning. Furthermore, there is not just one prize in a given contest but several. Indeed, in our complex and affluent society, affairs might even be so arranged that everyone would win something: there need be no losers.

This reply has some strength, but not enough to touch the basic points. Although there are many avenues of opportunity in our society, their number is not unlimited. The theory of equal opportunity must always be implemented within a set of conventions which favors some potentialities and discourages others. Persons who strive to develop potentialities that are not admired in a given society soon find their efforts tagged silly, or wrongheaded, or dangerous, or dysfunctional. This is inherent in any society, and it forms an insurmountable barrier to the full development of the principle of equal opportunity. Every society encourages some talents and contests, and discourages others. Under the equal opportunity doctrine, the only men who can fulfill themselves and develop their abilities to the fullest are those who are able and eager to do what society demands they do.

There is, furthermore, a hierarchy of value even among those talents, virtues, and contests that are encouraged: the winners in some contests are rewarded more handsomely than the winners in other contests. Even in a complex society, where many contests take place, and even in an affluent society, where it might seem that there had to be no losers, we know full well that some awards are only consolation prizes, not the real thing, and a bit demeaning to their winners. When the fat boy who finishes last in the footrace gets the prize for "best try," he has lost more than he has won.

The formula of equality of opportunity, then, is by no means the warm and generous thing it seems to be on first view. Let us now examine the doctrine from another perspective.

III

The equal-opportunity principle is widely praised as an authentic expression of the democratic ideal and temper. I shall argue, to the contrary, that it is a cruel debasement of a genuinely democratic understanding of equality. To argue that is also to imply, of course, that a genuinely democratic conception of equality is not widely held in the United States.

The origins and development of the principle are enough to throw some doubt on its democratic credentials. Plato gave the principle its first great statement, and he was no democrat. Nor was Napoleon, who was the first to understand that the doctrine could be made the animating principle of the power state. In the United States, the Jacksonian demand for equal rights was assimilated by the Whigs and quickly converted into the slogan of equal opportunity. It soon won a secure place in popular political rhetoric. Whig politicians used the slogan to blunt popular demands for equality—interpreted as "levelling equality"—while defending the advantages of the wealthy.

This argument from origins is, of course, merely cautionary, not conclusive, but other, more systematic considerations, lead toward the same conclusion.

The doctrine of equality of opportunity is the product of a competitive and fragmented society, a divided society, a society in which individualism, in Tocqueville's sense of the word,[3] is the reigning ethical principle. It is a precise symbolic expression of the liberal-bourgeois model of society, for it extends the marketplace mentality to all the spheres of life. It views the whole of human relations as a contest in which each man competes with his fellows for scarce goods, a contest in which there is never enough for everybody and where one man's gain is usually another's loss. Resting upon the attractive conviction that all should be allowed to improve their conditions as far as their abilities permit, the equal-opportunity principle insists that each individual do this by and for himself. Thus, it is the perfect embodiment of the Liberal conception of reform. It breaks up solidaristic opposition to existing conditions of inequality by holding out to the ablest and most ambitious members of the disadvantaged groups the enticing prospect of rising from their lowly state into a more prosperous condition. The rules of the game remain the same: the fundamental character of the social-economic system is unaltered. All that happens is that individuals are given the chance to struggle up the social ladder, change their position on it, and step on the fingers of those beneath them.

A great many individuals do, in fact, avail themselves of the chance to change sides as offered by the principle of equality of opportunity.[4] More than that, the desire to change sides is probably typical of the lower and middle classes, and is widely accepted as a legitimate ethical outlook. In other words, much of the demand for equality, and virtually all of the demand for the kind of equality expressed in the equal-opportunity principle, is really a demand for an equal right and opportunity to become unequal. Very much of what goes by the name of democratic sentiment—as that sentiment is molded within the framework of an individualistic, competitive society and expressed in the vocabulary of such a society—is really envy of those who enjoy superior positions combined with a desire to join them.[5]

This whole way of thinking leads effortlessly to the conclusion that the existence of hierarchy, even of oligarchy, is not the antithesis of democracy but its natural and necessary fulfillment. The idea of equality of opportunity assumes the presence of a mass of men of average talents and attainments. The talents and attainments of the superior few can be measured by comparison with this average, mass background. The best emerge from the democracy, the average, and set themselves over it, resting their position securely on the argument from merit and ability. Those on top are automatically justified because they owe their positions to their natural superiority of merit, not to any artificial claim derived from birth, or wealth, or any other such basis. Hence, the argument concludes, the workings of the equal-opportunity principle help the democracy discover its own most capable masters in the fairest and most efficient way. Everybody gains: the average many because they are led by the superior few; the superior few because they can legitimately enjoy rewards commensurate with their abilities and contributions.

So pervasive and habitual is this way of thinking today that it is virtually impossible to criticize it with any hope of persuading others of its weaknesses. One is not dealing with a set of specific propositions logically arrayed, but with an atmospheric condition, a climate of opinion that unconsciously governs articulate thought in a variety of fields. Something like this cluster of opinions and sentiments provides the framework for popular discussion of the origins and legitimacy of economic inequality. We are easily inclined to think that a man gets what he deserves, that rewards are primarily products of one's talents and industry, secondarily the consequences of luck, and only in small part the function of properties of the social-cultural structure. Somewhere around three-fourths of all personal wealth in the United States belongs to the richest fifth of our families.[6] There is no evidence, in the form of major political movements or public policies, that this distribution shocks the American democratic conscience—a fact suggesting that the American conscience on this matter simply is not democratic but is, rather, formed by the rhetoric of equal opportunity. Similarly, the giant public and private bureaucracies of our day could not justify for a minute their powers over the lives of men if the men so used did not themselves believe in the justness of hierarchy based on merit—merit always defined as tested competence in a special subject matter, tested mastery of a special skill or craft. Most modern writers on the theory of democracy accept this argument for elitism and point out happily that no serious moral or political problems arise so long as avenues for the movement of members into and out of the hierarchies are freely provided. The principle of equal opportunity, of course, does just that.

The basic argument is not new. What is new is the failure to appreciate the profoundly antidemocratic spirit of the argument. This failure is the specific novelty of the "democratic" thought and sentiment of our day, and it makes today's democrats as amenable to domination as any men have ever been. It is only necessary to persuade the masses (usually an easy task) that the hierarchs possess superior merit and that anyone (one naturally thinks of himself at this point) with the requisite ability can join them.

All that can be said against this orientation is that a genuinely democratic ethic and vision rejects oligarchy *as such*. The democrat rejects in principle the thesis that oligarchy of merit (special competence) is in some way different in kind from oligarchy of any other sort, and that this difference makes it nobler, more reasonable, more agreeable to democracy, than oligarchies built on other grounds. The democrat who understands his commitment holds oligarchy itself to be obnoxious, not merely oligarchy of this or that kind.

The argument for hierarchy based on merit and accomplished by the method of equal opportunity is so widespread in our culture that there seems no way to find a reasonable alternative to it. We automatically think that the choice is either-or: *either* hierarchy and orderly progress *or* anarchy and disorderly stalemate. But that is not so. It is hardly even relevant. The fact that it is thought to be so is a reflection of the crippling assumptions from which modern thought on these matters proceeds. It is thought that there must be hierarchies and masses, elites and non-elites, and that there can be no more democratic way of selecting elites than by the method of equal opportunity. The complexity of affairs demands elites; and democracy and justice require selection of those elites by merit and equal opportunity.

Of course there must be hierarchy, but that does not imply a hierarchical and bureaucratic mode of thinking and acting. It need imply no more than specialization of function. Similarly, the fact that complexity demands specialization of function does not imply the unique merit and authority of those who perform the special functions. On the contrary: a full appreciation of complexity implies the need for the widest possible diffusion of knowledge, sharing of views, and mutual acceptance of responsibility by all members of the affected community.

Of course there must be organization, and organization implies hierarchy. Selection of the hierarchs by the criterion of merit and the mechanism of equal opportunity seems to reassure the worried democrat that his values are not being violated. But hierarchy may or may not be consonant with the democratic spirit. Most of today's democratic thinkers soothe themselves on this question of democracy and organization with the assertion that everything that can be done is being done when organizations permit factions, provide channels of consultation, and protect individual rights by establishing quasi-judicial bodies for hearing and arbitrating disputes. Certainly these guarantees are valuable, but they have little to do with making organizations democratic. They are constitutionalist devices, not democratic ones.

Before there can be a democratic organization, there must first be a democratic mentality—a way of thinking about the relations among men which stresses equality of being and which strives incessantly toward the widest possible sharing of responsibility and participation in the common life. A democratic orientation does not grow from and cannot coexist with the present bureaucratic and "meritorian" ethic. It is an alternative to the present ethic, not an expansion or outgrowth of it. When the democratic mentality prevails, it will not be too hard to find the mechanisms for implementing it.

IV

I hope my argument will not be interpreted as some sort of mindless demand for the abolition of distinctions or as a defense of the ethic of mutual aid against the ethic of competition. The argument was mainly negative in intention, attempting to show that the idea of equality of opportunity is a poor tool for understanding even those sectors of life to which the notion of equality is applicable. It is a poor tool in that, whereas it seems to defend equality, it really only defends the equal right to become unequal by competing against one's fellows. Hence, far from bringing men together, the equal-opportunity doctrine sets them against each other. The doctrine rests on a narrow theory of motivation and a meager conception of man and society. It reduces man to a bundle of abilities, an instrument valued according to its capacity for performing socially valued functions with more or less efficiency. Also, the doctrine leads inevitably to hierarchy and oligarchy, and tries to soften that hard outcome by a new form of the ancient argument that the best should rule. In all these ways, the idea of equality of opportunity constitutes a thorough misunderstanding of a democratic conception of equality.

It is not the primary task of this essay to set forth a genuinely democratic conception of equality: that is a work for another time. Still, enough should be done in the second part of this essay to arrest the most obvious and most likely objections to the first part.

The equal-opportunity principle is certainly not without value.

Stripped of its antagonistic and inequalitarian overtones, the formula can be used to express the fundamental proposition that no member of the community should be denied the basic conditions necessary for the fullest possible participation in the common life, insofar as those conditions can be provided for by public action and through the use of public resources. This formulation will take one some distance toward a democratic conception of equality, but it must be interpreted carefully, for it can easily turn into just another defense of the equal right to become unequal.

Still, the formulation does provide some useful guidelines. It obviously implies equality in and before the law. It also implies a far greater measure of economic equality than is the case today. The issue here is not material comfort. Nor does it have anything to do with the notion that justice is served when economic goods are allocated according to the actual work (in the customary definition) each man does. That is impossible. We may urge that each should contribute according to his ability; we must surely insist that each be provided for according to his need.

What the criterion of a substantial degree of economic equalization requires is the establishment of the material conditions necessary for a generous measure of freedom of choice for all members of the community and the establishment of the conditions necessary for relations of mutual respect and honesty among the various economic and social groups within a society. This is not some kind of levelling demand for equality of condition. It is no more than a recognition of the obvious fact that the great material inequality that prevails in America today produces too much brutishness, impotence, and rage among the lower classes, and too much nervous vulgarity among the middle classes. There is no assertion here that economic equalization is the sufficient condition for the democratic New Jerusalem. Rather, the assertion is negative. As Arnold put it, "equality will never of itself alone give us a perfect civilisation. But, with such inequality as ours, a perfect civilisation is impossible."[7]

The equality-of-opportunity principle, as formulated above, also implies the equal right of each member to share in the political life of the community to the fullest extent of his interest and ability. But this is the point at which the principle, no matter how carefully formulated, easily leads one away from a democratic view. The equal-opportunity principle as employed today in, for example, discussions of representation and voting rights, really does nothing more than fortify the prevailing conception of political action as just another of the various steps individuals and groups take to secure and advance their own interests and advantages. In this view, politics is but another aspect of the struggle for competitive advantage, and men need political power in order to protect and advance their private powers. This conception of politics is drawn from the economic sphere, and never rises above the ethical and psychological possibilities of that sphere.

When it is understood that the principle of equal opportunity is in our time an expression of the competitive, capitalistic spirit, and not of the democratic spirit, then the boundaries of its applicability begin to emerge. To the extent that competition is inescapable, or socially useful, all competitors should have the same advantages, and this the equal-opportunity principle guarantees. In any competitive situation, some will do better than others, and it seems just that those who do well should be rewarded more generously than those who do poorly. This too the principle guarantees.

The basic question, however, is not whether competition should be praised or condemned, but where and under what conditions competition is a desirable principle of action and judgment and where and under what conditions it is not. Some kinds of competition actually draw men more closely together whereas others produce antagonism and isolation. The problem is to distinguish between these kinds, encouraging the former and discouraging the latter. Peace is but a euphemism for slavery unless men's competitive energies are given adequate outlet. Most people probably have some need for both inward and outward striving. Perhaps the struggles against other people and the struggles within the self can be brought to some kind of balance in each individual and in society as a whole. Ideally, we might strive toward a truly pluralistic society in which nearly everybody could find a specialty he could do fairly well and where he would enjoy friendly competition with others. Judged by this imaginative possibility, our present social order is a mean thing. It is a kind of institutionalized war game, or sporting contest, in which the prizes are far too limited in kind, the referees and timekeepers far too numerous, and the number of reluctant and ill-adjusted players far too high. We need a social order that permits a much greater variety of games. Such a social order could, I think, be based on an effort to find a place for the greatest possible range of natural abilities among men. The variety of available natural abilities is enormous and worth much more exploration than any of the currently dominant conceptions of social order are willing to undertake. In the United States today, the fundamental justification of the equal-opportunity principle is that it is an efficient means for achieving an indefinite expansion of wealth and power. Many men are unsuited by nature for that competition, so that nature herself comes to seem unjust. But many of the injustices we regard nature as having perpetuated on individuals are actually no more than artifacts of the narrow view we take of nature's possibilities and a consequent distortion of the methods and ideals by which we attempt to transcend nature. For example, in defining intelligence as what I.Q. tests measure, we constrict the meanings of intelligence, for there are many modes of intelligence that the tests do not capture—nature is more protean than man's conception of her. Furthermore, having defined intelligence in a certain way, we then proceed to reward the people who have just that kind of intelligence and encourage them to use it in the pursuit of knowledge, which they are likely to do by building computers, which in turn give only certain kinds of knowledge. Thus our constricted definition of nature is confirmed by the methods we use to study nature. In this special sense, there might still be something to say for the eighteenth-century idea that society should imitate nature.

We must learn to ask questions like these about the method of competition and the principle of equal opportunity. The task is to define their proper spheres of action, not to treat them as blocks to be totally accepted or rejected. At the outer limit, it seems clear that whereas every society is to some extent competitive and competition in some spheres is socially and individually valuable, no society ought to exalt the competitive spirit as such, and the equal-opportunity principle that implements it. Both conceptions tend naturally toward selfishness unless carefully controlled.

V

In addition to equality of opportunity, there is another kind of equality that is blind to all questions of success or failure. This is the equality that obtains in the relations among the members of any genuine community. It is the feeling held by each member that all other members, regardless of their many differences of function and rank, belong to the community "as fully as he does himself."[8] Equal opportunity, far from strengthening this kind of equality, weakens it.

When this point is reached, when the discussion turns to the meanings of equality involved in a democratic conception of membership and a democratic conception of ruling and being ruled, the equal-opportunity principle—no matter how carefully formulated—begins to mislead. A fuller conception of equality is needed, one stripped of the antagonistic and privatistic overtones of the equal-opportunity principle. That fuller conception, in turn, requires a broader view of politics than is afforded by the "who gets what, when, how" perspective.

Political life occupies a middle ground between the sheer givens of nature and society on the one side, and the transcendental "kingdom of ends" on the other. Through political action men publicly strive to order and transform the givens of nature and society by the light of values drawn from a realm above or outside the order of the givens. Men, acting together, define the ideal aims of the common life and try to bend realities toward them. Through acting with others to define and achieve what can be called good for all, each realizes part of his own meaning and destiny. Insofar as man is a being that wants not merely to live but to live well, he is a political being. And insofar as any man does not participate in forming the common definition of the good life, to that degree he falls short of the fullest possibilities of the human vocation. No man can assign to another dominion over how he shall live his life without becoming something less than a man. This way of thinking about political action leads to an idea of equality whose tone and implications are very different from those of the equal-opportunity formulation.

Other features of political action lead in the same direction, and, specifically, require a rejection of all claims to rulership based on the ancient analogies between the art of ruling and other arts. When one contracts with a carpenter to build a house, he may assume that the carpenter's skills are sufficient to the work that is to be done. But when citizens elevate some among them to places of political authority the case is different. Politics has so few givens and so many contingencies and complexities, contains so many dangerous possibilities and so few perfect solutions, and is such a baffling mixture of empirical, prudential, and ethical considerations that no man or group of men has knowledge and skill sufficient for all situations. As John Winthrop said, no man can "profess nor undertake to have sufficient skill for that office."[9]

Winthrop's comment, grounded as it is on a solid understanding of the political vocation, is a just rebuke to all claims for political authority based on technical competence. Relations between politician and citizen are very different from those between craftsman and employer. Politicians cannot be said to serve or to execute the will of citizens in the way that craftsmen can be said to serve their employers. Nor can politicians claim authority over their work and over other persons engaged in that work on the grounds of technical competence. The relations between politicians and citizens, in sum, are relations among equals in a number of important senses. Above all, their relations are built on premises that, when properly understood, encourage genuine conversation among the participants, not merely the transmission of information and commands up and down a line. This way of thinking about the matter presumes equality among citizens in the sense most basic to a democratic understanding of the relations among the members of a political community— in the sense of equality of being—and hence presumes the widest possible participation in and sharing of responsibility for the policies that govern the whole community.

Just as political authorities may not lay claim to superior rights on the ground of special merit, neither may ordinary citizens absolve themselves from partial responsibility for public policies on the ground that their task is done when they have selected those who will take active charge of the affairs of the polity. The democratic idea offers no such easy absolution from shared responsibility and guilt.

This sharing of responsibility and guilt may be one of the reasons why a genuinely democratic conception of equality is not easy to accept even by those who call themselves democrats. It is comforting to men to think that someone else is competently in charge of the large and dangerous affairs of politics: somebody else rules; I just live here. Hierarchy and oligarchy provide subjects with that comfort and with easy escapes from shared responsibility and guilt. This freedom from political responsibility is very valuable to men who would much rather devote themselves to their private interests anyway, than share the burden of caring for the public good. The doctrine of equality of opportunity, tied as it is to the principle of hierarchy, easily leads to moral arrogance on the part of the winners and to the taking of moral holidays by the losers.

A proper view of equality still leaves wide scope for the existence of necessary and just superiorities and differences, but it brings a different mentality to their appraisal. Certainly, some things *are* better than others, and more to be preferred. Some vocations and talents are more valuable than others, and more to be rewarded. The implication here is only that the more highly skilled, trained, or talented man has no ground either for thinking himself a better *man* than his less-favored fellows, or for regarding his superiorities as providing any but the most temporary and limited justification for authority over others. The paradigmatic case is that of the relation between teacher and student. The teacher's superior knowledge gives him a just claim to authority over his students. But central to the ethic of teaching is the conviction that the teacher must impart to students not only his substantive knowledge but also the critical skills and habits necessary for judging and contributing to that knowledge. The teacher justifies his authority and fulfills his duty by making himself unnecessary to the student.

Perhaps this at least suggests the outlines of a democratic conception of equality and draws the boundaries of its applicability. The heart of such a view of equality is its affirmation of equality of being and belonging. That affirmation helps identify those sectors of life in which we should all be treated in a common or average way, so that the minimal conditions of a common life are made available to all: legal equality, equal rights of participation in political life, equal right to those average material provisions necessary for living together decently at all. It also stresses the greatest possible participation in and sharing of the common life and culture while striving to assure that no man shall determine or define the being of any other man.

This is what equality is all about, and it is a great deal.[10] But it is far from everything. Beyond the realm of the average and the comparable lies another realm of relations among men where notions of equality have no relevance. Hence, a fair understanding of equality requires a sense of the boundaries of that realm in which equalitarian categories do not apply.

Those boundaries begin where we try to define man himself. Every attempted formulation of equality stumbles on the mystery and the indefinability of the creature for and about whom the formulation is made. In the end, it makes no sense to say that all men are equal, or that any two men are, because it is impossible to say what a man is. It is easy to abstract a part from the whole, and define that part in terms that make it commensurable with the same parts abstracted from other whole men. Thus, one can define an American citizen in terms that impart perfect sense to the proposition that all American citizens are equal. But when it comes to talking about whole men and about man, the concept of equality is mute. Then there is only the mystery of being, the recognition of self and others. Lawrence has expressed the idea perfectly, and he should be permitted the last word:

One man is neither equal nor unequal to another man. When I stand in the presence of another man, and I am my own pure self, am I aware of the presence of an equal, or of an inferior, or of a superior? I am not. When I stand with another man, who is himself, and when I am truly myself, then I am only aware of a Presence, and of the strange reality of Otherness. There is me, and there is *another being.* . . . There is no comparing or estimating. . . . Comparison enters only when one of us departs from his own integral being, and enters the material mechanical world. Then equality and inequality starts at once.[11]

NOTES

1. Michael Young, *The Rise of the Meritocracy* (London: Thames and Hudson, 1958). Young's book imaginatively explores the conditions under which Jefferson's lovely dream of rule by the natural aristocracy turns into a nightmare of banality and outrage. The main condition, of course, is the dedication of virtually all creative energies to the goal of material abundance.

2. Success is a function of both inborn talent and the urge to do well, and it is often impossible to tell which is the more important in a particular case. It is certain that the urge to do well can be stimulated by social institutions. How else can we account for Athens or Florence, or the United States?

3. *Democracy in America* (New York: Vintage Books, 1945), vol. 2, pp. 104–5.

4. Some civil rights leaders are suspicious of open enrollment plans to combat de facto segregation for precisely this reason.

5. "The greatest obstacle which equality has to overcome is not the

aristocratic pride of the rich, but rather the undisciplined egoism of the poor."
Proudhon, as quoted in James Joll, *The Anarchists* (Boston: Little, Brown,
1964), p. 67.

6. Oscar Goss, "The Political Economy of the Great Society," *Commentary,* October 1965, p. 37.

7. Matthew Arnold, "Equality," in A. L. Bouton, ed., *Matthew Arnold: Prose and Poetry* (New York: Charles Scribner's Sons, 1927), p. 362.

8. John Plamenatz, *Man and Society* (New York: McGraw-Hill, 1963), vol. 2, p. 120.

9. John Winthrop, "Speech to the General Court," July 3, 1645, in Perry Miller, ed., *The American Puritans: Their Prose and Poetry* (Garden City, N.Y.: Doubleday Anchor, 1956), pp. 91–92.

10. As Paine said, with permissible exaggeration, "inequality of rights has been the cause of all the disturbances, insurrections, and civil wars, that ever happened. . . ." Thomas Paine, *Works,* ed. J. P. Mendum, 3 vols. (Boston: 1878), vol. 1, pp. 454–55.

11. D. H. Lawrence, "Democracy," as quoted in Raymond Williams, *Culture and Society, 1780-1950* (New York: Columbia University Press, 1958), p. 211.

ARNOLD A. ROGOW
The Revolt Against Social Equality

> I do not mean that there is any deficiency of wealthy individuals in the
> United States; I know of no country, indeed, where the love of money has
> taken stronger hold on the affections of men, and where a profounder con-
> tempt is expressed for the theory of the permanent equality of property.
> —Alexis de Tocqueville, *Democracy in America, 1835.*

I

My thesis is that the United States is moving simultaneously toward and
away from social equality, and that the tension between the two movements is to a large degree responsible for the present social and political
mood. The movement *toward* equality is expressed in rising living standards, and it has been significantly accelerated in our time by broad
trends in the economy, the New Deal, World War II, and the current
mixture of defense spending and welfare programming that constitutes
the Warfare-Welfare State. The movement *away* from equality is

Source: Dissent 4 (Autumn 1957): 365-71. Copyright 1957 by Dissent Publishing
Association. Reprinted by permission of publisher and author.

represented in certain types of conspicuous consumption, anti-civil rights sentiment, and political behavior. I will also argue that the latter movement has been partly responsible for the failure of radical politics in the United States, and the related demise in some intellectual circles of a radical and reforming spirit.

Viewed superficially, the movement toward social equality has deep roots in the ideological and institutional past. The egalitarian theme, so viewed, permeates Jeffersonian and Jacksonian democracy, the abolition of slavery, the rise of trade unionism, and modern reformist politics. The imperative claim that "all men are created equal" has seemingly provided premise and goal for efforts to extend the suffrage, emancipate the Negro, develop a system of mass education, and promote equal economic opportunity. The American Creed, according to Gunnar Myrdal, not merely espouses equality, but has lodged it firmly in the national conscience to such an extent, for example, that discriminatory treatment of Negroes gives rise to profound guilt feelings (which are assuaged by further ill-treatment). Interpreted in this fashion, the movement toward social equality would appear to be unambiguous, uninhibited, almost deterministic.

The ambiguities and inhibitions exist, however, and they have become more pronounced in the last twenty years. They derive from the other themes which make up the ideological and institutional context: individualism and competition, the profit motive, and the importance in America of material success. Translated into personal aspiration, these themes have generated much less a desire for equality than a desire for economic gain, advancement, and higher social status and position. From the earliest days of the Republic, the business ethic has been the dominant ethic. The typical American, therefore, has never regarded the possession of wealth as inherently immoral, and even the poorest of Americans have never sought to reduce the wealthy to their own economic and social position. Depressions, financial panics, recessions, and the prevalence of poverty amidst plenty, have never undermined the faith in America as the land of *individual* opportunity.

By and large, the rich have been more imitated than envied, and more envied than disliked. But in essence, they have been imitated and envied not merely because they were rich, but because they were richer *than*. In America as an acquisitive society, the envy of the rich has been, at least in part, an envy of the select status and prestige of the rich, apart from envy of their material possessions. And in seeking wealth for himself, the American has sought the status and prestige that go with wealth. Put another way, he has tended to think in terms of advancement not as part of an advancing group or class, but of individual advancement *relative to the condition of the mass of citizens.*

In an important sense, however, a continuing general improvement of condition is an imperative of a viable capitalist system (as it is also an imperative of other viable systems). Such a system is dependent upon rising levels of mass consumption which increasingly transform the so-called luxury goods into mass produced and consumed commodities. It is not merely that full employment and higher wages create demand for higher-priced goods, although these are important factors in the trans-formation. The producers of such goods are both tempted and forced to increase their output, both as a way of making maximum use of capital investment (and re-investment), and as a way of maximizing profits. Furthermore, in certain cases (e.g., automobiles, boats, household furnishings, sporting goods, etc.), the "luxury market" is fairly easily and quickly supplied, and in such instances the market must be expanded if current output is to be maintained. Hence the "luxury market" must be steadily transformed into a mass market, through advertising, through the broadening of installment-buying plans and personal consumption loans, and, occasionally, through price reductions. In this fashion, the luxury goods of fifty years ago became the mass necessities of our time. Ultimately, if the economy is to continue to function at a high level (and leaving aside the relationship of the "expanding" economy to international developments), everything must be sold to everyone.

II

Meanwhile, the relative prosperity of the last decade has made possible a substantial measure of economic equality. The living standards of American workers are closer to those of the middle class, and the living standards of Negroes closer to those of the white population, than was the case before World War II. The Irish, Italian, and Polish descen-dants of the later immigrants have decreased the economic distance be-tween themselves and the older established Americans. Slum dwellers have moved in increasing numbers to the suburbs adjoining large cities. Paralleling these changes have been shifts in the class and ethnic com-position of college students, business, and the professions. Of course, there are millions of Americans whose economic position is still marginal, but it can hardly be denied that the majority of the population has made significant gains.

It may be suggested, however, that there is widespread dissatis-faction with these gains, not because they have been too limited but be-cause they have not been limited enough. The discontent stems from the fact that in a society whose supreme value is individual success in terms of money, no one gains if everyone gains, because in that event no one is left behind. One's allegedly no-account neighbors in the slum become one's apparently equal neighbors in the suburb, reducing the sense of individual achievement and mastery. Some part of the satisfaction of Cadillac ownership is denied, when it is observed that Negroes are driving Cadillacs.[1] The anticipated pleasure in the "night out" evaporates rapidly when the favored restaurant no longer appears to cater to a "select" clientele.

The revolt against social equality finds expression in a variety of ways. In its most overt form it consists of coercive efforts to maintain a separation between economic and social equality. Thus Negroes and other minorities who can afford better housing are denied access to such housing in white neighborhoods through "restrictive covenants," despite the fact that such covenants are not enforceable by the courts. Similarly, the economic gains of certain minority groups are rarely reflected in their admission to the more costly, exclusive recreational facilities: hotels, restaurants, dining clubs, country clubs, college fraternities and sororities, etc.; in various parts of the country such social segregation applies to Negroes, Jews, Catholics, Orientals, Mexicans, Italians, Slavs, and Puerto Ricans.

There is evidence from public opinion polls and attitude studies that racial and ethnic tolerance increases with education and income, i.e., evidence that the middle class is more tolerant than the working class. It is possible, however, that the relative tolerance of the middle class is a function, in part, of its relative immunity so far from the consequences of demands for social equality. The claims of Negroes and others for equal housing, education, and recreational facilities have been directed mainly at the working class. In Montgomery, Alabama, for example, the principal users of bus transportation are lower income white people. The real test of middle-class tolerance will come when Negroes and other racial and ethnic minorities are financially in a position to demand equality with the white middle class in respect to housing, education, and recreation. Thus far, the white working class has borne the brunt of egalitarian trends in racial and ethnic relations.

Within the white population the revolt against social equality is expressed, in one fashion, through indulgence in ever more conspicuous and initially confined consumption tastes. There is apparel snobbery, illustrated in *The New York Times* report of last Fall that there was greater demand for the more expensive types of clothing, including custom-tailored clothing, than for the cheaper ready-made varieties. There is gourmet snobbery, expressed in a quest for ever more exotic recipes and methods of cooking and serving food. There is decorator snobbery, in the preference for "high-brow" as opposed to "low-brow" modern furniture, and in the taste for original art, however mediocre, over the popular prints of the Masters. There is the "luxury cruise," the "red carpet" airline service, the "exclusive" island resort or remote vacation spot, the sofa trimmed with mink (in a recent *New York Times* advertisement), the $2,500 collection of pipes; the automobile "in the prestige price class" (Chrysler Imperial). In essence, the contemporary culture defines the non-conformist as the man who can *afford* to be different, and in a sense that definition of non-conformity has come to express the entire meaning of popular non-conformity in the nineteen fifties. But aside from the question of cost, such non-conformity is less an expression of individuality than a rejection at all income levels of social parity with peer income groups.

III

The revolt against social equality has been, in political terms, a revolt against the egalitarian politics of the New Deal. To be sure, few people vote for or against equality, but related issues have played a prominent role in recent campaigns. Thus the white collar group, which was significantly attracted to Eisenhower in 1952 and 1956, is hostile to one of the main beneficiaries of egalitarian politics, the trade union movement. It is probable that the identification of part of the Democratic Party with civil rights had a good deal to do with the partial swing of *white* Americans North and South toward the Republicans (this is not to deny that many Negroes now identify the Republican Party with civil rights). In both 1952 and 1956, a favorable view of New Deal economic policies was correlated with Democratic voting, and a negative attitude with Republican. Despite the role of the New Deal as a curb on the depression and the beneficiary of all economic groups in the population, there is no general disposition to identify the Democratic Party with prosperity and economic well being. On the other hand, the Republican Party is widely regarded as the party of aspiration. It may at least be questioned whether it is not also recognized, at least intuitively, as the party of inequality.

Thus culture and politics both express a revolt against social equality, and at another level the consequences of such a revolt in historical perspective have been no less important. I refer to the impact of the anti-equality revolt and certain related phenomena upon intellectuals. Until fairly recently the American intellectual's view of the common man was essentially Jeffersonian. In this view (which through the writings of Beard, Parrington, and J. Allen Smith has had a marked effect on American historical interpretation) the common man and the political movements he originated or supported were basically characterized by a faith in such values as tolerance, liberty, and equality.

The popular spirit, from Jefferson to Franklin D. Roosevelt, was regarded as a liberal, humanist spirit, and the main political tradition of America was therefore thought to be—and in some circles still is thought to be—a liberal tradition.

More recently, however, there have been a number of studies in history and sociology muckraking the so-called liberal tradition. The historians have discovered, or are rapidly discovering, that the various common man movements of the past were heavily influenced by narrow self-interest, status considerations, nativism, isolation, anti-Semitism, and anti-Negro feeling. So far the "new history" has focused on Populism and Progressivism, but we may expect the approach to be carried back eventually to Jeffersonian and Jacksonian Democracy.[2] It will then be discovered that there were significant illiberal and anti-democratic elements in these social movements and in their political expressions.

At the same time, a number of sociologists have found that there is a considerable gap between normative democratic theory and concrete democratic practice, at least as reflected in voting behavior and public opinion formation. According to theory citizens in a democracy vote on issues, but issues, it has been found, have relatively little to do with voting. Citizens are also supposed to seek information and enlightenment with respect to the problems of the day, but typically they do not seek to become informed, and most of them cannot identify the important problems. American public opinion, according to various studies, is ignorant, irresponsible, and easily manipulated. Finally, there have been some recent books which suggest that the wealthy, educated, and formerly suspected "interests" are more civil libertarian, more internationalist, and less prejudiced than the poorer, less educated masses.

These studies are both cause and consequence of the collapse of intellectual radicalism in our time. On the one hand, they suggest that the liberal and radical approach has always lacked a popular base, that, in essence, the liberal tradition has been a confined minority, perhaps elitist, tradition. On the other hand, they reflect a projection backward of the hopelessness and despair with which many intellectuals regard the contemporary American scene. The typical liberal intellectual is apt to experience a shocked betrayal with every report that the ordinary American is neither self-less nor idealistic. The materialism, conservatism, and indifference of the common man, both past and present, has tended to undermine the liberal intellectual's traditional faith in popular, democratic reform and change.

The betrayal to which the liberal intellectual responds, moreover, has not been immediate or sudden, but cumulative. For in large part the liberal and radical approach has been based on the assumption of a "hero class" which would act to implement the approach and provide it with a mass, or quasi-mass, base. But a "hero class" has never developed in America (or perhaps anywhere else), and successive rejections of the approach, by the farmers in the earlier period and the workers later on, have called into question the approach itself.

It is probable, in fact, that the current radical *malaise* owes much more to the failure of radicalism at home than the failure of radicalism abroad. The Soviet perversion of socialism and the puppet role of the American Communist Party have been important in framing the contemporary intellectual mood[3] but less important, perhaps, than the long-standing failure of *all* types of radicalism to attract significant support in the United States. The failures of radicalism in twentieth-century America have been particularly striking, whether in the form of rejection of radicalism at the polls even in periods of economic crisis, or rejection in the trade union movement. Nor has conventional liberalism proved much more viable or enduring. Just as little remained of Progressivism in the nineteen twenties, so little remains of New Dealism in the nineteen fifties. Hence the defeatism, pessimism, and fatalism of many radicals and liberals alike—excepting those who have abandoned the old faith for the "new conservatism" or, in Mills' phrase, "the American Celebration."

Yet all this may be admitted with reference to the past and present, and it may even be assumed, with Norman Thomas and some of the "new conservatives," that socialism has become respectable, and perhaps even Republican. There are still the consequences of the revolt against social equality which, unless tempered or reduced, can prove fatal to the value of conservatives and radicals alike. Social equality, whatever form the economy takes in the future, must ultimately be accepted or rejected, but any rejection will almost certainly require an enforced, coercive stratification. If, on the other hand, social equality is ultimately to be accepted, it must be given more ideological and institutional support than it now receives. Without that support, each successive achievement in reducing economic inequality (whether deliberate or not) will aggravate the revolt against social equality, and, in the end, political democracy itself.

NOTES

1. Not long ago, for example, a Westchester auto salesman informed me that automobile dealers in Westchester were having difficulty selling Cadillacs. He attributed this to the fact that "Negroes drive Cadillacs," and that, therefore, the former Cadillac class of citizens is tending to buy the more exotic makes of foreign and domestic cars. He added that the dealers in these cars make it a rule not to sell to Negroes.

2. The most recent example of the "new history," in the form of an attack on Beard's *Economic Interpretation of the Constitution of the United States,* attempts to show that there were no major ideological differences between the Founding Fathers and the yeoman farmers in 1787, that in a word, everyone at that time was interested in protecting property rights. Robert E. Brown, *Charles Beard and the Constitution* (Princeton, N. J.: Princeton University Press, 1956).

3. The mood also reflects, in addition to disillusionment with Stalinism, the growing conviction that Soviet man does not behave much differently than his American counterpart, i.e., that he, too, is conformist, commodity-centered, and indifferent to values other than materialist values. There appears to be an increasing suspicion in intellectual circles that Socialist Man *everywhere in the world* is essentially Economic Man in a slightly different guise.

JOHN WILLIAM WARD

The Problem of Violence and American Ideals

At this point, an unwary reader may breathe a sigh of relief, glad that Berkman has come to recognize the inhumanity of his revolutionary ideal and the political inconsequence of direct violence, especially in the United States. But that is a false moral and a sentimental conclusion to draw from *Prison Memoirs.* Berkman is not saying that violence has no place in American life. He is saying that violence cannot be understood by Americans because of the ideology which holds captive even those who are the oppressed. The American creed of an open, egalitarian society means that there can be no violent protest against the conditions of American society because there can be no real cause for it. The act of violence cannot be understood. It must be the act of a deranged and mad individual. It escapes historical understanding.

To say that because of our ideals violence should not happen here is not to say that it does not happen here. Statistically, both in individual and collective acts of violence, the United States far surpasses any other Western society. In the straightforward language of the final report of the National Commission on the Causes and Prevention of Violence, "The United States is the clear leader among modern stable democratic nations in its rates of homicide, assault, rape, robbery, and it is at least

Source: Excerpt from John William Ward, "Violence, Anarchy, and Alexander Berkman,"*New York Review of Books* 15 (November 5, 1970): 25–30. Reprinted with permission from *The New York Review of Books* and the author. Copyright ©by John William Ward. This is the last section of Professor Ward's review of *Prison Memoirs of an Anarchist: Studies in the Libertarian and Utopian Tradition* by Alexander Berkman published by the Frontier Press and Schocken in 1970, which has been retitled for this volume.

among the highest in the incidence of group violence and assassination."
In that context, the use of the word "stable" may seem rather heavy-
handed irony, but it points to a curious aspect of the phenomenon of violence in America: the violence which has marked our history has rarely
been directed against the state. Our political institutions have been little
affected by it. Which is what Berkman pointed out: violence has had no
political meaning in American consciousness. Berkman hints at why this
is so: Americans believe deeply that they enjoy self-government and personal independence.

When Americans insist that American society is free, they generally
mean that American society is a society in which each individual, irrespective of extrinsic associations of family, neighborhood, class, race,
or ethnic origin, is free to make of himself what he can. More is involved
than classical liberalism or laissez-faire capitalism. As Emerson put it,
"Government will be adamantine without any governor." That was the
millennial promise of America, a benign anarchism in which each individual was to be the bearer of his own destiny and society no more than a
collection of individual wills. It was that very dream which drew
Berkman to America: "There, beyond the ocean, was the land of noble
achievement, a glorious free country, where men walked erect in the full
stature of manhood."

A society which believes that it is the result of the actions of free and
equal and self-reliant individuals has, logically, no reason to suppose that
the state and the institutions of society are important. To the degree one
believes that America is a uniquely free society, that each person is unen-
cumbered by forces beyond the determination of his own personality, to
the degree such an ideal has power over one's mind and imagination,
there is no way to understand violence except as irrational and aberrant.
Our difficulty in understanding violence in America is, in part at least, a
consequence of our insistence that ours is a society of equality and opportunity and individual freedom. To ask questions about the reality of
violence would force us to ask questions about the reality of our ideals.

Furthermore, our ideology, to the degree it is believed in and acted
upon, leads to intense frustration which easily spills over into violent behavior when the social situation, the daily, lived experience of actual
people, blocks and prevents them from acting out what they are told is
ideally possible. After the ghetto riots in Watts and Newark and Detroit,
a study was made of those who could be identified as participants. In the
Detroit study, blacks who were actors in the riot, that is, those who were
apprehended in overt acts from breaking a window to sniping, were asked
whether they believed that if one had sufficient will and desire he could
make of himself what he wanted in American society. A majority of
those ghetto blacks said yes. There is a fact. What is one to make of it?

Not too much, perhaps, without knowing more. Was it a white man or a black man who asked the question? The blacks who answered were in the hands of the police and might well have wanted to assure everyone of their benign disposition toward American society. But to accept the fact on its face, one conclusion is that the most aggressive blacks were precisely those who believed they were free to seize the advantages of American life and, when blocked from doing so, reacted with rage and violence. One sociologist put it, as sociologists like to put it, that violence varies inversely with the presence of avenues to status and power, and avenues of legitimate modes of protest.

At yet a lower level, as Herman Melville put it, our ideals and values are even more deeply involved in the high incidence of violence in America. The traditional American emphasis on individualism and self-determination entails a weakening of institutional forms of restraint with the consequence of a relatively high statistical incidence of aberrant behavior. To put it paradoxically, a liberal, free society must be a repressive society: Freedom from external restraint means that the individual must internalize the values of the culture, and restrain himself. He must be, as we say, self-governing; he must repress his antisocial impulses in order to remain free.

A society such as ours, which increasingly rejects the sanctions of tradition, the family, the church, and the power of the state, necessarily must create the kind of personality who is self-governing, self-restraining, self-repressive. The founding fathers, following the Roman model, defined the essential quality as virtue; Emerson called it character; the Protestant evangelical tradition named it benevolence. The tradition is a long one, and we may respond warmly to some of its phrases, but we should not in our self-congratulation ignore the enormous psychic burden such an ideal places upon the individual. Until we reach the millennium of American democratic hopes, we must accept the probable instability of our society, especially when it denies the opportunity and self-respect which its ideology constantly celebrates.

Most interestingly, the rejection of violence as somehow un-American blinds us to the forms of violence, both official and private, which have in fact dominated American history. Consider the occasion of Berkman's deed: the Carnegie Steel Company imported a private army of 300 Pinkertons, the *condottiere* of industrial warfare in the late nineteenth century. The company held back its ultimatum to labor until it completed an order for steel plate for the United States Navy, whose power was needed to shield American commercial expansion. A lynch mob after Berkman's assassination attempt [on the life of Henry Clay Frick, the industrialist. Ed.] pillaged and destroyed a utopian anarchist community outside Pittsburgh. Finally, the state militia, welcomed by

the Homestead workers who believed that the state was a neutral umpire, broke the strike and escorted scabs back to work. Such particulars
support an important generalization: violence has been used again and
again to support the structure of authority in American society. We are
only puzzled when violence is used to attack that structure.

Our ideals are involved even here. The insistence that all men are
free and equal leads to the curious consequence of a mass conformity
and a mood of intolerance for dissent in any form. Tocqueville provided
the classic statement, which still holds, that the energetic individualism
and the tyranny of the majority in America both derived from the ideal of
equality. The necessary obverse of the belief that "I'm as good as you
are" is acceptance of the fact that "You are as good as I am." The basis
of one's own self-trust and self-sufficiency must be extended to all the.
equal others in society. So, if one is in a minority, one has no claim
against a tyrannous majority. The very ideal of the equal worth of every
man, which promises a world of manly, independent, and free men,
perversely leads to the mind and mood of the mass man who is intolerant
of any deviation from what he thinks. That majority may be silent, but it
has throughout American history been ready always to wreak its own
repressive violence on the rash individual who dares to challenge it or call
into question the ideology which creates and sustains it.

The fault, as Berkman would have it, lies in American consciousness: "that is the subtle source of democratic tyranny, and, as such, it
cannot be reached with a bullet." If that is so, the keepers of that consciousness, American intellectuals, have dismally failed in their responsibility to American society. One of the functions of the intellectual is to
raise to consciousness the ambiguities inherent in the professed ideals of
society, and to make clear the meaning of the social forces implicit in the
actions of society which contradict those ideals. We have failed to see
that the ugly violence of our society is not an aberration of an otherwise
sound and healthy society, but the unintended, and unforeseen consequence of our most cherished ideals. We must act on our ideals, or
change our minds. . . .

ANDREW KOPKIND

White on Black: The Riot Commission and the Rhetoric of Reform

"As America gets worse and worse," Murray Kempton once wrote, "its reports get better and better." No report of a commission investigating America's recent crises has found so warm a public welcome as the Kerner Commission's study of the season of civil disorders in the summer of 1967. In its official and private editions the "Riot Commission" Report has sold almost two million copies. Countless critiques and analyses have greeted it in the press, and it has turned to grist for thesis-mills in the nation's graduate schools and colleges. The careers of several Commissioners, staff officials and consultants have been considerably enhanced by their association with the Report (and only a few reputations have suffered). All in all, the Report has become a basic document in the platform of American liberals for social reform, a catalogue of problems and a program of solutions.

But by and large, those who were cheered by the Report's solemn platitudes or impressed by its torrent of statistics missed its essential political functions and its crucial social consequences. It presented—and legitimized—a specific view of the riots and a particular understanding of America that now constitutes the standard approach to the treatment of social ills. The Commission was able to do that job because of the way it was set up, staffed, manipulated and terminated; because of the promises and rewards it offered those who worked for it; because of its punishments for criticism and dissension; and because of its calculated presentation to the public through press and mass media.

Reportage and analysis of the Commission's work have largely failed, and for the same reasons: Reporters and analysts became deeply implicated in the "success" of the Report. Although there was an unusual amount of reportable conflicts during the Commission's seven months of operation, reporters never got past the vague rumors of friction between liberal and conservative forces, or the whispered hints of White House interference. The firing of 120 staff members in late 1967 was never explained; the substantial hostility of black staffers towards the Commission's own "institutional" racism was never mentioned; the "underground" Commission document, "The Harvest of American Racism," was never examined; the White House veto on employment of staff and consultants active in anti-war work was never disclosed; the tacit agreement to "forget" the war in Vietnam throughout the Commission's investigations and its Report was overlooked; and the secret

Source: Hard Times 44 (September 15–22, 1969). Copyright by Andrew Kopkind. Reprinted by permission of Andrew Kopkind.

plan of Commissioner Charles ("Tex") Thornton to torpedo the Report just before launching is still an untold story.

In similar ways, the political analysts who pored over the long document never got past its liberal rhetoric and its profuse programmatics to see its political role. No one has yet detailed the Report's lasting effect on the set of signals it delivered to corporations, foundations and government planners to manage urban affairs on the model of foreign aid and counter-insurgency programs of the early sixties.

For the Report does not exist outside of its political context. It can logically escape neither the conflicts which informed its operations, nor the uses to which it will be put. Strictures on thinking "unthinkable" thoughts about Vietnam (among other unthinkables) made impossible a realistic assessment of the nature of riotous America. Total concern for the way resources of the society are allocated—rather than control of the allocation process—eliminated discussion of the possibilities of serious social change. Acceptance of pluralistic myths about the operation of American institutions limited the Report to the exposition of a narrow ideology. Failure to analyze in any way the "white racism" asserted by the Commissioners in the Report's summary transformed that critical category into a cheap slogan. And overall, the Report's mindless attention to documenting conventional perceptions and drowning them in conventional wisdom made meaningless the Commissioners' demands for social reconstruction.

The very acceptance—and acceptability—of the Report is a clue to its emptiness. It threatens no real, commanding interests. It demands, by implication or explication, no real shifts in the way power and wealth are apportioned among classes; it assumes that the political and social elites now in control will (and should) remain in their positions. By avoiding an approach to the riots as events of political insurrection, or as part of a worldwide response to an overbearing US empire, the Report makes sure that social therapy will be applied only to surface effects, not systemic faults.

President Johnson chose eleven members for his National Advisory Commission on Civil Disorders, a collection remarkable chiefly for its predictable moderation. There could, and would, be no surprises. The list was comprised of men (and one woman) representing various aspects of economic and political elites in the US: expansive corporatism (Charles B. Thornton, the president, director and chairman of Litton Industries); bureaucratic labor (I.W. Abel, president of the United Steel Workers); the pre-1965 civil rights establishment (Roy Wilkins, executive director of the NAACP); Republicans (Rep. William M. McCulloch, of Ohio, and Sen. Edward W. Brooke, of Massachusetts); Democrats (Rep. James Corman of California, and Sen. Fred Harris, of Oklahoma); old-style machine politics (Chairman Otto Kerner, governor of Illinois); new-style urban politics (Vice-Chairman John Lindsay, mayor of New York City); the police (Chief Herbert Jenkins, of Atlanta); and women-in-politics (Katherine Graham Peden, then commerce commissioner of the State of Kentucky).

Like all presidential commissions, the Kerner panel was designed not to study questions but state them, not conduct investigations but accept them, not formulate policy but confirm it. Although the Commission conducted hundreds of hours of official "hearings" and traveled in groups of two and three Commissioners to riot cities, the basic work was done by the staff—and by the scores of outside consultants, specialists and experts who were directed into the really critical policy-making roles. Together, the outsiders made up the elite of professional "urbanists" which has become the command-group for the management of social crises.

Staff Director David Ginsburg was chief political cadre for the Administration. His assignment was to manipulate the internal and external operations of the Commission so as to produce a forward-looking report and avoid the worst pitfalls of controversy, bickering and career damage. President Johnson himself appointed Ginsburg as the Director, shortly after he announced the names of the Commissioners. It was an unusual move, and a source of some suspicion afterwards; commissions like to hire their own hands. But the job of political organizer was too important to be left to any old bureaucrat. The White House had to keep control of the Commission, even indirectly—*preferably* indirectly. David Ginsburg filled the required role to perfection. A quiet, commanding West Virginia lawyer, he had first met Johnson in New Deal days, and became one of his pool of Jewish lawyers (c.f. Abe Fortas, Edwin Weisl) who are always available for odd jobs, big deals and general counsel (myths of ethnic attributes grow tall in Texas).

As Ginsburg was the political manager and manipulator of the Commission, his deputy, Victor Palmieri, was the administrator and theoretician. Palmieri was a young Southern California lawyer, very much in the hard-living, aggressive Kennedy style. By the time he was thirty-five he had become president of the Janss Corporation, one of the West's biggest land holding and development corporations.

If Ginsburg had a broad rhetorical view of the Commission's purposes, Palmieri had a much more specific notion of what it was supposed to do: "We thought we had a damn good chance of moving to a major racial conflagration. ... The most important thing was what the response would be in the white police forces. The objective was to affect the posture of local authorities in the next summer."

President Johnson had called for two separate products from the Commission: an "interim" document in March, 1968, and a final Report by August 1. But Palmieri and Ginsburg came to believe that the schedule of separate reports would have to be discarded, if the Commission was to influence events in the summer of 1968.

It fell to Palmieri to assemble a crew of social scientists to document and analyze the "causes" of the riots, on which everyone had agreed before the Commission's work ever started. President Johnson's television speech on July 27—written in part and edited by Justice Abe Fortas—asserted that the riots then engulfing scores of cities were "caused" by "ignorance, discrimination, slums, poverty, disease, not enough jobs."

It should not have been difficult to find social scientists who accepted the Commission's premises. Until very recently, there has been no tradition of radical analysis in the social sciences. Many of the most important figures in academic and political social science in the US came of age in the late forties and fifties, when the "end of ideology" was proclaimed. But while many social science stars agreed to "consult" with the Commission, none would undertake a full-time commitment. The staff finally had to settle for a National Institute of Mental Health psychologist, Robert Shellow, who was a commissioned officer in the Public Health Service.

There was also some question about the acceptability to the Administration of those academics who agreed to work in any capacity on the Report. Herbert Gans, for instance, was "vetoed" by the White House as a regular consultant because he had indulged in anti-war activities. Palmieri (who was personally very much against the war, too) succeeded in hiring Gans on a "contract" basis. The White House veto operation was run by Presidential Assistant Marvin Watson, the notorious hatchet man of the late Johnson years, who kept names of anti-war activists in a computer-file in the basement of the executive offices. Gans' name turned up as a member of a group of artists, writers and academics who declared that they would refuse tax payments as a protest against the war in Vietnam.

Within the Commission staff, Palmieri tried a management device designed to provide alternate circuits and prevent overloading of the "social science input." He laid out his system of "fail-safes" in an attempt to treat conclusively the data received from field researchers. According to Palmieri's plan, the investigative and research material would be worked over in three ways: sociologically, by Robert Shellow; journallistically, by Robert Conot, co-author of a book on the Watts riots of 1965; and practical-politically, by staff lawyers, such as Ginsburg, Palmieri and Stephen Kurzman.

What happened in the end, as Palmieri once said, was that the system had an "abort" in its critical center—the social scientific, "intellectual" effort. The fail-safe failed. To Palmieri's way of thinking, that failure gutted the whole Report. The journalistic accounts, the statistical tables and the political suggestions were never bound in a coherent analytical structure.

It was more than a month after the Commissioners were appointed that the "critical" social scientific staff began its work. Having failed to enlist the undivided attentions of the top men at the universities and research centers around the country, Director Robert Shellow called for their recommendations for bright young assistants to round out his department. In time, he was provided with a half-dozen full and part-time men, three undergraduate "interns" from Antioch College, and scores of consultants who would fly to Washington at $100 or $150 per diem.

Like many government agencies, bureaus and departments plowing the new fields of "social technology"—education, urban development, anti-poverty, welfare, health and civil rights—the Commission drew to it every academic entrepreneur with a scheme to sell. Some were more successful than others: Washington is full of small research firms where returned VISTAs, Peace Corpsmen or Appalachian Volunteers can earn 12 or 15 thousand dollars a year trading on their brief associations with the poor, black and oppressed. Such operations are often run by the returnee's old bosses at the various government agencies which funded the volunteer projects in the first place.

The Commission signed a contract, quite early in the game, with the TransCentury Corporation, a Washington-based research, training and job-placement company run by Warren Wiggins, a former deputy director of the Peace Corps, and staffed in large measure by returned volunteers and their friends. Several TransCenturions joined the Commission staff. The company itself won its $18,000 contract to recruit staff.

Hundreds of thousands of dollars went into research contracts. The Bureau of Applied Social Science Research at Columbia (where several Commission contractors and consultants, including Herbert Gans, now work) got $45,540 for a study of arrest records of rioters. A University of Michigan spin-off research department got $45,488 for a study of the life habits of rioters. The International Association of Chiefs of Police won a $38,000 contract for a study of police preparedness.

One of the most important Commission research contracts was given to Systemetrics, a subsidiary of the Real Estate Research Corporation, of Chicago. Systemetrics is run by Anthony G. Downs, an old friend of Palmieri's. Downs is on the "new breed" side of a family connected with Mayor Daley's Chicago. He is a major ideologist of "downtownism" and "urban land reform."

Systemetrics was assigned two jobs: to design research and management programs for the Commission, and to combine and summarize the field research reports on twenty-four riots in twenty-three cities. The way

the Systemetrics researchers perceived the riots in the twenty-four summaries could profoundly affect the Commissioners' understanding of the
processes of conflict. If the summaries portrayed ghetto blacks as
pitiable victims, surrounded by rats and roaches, and put upon by evil
and prejudiced predators, that would be how the Commissioners ultimately would perceive the situation.

Systemetrics did use that approach, of course, and it was the theme
of the final Report. That theme grows out of the "middle position" between reactionary and revolutionary ideologies. It expresses the notion
that since the conflicts of black and white America are non-ideological,
no real shifts of power are needed to correct them. The problems which
were seen in the American cities in the summer of 1967 did not represent
contradictions within the whole political economy, but malfunctions of
one or another institution—the failure to get food or money or jobs to
the black people and whites in the same income group, to establish lines
of communication between "control authorities" and the people they
"serve." Racial prejudice, practiced by individuals alone or in groups,
compounds the problems. But there is no real answer to prejudice; the
"solution" to racial and urban problems must always be put in technical
terms. And although it may be extremely difficult, solutions can be
produced by the existing political elites.

Much of the foundation for that "middle position" was laid in an
early paper written for the Commission by Howard Margolis, of the Institute for Defense Analysis, the secret war research corporation. The
memorandum—never made public—reportedly laid out three possible
perspectives for the Commissioners to ponder: 1) the "right wing" theory
that a conspiracy lay behind the riots, and that program recommendations should emphasize the restoration of "law and order"; 2) the "left
wing" theory, that the riots represented a para-political rebellion of the
black poor in America, and that only radical social change could integrate that rebellion into a new American "system"; and 3) the "middle
position," focusing on the presumably "neutral" problems of migration,
urban overpopulation, and historical Negro underprivilege. Programs
designed to deal with those problems implied no threat to the current organization of corporate capitalism in America.

The central contradiction of the entire Commission operation was
embedded in the "middle position." As Margolis—and other staff assistants who read it in the first months of the Commission's autumn—
understood, the position did not fit the realities of the black rebellions of
the summer. The problem was not that it was "wrong," but that it didn't
represent the forces at work in the country. Its presentation was meant
to serve a single political purpose.

For that reason, its unquestioned reception created a constellation of problems for the Commission staff, for the Commissioners themselves, and for the final Report. The contradiction between theory and reality hampered the work of the field investigators, who felt themselves pulled apart between the blacks they were interviewing and the Commission they were serving. It created fatal tensions within the social science section, which was charged with integrating research materials and historical perspectives in a framework which was abstracted from real conditions. It made the official "hearings" before the full Commission quite irrelevant, for it gave values to the parameters of testimony before anyone ever was heard. And finally, it denied meaning to the Report, for it based programs on unrealistic theories.

The field investigation teams were the first to feel the tensions. Teams of six investigators were sent to each of twenty-three cities. In each city, "sub-teams" of two people would speak with officials, private citizens in positions of power, and ghetto residents and activists. The teams were organized on racial lines. According to a memorandum from David Ginsburg to the Commission staff, it was to be assumed that "only Negroes would be able to obtain information from residents in the ghetto areas." Whites, Ginsburg added, would be sent to interview officials and private citizens.

It was not long, however, before the black investigators began to sense that they were being used for purposes of which they were at least partly suspicious; specifically, they were worried that the reports of their interviews would be misrepresented when shown to the higher levels of the Commission staff, or that information on militants might ultimately be passed on to law enforcement agencies, despite official assurances that it would go only as far as the National Archives.

Many black staffers remained convinced that "the whole thing was a racist operation," as one of the field investigators put it. All the top policy-making jobs were held by whites, except for the post of general counsel, which had been given to a black man, Merle McCurdy. There were only a few "token" black consultants in the long list appended to the Report. Overall, the Report was always thought of as a white document written by white writers and aimed at a white audience—*about* black people. It was primarily a response to the white response to the riots. It was supposed to prescribe policy for black people, not for whites. Although it named "white racism," it did not describe white racist society.

The central contradiction of the Commission—between what was politic and what was real—was felt most strongly by the social science section, under Research Director Robert Shellow. It was expressed primarily in the drafting of the document, "The Harvest of American Racism," and "Harvest's" eventual rejection by Palmieri; and by the firing of Shellow and his entire staff in late December, 1967. Although perceptions of the reasons for the firings differ widely, the context of contradictions is hardly arguable: The Report was intended to serve particular political ends, and "Harvest" and the social scientists interfered.

Shellow had four assistants working on "Harvest": David Boesel, Louis Goldberg, Gary T. Marx and David Sears. All of them were young social scientists with liberal or radical tendencies. To them, the riots were not incoherent freakouts, but rather specific (though unplanned) responses to oppression. They could not be understood without a conception of black struggle against white domination; and the "causes" could not be found in the obviously bad living conditions, but in the distribution of power in the total system. In other words, the riots were rebellions.

By early November, the Shellow section began to feel the critical press of time. No underlings had yet been told that there would be only one Report—instead of the March interim document and the August final version—so the summary analysis of the whole summer of riots would have to be finished by the end of November to meet the interim deadline. "We were working around the clock," Boesel said. "We slept in our offices—they brought in cots—and we never left. It was crazy. We'd be found in our underwear darting across the hall in the mornings, just before people came to work. But we were really excited. We thought our case studies would be the guts of the Report. We thought our original doubts about how the Commission would operate were proving unfounded, and that we'd be able to say what we wanted."

What they wanted to say was contained in a 176-page document of forceful impressions, if somewhat limited analysis. "The Harvest of American Racism" was hardly the kind of work that a government agency would be happy to endorse. It did not couch its ideology in the conventions of "neutrality," but stated its positions boldly. It also was confused and inconsistent even in its own terms, and mixed traditional liberal assumptions which even the Commission would find perfectly acceptable with radical notions about the nature of oppression and the development of rebellion. The most extraordinary part was the last chapter: "America on the Brink: White Racism and Black Rebellion." Written in rather heated language, it went further than most top staff officials thought prudent in charging that racism infused all American institutions, and characterized the riots as a first step in a developing black revolution, in which Negroes will "feel it is legitimate and necessary to use violence against the social order. A truly revolutionary spirit has begun to take hold ... an unwillingness to compromise or wait any longer, to risk death rather than have their people continue in a subordinate status."

Both Palmieri and Ginsburg admit that they were appalled when they read "Harvest." Ginsburg, who was thought to be the soul of genteel manners and quiet control, spoke of the document in four-letter words. Palmieri said he fairly threw it across the room when Shellow gave it to him. The real problem was not that it was poorly done (it was no worse a job than much of the finished Report) but that it defied the categories that the top officials had established for the "social science input."

Palmieri "fired" Shellow on the spot, although the actual process of separation was much more ambiguous and drawn out. But from that point on, Shellow was excluded from all important Commission activities. "Harvest" was popped down a memory hold.

At length, Palmieri gave up entirely on "social science input," a notion in which he once placed so much confidence, and gave the analysis section of the Report to Stephen Kurzman, a lawyer who was a deputy director of the Commission, to complete. Kurzman turned out a quick, lawyer-like job, incorporating those notions in the "Harvest" thesis which were acceptable from the start, but removing the more threatening ideas.

Many of the 120 investigators and social scientists "released" from the Commission staff in December 1967 will always believe that the firings were ordered by the Johnson Administration. But there is every reason to believe that the action was undertaken by Palmieri (with Ginsburg concurring) because of the failure of Shellow's group to produce an "acceptable" analytical section.

The Commissioners themselves knew little of the firings, or of the controversy surrounding them, until the few speculative reports in the press were seen. On December 8, Ginsburg gave the Commission the news: "It was simply flabbergasting," a staff member reported. "Ginsburg said that the publication of the Report in March wouldn't really mean the end of the Commission, that there would be supplemental reports and such. And the Commissioners allowed themselves to be deluded. 'Oh, well,' Kerner said, 'if it's not really going to be the end of the Commission, then I guess it's all right.' He fell right in line, then Harris behind him, then Brooke. The rest of them sort of looked at one another. The decision was made in just fourteen minutes."

From the beginning, it was clear that John Lindsay was the chief spokesman for the liberal position, and Tex Thornton was the heavy for the conservatives. Lindsay's closest allies were Senator Harris, Chief Jenkins, and Roy Wilkins. Thornton had only Mrs. Peden as a full-time cohort. The others roamed around the middle, or, like Brooke, who had the worst attendance record, roamed elsewhere.

What the "liberal" side meant first of all was a full acceptance of the "middle position" as laid out long before in the Margolis memo. Beyond that, it entailed a rhetorical emphasis on the horrors of life for ghetto blacks, and a sense—as Hubert Humphrey once expressed it—that things were bad enough to explain (but not excuse) rioting. There was no agreement, however, that the riots were a positive or beneficial political act (as "Harvest" had proposed); nor, of course, was there any idea that the failure of black Americans to achieve equality with whites was a structural failure of the American political and economic system.

The "conservative" side grudgingly accepted that same "middle position" thesis, but emphasized the bad character of the criminal element in the ghettoes rather than the conditions of life there. Secret minutes of a Commission meeting of November 10, 1967, taken by a staff member, illustrate Thornton's attitudes; in this instance, he was responding to a discussion on "what causes riots":

In re "bitterness and despair": We're playing right into the hands of the militants who will use it as justification for violence. Maybe bitterness and an element of despair; but only two or three percent actually start the riots. It's also the rewards, the benefit from free burglary. Put in . . . "an increasing lack of respect for the law": That's what it is, and the Report has to bring this out loud and clear. There's little restraint to participation in disorders. . . . Improve the police departments: The military should train soldiers about to come out of the service in law enforcement work. Help solve big recruitment problem. There are up to 60,000 coming out per year. . . . No question that show of restraining force, quickly applied, actually has restraining effect. Show of military force (even with no bullets or bayonets fixed) quickly stopped militants. We should provide maybe that federal troops be made available on standby basis as a precautionary measure.

Let's not mention about the slave background and the poor Negro. Sins of forefathers idea will fall on deaf ears. Only 10 to 15 percent of whites had slave-owning forefathers.

No law and no courts will change the attitude of the whites. Labor unions have this very bad attitude, as does the so-called establishment. . . . If we voice poverty, etc., as a cause of riots, 30 million poor people will use it as an excuse to riot.

On the other hand, Lindsay thought that the Report, even in its finished form, was "wishy-washy." He was particularly angry that no mention was made of the war in Vietnam as a contributing factor to the riot process. But in a meeting of the Commission to debate the point of "mentioning" the war, Lindsay was voted down. Although there is no reason to think that President Johnson directed Ginsburg to avoid mention of the war, it is clear that Ginsburg was doing Johnson's bidding: That, indeed, was his function, and the reason he was picked to head the Commission staff—by the President himself. Early fears that Lindsay entertained about Ginsburg's "daily" contact with Johnson were irrelevant. Ginsburg didn't *have* to see Johnson.

There was, however, one exception. Late in 1967, Thornton grew anxious about the final Report's "liberalism." He was particularly worried that it would suggest legislation for enormous federal expenditures; and, more than that, that it would generate "expectations" in the black community which could never be fulfilled, and which would lead to more rioting. Thornton went to George Mahon, the Texas Democrat who heads the House Appropriations Committee, and asked him to intercede with the White House on behalf of the "conservative" side of the Commission. Mahon, Thornton and the President were, of course, all Texans. Mahon and Thornton were also allied through Litton Industries' interest in government appropriations.

On the night before the final meeting, Lindsay and his personal staff put together what he describes as an "end game." The plan was that Lindsay would "assume" at the next day's meeting that a summary would preceed the full Report. He would then read just such a summary—written in an all-night session by his aides. In promoting the summary, Lindsay would tell how deeply he felt about the issues it raised. The implication was that he would not sign the Report if the summary were not included. The move had three objectives. First, Lindsay's "support" of the Report (with summary) would put the burden of "dissent" on the conservative side. Second, Lindsay got his own summary into the hopper before any others. Finally, the gambit would lay the emotional and intellectual basis for Lindsay's personal dissent, should his summary be defeated, or if the conservatives won their points.

But the game worked smoothly. At first, Thornton and Corman argued against Lindsay's summary, but Thornton's attempt to put together a majority against it (and, by implication, against the Report as it stood) came to nothing.

Could the Report have gone either way? Palmieri, for instance, thought there was a real danger that it could turn into an obviously illiberal document. But the structure of the Commission and the context in which it operated suggest that its tone could have hardly been other than "liberal." The finished product almost exactly reproduced the ideological sense given it by President Johnson more than half a year earlier. The choice of Commissioners, staff, consultants and contractors led in the same direction. The political constituency foremost in the directors' minds—the audience to which the Report was played—had been conditioned to expect and accept a catalogue of ills and a list of reforms.

According to the directors, the real fights in the Commission came over the introduction to the "Recommendations for National Action." That seventy-page chapter was supposed to outline the scope of a national program of social reforms, in employment, education, welfare and housing, with no "price tag" attached.

The chapter was based on a thorough memorandum of program recommendations drawn up for the Commission by Anthony Downs, of Systemetrics.

The importance of the Downs strategy is not in the specifics of its programs, which in many cases are considered desirable by most right-thinking people, but in the nature of its political demands. Continuing, reinforcing—and to some degree setting the ideology of the Commission, it assumes the dominance of the same elites now in power, minus the old fogeys and plus the new technocrats. While its theory of programming may be dynamic, its theory of power is static.

PAUL GOODMAN

Reflections on Racism, Spite, Guilt, and Violence

White Racism

The premise of the Kerner report on civil disorders [*Report of the National Advisory Commission on Civil Disorders* with an Introduction by Tom Wicker, Dutton, 609 pp., $7.95 (Bantam paper. $1.25.)] is, "Race prejudice has shaped our history decisively. ... White racism is essentially responsible for the explosive mixture which has been accumulating in our cities since the end of World War II." Both parts of this are not true. Since the end of World War II it was a rapacious policy of rural enclosure and, in Puerto Rico, a rapacious mercantilism that drove unprepared colored peoples north in unassimilable quantities, whether their reception would be racist or not; and add the whites disemployed out of Appalachia. To account for the explosive mixture, one does not need fancy new concepts like white racism; the old story of criminal neglect of social costs for private gain is more to the point. Further, historically, with notable exceptions, the northern whites have not been racially prejudiced—though they have been something else, perhaps more disastrous. It is best to get rid of these cliches and call each thing by its right name.

In classical psychology, race prejudice is a projection onto others of

Source: The New York Review of Books 10 (May 23, 1968): 18–23. Reprinted with permission from *The New York Review of Books* and the author. Copyright © by Paul Goodman.

one's own unacceptable traits. It is a species of paranoia, the repressed traits returning as floating threats. It is characteristic of the authoritarian personality, brought up with severe inhibition of the child's initiative and animal nature; and the paranoia is excited by economic or other insecurity that makes the adult ego labile. Typically, a failing petty bourgeoisie with puritanic upbringing will have racial prejudices. The Germans were classically racist, with a full-blown ideology of Aryan supremacy that made them feel grand, whereas the Jews poisoned the bloodstream and were responsible for the Versailles treaty. Degraded by the Civil War, southern whites developed the full-blown racism of the Ku Klux Klan; they had to be better than somebody, and niggers were inferior, apelike, a threat to southern womanhood.

In this classical sense, the northern white middle class has hardly been racist at all. Their upbringing, though not free, has been unrestrictive by European standards. They certainly have not failed economically. Where there *is* more authoritarianism and insecurity, as among newly prosperous blue-collar workers—e.g., Poles, Italians, Irish, or Appalachians in Chicago—there is more racial prejudice; the same holds for retired rentiers like the Californians, threatened by inflation. (In England, prejudice is loosed at the more bitter level of job-competition among the poor). But the usual majority objections to blacks that have caused the suburban flight have not been "prejudices" but a Gradgrind kind of facts, narrowly realistic. Blacks do downgrade the schools and make it hard for junior to compete for MIT; they make streets unsafe; they swell taxes by being on relief and not pulling their oar; they are not prepared for better jobs that have (irrelevant) mandarin requirements. By contrast, in the important area of discrimination in unionized semi-skilled jobs, there have been strong prejudices by blue-collar workers; and the most vehement opposition to open housing has come in rentier neighborhoods.

In many cities the police are recruited from just the most prejudiced classes, and this has been calamitous. And everywhere, of course, police are subject to the factual prejudices of their dangerous craft; poor suspects of any color have never gotten loving care from cops. (It happens that hippies and vocal pacifists are the worst treated of all, but this is an effect of paranoiac prejudice, since these pose an inner threat to the policeman's manly perfection.) Schoolteachers are a striking example of a kind of factual prejudice produced by narrow craft idiocy: probably most of them start out with fairly innocent attitudes, but when little black children do not learn to read *Dick and Jane,* the teacher's annoyance and anxiety, fearful of the supervisor, can come close to hatred.

Historically, there has been, and persists, a northern middle-class exclusiveness, provincial and conformist, that could reasonably be called "racist." But let us look at this, too, accurately, for the remedy depends on the diagnosis. Blacks have always been strange. There were few in the eastern and middle-western country and towns from which many of the whites came. Their mores were not necessarily inferior, ludicrous, or bad, but unknown. When blacks were hired as domestics, for instance by New York Jews, they were not looked down on but treated like articles of furniture. Not in business, they did not belong to clubs. Living in their own neighborhoods, they did not belong to white churches. But to be socially excluded has been the common fate of immigrant poor. Color is not the decisive factor: black Puerto Ricans, even with their culture of poverty, now make an easier adjustment. But Negroes have been continually recruited from an entirely inappropriate slave and depressed-rural background, and their exclusion has been fatally cumulative. Then, with the recent overwhelming influx of new immigrants, and their teeming offspring, the familiar atmosphere of the northern cities has changed drastically; strangeness has become menace; panic flight has ensued.

What picture of the white middle class emerges from this analysis? It is not so much racist as narrow, self-righteous, and busy. But of course. This is the same tribe that, north and south, displaced the Indians, had Negro slaves in the first place, needlessly bombed Hiroshima, and destroys Vietnamese. Whether one calls it brash enterprise or imperialist arrogance, to these people their victims are not quite persons. If the deviants shape up, fine, one does business with them—and even extraordinary efforts are made to help them to shape up. But if they persist in being themselves, they are exterminable. "Essentially," as the Kerner report puts it, busy self-centered people do not want to be thwarted or bothered. This bleakly explains more than "racism" does.

On the other hand, the Americans have the virtues of their defects, and these are more promising. Being busy, self-interested, independent, and successful, they have also been spectacularly extraverted, pragmatic, and generous. They will pay enormous sums to convert the heathen, wash the unwashed, and teach the mentally retarded to spell. And there has been an absolute contradiction in their racial attitudes. For instance, on the one hand there was the smug silence about the Indians and Negroes in classical New England literature; on the other hand there was the pan-humanism of Cooper and Walt Whitman. The framers of the Declaration of Independence obviously meant it when they said all men were created equal; yet some of the same authors allowed the organic charter, the Constitution, to speak of "three-fifths of a person." (This was exactly the kind of detail on which Gandhi would have fasted to the death.) The bother with the premise of the Kerner report is that, if it were true, nothing less would avail than psychiatry for epidemic paranoia, probably including shock treatment—and this is, of course, the proposition of the black terrorists. A more prima facie diagnosis allows us to appeal to the outgoingness, the pragmatism, the enlightened self-interest of Americans.

Unfortunately, in modern conditions, we must notice the *increasing* anxiety and privatism of the middle class. As businesses become more centralized and the standard of living more demanding and complicated, independence and enterprise are severely constricted. And more and more we see that American horse-sense and generosity, which have been saving graces, give way to a desperate need to keep things under control. Self-righteousness can then become "efficient," a cold violence that has no inner check. There is a fanaticism of business as usual, called Preserving Law and Order, manner of Mayor Daley. If citizens fail to social-engineer the deviant into conformity, they quickly resort to mechanical measures, police, tanks, marines, bombers. When the threatened victims respond with desperate counter-measures, it is necessary to up the ante and there can be a massacre. Yet in modern conditions, it is again not necessary to speak of "white racism"; what is evident is a *general* drive to dispossess, control, and ignore human beings who are useless and bothersome, whether small farmers, displaced coal-miners, the aged, the alienated young, the vastly increasing number of "insane." And unassimilable racial minorities.

But modern conditions also have advantages. The very centralization and affluence that dehumanize allow also for pragmatic remedies on a grand scale: an 800 billion Gross National Product and the mass media can mount "crash programs." Second is the remarkable moral development of the young, sophisticated and free of economic pressure. In their own way they are as ignorant and self-righteous as the day is long, but they are not narrow, mechanical, or privatist, and they disregard caste and color. Finally, there is evidence that there is still life in the American democratic process itself, that peculiar mixture of morality, civil liberties, self-interest, and sporadic violence, swelling to make institutional change. Led by the young, the blacks, and the increasingly impatient "new class" of intellectuals, there is a revival of populism. Even the mass media, which have done so much to brainwash us, now seem—sensationally and inaccurately—to be informing us, because the journalists are new intellectuals. It is an odd "System."

Black Racism

In the nature of the case, blacks in the United States are, by and large, racist, from Uncle Toms to Black Muslims. Whites can disregard blacks, but blacks can hardly disregard the power that owns and runs everything. Whiteness, as Fanon points out, inevitably invades the unconscious. Frustrated and deprived, blacks project onto the whites the putdown and hostility that they themselves feel. It would be too bitter to see truly the indifference that is usually really there.

(It is hardly necessary to discuss racial relations in order to make a catalogue of human sadness. But on the black side, lack of acquaintance, and mutual misunderstanding of manners and signals, must be especially devastating. For instance, willing to be friendly but being suspicious and vulnerable, he may start out with testing, either boring politeness or probing insult. But if the white is a simple person, he will be bored or annoyed, and shrug and sign off, and the world is so much worse than it was. This can quickly spiral downward to general mutual avoidance and fear. Yet, given ghetto conditions, it would be unusual for a black child *not* to grow up with suspicion, if the only whites he is exposed to are not simple persons, but police, schoolteachers, and bill-collectors.)

The sophisticated ideology of Racism itself has been picked up by intelligent blacks from white paranoids; it is a fairly recent invention of Germans, Boers, and the Ku Klux Klan. (Until the nineteenth century, race was not much used as a projection-screen, though religion, caste, and nationality were vastly overworked. Even anti-Semitism was mainly religious and could usually be alleviated by conversion.) And now we see that the artifact of a "racist society" is picked up from black militants by the Kerner report. Presumably the report's rhetorical purpose in this is to sting white guilt in order to get action, but, as we shall see, this is a slender reed to lean on.

At present, southern blacks are less racist than northern blacks. Being more acquainted with real white madmen, they themselves have less paranoia and more sense of plain injustice; whereas northern blacks have to cope with bland unconcern or downgrading by neutral rules, at the same time as they are suffering. A case in point is "Law and Order." A Jim Crow law is mad on the face of it; but to northern middle-class whites, due process is only reasonable, it provides a neutral forum for discussion and legislation. They cannot see that to dispossessed people due process is precisely the usual runaround that they have been getting. Besides, northern blacks are now a more failing class than southern. The excessive urbanization is fiscally and physically unworkable, and is unlivable. Religion and family are shattered. There is more anomie. The great bloc of immigrants and estranged youth may have a little more money but they are much worse off than they were in the rural areas from which they were driven.

A poignant example of the clash of black racism and white lack of empathy was the expulsion of white students from the civil rights and Black Power movements, e.g., from SNCC. Innocently righteous and confident in themselves, the white students took too much initiative and too much for granted. This made it hard for the blacks to run their own show, which was indispensable if they were to regain their own confidence. If the blacks had responded with fraternal, even if angry, competition, it might have cemented a deeper friendship. Instead they responded with jealousy, including sexual jealousy, and expulsion. The possibility of free cooperation has been foreclosed. Yet, since the blacks still need help, for instance funds and facilities and to swell a demonstration, there now develops the ugly situation that sympathetic whites are manipulated, hustled, or lied to; and it must be a further humiliation for blacks to do this.

During the recent fracas at Columbia, the blacks invited their SDS allies out of a joint action because, a leader said, "They were shaky and would vacillate and panic and could not be depended on. With black kids the issue is clear, to fight racism." (One is struck by the testimonial to Socrates' definition of courage, to have an idea.) My guess is that the whites had a more complicated idea; but in fact the more structural issue of the action, to fight military infiltration of the university, did get lost in the shuffle, so the blacks were proved correct.

Generally speaking, it has been a mistake, in my opinion, for black militants to try to make "integration" and "black power" absolute and incompatible. The basic theory behind it is nonsense, to lay stress on the color of civilization as the Germans laid stress on its nationhood; and, practically, too much science and wisdom, as well as wealth, resides in the dominant community to try to dissociate from it without being continually phony. It is stupid to regard Galileo or Faraday as "white" rather than as human—and to be saying it into a microphone. And negatively, it would be stupid to have a black and white committee against nuclear fallout or cancer. (By contrast, draft resistance warrants separate committees, since those with and those without student-deferments have different problems.) I doubt that, outside the South, there are many middle-class whites who have any feelings at all about being "white" as such. To the extent that to belong to a racial or national group is indeed a cause of pride—frankly, as a child of the Enlightenment, I think this is thin gruel—the minority group will thrive best in a mixed society where it has influential soul-brothers or *Lands-männer*. And politically, the majority of blacks and the best of the whites in fact want "integration" and will insist on it.

Nevertheless, illogic has its place. *Le coeur a ses raisons que la raison ne connait pas.* It is now thinkable that there *could* be a black committee against nuclear fallout, whereas ten years ago it was impossible to mount a protest in Harlem on this issue at all. People have to humanize themselves in their own way. It produces a curious dilemma.

For example, at the Conference for New Politics, just the most energetic of the blacks insist on the official recognition of their caucus; whereas just those whites who are most thoughtful and most deeply committed to social justice are embarrassed and do not know what to do with this demand, because in fact the unity of mankind is the truth.

Spite

The actual situation, without fancy constructs, is that some are hurting and the others don't care. Starting from this obvious premise, for the oppressed a primitive method of coping is spite. Spite probably played a part in the expulsion from SNCC—"you aren't invited": it is the chief ingredient in the black theater of insult, genre of LeRoi Jones; and I think it has been an important factor in the riots—"burn, baby, burn." Spite is the vitality of the powerless; it is a way of not being resigned, of keeping a lost fight alive by preventing the dominator from enjoying his domination.

(Needless to say, let me say at once, there are other factors in the riots. In some cities there has been evidence of a political plan for insurrection, part of a plan for world insurrection. The looting speaks for itself as reasonable free appropriation by people who are hopelessly poor. Burning white businesses in the ghetto makes a rational, though desperate, political point. There is a spontaneous explosion of frustration. In any culture of poverty there is a carelessness about one's own possessions and life, just as the homicide rate is high. On the part of the intelligent and energetic young, who have played a big role, rioting is exactly equivalent to white youth uprisings on campuses and streets around the world, in fascist, corporate liberal, and communist countries: it is an *acte gratuit* of freedom in the face of irrational authority; the youth component is more important than the racial or ideological component.)

Commentators seem to be unwilling to say the word spite; yet it is not an ugly or useless passion. It is a means of preserving or even of finding identity. Saul Alinsky especially has often tried to use it for community development, e.g. by organizing dispossessed and fragmented people simply to take revenge on shortweight grocers. But the trouble with spite, of course, as Alinsky also knows, is that its victories do not add up, and the letdown can lead to worse despair.

Spite is often self-destructive, "biting off one's nose to spite one's face"; one burns down one's own neighborhood partly because one cannot burn down theirs, but also to make them feel bad. This purpose usually fails; to "natural calamities" the affluent Americans promptly respond with clothing and canned goods, and do not feel bad but good.

To hit home, it is necessary to produce an apocalypse as when Malcolm X, during his fanatical period, prayed for an atom bomb to destroy New York, Allah's revenge. But I have heard, too, of a "political" purpose of self-destruction, to make precisely the unengaged blacks worse off and so swell the cadres of revolt. This motive, if it exists, is evil.

Somewhat more practical is spite-work as blackmail. It is possible that some riot areas, like Watts or Newark, have received a tangible payoff, as well as sociology. C. V. Hamilton puts it formally when, in a recent essay, he speaks of a quid pro quo: "Blacks receive economic support and political power; whites receive a chance to live in a healthy, developing, equitable society." But the results have been meager, and, as a political proposition, shakedown must finally produce a devastating backlash. Nevertheless, the same substance can be put in a theoretical form that is quite acceptable political science, and hopefully workable: "For the commonweal of a pluralistic society, it is necessary for every group to flourish, and every group has the duty to throw its weight around to get justice for itself and the whole." It is not newsy in American history that this might involve some violence; consider, for instance, the burned barns and derailed trains of 1885 agrarianism, or the defiance of court and police in the labor movement, with many killed. Hamilton has to use the language of blackmail because he cannot speak of commonweal: he seems to need the ideology of race war in order to organize a following.

In my opinion, we would be much further along if Black Power had long ago presented its concrete political program, e.g., local control of police, schools, and other services; the underwriting of local small businesses and cooperative housing. Such things are perfectly plausible and, if fought for, would by now have been won. (I have been plugging them for twenty years, but I have no troops.) If a decade ago, as we urged, the integrationists had asked for the guaranteed income for all Americans instead of welfare, we would now have it; liberals get used to anything, once they hear the words. Five years ago, the March on Washington should have highlighted the Vietnam War, as some of us again urged. But moderate black leaders insisted that these things were too far out. And militant black leaders insisted on the spiteful recourse of sulking and putting on the whites the burden of guessing what is needed and coming across to prove their good will. Blacks shouted "Black Power!" and puzzled sympathetic whites asked, "What is Black Power?" A painful example has been James Baldwin's gambit: he forces the white interlocutor to ask, "But what do you want?" "You know what we want." "No, I really don't." "We want just what you want." Perhaps Baldwin says this ingenuously, but he is in error; for usually the white man does not think of himself as a "white man," but just as an individual in his own state of confusion and misery, in which being white does not help at all. Unless he is very empathetic, he does not see the disadvantage of being *not* white. If Baldwin would say, "We need thus and so to live better. How can *you* be of use in *our* getting it?" then the white man will either help according to his abilities or confess that he doesn't care enough to put himself out. Of course, a psychological use of the spiteful gambit is to avoid the risk of rejection.

But this is water under the bridge. Concrete programs for local control *are* emerging, there is certainly more acquaintance, and despite spectacular militant tactics there seems to be diminishing backlash. One has the impression that, in the white community, private groups small and large are far ahead of the political officials and Congress. These include, let me say wryly, big business corporations which have a natural self-interest in fire-prevention and will even make an extra buck out of racial harmony—you'll see.

But to account for the slow emergence of concrete demands, we must bear in mind, too, that dispossessed and dependent people are disoriented and do not themselves know what they want. If something positive is given, it is suspected as second-rate or a trap or a token never adequate to need. If something is taken or achieved by one's own effort, it thereby becomes degraded, or is a cause of envy among one's fellows and proves that one has been "co-opted." This is the neurosis of the victimized that Robert Jay Lifton has been studying.

Sensitive minds, like James Baldwin again, understand perfectly that just to get into the middle-class American mainstream is not humanly good enough; but then it is hard for him to explain to poor people what, these days, would be humanly good enough. Consider the current social imputation of many jobs as "menial." When I was young, driving a bus or trailer-truck was manly, difficult, and responsible; now when there are many black drivers, it is ordinary. Construction work used to be skilled; but a black or Spanish bricklayer or mason tends to be considered unskilled. White road-workers in Vermont have a decent job; black road-workers with the same equipment have a menial job. Postman, a job requiring unusual tact and judgment, has always been a dignified occupation; now that, like other Federal employment, it is open to many blacks, my guess is that it will be considered drab. A German or Jewish waiter is a mentor or kibitzer; a black waiter has a servile job. This social imputation of worth is made, of course, by both whites and blacks. Whites, however, usually do not give it a second thought, as their young move into other jobs. The question is why the blacks go along with the same imputation. The dismaying thing is that objective criteria like the kind of work, the worth of the product or service, and often even the wages count for very little. In this frame of mind, it is impossible to be free and independent.

But this subjective evaluation by the standards of public relations is endemic in American society. Nothing is regarded as itself, on its own merits. Thus, in the present essay which ought to be on politics and ends and means, I find myself discussing emotions and unconscious emotions, like racism, spite, revenge, and guilt. I find this pretty sickening. Perhaps the chief hope in the young, with their flesh-and-blood interests, simplifications of the standard of living, casteless friendships, and direct action, is that they will bring us back to objective reality, however crude.

Guilt

A chief use of spite is to make the others feel guilty; this not only prevents their enjoying their domination but may result in tangible "amends." It is clear that with many middle-class whites, this ruse has disastrously succeeded. Disastrously, because no good has ever come from feeling guilty, neither intelligence, policy, nor compassion. The guilty do not pay attention to the object but only to themselves, and not even to their own interests, which might make sense, but to their anxieties.

Psychoanalytically, guilt is repressed resentment and this is latent dynamite. For a time the guilty may forbear retaliation for annoyance or insult and may pay token amends, but soon they turn a deaf ear and then resentfully get even.

The dilemma is that blacks are indeed victims, of a system of property relations and policing, but the present-day northern whites, as persons, are not consciously nor importantly victimizers. There is exploitation of black people in their own neighborhoods, which can be helped by phasing out of their neighborhoods; but such exploitation is trivial in the Gross National Product and is overwhelmingly outweighed by the general tax-cost in black social services, special services, special policing, etc. Since they are not economically necessary, blacks cannot get redress by striking and bargaining. Since most whites are not exploiting them, they cannot give them redress by stopping their exploitation. When there is disorder and the cops crack down, the whites feel that *they* were aggressed on, and this is technically true. The black demand "Just get off our backs" makes sense in asking whites to stop running the ghettos through the school bureaucracy, the welfare bureaucracy, the police, and slumlords; but it is a poor slogan since, in the inflationary urbanism and high technology, blacks simply must have white subsidy, professional help, and jobs in the only economy that there is.

Almost all whites now agree blacks ought to get preferential treatment and there are stirrings in this direction. But this cannot come to much if it is done by guilt, to make amends; it must be done for political motives, self-interest, decency, commonweal, and justice. Unhappily, the Americans, who neglect other public goods, whose rivers stink, whose towns are hideous, whose countryside is despoiled, and whose children are mis-educated, neglect this public good too. My guess is that, just beneath the surface, it is they who have the slogan, "Get off our backs."

Really to remedy our domestic colonialism (and our foreign colonialism) requires profound institutional changes and structural changes in the economy. We would have to divert the military technology to useful production; control the inflation that makes poor people poorer; reverse the policy of rural enclosures that swells the cities; manage the advertising, design, and pricing of consumer goods so that people can live decently without being in the rat race; get rid of the irrelevant mandarin diplomas for licensing and hiring. To stop being exclusive, American society would have to be about human beings rather than the Gross National Product, and the privatist competition for a cut. It would have to give up its delusion of social-engineering everybody, and tailor its help to local needs and local social organization. But all this amounts to a religious conversion and seems hopeless. It is possible that we cannot have such a conversion without convulsions; unfortunately I do not hear of any convulsions that would lead to the relevant conversion. The violent champions of Che or Lenin rarely say anything relevant to the real problems of a country like ours. It is understandable that blacks are hung up on their gut issues of being hemmed in and pushed around, but it is distressing that the Peace and Freedom Party or Students for a Democratic Society cannot get beyond gut issues. Radical liberals, like Harrington, Keyserling, or Rustin, propose New Dealish remedies like more public housing, schooling, and transit, that would recreate the same problems bigger and worse. Liberals feel guilty. "Conservatives" arm the police.

Non-Violence

Meantime, we must live with the immediate problem: what to *do* when some are hurting and others, who have power, don't care? *How* to make narrow, busy, and self-righteous people understand that other people exist?

It was exactly for this problem that Gandhi, A. J. Muste, and Martin Luther King devised and experimented with the strategy of active massive non-violent confrontation, both non-violent resistance and aggressive non-violence. In my opinion, this is the only strategy that addresses all aspects of the situation. It challenges unconcern. It attacks institutions and confronts people as well. It personalizes the conflict so that habitual and mechanical responses are not easy. It diminishes strangeness. It opens possibilities for the narrow to grow and come across, instead of shutting them out. It interrupts the downward spiral of the oppressed into despair, fanaticism, and brutality. Most important, it is the only realistic strategy, for it leads to rather than prevents the achievement of a future community among the combatants. We will have to live together in some community or other. How? In what community? We really do not know, but non-violent conflict is the way to discover and invent it.

Non-violence is aggressive. Since the injustices in society reside mainly in the institutional system, though the personal agents may be innocent or even quite sympathetic, it is necessary to prevent the unjust institutions from grinding on as usual. It is necessary not to shun conflict but to seek it out. So Gandhi, Muste, and King were continually inventing campaigns to foment apparent disorder where things apparently had been orderly.

Naturally, aggressive massive non-violence is not safe. (Gandhi lost thousands.) If only mathematically, when there is a big crowd, some will be hurt—sometimes because of one's own young hotheads, more usually because the police panic and try to enforce impossible Byzantine restrictions, Law and Order. On the other hand, actions of this kind are far less likely to lead to a shambles. In the present climate of cold violence armed with a lethal technology, this is a major consideration.

I do not think that non-violence is incompatible with fringes of violence or flare-ups of violence, so long as its own course is steadily political, appealing to justice, self-interest, and commonweal, and if the political object of the campaign speaks for itself. Gandhi, of course, was a purist about avoiding violence, though he said that it was better to be violent against injustice than to do nothing; both Muste and King were willing to cooperate with violent groups, if they did not try to take over. Psychologically, indeed, it is probably an advantage for a non-violent movement to have a group like the Black Panthers in the wings, committed to violent self-defense, for this quiets down the more rabid opposition and makes a calmer zone for real political and economic confrontation. (Sometimes it doesn't work out so smoothly.)

Non-violence, and King's own campaigns, do not necessarily prejudge the issue between "integration" and "black power." Separatism is ruled out, however, since the point of confrontation is to come to mutual recognition and commonweal. It is not necessary to "love" one's enemies, but there must be a belief that common humanity is more basic than racial difference; and this belief must be bona fide or non-violence becomes a mere tactic and has no energy. Certainly King's followers took his universalist Christian rhetoric at face value. (So did I.) As I have said, it is the only realistic position; it is the tendency of history. In the world, we cannot continue to have "peaceful" co-existence, which is really cold war; we will come to community or perish. In this country, it is not the case that there could be two societies, as the Kerner report threatens. Either the dominant group will hem in the blacks in apartheid reservations, which is unthinkably abhorrent, or there will be a democratic pluralism or general miscegenation, each of which has attractions.

In the northern cities, however—and this is a grim complication—there are two distinct problems which somehow have to be solved at the same time. The first is the one we have been discussing, how to get whites to pay attention to blacks as existing, and for this, aggressive non-violence makes the most sense. But the second problem is that we have allowed, in the ghettos, the formation of what Oscar Lewis calls a Culture of Poverty, insulated, ingrown, dependent; and how can such a culture become free and independent? I don't know; but it is possible that rioting, burning, hurling insults, apparently stupid militancy, and an extravagant black racist ideology are indeed means of regaining confidence at this level of dispiritment. King, as he came to deal with northern problems, had begun to take this factor into account, though it clearly pained his heart and mind. And it is encouraging that whites, and white officials like Lindsay, may be finding the compassion that is here the only relevant thing we have to give.

The violent who are interested in insurrection and "revolutionary" overturn inevitably consider non-violence as "reformist." According to their theory, since it is piecemeal and does not aim to demolish the System and replace it (with what?), it cannot change anything. In my view, especially in complicated and highly organized societies, it is only by opening areas of freedom piecemeal that we will transform our lives. "Seizing power" in such societies is precisely counter-revolution and stops the social revolution short. But the human contact of aggressive non-violence is exquisitely relevant to the deepest danger of modern times, the mechanical violence of 1984. Because of it and the new spirit of the young, we will not have 1984.

Finally, it is said that non-violence might suit the Hindus but it is contrary to American spirit and tradition. Quite the contrary. It seems to me to be simply an extension of traditional American populism, the democratic process as conceived by Jefferson, that has always revived in times of great crisis: acting "illegally" and "petitioning," rousing the general will, protected by the Bill of Rights, with fringes of violence, and ending up with important institutional change. In every major country in the world, power is terribly deeply entrenched; but America is the most likely place for a non-violent movement toward freedom to succeed.

Since I have this occasion, let me say a word about the death of Martin King. He was a stubborn, reasonable man, and political without being a fink. I do not know any other national leader for whose death I would have wept.

In my opinion, the extraordinary general grief of the Americans was not, as has been charged, hypocritical or empty. The grief for death and sympathy for survivors is one of the few emotions that bring all people, even divided families, together. I think that whites now recognize blacks a little more as persons than they did before, and this should have consequences.

Part Five

The Emergence of Technocratic Ideology in the Superindustrial Society

Ivan Illich has observed that the "university graduate has been schooled for selective service among the rich of the world."[1] Students should take time to reflect upon the international as well as national implications of this prospect. Perhaps student concern in recent years with selective service and the Vietnam War should be put into this larger context. Yet amid the everyday busyness of "schooling" it is not easy to identify and pursue the fundamental political problems of thought and action in the surrounding technocorporate society. The essays in this section help to identify political functions of university culture and academic institutions.

The role of the university in fitting people for selective service among the rich has been obscured by the increasing emphasis on narrow technical knowledge in higher education. In the social sciences, political problems are often falsely interpreted as engineering problems to be solved by experts applying specialized techniques. The notion that elites have the means and the will to act in the interest of all sectors of society increases the tendency for public debate to degenerate into bargaining between those who already have power. The full development of human rationality is, of course, blocked by this tendency. Some students may find contentment in the conclusion of the authors of one American government textbook that the "future of American democracy depends on the wisdom, responsibility, and resourcefulness of the nation's elite."[2] There will be plenty of encouragement from academicians, keeping a faith probably going back to Plato, that if the total number of significant "actors" is small enough, then somehow they can make an "input" of "objective knowledge" to rationalize life into a democracy of merit. On the other hand, it may be worthwhile to work toward a *critical* theory of why the

1. Ivan Illich, *Deschooling Society* (New York: Harper & Row, Harrow ed., 1972), p. 49.
2. Thomas R. Dye and L. Harmon Zeigler, *The Irony of Democracy* (Belmont: Duxbury Press, 1971), p. 339.

public realm is becoming a place of little more than what Edelman has called "symbolic reassurance."

John McDermott suggests that we will be blind to these problems as long as we assume that the development of scientific and technical knowledge and the growth of freedom are inextricably linked in our society. He sees a *political* need for a new concept of reason and social purpose, one which goes beyond both the seemingly mindless technical rationalism of the politico-economic elites and the seemingly mindless irrationalism of America's "underclasses." McDermott provides important insights into the development of technocratic ideology and its relation to the growing despair of popular political culture.

There is today growing discussion and debate, at least on the campus, about the question of "technocracy" on the one hand, and about a "new populism" on the other. Those who are troubled by McDermott's criticism of the "anti-Populism of university-based intellectual culture" may indeed argue that he makes some uncritical assumptions about the nature of popular egalitarianism in the United States. Traditional and recent ideological trends obscure the relations between the types of knowledge developed in a society and the groups that use this knowledge in the pursuit of interest. American culture has become increasingly industrialized *and* ideologized and, so, American society may better be called "superindustrial" than "postindustrial." In this context Hansen and Weisbrod show the fictional nature of the claim that the American system of higher education contributes to equality of educational opportunity. Schaar noted that the principle of "equality of opportunity" justifies the myth that American education fosters a genuinely democratic, merit-based hierarchy. The view persists that the "unnatural" bases of socioeconomic inequality may be removed by more sophisticated approaches to public education, which is to say: without attacking directly its *chief* institutional sources in economic privilege.

The American liberal-capitalist worldview seems to be entering a new phase of technocratic ideology, the intellectual core of which is a deification of science. Perhaps this development of science and technology as ideology is, in part, a response to the need to fortify mainstream bureaucratic authority against chaotic and fragmented elements of "countercultural" protest, minority-group unrest, and counterrevolutionary pressures toward increased state repression and violence. The hegemonic apparatus of the superindustrial society seems to manipulate different forms of discontent with varying degrees of success. But the distinctive, long-range effect is the muting of fundamental political debate. Whether the institutional medium is advertising or the army, the apparent goal is "to bring society under control in the same way as nature by reconstructing it according to the pattern of self-regulated

systems of purposive-rational action and adaptive behavior."[3] Perhaps this is
not so easy to grasp for students who have been taught that a career as a specialist within a bureaucracy will give them high status and self-fulfillment. A
critical, historical perspective is not forged easily in such a milieu. Nevertheless, if control-oriented systems are extended, the actual choices of college
graduates will be narrowed.

Louis Kampf's indictment of how the humanities accommodate young
people to the falsification of experience and the compartmentalization of behavior must be assessed in terms of the ascendancy of the technician over the
intellectual in our institutional life, and the ways in which an uncritical democratic rhetoric obscures the authoritarian structures of bureaucracy. Vidich
and Bensman provide concrete evidence of the way in which bureaucratic
language papers over conflicts and promotes total administration of life. It
would appear that the university cultivates a "technological ego" adapted to
the concealed "machine ideal" of most bureaucracies. Dominant structural,
political, and ideological relations of the university to other institutions often
facilitate the kind of programmed control over human activity which serves
the interests of military and business elites.

Theodore Lowi says of the contemporary politics of higher education:
"Pressures are on, inside and outside the universities, to convert every aspect
of American culture into a series of service stations, putting everything into
mesh."[4] These pressures may be viewed collectively as the process of
technocratization. The technocratization of the curriculum, teaching, and research of social scientists tends to mean generally that the "problems"
confronting the institutional managers of the society are "solved" by creating
an order congruent with their specific objectives and interests. As another
"tool" in this cultural regime of industrial empiricism, political theory becomes
the management of the immediate, concrete tensions of people reduced increasingly to the role of passive consumers.

This theme is central to Edgar Litt's study of *The Public Vocational
University*[5] which shows how the university often tends to promote and sustain an "anti-developmental curriculum." Insofar as this is the case, the
university facilitates the growth of administrative power at the expense of
citizenship. The university curriculum might cultivate instead the concepts

3. Jurgen Habermas, *Toward a Rational Society,* trans. Jeremy Shapiro (Boston:
Beacon Press, 1970), p. 117.
4. "The Politics of Higher Education: Political Science as Case Study," in *The
Post-Behavioral Era,* ed. George Graham and George Carey (New York: David McKay,
1972), p. 36. On technocratization in general, see Max Horkheimer, *Eclipse of Reason*
(New York: Oxford University Press, 1947).
5. New York: Holt, Rinehart & Winston, 1969. This work is subtitled "Captive
Knowledge and Public Power." See also the discussion of political education in Robert
J. Pranger, *The Eclipse of Citizenship* (New York: Holt, Rinehart & Winston, 1968).

and perspectives for criticizing the politics of everyday life, as suggested by McDermott. It may well be an ironic sign of health in American political culture that an increasing number of students seem unwilling to live complacently in the ideological mainstream of American life. Using a theme from the work of the young Walter Lippmann, it appears that, while they may be willing to give up the ideal of total *mastery* of historical processes popular with older generations and with techno-bureaucrats, students are not prepared to submit to political *drift* in the turbulent waters of contemporary social and economic life. On the other hand, some—in trying to turn "up the mainstream"—seem unable to avoid the whirlpools of instant entertainment and privatistic gratification that populate the technocorporate landscape with political "dropouts."

The struggle "up the mainstream," pursued seriously, requires political imagination, discipline, and courage. Regarding the ideological mainstream as *nothing but* a menace would seal us off in a position similar to the technocrats' insistence on dealing not with persons and politics but with "hard data" and "technical models." The American political tradition is not unitary and its meaning should not be allowed to be monopolized in mainstream ideological versions. The monopolization of the cultural process has been an essential aspect of the economic and political domination of societal development by American business elites and their spokesmen. The elite's foreclosure of alternative lines of development based on different ethical, aesthetic, and political values has stifled the critical spirit necessary for the democratic reconstruction of human relations. As Enzo Paci has put it, "Present society needs the history of the past so that it can rediscover and reactivate its genesis in it."[6] Mainstream rationales for "technological society" and our "high standard of living" promote social conformity and standardized personality. Under the cloak of scientific and technical jargon, the old themes of private gratification and selfishness are exploited to secure obedience to bureaucratic dictates. Elite domination of various institutions depends *partly* on a general life style characterized by futility, which fosters a cult of the present opposed to genuine political orientation and action. Public forums do not function to raise basic questions. The political and economic mainstream from the time of its rise in the new land has flowed, though never without opposition, toward such a "post-communal" culture.

Alexis de Tocqueville sensed this when he foresaw the possibility of a new, rather benign form of despotic society:

> Each of them, living apart, is as a stranger to the fate of all the rest,—his children and his private friends constitute to him the whole of mankind; as for the rest of his fellow-citizens, he is close to them,

6. *The Function of the Sciences and the Meaning of Man*, trans. Paul Piccone and James Hansen (Evanston: Northwestern University Press, 1972), p. 278.

but he sees them not; he touches them, but he feels them not; he exists but in himself and for himself alone; and if his kindred still remain to him, he may be said at any rate to have lost his country.[7]

Several decades before Tocqueville, in England, it was noted:

The Law locks up both man and woman
Who steal the goose from off the common
Yet turns the greater felon loose
Who steals the Common from the goose.

Against the forceful currents of the mainstream, some Americans will continue to probe in thought and action for the foundations of the Common, not only on behalf of the "goose" but for us all and for our future generations. Lacking new dimensions for the conduct of public life, we seem quite likely to fulfill Tocqueville's vision. "It is the task of the political and sociological imagination to conceive men's private troubles in the contexts of public concern and to furnish bridging concepts which will enable individuals to translate their private uneasiness into public speech and political action."[8]

In a critical analysis of our "pursuit of loneliness," Philip Slater suggests that there is a close relationship between the "need to triumph over each other and the tendency to prostrate ourselves before technology," and that we "turn continually to technology to save us from having to cooperate with each other."[9] Americans have been taught to lack confidence in genuine communication with others and to ignore and fear the democratic uses of variety and conflict. Important changes in these motivations are in evidence, but it is not at all clear that they will be channeled into agencies of political education and change that can mount effective challenge to the expanding domains of the technocorporate elites. There is something deeply narcissistic in the way many of us have participated in developing and institutionalizing our elite-dominated technologies. Few people "have found a way to be American that does not involve the denial either of the claims or the humanity of somebody else."[10] Sensing this to be true, some "liberal" academicians respond by arguing or assuming that the dehumanizing foundations of our institutions must be shielded from political criticism and public debate. Academic contempt for "nonprofessional" people is widespread. The social engineering bent of the academician's "technological ego" blots out democratic visions. Among other things, the fear of the alleged

7. *Democracy in America* ed., Richard D. Heffner (New York: Mentor Books, 1956), p. 303.
8. This quote is from John O'Neill's excellent essay "Public and Private Space" in *Agenda 1970: Proposals for a Creative Politics,* ed. Trevor Lloyd and Jack McLeod (Toronto: University of Toronto, 1968), pp. 74–93.
9. *The Pursuit of Loneliness* (Boston: Beacon Press Paperback, 1971), p. 133.
10. Jervis Anderson, "Black Writing: The Other Side," *Dissent* 17 (July–August 1970): 242.

authoritarianism of "mass movements" seems to have dimmed perception of the developing conditions susceptible to a new technocratic type of authoritarian polity. The attempt to implement the technocratic model of politics will perhaps only increase the probability of the coercive imposition of a nationalistic myth of purified community. Demands for meaningful participation will be short-circuited increasingly into the consumption of "politics" as just another manufactured product. The articles that follow try to help mark the distance we have already floated or drifted on this journey down the mainstream, and the work to be done in changing course.

W. LEE HANSEN and BURTON A. WEISBROD

Bottom Dogs Subsidize Top Dogs: The Equality Fiction in Higher Education

The claim that the American system of higher education contributes to equality of educational opportunity is largely fiction. This year well over $11 billion of tax funds spent on higher education will seriously violate the egalitarian principle. Seemingly, public colleges and universities are open to all, but the truth falls far short of this. In practice, a perverse redistribution of higher education subsidies from low-income to high-income families takes place. Those with the most need for higher education are getting the least in terms of public benefits.

Studies of public higher education have recently been completed for the states of California, Florida, and Wisconsin. Because our study of California is most comprehensive we shall focus on it.

The following material is drawn from our book, *Benefits, Costs, and Finance of Public Higher Education,* Markham Publishing Company, Chicago, $3.95, published September 1 [1969].

California possesses a vast and in many respects a model system of public higher education. Tuition is zero. College campuses abound, with at least a junior college in every sizeable community. And it has the largest percentage of any state's high school graduates going on to college. Undergraduate students all receive large public students subsidies, although the amounts differ greatly with the type of school attended. A student fortunate enough to attend the University of

Source: The New Republic, September 13, 1969, pp. 23–24. Reprinted by Permission of *The New Republic,* © 1969, Harrison-Blaine of New Jersey, Inc.

California in the mid-1960s received an average subsidy of about $5,000, but a California State College student only $3,000, and a junior college student about $1,000. Of course, some got even larger subsidies: a student completing four years at the university received a total subsidy of over $7,000. By "subsidy" we mean the difference between tuition—which in California is zero—and the sum of average instructional costs (professors' salaries, operating expenses, etc.) and capital costs (the value of services provided by building, equipment, and land).

Many youngsters, however, receive no subsidies at all, because they do not go to college (or, at least, not to a public college in their own state), and many others receive little, because they are in college only briefly.

The highest subsidies go to students at the University of California (UC). But UC accepts only the upper eighth of all high school graduates, and these are largely children from well-to-do family backgrounds. Students from families with incomes above $25,000 are four times as likely to be eligible as are those from families with incomes below $4,000. Moreover, among eligible students, twice as large a percentage from high-income families actually attend the UC as do those from low-income families. The selectivity process restricts the availability of large subsidies to all but high-income families. The end result is that California's three higher education systems—the University, the State Colleges (SC), and the Junior Colleges (JC)—educate three different general classes of students and, in turn, provide three different levels of subsidies. (The same is true for many other states—including Florida, Wisconsin, Michigan, and Illinois, to name a few—that have a multiple-tiered higher education system.) The UC has the highest-incomes average—more than $12,000—and provides the largest subsidies—$5,000 per student. Meanwhile, the JCs attract the lowest-income students—with $8,800 average family income—and provide the lowest subsidies—about $1,000. The SC students are in between, with family incomes of $10,000 and subsidies of $3,800. Thus the average subsidy received by students at the UC is 30 percent greater than that received by SC students, and is 400 percent greater than the JC subsidy—in spite of the fact that "need," as reflected by family income, runs in the opposite direction.

The upshot: even in California, with its extensive higher education system, over 40 percent of families with college-age children receive *no public subsidy at all,* while a most fortunate 10 percent receive subsidies over $5,000.

Consideration of the taxes people pay does not alter these striking redistributional effects. There is no satisfactory way to isolate the taxes that go for education, and so we can only compare *total* state and local taxes (for all public services) with the subsidies provided by public higher education. However, higher education consumes roughly ten percent of state and local tax revenue in California, whose state-local tax system is essentially proportional to income over most of the income range.

The inescapable conclusion is that the structure and financing of their public higher education in California heightens rather than narrows inequalities in economic opportunities. The situation is no different in other states. State tax systems are either proportional (to income) or regressive (i.e., high-income taxpayers pay a smaller percentage of their income in taxes than low-income persons).

Nationally, a larger percentage of low- than of high-income youngsters drop out of high school and so are not eligible to receive any higher-education subsidies. Those low-income students who are eligible to go to higher educational institutions most often wind up at institutions where the education subsidy is lowest. And they are more likely to drop out before graduation. For these and other well-known reasons, the cards are stacked against low-income youngsters. Yet because tax revenues are used to support higher education, the anomalous result is lower-income families not only do not receive significant amounts of public higher-education subsidies but actually pay a larger fraction of their income in taxes to support higher education than do more affluent families. At a time when pressures are mounting to reduce disparities between privileged and disadvantaged, it is clear that something has gone awry. The mythology of equal educational opportunity for all is just that: mythology.

It is clear that the present structure and financing of public higher education needs to be reformed. One important possibility is to revamp the tax structure, making state and local taxes more progressive. This would increase taxes most for higher-income families and wipe out some but not all of the redistributive effects. But it wouldn't discriminate between families with and without children in college, or between those in public and in private colleges.

Another approach is to set tuition much closer to the full instructional and capital costs of college, and then to provide financial aid to students who cannot afford the full cost. This is essentially what private schools now do through their financial aid programs. Judging from the recent actions of state legislatures in raising tuition and fees, there is some sentiment for moving in this direction even at public colleges. Unless, however, every increase in tuition for those who can afford it is accompanied by an increase of loan and scholarship funds for those who cannot afford it, the goal of greater equality of opportunity will continue to be only a distant vision. Unhappily, while tuition rates at public colleges are rising rapidly, student-aid funds are lagging and federal student-loan and scholarship funds are actually drying up.

More important than either of these reforms, public subsidies should be available to *all* young people, not just college students. Those for whom the best way to increase earning power is through apprenticeships, on-the-job training, or night school deserve an equal chance in their struggle for productive and satisfying lives.

LOUIS KAMPF
The Humanities and Inhumanities

American higher education, like any institution, lives by myths. Still feeling threatened by the seriousness of purpose shown by students during last spring's campus rebellions, the educator's myth of the moment informs us of both the practicality and the transcendent beauty of a liberal (or humanistic) education. The same noble speech is being (or has recently been) addressed to thousands of freshmen: whether at West Point, Swarthmore, the Texas College of Mines, M.I.T. or the University of Michigan hardly seems to matter. It informs them of the primacy of a liberal—rather than a specialized, or technical—education. The humanities, the speech continues, release us from irrationally held prejudices; they open our minds; they teach us to be generalists instead of specialists. In short, a liberal education transforms the narrow career-oriented youth into a free, though of course responsible, man or woman of culture.

The underlying assumption of the speech is that four years of exposure to a balanced curriculum will produce young men and women who are objective, rational, yet not without feeling; who being free of ideological blinders will be blessed with a sense of their own autonomy. Having been made intellectually independent by their study of Homer, the Renaissance, atomic particles, Wordsworth, brain waves, Pop art and total environments, they are capable of discovering the relevant past and applying it to the problems of the moment. They are prisoners neither of history nor of the imperatives of current urgencies. Consequently they are eminently capable of dealing with the insistent pressures of change. Having absorbed the best civilization has to offer, they will be able to retain their humanity though practically engulfed by inhuman events. Briefly put, they will be liberal. Certainly, they will not resort to the barbarism of riots.

Source: The Nation 207 (September 30, 1968): 309–13. Reprinted by permission.

I suppose there is a grain of truth at the center of this hollow rhetoric. Certainly the motives which generate such words are often decent enough. Yet I suspect that the hearts of most academics attending freshman orientation sink as they hear the noble sentiments being piled on. There is a moment when one expects the dean of freshmen either to burst into tears, to choke on his own words, or perhaps to double up with laughter. He knows that his colleagues know his words are fake; and I suspect that most of the students see us all—teachers, deans, administrators—for the frauds we are. Is it not time we forgot about the nobility of the humanities and asked what their real function is, what social purposes they, in fact, serve?

Hardly a day passes without some representative of the industrial elite letting us know that America's corporate enterprises, not to speak of its government agencies, need managers who are not only steeped in the techniques of operations research but who are equally adept at quoting John Donne or T. S. Eliot. At M.I.T., the Sloan Fellows in Industrial Management are expected to devote a fairly substantial amount of their time to the study of literature. The exposure to literature, we are to assume, makes them better—indeed, more enlightened—managers. But who are these managers? What is their task?

No one knows who will live in this cage in the future, or whether at the end of this tremendous development entirely new prophets will arise, or there will be a great rebirth of old ideas and ideals, or, if neither, mechanized petrification, embellished with a sort of convulsive self-importance. For the last stage of this cultural development, it might well be truly said: "Specialists without spirit, sensualists without hearts; this nullity imagines that it has attained a level of civilization never before achieved."

The melancholy words are Max Weber's. The occupants of his cage are the functionaries of the bureaucracy bequeathed us by the Protestant ethic and the spirit of capitalism. The culture he feared was one in which rationalization of the profit motive, rather than the simple urge to earn money, becomes its own end, and efficiency is pursued with religious—yet mechanical—zeal. To further such ends, traditional education is replaced by training programs for technicians and efficiency experts. M.I.T., the Harvard Business School, and their brothers and sisters were fathered by the needs of industrial capitalism.

But today such an analysis may seem naive, even simple-minded. We know that our business schools give courses in social responsibility; moreover, our industrial managers conduct seminars on the needs of the Third World and the family structure of the poor. And who would doubt that this derives from anything but the best of motives? But before we congratulate ourselves on our good luck, we might take a closer look at modern capitalism. Clearly we have moved beyond that stage of rationalization which merely involves problems in engineering. Moreover, the complexities of modern finance—the mother of industrial development—involve a subtlety of human manipulation undreamed of by Weber's contemporaries. And as the complexity insinuates itself into all areas of the social system, we reach a point where our corporations and financial institutions effectively control most public—as well as private—institutions. As Kenneth Galbraith has pointed out, in this situation the main function of the American Government is not to promote the public sector but to keep the social order stable enough for business to do its business. Its second large task is to see that America's educational institutions provide the corporate machine with enough functionaries to keep it oiled.

The function of higher education, then, is to turn out those industrial cadres, rocket engineers, researchers, planners, personnel managers and development experts needed by the economy. But not only this; our colleges and universities have also been charged with the task of shaping the more ordinary functionaries: the kind who were once not subject to a four-year grind through the educational mill. Looked at in terms of real industrial need these four years of classes, laboratories, football games, hours in the library and bull sessions seem entirely superfluous. But that is not the point. For beyond immediate mechanical requirements there are the larger social imperatives. Social order must be maintained, and the whole fabric of traditions which gives a society its continuity must be kept intact. If this proves to be impossible, then at least appearances must be kept up; patches covering up the rents must be made invisible. As ordinary mechanical tasks multiply, as more of the labor force takes on white-collar jobs and finds itself pushed into the middle class, the process of acculturation becomes increasingly difficult. Formerly, those few who climbed the social ladder learned their manners—were educated to the proper social style—by their gradual exposure to the more or less culturally advanced. This was a slow and haphazard process; many fell by the wayside and never attained the style of life appropriate to their economic station. If the production of consumer goods is to expand, the goods must be consumed. To accomplish this, the new industrial cadres must be prepared for an "enriched"—that is, a cultured—style of life. Above all, the new class must never be allowed to feel that it constitutes a new industrial proletariat.

Let me return to Weber's metaphor: the animals in the bureaucratic cage must be civilized. Yet having consciousness, the task of civilizing tends to go beyond the development of conditioned reflexes. It must concern itself with the inescapable fact of human creativity and with the reality of man's historical memory. Both are, after all, basic components of what we call culture; they are integral to man as a species. The ordinary functionary, then, must be convinced that the rationalized task he performs—his ordinary, and inexplicable, job of work—is somehow connected to traditional culture—to all those monuments, both artistic and social, which represent our historical aspirations. What had formerly been the property of an elite now also belongs to the bureaucrat; for he, after all, has become a member of that elite. Or so he thinks. In any case, he knows he has his place in the traditions of the social system—and it is good. Consequently, there is no point in directing the anger of one's frustrations, of one's secret dissatisfactions, at the system itself, for one would be turning them against oneself—against that historic culture one has attained.

And therefore the future home economist, insurance salesman, even department store floorwalker must be made to believe that these tasks are—however mysteriously—connected to Homer, the Athenians, the Judeo-Christian tradition, and the rest of our cultural baggage. The connections may not be clear, but we feel a terrible guilt if we do not perceive them.

To perform this job of acculturation requires an expanding system of colleges and universities; to run them, a force of educational functionaries whose size seems to have no limit. The opportunities for administrators, professors, research executives, even writers, painters and composers are getting better every day. If nothing else, our colleges provide a marvelous haven for Cabinet members, mayors, Presidential advisers and generals, who are temporarily out of work. They, like their fellow humanities professors, are also students of the liberal arts. But, once more, this job of training and acculturation must proceed without upsetting our traditional notion of the university's function. The educational cadres must believe that they perform the humane tasks of scholarship. So they all write articles, and monographs, and books, and reviews of books and bibliographies of these reviews. At the highest level, in our important graduate schools, they train people like themselves to train people like themselves, to train people like themselves, to train people like themselves. . . .

Far from teaching young people to become aware of their capacities, a liberal education allows them—worse, forces them—to ignore themselves. As for the nagging reality of a world desperately in need of social change, the ordinary liberal education pretends either that the need does not exist, or that it can be taken care of painlessly, as a matter of ordinary academic routine. One thing is certain: change must do no violence to the traditional humanistic values embedded in the curriculum. These foundations of a liberal education are sacred. Thus the master task of the humanities becomes one of accommodating students

to the social dislocations of industrial society by hiding their painful ap-
prenticeship—their rite of admission to an appropriate office—behind
the mask of a traditional culture. Confronted by the radical transformation of roles played by the educated, the liberal arts must assure us
that the status quo is, after all, being maintained.

An odd development. Matthew Arnold once taught us that the
object of studying the best that had been thought or said is to criticize
our present mode of life, to make us see the object as it really is. Instead
the study of our classics seems to provide us with ideological blinders. It
mystifies—to use R. D. Laing's phrase—the very basis of our experience: our way of seeing, feeling, knowing. The humanities have been
the educational system's unwitting collaborators in destroying our experience—that is, our humanity. For by blinding us to social mechanisms
they have made us unconscious; they have made us the victims of a myth:
they have kept us from seeing things as they really are. And, to quote
Laing again. "If our experience is destroyed, our behavior will be
destructive." And so it is. It is so because our culture has taught us to
disguise competitive aggression as social benevolence, oppression as
freedom, hate as love. These marvelous transformations have been
effected not only by those who control our most powerful institutions but
by our educators—our experts in acculturation. The lesson concerning
the relationship of culture to aggression taught us by *Civilization and Its
Discontents* seems not to have sunk in. Or perhaps it has sunk in all too
well. As Freud observed, we desperately stand in need of our defense
mechanisms.

But perhaps we are running out of defense mechanisms. Perhaps the
contradictions liberal education creates for students are beginning to
turn on us; perhaps the young will make us ask those questions we have
so long refused to ask.

How so? The meaning of life is in action—whether the acts be
physical or mental. Fulfilled action frees us; it makes us independent.
When we can relate our thoughts, our yearnings, to activity; when our
vague projections issue in conscious work—then we may rightly feel that
we have our lives under a measure of control. Formerly the purpose of a
traditional liberal education had been to train a cultured—and humane—
elite. The act of ruling, of governing and giving guidance, was the activity
which gave life its meaning; it fulfilled the objectives of the education.
Clearly we still have the same goals in mind for the liberal arts today.
Supposedly they teach us to be creative and to act humanely. And are
these not the standards we set for our elite? But consciousness has made
a fool of our objectives; for the young—or at least for some of them—the
ideological fog has been cleared by the very contradictions of their education.

Precisely because we have been liberal in our education, our best students have come to understand that their deepest intellectual concerns—their very enthusiasms, their most intense involvements—cannot issue in any sort of activity which makes a claim to any social relevance beyond acculturation. And if there be no such social relevance, how can activity be fulfilling? Thus there is an almost inevitable split between thought and action. Thought may be free, but activity is controlled; stated educational objectives may be ethical, but actions immoral. The thoughts and feelings engendered by liberal education—the cultural enrichment we offer the young—become ideological masks for the politics of those who rule.

And the best of our students know this. They know that their studies are divorced from meaningful activity. They know that their courses are not intended to further their self-development; rather they become a part of the students' property, their capital. Their knowledge—technical or humanistic—makes them a product. As the material and cultural embodiments of this knowledge grow—and recall, these embodiments are products of man's self-formation, actualizations of his ideas—our practical activities, in a most ironic fashion, become ever more faintly related to our thoughts and feelings; their connection to the meaningful development of ideas and passions becomes more and more tenuous. Consciousness has once more played us for the destructive fools we are. For the object of a liberal education, we tell ourselves, is the fulfillment of individual capacities, of ideas and passions. Through such fulfillment, we assume, men can become whole, sane, peaceful and free—that is, humane.

But the split we have created in the student's life has allowed him to see his education for what it is. He knows that his studies—especially those in the humanities, he is informed by our managers—make him a more valuable piece of private property. He knows that his labor in the classroom transforms him into an object; that he makes of himself a product.

Since it is the student himself who becomes the product of his own labor, he is in tension with himself; he is split. He sells those treasures which, we have taught him, best represent his humanity—that is, his civilization, his culture, his liberal education. And so he is at war with his own being, for the battle over this piece of private property is a battle over himself. For the best of our students the study of the humanities creates a more intense consciousness of this situation. Indeed, self-knowledge creates a condition which puts that very education—the act of preparing oneself for one's role—beyond endurance. What truly liberally educated human being can bear to be a commodity with consciousness?

Such are the ends of a liberal education—or at least one of the unintended ends. In their attempt to use the traditional liberal arts to gain social consent, our managers have created a situation where students must risk their sanity in order to enact the lessons of their education; or they must turn into commodities, accommodating themselves—consciously or otherwise—to the lie on which their education is based.

In seeking alternatives, the educator's first impulse is to suggest curricular reform: jiggle the mechanism a bit, make a great-books course out of freshman composition, even have them reading Norman Mailer and Mao Tse-tung. Such reforms, we assume, will effect a fundamental change in the lives of our students. I doubt it. Changes in the curriculum—though often valuable and necessary—may have the ultimate effect of making the acculturating mechanisms more efficient. They may make the beast more cultured, but will not change its objectives. To break out of Weber's cage, to face the imperatives of fundamental change without dogma—if these are the conditions to which we hope our students will aspire, we shall need a most fundamental critique of the very social basis and function of higher education. Much academic political science will serve as an example. Aside from its more gross involvements with the CIA, the field's major object is to put government *policy*—unlike the more trivial matter of its *execution*—beyond criticism: to harden ideologies like the "national interest" into unassailable dogmas. Political science has done its job well, for it has succeeded in putting real political inquiry beyond the pale of academic respectability. This situation will not be changed by curricular reforms alone. If students are once more to ask meaningful questions about the state, and if they are to meet these questions with programs they can translate into action, the very *ends* we set for political science will have to be changed. [See "Political Science Discovers Politics," *The Nation,* September 23, 1968.]

The objective of a liberal education, it seems to me, should be the harmonious reconciliation of philosophy (that is, our ways of thinking), action and nature (the world; what there is). This condition, is possible only when we do not feel estranged from the products of our thoughts and actions, when we do not feel separated from the nature we have helped to create. Unhappily, industrial capitalism is rooted in these divisions. In our divided state, philosophy (our principles of education) must not be allowed to become an integral expression of culture; it must not serve to rationalize the divisions induced by the industrial system. It can remain philosophy, rather than ideology, only as it is *critical.* And so for the humanities or liberal arts.

How is this criticism to be expressed? Most often, I suspect, in acts which appear irrational, if not deranged. On October 16, 1967, while watching nearly 300 students turning in their draft cards at Arlington Street Church in Boston, I understood—and was saddened by that understanding—that these young men were involved in a desperate act of rejecting a civilization. The moral outrage required for this heroic act is disfiguring; it warps one's sense of reality; it too makes one's view of the world partial. Yet this seemingly mad act of rejecting an illegitimate and immoral authority was really an attempt to relate thought to action; to assert that the products of one's actions are one's own; that freedom—or at least the struggle for it—is a human necessity. Saying "Hell, no, we won't go!" is one way for the student to expose the lie of his education. Exploiting the class privilege of one's college deferment is, after all, a moral fraud—a fraud to which higher education not only closes its eyes but which it encourages. Ironically, in their act of criticism, in their act of rejection in willfully separating themselves from society these draft resisters tried to assert their wholeness.

Yet what of the madness of this act? Recent studies of schizophrenics have shown that insanity may provide the morally sensitive with the only means of staying alive in a disordered world. The ordering principle imposed by insanity on destructive chaos keeps one from suicide. This is one way of relating thought to action; or, more simply, to *act*—rather than turning inward self-destructively. Yet there is an alternative to pathology. And the students who take their education seriously and resist the draft have pointed to that alternative. Our ordering principle as educators must be criticism or, going further, counteraction, resistance. This may not sound much like the detachment, the wholeness, we associate with the humanities. Indeed, we know criticism tends to induce disorder and most of its serious practitioners often act like uncivilized madmen. But consider that the only real choice may be whether to be mad (though civilized) on society's terms, or on one's own.

If resistance be madness, it is at least human madness, not the rationalized lunacy of an abstract process. If our students are to retain—or perhaps discover—their humanity, they will have to oppose the system of acculturation and spiritual servitude which our colleges encourage. And opposition to abstractions constantly tempts one into irrational confrontations; the bars of the cage are beyond rationality.

Surely, the truly humanistic educator must strive to create a world which does not demand of our students acts of madness as the price for spiritual wholeness. Our primary need then is not for a liberal education but for one which is actively committed to an end. If we are to break out of the empty rhetoric of liberal educational reform, scholarship may need to become allied with activism.

Activism on what front? Not on the campus alone. For one thing, the university is not the place where students and their teachers are most likely to liberate themselves from the shackles of ideology. For higher education's institutional nature has shaped it into an instrument of perpetuation for our most cherished—that is, humanistic—ideologies: the university and most of its faculty has a vested interest to protect. And if we are to take Richard Hofstadter's commencement address at Columbia as an index, that vested interest will be defended against campus activists in the name of free scholarly inquiry. For it is the student strikers, Professor Hofstadter would have us believe, who are the chief threat to the values of humane scholarship.

Those scholars concerned with liberating themselves from such academic dogma and effecting fundamental change in the role played by the liberal arts, might have to begin by forming political groupings (such as the New University Conference) which create alliances both within and outside the university. These groupings will have to gain a sense of identity by taking clear, strong and public stances on the most important moral issues which confront our students: Vietnam, the draft, race, poverty, the nature of higher education, the uses of scholarship. Or to go deeper: American imperialism, war itself, the function of private property, sex and aggression. What is more, analyses should be complemented by meaningful political action. Such activity may, in some cases, involve divisions within the faculty. But this surely must be the first step if our philosophy is to relate to our acts. Some things cannot—and must not—be smoothed over. Surely one thing our students must learn is to take their thoughts seriously.

The special urgency and occasional violence of the students' demands for university reform derive, I think, from an intuition that the liberal arts, rather than being the property of educational establishments, should embody our civilization's highest achievements. This intuition makes the integration of the liberal arts into the students' daily lives a condition toward which they (and we) desperately yearn. Yet if we are to see the object as it is, in Matthew Arnold's sense, we must look at the liberal arts within their social context. If liberal education is to perform its proper function—to help the students see things as they are, to face them humanely and freely—then that education must be placed within an appropriate social context. Creating this context becomes, consequently, the foremost task for the liberal arts.

This involves a transformation of consciousness, a transformation which must be radical—that is, it must take hold at the root. To reach this goal, the economic and social conditions which enslave our students must also be radically transformed. Is this possible inside our educational institutions? Within the imperatives of our social system? I doubt it. Yet our society is being shaken; it changes radically in spite of ourselves, and in spite of our universities. Though we have no clear answers or directives for action, we must make the attempt. For only in the attempt will our analyses unfold, our activity become consciously meaningful.

JOHN McDERMOTT

Campus Missionaries: The Laying on of Culture

I

About a year ago I accepted an invitation to speak "against the war," at, let's call it, the University of Dexter. It is located in the city of that name, one of the major manufacturing towns of the Midwestern industrial belt. Since Dexter is somewhat off the main circuit for anti-war speech-making, I read up on the university and the town, and what I found made me look forward to my visit.

The university tended to draw most of its students from the town itself. They came heavily from working-class families and were often the first in their families to attend college. Frequently English was not the only language spoken at home. More significant was the fact that the city itself had at one time considerable fame for working-class militancy. One of the great early strikes of the depression was fought in Dexter, and the issue was not settled in the workers' favor until they had fought the National Guard to a draw in pitched street battles. Before that the city had been a center of Socialist Party activity, and still earlier, a stronghold of IWW sentiment. Thus I looked forward to my visit as an opportunity to talk to the kind of students seldom reached by Movement speakers.

It wasn't. Attendance at the well-publicized meeting was spotty; those who came tended to be about evenly divided between faculty and graduate students, almost all of whom were from outside the state. And there were no students at the party to which I was taken later in the evening, though they had helped plan the meeting, for student segregation is the campus rule at Dexter, no less within the Movement than outside it. Perhaps it was that or perhaps my disappointment at the absence of "normal" students at the evening's meeting; anyhow, I deliberately forced the party to become a meeting. It had taken no great

Source: The Nation 208 (March 10, 1969). Reprinted by permission.

powers of observation to note that the anti-war movement at Dexter, and, by extension, its Left, was largely a preserve of the faculty and some fellow-traveling graduate students, and I was interested to discover why that was so. In particular, I wanted to explore the role these teachers had adopted to their "normal" students and to examine with them the contradiction between that professional role and their wider political aspirations. I have taught in several universities, I've suffered the same contradiction and was unable to overcome it.

The most prominent feature of the discussion which followed, and of all the subsequent ones I've started on the same subject in similar situations, was that the faculty, to a man, still aspired to teach in elite schools. Dexter, after all, is what is popularly known as a "cow" college. A state school, it gets those students who, for lack of skill or money or interest, don't go to the main state university and couldn't "make" the liberal arts colleges in the area, even if they wanted to. Its students are very much vocationally oriented and still tied to their families. Most of them live at home.

Dexter is frequently under nuisance attack by some right-wing faction or other. It pays rather badly and is not in an attractive metropolitan area. Its library is inferior, it provides little research money, and the teaching loads are heavy. The administration is fusty and conservative, as is much of the faculty.

My faculty friends, obviously talented men and women, had not reconciled themselves to this exile. They depreciated the region, the town, the university and, especially, the students, even the graduate students. Loyalty and affection they reserved for the graduate schools from which they had come, and they reflected this feeling in their teaching and counseling by relating only to that one student in a hundred who might go on to one of those prestigious graduate schools. Those were the students who shared with them the culture of books and civility—and scorn for Dexter; who might by their success at a "good" graduate school justify the faculty's exile in Dexter.

Of course they didn't put it that way, and neither did I when I taught in similar places. They saw themselves as embattled missionaries to the culturally Philistine. They worked hard and creatively with the students who merited hope. As for the others, these men and women, in spite of their expressed scorn, nourished a vision, hesitantly expressed, of a society in which no student would be oppressed by cultural bondage to ignorance, vocationalism, anti-intellectualism and provincialism. In fact, that attitude and hope gave rise to and was expressed in their left-wing politics.

The guests at the party were woefully ignorant of the background of their "normal" students. They were vaguely aware that most of them came from working-class families, though what that might mean aside from greater resistance to formal education they had no idea. They had no knowledge either of Dexter's militant labor traditions. This was sad, for it penalized the faculty in a number of ways. To cite an apparently trivial instance, most of the faculty present were concerned over attacks made on the university by the right wingers in town. Respect for free speech and expression had an important place in their scale of values, and they tried to convey it to their classes, using all the familiar academic examples, from HUAC witch hunting and Joe McCarthy, to Stuart Mill, Milton and Sophocles.

Yet that they might relate the principle of free expression to the problems of Wobbly agitators in the 1910s or of CIO organizers in the 1930s (or of white-collar workers in the 1970s)—in short, relate it to the actual cultural history (or future) of their own students—never occurred to them. Instead, they were put off when the students responded to the alien and seemingly irrelevant world of HUAC and Milton and academic freedom with either passive unconcern or active hostility.

I believe this example successfully characterizes how the great majority of faculty behave in schools like Dexter, including, especially, the left wing of the faculty. Socialized like all their fellows into a rigid professional role by their university, graduate school and early professional experiences, they have neither the information nor the inclination to break out of that role and relate openly and positively to the majority of their students who cannot accept the culture of the university world as their own.

University professors as a group seem exceptionally uncritical of the limited value—and values—of a university education and the acculturation it represents. In their view, a student who is really open to his classroom and other cultural experiences at the university will, as a rule, turn out to be more sophisticated, more interested in good literature, more sensitive morally than one who is less open or who has not had the benefit of college. The student will also be free of the more provincial ties of home, home town, region and class. In short, most academics take it as an article of faith that a student benefits by exchanging his own culture for that of the university. It is by far the most common campus prejudice.

And it would be harmless enough if it were limited in its sanction to those students who allow their university education to "take," who do well at university work and will go on to graduate school and then to a place within the university world or, perhaps, into some other related profession. University attitudes and values are appropriate to that world. But what about the others, the cultural rednecks, the "normal" boy and girl at a place like Dexter? Do they really profit from acquiring the attitudes, values, life style, and so forth of the peculiar culture whose institutional base is the university? One way of attacking this question is to ask to what extent those values, attitudes and life style may be usefully transferred to other institutional settings—to little towns and big cities, to industrial or agricultural life, to life in a corporation or in government.

That was about as far as we went at that party a year ago. We agreed that we were part of a university system which was actively engaged at its Dexters in destroying whatever indigenous culture might remain among the American working class. We recognized that, consciously or not, we had assumed an invidious clerical relationship to our student laity. Like medieval priests or missionaries to the heathen, we dispensed a culture to all our students, despite the fact that a scant few could participate in it. For the others, the language of that culture, like Latin to the colloquial, was grasped largely in rote phrases, its symbols and doctrines recognized but only dimly understood. To the extent that this majority of students acquired the external trappings of the university, they seemed both culturally pacified and made culturally passive. Pacified because they were acculturated away from their own historical values and traditions; passive because they could at best be spectators of a culture whose home remained an alien institution.

II

In the year that has passed since my visit to Dexter my views of the relationship of general culture to political culture have very much developed under the influence of Edward Thompson's *The Making of the English Working Class.* [See review by Norman Fruchter, *The Nation,* April 6, 1964.] I find particularly persuasive and suggestive Thompson's demonstration of how certain aspects of the general culture of the English working class, over a period of time and under the stress of events, came to support a specifically political culture—that is, to enlarge its capacity to define its social interests and to struggle successfully in their behalf. I shall cite several instances of this, for I want later to use them to illuminate the problem at Dexter from a new and, I think, hopeful standpoint.

Thompson shows that the movement into the factories in England of the late eighteenth and early nineteenth centuries was made up of two distinct streams. One was the movement of poor, dispossessed rural persons to the city and the factory in search of opportunity; the other of highly skilled, often literate craftsmen being pushed down the social and economic ladder by the new forces of industrialism and technology. The former, abruptly torn from their rural poverty, had some reason to view the change as an improvement. The cultural shock of the transition, the traditional passivity to authority, the stimulus of urban life, and the novelty of cash wages might easily have disguised for a time the exploitative nature of their place in the new factory system. The urban craftsmen, however, having a sense of their own skill and worth, with still lively guild traditions, and a strong sense of declining status and economic position, were most unlikely to think of the factory experience as a road to opportunity. They knew it for the oppression it really was. It was the meeting of these two groups that proved so creative for the future of the working-class movement. The skilled printers, weavers and mechanics recognized that their lot was cast with the unskilled rural migrants, and they became a creative element among the larger mass. Their literacy, their talent for organization, their family and folk memories that working people had once lived secure in their homes, livelihoods and craftsmanship, were transferred over the years to the mass of working people. But they were transferred with a radical difference. By contributing them to the cause of the entire working class, what might otherwise have been merely a narrow defense of guild interests was instead universalized into a struggle for the rights of all Englishmen, a struggle for the rights of man.

Thompson also shows how important for the new working-class movement was the experience so many workers had in the Dissenting Churches. Men and women who, over the years, had learned to contend with the problems of maintaining a minister's salary, keeping up the church and parsonage, administering an active religious and social program, and organizing regional church activities were able to apply these skills to nascent working-class organizations. Of particular importance was their long experience of persecution at the hands of the Church of England. Both ministers and congregations had learned how to preserve their churches and beliefs in the face of official hostility and repression. Thus when Pitt, Burke and their successors attempted to destroy the new workingmen's organizations, these were able to go underground, preserving their organizations, maintaining their programs and extending their networks throughout the country.

Still another general cultural factor cited by Thompson as a primary support for the growing working-class movement was the belief among the English lower classes that they were "freeborn Englishmen." The phrase had no precise meaning, but it was habitually called into play to criticize or resist any arbitrary act against the populace and its organizations, any claim to special place by the upper classes, any innovation in government control over the speech, writing, travels or associations of the common people. It was a useful and eminently flexible weapon in the hands of the working-class movement against the power of the capitalists and the wiles of Edmund Burke.

What makes Thompson's work of more than antiquarian interest is the suggestive analogy it offers to situations such as that at Dexter. There is a double movement into such universities today, somewhat as there was a double movement into the factories of England two centuries ago. On the one hand, a flood of lower-class young people is moving into these universities, seeking entrée into the old independent professional middle class which university attendance supposedly affords. It is necessary to add "supposedly," for passage through a non-elite university no longer qualifies one for that kind of life. The jobs for which the Dexters and the junior colleges prepare students are elementary and secondary teaching, the lower levels of social work, white-collar hire, petty management—that is, employments which were once semi-professional, but which now are being rapidly industrialized by bureaucracy, managerial science and the IBM machine. Thus the lower-class boys or girls who go to Dexter only appear to escape from the world of industry; they are really taking the first vocational step into a new kind of industrial life.

The second movement into such institutions as Dexter is of a gifted minority of educated persons, who identify with the values, accomplishments and prestige of elite professions, but are forced by the economics of academic employment to take positions they consider beneath their skills, their sense of worth and accomplishment, their lively memories of the recent past.

But here the analogy with Thompson's English working class begins to break down, for these latter specifically and pointedly refuse to make common cause with the lower-class students with whom they share daily existence. This gifted Left minority does not help the students to develop an effective and vital popular political culture. On the contrary, it often occupies the vanguard of a university culture which, as I suggested above and now wish to argue more fully, pacifies lower-class students.

III

The most obvious political characterization of university culture is that it lives by, and presents to its students, the values and attitudes appropriate to its own upper-middle-class life style—a style that is part of the older, now declining, professional middle classes. As indicated above, a university education did once promise membership in the professional classes. This meant that university graduates could ordinarily expect a life of considerable social and economic independence, some measure of personal influence in local business and political communities, significant autonomy and initiative in carrying out their daily work, and thus the possibility of enjoying the pride that follows from personal accomplishment and craftsmanship.

Could it be clearer that no such life awaits the graduates of the nation's Dexters? Today a degree from a second- or third-line institution is a passport to a life style of high consumption and of reasonable job security. But it will probably be an industrial life style, characterized by social and economic dependence on a large institution, by little or no political or social influence, and by participation in rationalized work processes wherein one must try merely "to get by and not step on anybody's toes." Consider, therefore, how the professionally oriented values of the university's culture might function in such an industrial environment. High on the scale of university values, now and in the past, stands the virtue of tolerance—not only personal tolerance in the face of new or differing ideas, attitudes and values but the belief that tolerance itself is of greater personal and social value than the substance of almost any set of creeds. Such a value was useful in the professional worlds of the past, for it would normally help diminish conflict in a middle class made up of highly autonomous individuals. And in elite circles even today it diminishes the weight assigned to ideological differences and helps to harmonize the social and political relations of our pluralistic, semi-autonomous industrial, educational, government and other managers. It carries the advantage, too, that it opens managers to the merits of technological and organizational novelty in a political economy strongly oriented to such innovations.

But how does this belief function for the young men and women of Dexter, who will normally occupy the lower and middle levels of great institutional bureaucracies, and who may have reason to resist those very same innovations: speed-up, compulsory overtime, more and more alienating work processes, forced transfer to another city or region, institutional propaganda, Muzak and the other normal tyrannies of personnel managers? Is it a value that helps them to initiate or continue those collective struggles which are necessary to defend or enhance their interests; or does it rob them of the moral and ideological assurance which must support the beliefs of people who challenge the social legitimacy and retributive power of authority?

A second political aspect of university culture is its almost uniform hostility to the institutions of local and community life. Many churches, fraternities, veterans' associations, councils and boards upon which local and community life in America is built are havens of the narrowest sorts of provincialism, racism, intellectual baiting, babbittry and jingoism. For these reasons, and for reasons having to do with the demands of the national economy for college-trained persons, the tendency of university

experience is to propel the young away from local and community life
and toward national life and its institutions. A result of the university's
liberalism, cosmopolitanism and technologism, this tendency is supported by the national culture, by the students themselves, and by their
parents.

But it should be combated by those, like my friends at Dexter, who
are interested in building mass resistance to the prevailing currents of
American life. A young person from Dexter, unless extraordinarily
gifted or fortunate, has almost no means of gaining influence in national
politics. And to the extent that university culture directs great masses of
lower- and lower-middle-class young people into the institutions of national rather than local and community life, it assists in disenfranchising
them from political influence. Of course, the conventional representatives of university culture argue that the decline of local politics and local
institutions is inevitable, given the institutional needs of twentieth-
century industry and government, the gradual nationalization of
American life, and the march of technology—i.e., liberalism, cosmopolitanism and technologism. But we should begin to question whether
this inevitability amounts to more than advantageous prejudice. For the
kind of society which these university spokesmen describe as inevitable
appears to be coincidentally one in which the Ph.D. takes its place with
property and birth as a means to political influence and social status.

Similarly, the ignorance, racism and the like which characterize so
much of local life should not put us off. Given the preoccupation of the
Left, over the past epoch, with national rather than local concerns and
institutions, it is not surprising that local America has become a playpen
of unchallenged right-wing attitudes, persons and organizations. Of
course, one could not expect, even under the best conditions, that the life
style of local America will rival the faculty club in gentility, civility, humanist learning and other caricatures of university life. But that is not its
test, any more than the theological elegance of the Dissenting Churches
was the test of their usefulness to a struggling movement of ordinary
Englishmen. Those who are today concerned about a different kind of
economic barbarism and a similar kind of world-wide crusade should
draw the appropriate lessons.

A third political aspect of university culture is its latent hostility to
two of the more valuable and humane realities in current popular culture. One cannot move around this country without being impressed by
its egalitarianism, that is, the depth and vitality of the ordinary
American's feeling that he is as good as the next fellow. And the other
reality so important in our popular culture is the well-nigh universal
belief among our people that they possess an extraordinary range and variety of substantive rights. Like the belief in "the freeborn Englishmen,"

the belief in substantive rights is often vague and contradictory. Nevertheless, the history of popular political movements is the history of ordinary people acting in behalf of what they believe to be their substantive rights.

It would be too much to say that the university's culture is uniformly hostile to these popular realities, for the situation is ambiguous. However, it is not difficult to identify important hostile tendencies. Thus in contrast to the normal American acceptance of the principle of equality, the professoriat strongly values formalized differences of age, academic rank, scholarly reputation and, it may even be, accomplishment. The effect of this sort of deference is somewhat difficult to gauge and it may be tendentious on my part to believe that it influences student attitudes on legitimacy, authority and equality. Perhaps the issue is instead that university men and women, by failing to provide a living example of egalitarian relationships, merely fail to make common cause with the American people in their resistance to the hierarchic tendencies implicit in the social and economic system.

A more secure case can be made against the disposition in the university world to identify right not with substantive but with procedural matters. Peter Gay expressed this position in the Summer 1968 issue of *Partisan Review:* ". . . democracy is essentially procedural and what matters is not so much (important though it may be) what a given policy is as how it is arrived at. . . ." Persons as fortunately placed as Professor Gay, whose substantive rights are well established in easily available procedures, have an understandable tendency to overlook the fact that, for example, tenure, sabbaticals, choice of hours, and freedom of expression on the job—are virtually unknown outside the academic world. Obviously there are other, important and thorny issues here as well. Without going into them at any length, note that the test of Professor Gay's remark is its fidelity to historical fact. From that point of view, it tends to obscure the fact that the great libertarian and democratic turning point in postwar American political history, a turning point with great promise still, came not from the narrow defense of procedural rights by academic and other liberals against Joe McCarthy in the 1950s but from the assertion of substantive rights in the 1960s by mass movements of students, blacks, professors and ordinary Americans.

The students at Dexter, and a great part of their countrymen, rightly view the liberal and academic preference for procedural right as a defense of privileges which they themselves are denied. Many view the principle of academic freedom, for example, as they view some of the laws of property. It is a tricky device which enables professors to do things, like criticize the dean or the country, for which ordinary people can be fired; just as the law of property is a tricky device which enables installment houses and loan companies to do things for which ordinary people can be sent to jail. The goal is not to do away with academic freedom, or any other hard-won libertarian procedure. A better approach would be to shape a university culture which would help to extend Professor Gay's tenure, sabbaticals, and freedom of expression on the job to everyone, on campus and off.

The existence of hostile tendencies toward egalitarianism and the primacy of substantive right is very much related to still a fourth political aspect of university culture. Even though the university is the home and source of much of the libertarian ideology within our culture, it is often the source of authoritarian ideology as well. I have two cases in mind. The first has to do with the extensive commitment to technologism found among many faculty members. A considerable body of university opinion believes with Zbigniew Brzezinski that the promises of modern technology demand for their social realization a society characterized by "equal opportunity for all but . . . special opportunity for the singularly talented few." The evasiveness of the formula should not be allowed to obscure the authoritarian social and political processes which are envisioned and justified by it—processes today best exemplified in the area of national security, where the equal voting opportunities of all are nullified by the special bureaucratic opportunities open to a singularly talented few. The second of the university's authoritarian ideologies I call clericism. To borrow from Brzezinski's formula, it is the claim to "equal cultural rights for all, but special cultural authority for a singularly scholarly few." I refer to the still widespread (but declining) academic belief that, whatever else culture may include, it also includes the Western Heritage, the Western Tradition, the Literary Tradition, the traditions of reason and civility, etc., and that these are most fully embodied in the profession of academe and the written treasures of which academe is priestly custodian and inspired interpreter.

This principle underlies faculty sovereignty over curricular matters, justifies any and every required course, oppresses first-year graduate students, and received its most prosaic formulation in the observation by Columbia's vice dean of the graduate facilities that ". . . whether students vote 'yes' or 'no' on an issue is like telling me they like strawberries." Clericism and technologism have their good points; no one wishes seriously to derogate either the social or the moral value of good scholarship or competent technology. But as principles under which to organize cultural or political life they are distinctly hostile to the interests of great numbers of non-elite students, the social classes from which they are drawn, and especially the social classes they will constitute when they leave the university. For clericism and technologism, like the doctrines of apostolic succession and of property which they tend to replace, transpose major areas of social concern from the purview of all to the treasure house of the few. Culture, no less than politics, is a critical factor in the nature of social organization; in the distribution of power, reward and status; in the infliction of powerlessness, oppression and despair. This is becoming increasingly understood with regard to politics, where ten years of war, urban decay and increasing social chaos seem to have been the fruit of the same decade's obeisance to technology's claims. But I am not persuaded that clericist depredations on culture are similarly recognized.

As I think was made clear at the start of this essay, the faculty at Dexter did not feel called upon to know the specific cultural history and experiences of the students they taught. Neither they nor anyone in the academic profession consider it their task to use their own superior symbolic gifts and wider historical perspective to identify the specific historical culture of their students, to clarify its ambiguities, to criticize it, purging it of its moral (not geographical) provincialism, and thus to assist the students to develop a culture which is at once personally ennobling and politically self-conscious. On the contrary, at Dexter and elsewhere the faculty assume that it is their duty to replace the students' actual culture with an alien culture. Missionaries from these graduate schools, like clergy from colonial empires everywhere and in every time, feel confident that what they bring is good for the natives and will improve them in the long run. In culture, as elsewhere, this is manifestly not so.

Consider the matter of historical traditions. No acculturation worth the name should be permitted to block the transmission of Dexter's militant working-class traditions. Even granting, as is probably the case, that only a small minority of the Dexter students are children of depression workers or the earlier Wobblies, to assist, even if only negatively, in destroying these traditions is to minimize for most of the students the opportunity to discover the reasons for their attitudes on a score of moral and social questions, the reality of their social lives, and the possibility of rebuilding a more humane culture in Dexter for their own advantage. White intelligentsia recognize this danger when they peer across cultural lines at blacks or Vietnamese; why are they so blinded by the class lines of their own society? It should come as no surprise, therefore, that the anti-intellectualism of the students is often as deep and as bitter as the hatred exhibited by other colonial peoples toward foreigners and their works.

A university culture which related positively and creatively to the traditions and history of the working classes, blue collar and white collar, would find allies not only among the hippies and the leftists of Smith and Williams but from the squares of Dexter as well.

What is particularly disturbing about cultural pacification in the university is that it is not entirely an accidental phenomenon. At least since Herbert Croly's *Promise of American Life* (1909), America's dominant historians have been strongly nationalist, more interested in discovering and celebrating the American essence or character, the national mainstream, consensus or moral epic, or the peculiar quality of our national integration, than in emphasizing its divisions, especially those based on class. It has often crossed my mind that when liberal historians two decades hence write the chronicle of the southern freedom movement of the early 1960s or of the anti-Vietnamese War movement of today, they will find imaginative and persuasive reasons to show that the first was really part of the New Frontier and the second of the Great Society. It was thus that their predecessors have managed to reduce the richness and variety of popular revolt in the 1930s to the bureacratic dimensions of a Washington-based "New Deal."

Fortunately, some of the younger historians, such as Staughton Lynd and Jesse Lemisch, have begun to undermine the epic poetry of the Crolyites by reviving interest in the history of popular insurgency in America. Thus they have created the possibility that at least at some universities young people will be reacquainted with the real diversity and conflict of their past. More than that, and without exaggerating its importance or extent, this new scholarship provides a point of departure for a fundamentally different university culture than the one I have been describing.

IV

Faced with the vast social diversity of America and in opposition to the variety and strength of its Populist traditions, the thrust of university culture is to pacify its working-class "natives" and thus, I believe, to help preclude any fundamental change in national politics and priorities. Because of the surge of rebellion on campus since last spring, it is likely that this is understood better now among faculty than it was at the time I visited Dexter. But many university men and women, comparing the university's cultural values to those of industry, the mass media and the military, or to the restless hostility of lower- and working-class America, remain partisans and priests of academe, convinced that for all its faults it is, at least minimally, a humane alternative to its rivals.

The analogy I began earlier to the work of Edward Thompson points in a more hopeful and, I think, more realistic direction. A survey of recent campus rebellions would show that it is no longer only the Harvards and the Berkeleys which suffer serious student unrest; some of the most interesting and militant activity occurs at the non-elite schools.

In addition, scores of young men and women continue to be exiled by their elite graduate schools into a lifetime of work in the non-elite universities. The narrowest interests of these teachers and their most lofty professional and political aspirations lie in the same direction. It is to take up the task, in common with their students, of rebuilding the vitality of a popular resistance culture—that is, of a culture which will "enhance the capacity of ordinary Americans to identify their social interests and to struggle successfully in their behalf."

This is not a task which individuals can successfully undertake in isolation, nor one whose champions will be free of serious reprisal at the hands of university and political authorities. Nevertheless, there are already a handful of campuses where the work has begun, in critical universities, liberation courses, seminars in local and working-class history, student-taught courses for faculty, and research projects on local and campus decision making. It remains for others to add to these hopeful beginnings.

ARTHUR VIDICH and JOSEPH BENSMAN
The Bureaucratic Ethos

One important aspect of the New Society is the ever-increasing growth of the administrative structure of bureaucracy and of the scale of large organizations. Government, industry, education, trade unions, and churches carry out the internal and external operations of the society by use of the bureaucratic mechanism. It is critical to note that the exact counterpart of the growth of the middle class is the growth of the administrative structure of bureaucracy which administers this enormous productive and service-oriented society.

In describing the characteristics of bureaucracies and especially European political bureaucracies, Max Weber provided the foundations for the technical description of large-scale business organization. The key theme in Weber's description of bureaucracy is the separation of the administrator from the means of administration, just as the soldier in an earlier epoch had been separated from the ownership of his weapons, and the worker from the means of production. Bureaucracies are characterized by relatively fixed hierarchies and spheres of competence (jurisdictions), and they depend on files and legalistic regulations for specifying their operations. The entire bureaucracy depends on technical experts who are engaged in a lifelong career and who are dependent on their jobs as their major means of support. Thus discipline, obedience, loyalty, and impersonal respect for authority tend to become psychological characteristics of the bureaucrat.

Even more important, however, is the bureaucrat's habit of making standardized categorical decisions which are rationally calculated—in form if not in content—to administer thousands of cases which become relevant because they fall into a category predescribed by administrative regulation and procedure. Weber describes bureaucracy as a giant machine in which all individuals, both administrators and subjects, are cogs. This Weberian nightmare is so awesome and horrifying in its portrayal of the dehumanization of men and the disenchantment of society that it has been hard to swallow in all its implications. It is only Weber's academic style that has prevented him from being treated as another George Orwell.

For Weber, bureaucracy did not arise out of a devilish plot. Rather it was a dominant institution emerging from the administrative efficiency that results from size, scope, and categorical application of cases. Bureaucracy is adaptive to large-scale enterprises in all areas of society, as governmental and private activities expand in response to the growth of societies from localistic (feudal) and small units to giant large-scale enterprises that are national and international in scope. In many respects, Weber saw bureaucracy as almost self-generating, with one important qualification: the desire of leaders of large-scale enterprises to extend their own freedom, autonomy, and opportunity for rational decision-making by limiting the assertiveness, the interference, the power, and the irrationality of others within their sphere of administration. Thus those who control large-scale institutions limit the freedom of others in order to maximize their own freedom. Seen from the point of view of leadership, bureaucracy must always be something more than a technical system of administration. It is also a system for the organization and distribution of power and the formulation of policy within institutions, between institutions, and within societies. From this perspective, bureaucracy, in its full form, is diametrically opposed to the Jeffersonian and Jacksonian image of a viable democracy.

American social and political scientists did not find it easy to accept Weber's discussion of bureaucracy. For the most part they reacted against the image of the officious, legalistic bureaucrat and criticized Weber for universalizing the image of the uniform-happy, tyrannical German bureaucrat, later overdrawn in the image of the Prussian

Junker or the Nazi official. Americans contrasted the German stereotype to the oft-perceived style of the American official, who appeared to be easygoing, equalitarian, breezy, friendly, personal, and non-officious, even though a bureaucratic official. What they failed to realize was that the American tradition, stemming as it does from the Jeffersonian and Jacksonian frontier style, causes the power holder to conceal his power in proportion to its growth. The Weberian bureaucrat does not look like the American manager because the *cultural* style surrounding bureaucracy is different in America. As a result of this mask, the subordinate in any organization has at subliminal levels the ability to make precise estimates of the actual power positions of each officeholder in the organization. With this as his framework, the formal, equalitarian, personal, and friendly responses of co-workers are based on these estimates. In the American system the official knows how to be informal and friendly without ever intruding into the office of the superior, and the superior knows how to be equalitarian without ever losing his authority. Thus bureaucracy functions in the classical Weberian way while retaining an air of American friendliness and informality.

This special bureaucratic by-product of Jeffersonian and Jacksonian democracy creates a bureaucratic style in which it becomes a major requirement to mask authority relations. As a result, very substantial changes have taken place in the ideology of the social worker, the human relations specialist, the psychological counselor, the personnel officer, and in interpersonal relations in almost all bureaucratic job situations. In the United States a whole range of bureaucratic subspecialties have been created in welfare, government, and business bureaucracies for the express purpose of concealing bureaucratic authority. In American bureaucracy it is possible to sustain a rhetoric of agreement, respect for the individual personality, and rewards for technical ability as the critical factors governing the relationship between boss and subordinate.

In actual bureaucratic practice the subordinate is expected to agree voluntarily with his superior and to suggest the conditions for his subordination without ever openly acknowledging the fact of his subordination. The rhetoric of democracy has become the sine qua non of bureaucratic authoritarianism.

So complex is this masking process that in a literal sense a linguistic revolution has taken place that allows us to conceal from ourselves the inequalitarianism of bureaucratic social relations. Bureaucracy, like any dominant institution, has developed a structure of linguistic euphemisms which allow the retention of an equalitarian, friendly, personal ideology while concealing the authoritarianism and at times the harshness of bureaucracy. The following expressions, placed opposite their euphemisms, are intended only to suggest some of the possibilities.

EUPHEMISM	REAL MEANING
Obedience:	
We expect your cooperation.	Obey.
I'd like to have consensus on this issue.	I expect you to repress all differences.
Obligation and duty require this.	My job and responsibilities require your obedience.
Being reminded of one's place:	
It's a wonderful idea, but at the present we don't have the time to give your idea the attention and consideration if needs.	Drop it.
You're kidding, aren't you.	You're out of line.
That's an interesting idea that needs further developing.	Let's not discuss it now.
We must respect the autonomy and individual rights of others.	You're overstepping your authority.
You can do that if you want to, but I'll take no responsibility for it if it gets out of hand.	You do it at your own risk, but I'll take the credit for it if it's successful.
With some development and elaboration, the germ of your idea could be useful.	I'm stealing your idea; forget it, the idea is no longer yours.
That was a good idea you had at our meeting yesterday.	I'm giving it back to you.
Ways to get fired:	
You've been late three times in the past month.	Warning of forthcoming dismissal.
Your work is not up to your usual standards.	Warning of forthcoming dismissal.
You haven't reached your full potential in this job.	You're not fired, but don't expect a raise or promotion.
We feel that this organization can do no more to further your career.	You're fired.
We can't stand in the way of your growth.	You're fired.
You're too well trained for this job.	You're fired.
We'll give you excellent references.	Please leave without making a scene.
We'll give you an extra month's severance pay.	Please leave and forget you ever worked here.

EUPHEMISM	REAL MEANING
At other levels:	
Free lunch.	A small, somewhat ambiguous bribe setting the stage for bigger bribery.
Fringe benefits.	Fairly serious bribery.
Hanky-panky.	Serious bribery.
A preliminary meeting.	Setting out to rig a forthcoming meeting.
A well-organized meeting.	A rigged meeting.
An informal coffee meeting.	An incipient plot.
A private meeting.	A plot.

Although this whole area of linguistic usage is central to the functioning of society, few writers apart from George Orwell, Hannah Arendt, and Shepherd Mead have emphasized it. The bureaucratic aspects of the New Society could well be studied through the revolution in linguistics of which we have suggested only a few examples.

C. WRIGHT MILLS
The Rise of the Technician

The social developments centered upon the rise of bureaucracies and the ideological developments centered upon the continual demands for new justifications have coincided: together they increasingly determine the social position and ideological posture of the intellectual.

Busy with the ideological speed-up, the intellectual has readily taken on the responsibilities of the citizen. In many cases, having ceased to be in any sense a free intellectual, he has joined the expanding world of those who live off ideas, as administrator, idea-man, and good-will technician. In class, status, and self-image, he has become more solidly middle class, a man at a desk, married, with children, living in a respectable suburb, his career pivoting on the selling of ideas, his life a tight little routine, substituting middle-brow and mass culture for direct experience

Source: From *White Collar: The American Middle Classes* by C. Wright Mills. Copyright 1951 by Oxford University Press, Inc. Reprinted by permission.

of his life and his world, and, above all, becoming a man with a job in a society where money is supreme.

In such an atmosphere, intellectual activity that does not have relevance to established money and power is not likely to be highly valued. In the "capitalization of the spirit," as Georg Lukács has remarked, talent and ideology become commodities. The writing of memoranda, telling others what to do, replaces the writing of books, telling others how it is. Cultural and intellectual products may be valued as ornaments but do not bring even ornamental value to their producers. The new pattern sets the anxious standards of economic value and social honor, making it increasingly difficult for such a man to escape the routine ideological panic of the managerial demiurge.

The scope and energy of these new developments, the spread of managed communications, and the clutch of bureaucracies have changed the social position of many intellectuals in America. Unlike some European countries, especially central and eastern Europe, the United States has not produced a sizable stratum of intellectuals, or even professionals, who have been unemployed long enough or under such conditions as to cause frustration among them. Unemployment among American intellectuals has been experienced as a cyclical phenomenon, not, as in some parts of Europe, as a seemingly permanent condition. The administrative expansion of the liberal state and the enormous growth of private-interest and communications bureaucracies have in fact multiplied opportunities for careers. It cannot be said that the intellectuals have cause for economic alarm, as yet. In fact, amazing careers have become legends among them. Having little or none of that resentment and hostility that arose in many European intellectual circles between the wars, American intellectuals have not, as an articulate group, become leaders for such discontented mass strata as may have become politically aware of their discontent. Perhaps they have become disoriented and estranged, from time to time, but they have not felt disinherited.

The ascendency of the technician over the intellectual in America is becoming more and more apparent, and seems to be taking place without many jolts. The U. S. novelist, artist, political writer is very good indeed at the jobs for which he is hired. "What is fatal to the American writer," Edmund Wilson has written, "is to be brilliant at disgraceful or second-rate jobs . . . with the kind of American writer who has had no education to speak of, you are unable to talk at all once Hollywood or Luce has got him." No longer, in Matthew Josephson's language, "detached from the spirit of immediate gain," no longer having a "sense of being disinterested," the intellectual is becoming a technician, an idea-man, rather than one who resists the environment, preserves the individual type, and defends himself from death-by-adaptation.

The intellectual who remains free may continue to learn more and more about modern society, but he finds the centers of political initiative less and less accessible. This generates a malady that is particularly acute in the intellectual who believed his thinking would make a difference. In the world of today the more his knowledge of affairs grows, the less impact his thinking seems to have. If he grows more frustrated as his knowledge increases, it seems that knowledge leads to power-lessness. He comes to feel helpless in the fundamental sense that he cannot control what he is able to foresee. This is not only true of his own attempts to act; it is true of the acts of powerful men whom he observes.

Such frustration arises, of course, only in the man who feels compelled to act. The "detached spectator" does not feel his helplessness because he never tries to surmount it. But the political man is always aware that while events are not in his hands he must bear their consequences. He finds it increasingly difficult even to express himself. If he states public issues as he sees them, he cannot take seriously the slogans and confusions used by parties with a chance to win power. He therefore feels politically irrelevant. Yet if he approaches public issues "realistically," that is, in terms of the major parties, he inevitably so compromises their initial statement that he is not able to sustain any enthusiasm for political action and thought.

The political failure of nerve thus has a personal counterpart in the development of a tragic sense of life, which may be experienced as a personal discovery and a personal burden, but is also a reflection of objective circumstances. It arises from the fact that at the fountainheads of public decision there are powerful men who do not themselves suffer the violent results of their own decisions. In a world of big organizations the lines between powerful decisions and grass-roots democratic controls become blurred and tenuous, and seemingly irresponsible actions by individuals at the top are encouraged. The need for action prompts them to take decisions into their own hands, while the fact that they act as parts of large corporations or other organizations blurs the identification of personal responsibility. Their public views and political actions are, in this objective meaning of the word, irresponsible: the social corollary of their irresponsibility is the fact that others are dependent upon them and must suffer the consequence of their ignorance and mistakes, their self-deceptions and biased motives. The sense of tragedy in the intellectual who watches this scene is a personal reaction to the politics and economics of collective irresponsibility.

The shaping of the society he lives in and the manner in which he lives in it are increasingly political. That shaping has come to include the realms of intellect and of personal morality, which are now also subject to organization. Because of the expanded reach of politics, it is his own personal style of life and reflections he is thinking about when he thinks about politics.

The independent artist and intellectual are among the few remaining personalities presumably equipped to resist and to fight the stereotyping and consequent death of genuinely lively things. Fresh perception now involves the capacity to unmask and smash the stereotypes of vision and intellect with which modern communications swamp us. The worlds of mass-art and mass-thought are increasingly geared to the demands of power. That is why it is in politics that some intellectuals feel the need for solidarity and for a fulcrum. If the thinker does not relate himself to the value of truth in political struggle, he cannot responsibly cope with the whole of live experience.

As the channels of communication become more and more monopolized, and party machines and economic pressures, based on vested shams, continue to monopolize the chances of effective political organization, the opportunities to act and to communicate politically are minimized. The political intellectual is, increasingly, an employee living off the communication machineries which are based on the very opposite of what he would like to stand for.

Just as the bright young technicians and editors cannot face politics except as news and entertainment, so the remaining free intellectuals increasingly withdraw; the simple fact is that they lack the will. The external and internal forces that move them away from politics are too strong; they are pulled into the technical machinery, the explicit rationalization of intellect, or they go the way of personal lament.

Today there are many forms of escape for the free intellectuals from the essential facts of defeat and powerlessness, among them the cult of alienation and the fetish of objectivity. Both hide the fact of powerlessness and at the same time attempt to make that fact more palatable.

"Alienation," as used in middle-brow circles, is not the old detachment of the intellectual from the popular tone of life and its structure of domination; it does not mean estrangement from the ruling powers; nor is it a phase necessary to the pursuit of truth. It is a lament and a form of collapse into self-indulgence. It is a personal excuse for lack of political will. It is a fashionable way of being overwhelmed. In function, it is the literary counterpart to the cult of objectivity in the social sciences.

Objectivity or Scientism is often an academic cult of the narrowed attention, the pose of the technician, or the aspiring technician, who assumes as given the big framework and the political meaning of his operation within it. Often an unimaginative use of already plotted routines of life and work, "objectivity" may satisfy those who are not interested in politics; but it is a specialized form of retreat rather than the intellectual orientation of a political man.

Both alienation and objectivity fall in line with the victory of the technician over the intellectual. They are fit moods and ideologies for intellectuals caught up in and overwhelmed by the managerial demiurge in an age of organized irresponsibility; signals that "the job," as sanction and as censorship, has come to embrace the intellectual; and that the political psychology of the scared employee has become relevant to understanding his work. Simply to understand, or to lament alienation—these are the ideals of the technician who is powerless and estranged but not disinherited. These are the ideals of men who have the capacity to know the truth but not the chance, the skill, or the fortitude, as the case may be, to communicate it with political effectiveness.

The defeat of the free intellectuals and the rationalization of the free intellect have been at the hands of an enemy who cannot be clearly defined. Even given the power, the free intellectuals could not easily find the way to work their will upon their situation, nor could they succeed in destroying its effect upon what they are, what they do, and what they want to become. They find it harder to locate their external enemies than to grapple with their internal conditions. Their seemingly impersonal defeat has spun a personally tragic plot and they are betrayed by what is false within them.

JOHN McDERMOTT
Knowledge Is Power: Overclass/Underclass

The key to understanding the oppressive class structures now developing in American society is found less in the maldistribution of the nation's property than in the maldistribution of its knowledge. Whether in the form of raw data, esoteric scientific principle, advanced industrial technique or the judgments of scientific and technical elites, knowledge has become decisive, for it is rapidly displacing wealth, real property and individual entrepreneurial skills as the growth factor in industrial production, social organization and, most important of all, political power.

Source: The Nation 208 (April 14, 1969): 458–62. Reprinted by permission.

This increase in the importance of technical knowledge has been embodied in the expansion of the giant institutions which have come to achieve a near monopoly over its effective use. Segments of knowledge still belong to technical specialists and pieces of knowledge to the well educated, but only the very largest organizations are able to integrate these proliferating segments and pieces into systems of productive, effective or, more likely, profitable information. That is the meaning of technological progress: the systematic application of new knowledge to practical purposes. And it dictates a continual increase in the size, wealth and managerial capacity of the organizations which seek thus to apply the knowledge. Corporations, government agencies, universities and foundations have been quick to respond.

Not only has technological progress demanded the extraordinary growth in institutional scale witnessed in the years since World War II; it has also modified it in an unusual and important way. For beyond a certain size institutions need no longer confine themselves to their original spheres of activity. Their scope and wealth, the sophistication and ambition of their managements, the urge and capacity to profit from novel undertakings, the desire not to take second place to their rivals combine to produce the diversified corporate which has become the characteristic form of organization among the larger institutions of American society.

In the institutional world, the most successful corporate bodies are those that have most diversified their activities. Their managements have accepted the challenge and the opportunity to master an ever wider range of scientific and technical disciplines, and to weld them into production and distribution of ever more varied and sophisticated goods or services. Consider the variety of outputs now characteristic of our corporates and the range of knowledge they employ. A company like RCA manages missile tracking systems, does research in linear algebra, edits and markets new novels, plans new educational systems, and experiments with electronic music. The University of Michigan, another growing corporate, teaches students at Ann Arbor, advises welfare mothers in Detroit, and pacifies peasants in Thailand. The most impressive example of diversification is found, as one might expect, in the Department of Defense. High energy physics, transoceanic logistics, infantry tactics, elementary and secondary education, comparative linguistics, Greek political studies, psychiatry and astronomy are but a handful of the knowledges the Pentagon employs in its far-flung activities. Among corporate bodies like these, the words private and public, industrial and educational, national and international, military and civilian, no longer define significant distinctions; for, in the case of each pairing, a single group of managers, acting through bureaucratic hierarchy, has disciplined the babble of modern specialisms to its own expanding purposes.

That these facts, and their social consequences, are not more widely understood is in part tribute to the doggedness with which we cling to an inaccurate and outmoded conception of knowledge. Intellectual tradition still treats knowledge as the property of an individual man, its highest forms being humane learning, wisdom or science. This faces us in precisely the wrong direction to understand what has been happening to knowledge and its uses. The prevailing complaint is that the knowledge explosion has forced men to specialize so intensely as to lose contact with the general contours of knowledge and thus of human experience itself. But concern with this phenomenon has blocked our appreciation of a far more important one. As individual men have become microspecialists, less and less able to understand and act from general systems of knowledge, the great institutions have become generalists, increasingly able to integrate the discrete information of the specialists into technical and organizational systems which produce goods or services.

Thus the same explosion of information which has been so unkind to the makers of intellectual systems has been a boon to the makers of industrial systems. What has been for individuals a source of private alienation has been for institutions a source of social opportunity. What has been for the former an insurmountable barrier to understanding has been for the latter an indispensable aid to Gargantuan expansion. The mathematicians, sociologists, metallurgists and psychologists of the Defense Department may be alienated from their work, but in the higher echelons of the Pentagon, as throughout corporate America, knowledge is power.

These are not new facts and, in their outlines at least, they are frighteningly simple. America believes in *progress*. Hence it gives free rein to those very large organizations which have mastered *technology,* calling this *pluralism*. Its ethos is governed, ideally, by the principle of *equal opportunity* for enormous privilege, the result being a social system called *Meritocracy* or, by some, *Meritocratic Democracy*. (See "The Laying on of Culture," earlier in this volume.) It is the *American Way* adapted to the *World of Tomorrow*.

One cannot rest easily with the maldistribution of knowledge which is so essential a feature of the American Way. For the concentration of effective knowledge of and about American society in several giant organizations can lead to no other result than a substantial decline in the capacity of ordinary Americans to control that society and those organizations. In fact, one can already observe several important tendencies which mark that decline.

First, as the institutions have increased in size and enjoyed growing monopolies, both of information and of the products and services dependent on it, their relationships to the unorganized and hence uninformed individuals who make up their publics have undergone a subtle but radical change. Whereas previously these had been to some extent political or market relationships, implying some bargaining between the interests of the two parties, they now tend more and more to become administrative, implying subordination of the interests of the weaker party. The vague feelings of impotence so widespread in this country reflect the true state of affairs; for to be a consumer of, an employee of, a client of, a citizen of, a voter of, a taxpayer of, a draftee of, a reader of, a student of, or even a member of a large institution is, increasingly, to be its victim, not its master.

Second, just as institutions have improved their capacity to act on their various publics, their managers have improved their capacity to control the internal behavior of the institutions. Former Secretary McNamara's cost/benefit systems, which revolutionized and centralized budgeting procedures in the Department of Defense, are a startlingly cogent instance of a general trend. The increasing professionalization of middle management and the growing employment of data storage and retrieval systems are among a host of new techniques which enable senior managers to exert more selective control over the internal behavior of even the very largest and most diversified institutions. The combined result of these two tendencies is that the growing command of large institutions over the vital processes of American life measures the real power of their managers over the activities of Americans generally.

Third, as these institutions gather, process and apply wider and wider systems of information and steadily expand into novel spheres of activity, the distinction between (public) right and (private) privilege disappears. Whatever is done within the confines of an institutional bureaucracy becomes for that reason a private matter, of concern only to those technicians immediately involved and their hierarchic superiors. Whether an institution is privately or publicly controlled is not material; the laws and customs of private property or academic freedom guarantee the privacy of the former, while those of national security have spread to veil the latter.

As a result of these three tendencies, politics has lost its significance as a set of devices by which the general public rules over private hierarchy. It has become a shadow, uncertainly related to the real events of the private world it ostensibly controls. This summary point must be gone into at length, for it involves much more than the traditional tricks of the traditional parties.

Those of us engaged in "guerrilla journalism" over the war in Vietnam have learned that it is no longer possible to keep up politically with most areas of national life simply by reading the conventional press. However carefully one studies *The New York Times, The Wall Street Journal, The Washington Post,* etc., the newsweeklies and other mass sources of information, one is at a loss to pass judgment on events unless one also follows the relevant technical press. Perhaps an instance will suffice to document and clarify this lesson.

During 1965 repeated press stories reported that neutral Thailand was being used as the base from which most of the air offensive against North Vietnam was being launched. This should have been a singularly important fact for the public debate of the time. It not only made possible a quantitatively heavier offensive against the North but represented a qualitative escalation of the war as well. Once Thai bases were used, the conflict was no longer confined to Vietnam. And, since it was likely that the Thais had exacted some price for the use of their airfields, it was also likely that the diplomacy of the war had become more complex: presumably the Thais too would now have to be satisfied in any war settlement. Finally, of course, the bases raised the possibility that the North Vietnamese would henceforth feel justified in causing the Thai dictatorship some equivalent grief, thus increasing still further the military-political complexity.

This singularly important information about the bases never really penetrated the public debate, for it was never permitted to become a public fact. By the technique of issuing "unofficial," "informed sources," "nonattributable," "off-the-record," "official" and "attributable" denials—as the situation demanded—to accompany each new press report (which were dutifully printed by the newspapers in tandem with their own stories), the government managed to obscure from the public both the seriousness of the Vietnam escalation and the gravity of its probable development. However, no such clouding of the situation affected the technical press. Journals like *Air Force and Space Digest* early carried and soon confirmed the reports and, as if to underline my point, were careful to emphasize that the government was making a major effort to hide their importance from the general public. The reason for this difference in news dissemination is plain. The climate, geography, dust and logistic peculiarities of Thailand affected the procurement of technical equipment for the short future and its design for the middle future. Persons engaged in the aircraft and electronics industries had to know about the Thai bases because they were expected to develop and act on that knowledge. They belonged to the private institutional world, and in the private world one has rights based on function. No equivalent rights exist in the public world. It is a world which, increasingly in our society, has no function.

This leads to perhaps the most important of the tendencies encouraged by maldistribution of knowledge. Stripped of any relation of control or significance to the events of the real world, people's political responses have themselves become increasingly unreal and even paranoid. That explains, I think, the wild gyrations of public opinion polls, especially those dealing with international questions. It also partly explains the appeal of Goldwater and Wallace.

This apparent irrationality is widely misunderstood. Educated Americans tend to see in the primitive style of the Wallace movement, for instance, merely a projection of the primitiveness of its individual adherents. They explain its propensity to violent solutions for various questions as an acting out of the private frustrations and fantasies of its so-called "redneck" members. But the Wallace people are not reacting blindly out of the inadequacies and failures of their *personal* lives. They are trying to react rationally to the inadequacies of their *social* lives. Uneducated people and people at the social margin of this technically advanced society correctly perceive that politics is changing so as to reduce their power to act for the advantage or defense of their own interests. They recognize that the institutional processes which disenfranchise them have already advanced to a degree that conventional political channels are closed to them. Thus they forsake the conventional parties. Of course, the substitutes offered by Wallace and his cronies also fail to reach the heart of any problem—except perhaps the expression of resentment.

Deeply sensed political incapacity extends to the Left as well, especially to the educated liberal Left. In retrospect, it is evident that the combination of President Johnson's March speech, the opening of the Paris talks, and the McCarthy candidacy caused many liberals to channel the bulk of their political energies and hopes into the campaign leading up to the Democratic convention. Having channeled themselves it was easier for others to deflect them, with the result that the McCarthy candidacy gurgled to a docile end within the hostile and muddy confines of the Democratic convention. For what the McCarthy people failed to realize was that their strength within the Democratic Party was solely and directly dependent on their strength outside it. They never had the numbers, resources, skills or strategic position within the party to win the nomination or even a continuing minority position. Their real allies were the draft card burners, resisters and demonstrators, and the broad popular movement these "extremists"—not McCarthy, a late-blooming dove—had called into being. But the McCarthy people didn't see this; they saw their campaign as an "orderly" alternative to the "extremist" movement, rather than as the expression of that movement. It was only in the brief span of Chicago that the mutually supporting relationship which should have characterized the link between the party and nonparty people became apparent and effective. But the alliance came too late to accomplish anything more than Humphrey's defeat, and has not been maintained since.

The radical Left understood the situation very little better. In spite of some evidence to the contrary, it was largely the play of events, not conscious choice, which created their effective temporary alliance with party types in Chicago. As the McCarthy campaign illustrates, the overeducated Left fares no better than the undereducated Right when it comes to analyzing and acting effectively within the ghost world of contemporary public politics. And the reason for this is that we confront a social phenomenon, not a personal one. The very political language people use is seriously debased; loyalties they retain border on total unreality. Even the actual processes which they engage in, such as reading newspapers, belonging to political clubs and voting, have small ascertainable relevance. In short, the popular political culture has become so distant from the knowledges that influence the real world of decision making that the former is no longer able to deal with the latter in any effective and humane way.

America's developing class structure would appear to parallel this maldistribution of its knowledge. Within and around the great institutions which now constitute the core of our political, economic and social life, two distinct classes are taking shape, both defined by their relationship to the processes of those institutions. An overclass comprises those who manage the lives of great institutions, and an underclass those whose lives the institutions manage. By means of institutional place and institutional resources, the former normally amasses the technical, scientific and political information necessary for the direction of American life and the satisfaction of its own interests. For the underclass, largely buried in bureaucratic pigeonholes, a perspective on its own situation is, socially speaking, nearly impossible. For between them and the means to put the reality of their social lives in manageable order, to formulate their interests and to act effectively in their own behalf, stands almost the entire panoply of our largest, most prestigious and most powerful institutions.

In saying this, one must guard against two important misconceptions. First, the maldistribution of socially effective knowledge provides only a guide by which the outlines of the class system may be charted. The latter's substance rests in far more diverse phenomena, namely in the interaction between the explosion of technical knowledge and the capitalist and cold-war legacy within which that explosion has occurred. It is the institutional framework that is critical here. No amount of technical information pumped into the public life stream would be likely to correct the weaknesses of underclass politics, for the underclass now lacks the social, cultural and organizational framework within which that information can be assimilated and acted upon. As I have tried to stress, the problem is fundamentally a social one, not one of making individuals better informed. After all, Senator McCarthy and his followers were "smarter" than General Westmoreland, Mayor Daley and theirs, but not so powerful.

Second, we should purge ourselves of the all too prevalent view that the new importance of scientific knowledge promotes the growth of freedom. As Carol Brightman has pointed out (*Viet-Report,* January 1968), this is an old illusion in American life and one which has, unfortunately, a considerable following even today. Carl Becker spoke for several generations of American Progressives when he wrote in *Progress and Power* that

... the mastery of the physical world has been effected by scientists whose activities, *unhindered by the conscious resistance of their subject matter or the ignorance of common man,* have been guided by matter-of-fact knowledge and the consciously formulated purpose of subduing things to precisely determined ends, [while] the organization of society has been left to the chance operation of individual self interest and the uncertain pressure of mass opinion. (*Italics added.*)

Looking to the cure of our social ills, Becker shared with John Dewey and Robert Lynd the diagnosis that

those who have or might acquire the necessary matter-of-fact knowledge for adjusting social arrangements to the conditions created by technological progress have not the necessary authority, while those [elected representatives] who have . . . must accommodate their measures to a mass intelligence that functions most effectively at a level of primitive fears and taboos.

What is this but a literate statement of the ideological presuppositions behind which the new technocracy combines with the old oligarchy to remove public concerns to the institutional world of private decision making? Knowledge necessary "for adjusting social arrangements" has become almost exclusively the possession of a narrow and privileged class of men and women, residing in the commanding positions of America's great institutions and protected by law, ideology, custom, power and technique from the "conscious resistance" of an increasingly disoriented and feckless underclass intelligence.

For intellectuals concerned to mount effective attacks on this class system, two steps appear to have priority. First, the world of institutional behavior and the knowledges it employs must be charted far more precisely and more richly than has heretofore been the case. Current descriptions and explanations of corporate, government, municipal, union and foundation behavior are inadequate, for they do not permit a sufficiently reliable forecast of how and why institutions will act under specific circumstances. The Left is especially and perennially susceptive to explanations so general that they describe little more than anger and frustration. We are forever being surprised and undone by developments.

A good example of the low level of our understanding of institutional behavior is a little booklet which grew out of the Columbia University student strike last year and which has been circulated by SDS in the thousands to campus activists, students and faculty. *Who Rules Columbia?* is an excellent and important work of research on Columbia's Board of Trustees, and in this respect it should be, and has been, copied by other campuses. The character of the analysis it draws from this data is another matter. It tries to explain Columbia's interest in Defense-related research, CIA shenanigans, business education and the denial of student rights as a pure and simple function of the presence on the Board of Trustees of corporate, media, foundation, government and other Establishment figures. The influence of faculty ideology, alumni fears and professional administrative standards, as well as bureaucratic inertia (one of the main, designed-in "values" of bureaucracies that deal with ordinary people) is not even raised, much less explored. And the critically important role played by other university administrations, which urged Columbia's to hold the line (or the first domino) against a Red-anarchist-nihilist-nonprofessional plot, is also ignored. When one considers that *Who Rules Columbia?* is an approach to this kind of problem infinitely more sophisticated than the usual academic discussion—which equates a few pieties about academic freedom and the advance of knowledge with a worn-out theory of university governance—the problem is serious indeed.

But it is not fundamentally an intellectual problem, a matter of pure scholarship. Among the knowledges which large institutions have come to master are those which can be employed to disguise, prevent and manage conflict. Columbia, for example, might reasonably have been considered a bland, successful and liberal community of scholars until its carefully nurtured appearance was probed by the actions of student radicals. It was only then, as the Cox Commission itself pointed out, that under the stress of conflict the reality of Columbia began to emerge: ill-managed, torn by unresolved internal problems, unwilling and unable to deal forthrightly with the wishes of its student and black publics.

To the extent that the same situation holds in other corporate organizations, the response should be designed accordingly. Practically speaking, what is both needed and possible is not a disengaged scholarly literature about institutions apparently at peace with themselves and their world such as now strangles academic political science. Good scholarship here requires, I believe, a working alliance with insurgent political activity.

It therefore follows, as the second step, that the mutually destructive division between intellectual culture and popular culture should be ended. The anti-Populism of university-based intellectual culture, so evident in its attitudes toward Wallace followers, should be attacked. We should frankly recognize that that culture, comfortable in its adherence to the liberal social prescriptions of Dewey, Becker and Lynd, and confident that those once Progressive canons still contribute to the general betterment of mankind, now too often merely mask the social rapacity of the technological impulse.

Underclass assaults against American society, led by left-wing youth and right-wing adults, now pose a serious problem of orientation for intellectuals. One possible reaction was typified by George Kennan's recent widely publicized exchange with Princeton students. But the cultural exclusivity and intellectual clericalism espoused by Kennan can lead, I think, only to the destruction of any serious humanist role for intellectuals. It leaves the intellectual in the position of being a protected minority within the exploding multiversity, well away from its technological mainstream, and thereby under powerful sanction to shift roles from intellectual to intellectual technician. The difference in the two roles is fundamental: intellectuals contribute to people's self-knowledge and liberation; intellectual technicians con people while trying to control them.

A constructive alternative to Kennanism and Progressivism is not easy to describe. It requires an intellectual culture, such as has been lacking for many years, that is really knowledgeable about the concerns, activities and situations of popular life in the country. Intellectuals have to make contact with the views, experiences and problems of people who have no daily relationship to the university or who, if they have, are antagonized by it. The burgeoning radicals-in-the-professions movements, the New University Conference, draft counseling, and the various efforts to work with GI war protesters fit this description. It would help, too, if intellectuals would really face up to the fact that the gentler virtues are by no means a monopoly of the educated classes, and that there are decent visions behind the often violent and shortsighted slogans of underclass revolts. We should recognize that intellectual arrogance in these matters is a result of the same system which makes those revolts necessary.

Related Readings-
A Select Bibliography

Related Readings-
A Select Bibliography

*Part One: Mainstream Ideology as a System of Cultural
Hegemony: Political Domination in Everyday Life*

Baskin, Darryl. *American Pluralist Democracy: A Critique.* New York: Van Nostrand Reinhold, 1971.

Bluhm, William. "Lockean Theory: Naturalism as Tradition." Chapter 9 in *Theories of the Political System.* Englewood Cliffs, N.J.: Prentice-Hall 1971.

Boggs, Carl. "Toward a New Consciousness." *Liberation* 16 (January 1972).

Cruse, Harold. *The Crisis of the Negro Intellectual.* New York: William Morrow, 1967.

Devine, Donald. *The Political Culture of the United States.* Boston: Little Brown, 1972.

Dolbeare, Kenneth and Patricia. *American Ideologies.* Chicago: Markham, 1971.

Drukman, Mason. *Community and Purpose in America.* New York: McGraw-Hill, 1971.

Elson, Ruth. *Guardians of Tradition.* Lincoln: University of Nebraska, 1964.

Gramsci, Antonio. *Selections from the Prison Notebooks.* New York: International Publishers, 1971.

Hartz, Louis. *The Liberal Tradition in America.* New York: Harcourt, Brace & World, 1955.

Hartz, Louis, ed. *The Founding of New Societies.* New York: Harcourt, Brace & World, 1964.

Horowitz, Irving L. "The Sociological Textbook: The Treatment of Conflict in American Sociological Literature." *Social Science Information* 2:51–63.

Lasch, Christopher. *The Agony of the American Left.* New York: Vintage Books, 1969.

LeFebvre, Henri. *Everyday Life in the Modern World.* New York: Harper & Row, 1971.

Lowi, Theodore. *The End of Liberalism.* New York: Norton, 1969.

Marcuse, Herbert. *One Dimensional Man.* Boston: Beacon Press, 1964.

Mills, C. Wright. "The Cultural Apparatus." In *Power, Politics and People.* New York: Oxford University Press, 1963.

Reid, Herbert. "Contemporary American Political Science in the Crisis of Industrial Society." *Midwest Journal of Political Science* 16 (August 1972): 339–66.

Rogin, Michael. "Liberal Society and the Indian Question." *Politics and Society* 1 (May 1971).

Weinstein, James. *The Corporate Ideal in the Liberal State, 1900–1918.* Boston: Beacon Press, 1968.

Williams, Gwyn. "The Concept of 'Egemonia' in the Thought of Antonio Gramsci." *Journal of the History of Ideas* 21 (1960).

Wills, Garry. *Nixon Agonistes: The Crisis of the Self-Made Man.* New York: New American Library, 1969.

Wolff, Robert Paul. *The Poverty of Liberalism.* Boston: Beacon Press, 1968.

Part Two: Mythical Roots of Property and Power in the American Politics of Everyday Life.

Birnbaum, Norman. *The Crisis of Industrial Society.* New York: Oxford University Press, 1969.

Boorstin, Daniel. *The Image.* New York: Harper Colophon, 1964.

Burnham, Walter Dean. "Crisis of American Political Legitimacy." *Society* 10 (November–December 1972): 24–31.

DeBord, Guy. *Society of The Spectacle.* Published as *Radical America* 4 (1970).

Domhoff, G. William. "Historical Materialism, Cultural Determinism and the Origin of The Ruling Classes." *Psychoanalytic Review* 56:271–87.

Grant, George. *Technology and Empire.* Toronto: House of Anansi Press, 1969.

Hofstadter, Richard. *The American Political Tradition.* New York: Knopf, 1948.

Klare, Karl. "The Critique of Everyday Life, the New Left, and The Unrecognizable Marxism." In *The Unknown Dimension* ed. Dick Howard and Karl Klare. New York: Basic Books, 1972.

Leiss, William. *The Domination of Nature.* New York: George Braziller, 1972.

MacPherson, C. B. *The Political Theory of Possessive Individualism.* New York: Oxford University Press, 1962.

McConnell, Grant. *Private Power and American Democracy.* New York: Knopf, 1966.

Miliband, Ralph. *The State in Capitalist Society.* New York: Basic Books, 1969.

Regan, Michael. "Property, Power, and American Political Thought." Part One of *The Managed Economy.* New York: Oxford University Press, 1963.

Shapiro, Jeremy J. "One-Dimensionality: The Universal Semiotic of Technological Experience." In *Critical Interruptions,* ed. Paul Breines. New York: Herder & Herder, 1970.

Shonfield, Andrew. *Modern Capitalism,* especially chaps. 13 and 14. New York: Oxford University Press, 1965.

Weber, Max. *The Protestant Ethic and the Spirit of Capitalism.* New York: Scribner's, 1958.

Weinstein, James. *The Decline of Socialism in America, 1912–1925.* New York: Vintage, 1967.

Part Three: The American Dream and the Democratic Mirage: The Facts of Anti-Development

Benello, C. George. "Wasteland Culture." In *Recent Sociology No. 1,* ed. Hans P. Dreitzel. New York: Macmillan, 1969.

DeMott, Benjamin. *Supergrow.* New York: Delta, 1970.

Gall, Norman. "The Legacy of Che Guevara." *Commentary* 44 (December 1967): 31–44.

Gitlin, Todd, and Hollander, Nanci. *Uptown: Poor Whites in Chicago.* New York: Harper Colophon, 1970.

Harrington, Michael. *The Other America.* New York: Macmillan, 1963.

Henry, Jules. "Education for Stupidity." *New York Review of Books,* 9 May 1968.

Houghton, Neal D., ed. *Struggle Against History.* (New York: Simon & Schuster, 1968). See especially the selection by Robert Heilbroner which appeared originally in *Commentary* under the title "Counter-Revolutionary America?"

Howe, Louise, ed. *The White Majority: Between Poverty and Affluence.* New York: Random House, 1970.

Kolko, Gabriel. *Wealth and Power in America.* New York: Praeger, 1962.

Marine, Gene. *America the Raped: The Engineering Mentality and the Devastation of a Continent.* New York: Avon Books, 1970.

Melman, Seymour. *Pentagon Capitalism.* New York: McGraw-Hill, 1971.

Miller, Herman. *Rich Man, Poor Man.* New York: Crowell, 1971.

O'Neill, John. "Public and Private Space." In *Agenda 1970,* ed. Trevor Lloyd and Jack McLeod. Toronto: University of Toronto Press, 1968.

Parenti, Michael. *The Anti-Communist Impulse.* New York: Random House, 1969.

Pranger, Robert. *The Eclipse of Citizenship.* New York: Holt, Rinehart & Winston, 1968.

Sexton, Patricia and Brendan. *Blue Collars and Hard Hats.* New York: Random House, 1971.

Slater, Philip. *The Pursuit of Loneliness.* Boston: Beacon Press, 1970.

Terkel, Studs. *Division Street: America.* New York: Avon Books, 1967.

Part Four: The Rhetoric of Equality in the Mobilization of Political Bias and Official Violence

Bachrach, Peter, and Baratz, Morton. *Power and Poverty.* New York: Oxford University Press, 1970.

Christoffel, Tom. "Black Power and Corporate Capitalism." *Monthly Review* 20 (October 1968).

Coser, Lewis. "The Visibility of Evil." *Journal of Social Issues* 25 (1969): 101–9.

Levin, Murray. *Political Hysteria in America.* New York: Basic Books, 1971.

Lichtman, Richard. "The Facade of Equality in Liberal Democratic Theory." *Inquiry* 12 (1969).

The Autobiography of Malcolm X. New York: Grove Press, 1964.

Mason, Gene L., and Vetter, H. Fred, eds. *The Politics of Exploitation.* New York: Random House, 1973.

Nelson, Benjamin. *The Idea of Usury: From Tribal Brotherhood to Universal Otherhood.* Chicago: University of Chicago, 1969.

Poirier, Richard. "The War Against the Young." *Atlantic Monthly* 222 (October 1968): 55–64.

Rogin, Michael Paul. *The Intellectuals and McCarthy: The Radical Spectre.* Cambridge, Mass.: Massachusetts Institute of Technology Press, 1967.

Rubenstein, Richard. *Rebels in Eden.* Boston: Little Brown, 1970.

Sanford, Nevitt, and Comstock, Craig, eds. *Sanctions For Evil.* San Francisco: Jossey-Bass, 1971.

Schaar John. "Legitimacy in the Modern State." In *Power and Community,* ed. Philip Green and Sanford Levinson. New York: Vintage Books, 1970.

Schattschneider, Elmer E. *The Semi-Sovereign People.* New York: Holt, Rinehart & Winston, 1960.

Schuman, Howard. "Sociological Racism." *Trans-Action* 7 (December 1968): 44–48.

Taylor, Charles. *The Pattern of Politics,* especially chap. 5. Toronto: McClelland & Stewart, 1970.

Willhelm, Sidney. *Who Needs the Negro?* Garden City, N.Y.: Doubleday Anchor, 1971.

Wolff, Robert Paul. "Tolerance." In *The Poverty of Liberalism.* Boston: Beacon Press, 1968.

Part Five: The Emergence of Technocratic Ideology in the Super-Industrial Society.

Barber, Benjamin. *Superman and Common Men.* New York: Praeger, 1971.

Bazelon, David. "Scientism—the Stultifying Style." Chapter 7 in *Power in America: The Politics of the New Class.* New York: Macmillan, 1967.

Birnbaum, Norman. "The Problem of a Knowledge Elite." In *Toward a Critical Sociology.* New York: Oxford University Press, 1971.

Dreitzel, Hans P. "Social Science and the Problem of Rationality: Notes on the Sociology of Technocrats." *Politics and Society* 2 (Winter 1972): 165–82.

Fischer, George, ed. *The Revival of American Socialism.* New York: Oxford University Press, 1971.

Gross, Bertram. "Friendly Fascism: A Model For America." *Social Policy* 1 (November–December 1970).

Gurvitch, Georges.*The Social Frameworks of Knowledge.* New York: Harper & Row, 1972.

Habermas, Jurgen. *Toward a Rational Society.* Boston: Beacon Press, 1970.

Howton, F. William. *Functionaries.* Chicago: Quadrangle Books, 1969.

Kress, Paul. "Politics and Science: A Contemporary View of an Ancient Association." *Polity* 2 (Fall 1969).

Lasch, Christopher. *The New Radicalism in America,* especially chap. 9. New York: Vintage Books, 1967.

Litt, Edgar. *The Public Vocational University.* New York: Holt, Rinehart & Winston, 1969.

Marcuse, Herbert. *Counterrevolution and Revolt.* Boston: Beacon Press, 1972.

McDermott, John. "Technology: The Opiate of the Intellectuals." *New York Review of Books,* 31 July 1969.

Megill, Kenneth. *The New Democratic Theory.* New York: Free Press, 1970.

Miles, Michael. *The Radical Probe: The Logic of Student Rebellion.* New York: Atheneum, 1971.

Raskin, Marcus. *Being and Doing.* New York: Random House, 1971.

Schaar, John, and Wolin, Sheldon. *The Berkeley Rebellion and Beyond: Essays on Politics and Education in the Technological Society.* New York: New York Review, 1970.

Schroyer, Trent. "Toward a Critical Theory of Advanced Industrial Society." In *Recent Sociology No. 2,* ed. Hans P. Dreitzel. New York: Macmillan, 1970.

Touraine, Alain. *The Post-Industrial Society.* New York: Random House, 1971.